2nd Edition

CW01597594

ESSENTIALS FOR LIVING

Eilis Flood

Gill & Macmillan

Gill & Macmillan Ltd
Hume Avenue
Park West
Dublin 12
with associated companies throughout the world
www.gillmacmillan.ie

978 0 7171 4671 0

Design and print origination by Design Image, Dublin
Artwork by ODI, Oxford

The paper used in this book is made from the wood pulp of managed forests. For every tree felled, at least one tree is planted, thereby renewing natural resources.

Contents

Unit 4 Resource management and home studies

Unit 5 Textile studies

Unit 6 Options

Acknowledgements

I would like to express my sincere thanks to all who assisted in the production of this book. In particular, I would like to thank my husband John for his very practical support and my sons Luke and Mark for their understanding. A sincere thank you to my sister Fiona, who I inexplicably forgot to thank in the first edition of this book and who didn't hold it against me! I would also like to thank everyone at Gill & Macmillan, especially Anthony Murray, Aoileann O'Donnell, Emma Farrell, Kristin Jensen, Neil Ryan and Esther Kallen. Thanks to Richard in Oxford Designers and Illustrators for the illustrations.

Finally, I would like to acknowledge the support of my late mother, Maura Flood.

Eilis Flood
March 2010

For permission to reproduce photographs the author and publisher gratefully acknowledge the following:

© Advertising Archives: 100BL, 180TL, 180TR, 180BL, 180BR, 181TR, 181CL, 285TR; © Alamy: 5BC, 7BR, 9TR, 9BR, 12BR, 13TCL, 25BR, 32C, 39BC, 48TL, 50, 55BC, 57BR, 58TL, 69CL, 71TR, 71CB, 73CR, 76BR, 79TL, 79TR, 81CL, 81CR, 81BL, 84TR, 90TL, 90BC, 91TCLL, 91TCL, 91TCR, 91TCRR, 91TRC, 93TL, 93TCL, 93TCR, 93TR, 96TTC, 96CL, 99CR, 100TL, 101TR, 103TL, 103TR, 103BL, 103BC, 103BR, 104C, 104CR, 106BR, 109CL, 109C, 109CR, 109BL, 109BC, 114BL, 117BR, 118TL, 119BR, 122CL, 125TR, 129, 131, 134, 135, 136, 137, 141, 143, 144, 146, 147TR, 148, 152, 153, 158, 160, 161, 170CL, 170BL, 174TL, 174TC, 174C, 174TR, 174CL, 174CR, 175BL, 175BC, 176BL, 179, 182BR, 184, 185, 191TC, 191CL, 191BC, 191BR, 191BL, 192LC, 192CL, 192CR, 192RC, 192BL, 193BL, 196, 198TL, 203BL, 203BC, 203BR, 204TL, 204TR, 210, 215BR, 216BR, 219BR, 221BL, 222, 224, 225, 226BL, 227TR, 227CR, 235, 237TL, 239TR, 240, 242TL, 242CL, 244BL, 245BR, 247CR, 248TL, 248CL, 248BL, 248BC, 248BR, 249TR, 249CR, 249BR, 250, 251CR, 251CL, 251BR, 252TL, 252CR, 252CL, 253, 254BR, 255BL, 257BR, 259C, 259CR, 262BL, 264TL, 264BL, 264BC, 264BR, 265, 266TL, 266TCL, 266BCL, 266B, 270, 274TC, 279, 280CL, 282, 283CL, 283C, 283CR, 283BL, 283BC, 286TCL, 286TCR, 290CL, 291TL, 292CL, 292BR, 293CR, 294BL, 296TL, 296CL, 296CL, 296CR, 300CR, 300BL, 302TL, 302CL, 302BC, 307BL, 311BR, 324L, 331L, 332TL, 333TR, 333BR, 335; © Australian Wool Innovation: 186TL, 289TCR, 289TR; © Avent: 330TL; © Bank of Ireland: 177CR, 198CL; © British Standards Institution: 189BR; © Coeliac UK: 32TR, 89CR; © Consumers' Association of Ireland: 188CL; © Corbis: 7CR, 10, 23TL, 25TR, 321TR, 324TC; © Credit Union Ireland: 197; © David Timmons: 344CR; © Ecobaby: 333CR; © eco-label.com: 273BR; © Excellence Ireland Quality Association: 189CL; © François Micheloud: 57CR; © Fresh Food Images: 39CR, 39BLC; © Getty: 2C, 3R, 5BR, 6BC, 7TR, 11TR, 11BR, 13TL, 13TR, 21TR, 23TR, 48TC, 48CL, 57TR, 69TC, 69CR, 84BL, 89BL, 98BL, 110TL, 119CB, 181TL, 198BL, 237TR, 238TL, 254BC, 259CL, 266CL, 266BL, 267CL, 267C, 267CR, 269TR, 274TL, 280TL, 284TL, 284BL, 285CL, 287, 289CR, 290TL, 291TR, 291BR, 316B, 325TR, 325BR, 326TR, 326BR, 327CL, 327BR, 330C, 331TR, 332BR, 356; © Glanbia foods: 81TL, 82; © Guaranteed Irish: 186TCL, 189C; © Imagefile: 5BL, 6BL, 37, 38, 39BL, 45, 48C, 55TC, 56, 57CL, 58BL, 69TL, 69TR, 69C, 69BL, 69BC, 70TL, 70CR, 71CR, 73CL, 76BL, 81CRR, 84TL, 84BR, 88TL, 91TLC, 99TR, 99CL, 101TC, 101CR, 104CL, 106BL, 111BR, 118CL, 119TR, 119CR, 120TL, 125CL, 126, 138TR, 147CL, 155, 166, 171, 202CL, 208BL, 212CL, 216BL, 220BL, 221BCL, 221BCR, 236, 237CL, 238CL, 238BL, 238BR, 239CL, 239CR, 242BR, 243BR, 251TR, 251BCR, 254BL, 271, 272CL, 272CR, 278, 281BL, 283BR, 286L, 286BCL, 286BCR, 286R, 294TL, 294CL, 295BR, 300TL, 321CR, 321BR, 322TL, 324BR; © Irish Inspiration: 344C; © Lakeland: 140; © Leah Hennen: 347CL; © Mother and Baby Picture Library: 329CR, 330CL; © National Consumer Association: 188TL; © Nicholas Mosse: 344CL; © Northern Foods: 77TR; © National Standards Authority of Ireland: 189CR, 255TR, 261TR; © Panos: 2R; © Science Photo Library: 2L, 3L, 5TC, 6BR, 9TL, 11CR, 12CL, 12BL, 13TCR, 21BR, 22, 23BR, 30, 36, 41, 213CR, 220CL, 226TL, 269CR, 301BR, 320TL, 320CL, 320BL, 328TL; © Shamrock Foods: 89TC, 89TL; © Simplicity: 349BR; © Sportsfile: 276; © State Examinations Commission : 96LB; © Sustainable Energy Ireland: 252BL; © The Irish Payment Services Organisation Limited: 177TR; © TopFoto: 58CL, 151, 221BC, 221BR, 229, 234BL, 306TL, 324C; © Wikimedia Commons: 109BR, 191CR, 255CR.

eTest.ie – what is it?

A revolutionary new website-based testing platform that facilitates a social learning environment for Irish schools. Both students and teachers can use it, either independently or together, to make the whole area of testing easier, more engaging and more productive for all.

Students – do you want to know how well you are doing? Then take an eTest!

At eTest.ie, you can access tests put together by the author of this textbook. You get instant results, so they're a brilliant way to quickly check just how your study or revision is going.

Since each eTest is based on your textbook, if you don't know an answer, you'll find it in your book.

Register now and you can save all of your eTest results to use as a handy revision aid or to simply compare with your friends' results!

Teachers – eTest.ie will engage your students and help them with their revision, while making the jobs of reviewing their progress and homework easier and more convenient for all of you.

Register now to avail of these exciting features:

- Create tests easily using our pre-set questions OR you can create your own questions
- Develop your own online learning centre for each class that you teach
- Keep track of your students' performances

eTest.ie has a wide choice of question types for you to choose from, most of which can be graded automatically, like multiple-choice, jumbled-sentence, matching, ordering and gap-fill exercises. This free resource allows you to create class groups, delivering all the functionality of a VLE (Virtual Learning Environment) with the ease of communication that is brought by social networking.

Unit 1

Food

CHAPTER 1

Nutrition

Teacher's CD-ROM: Slide presentation • Student activity pack – with revision crossword • Class test

Why we need food

Food serves three functions in the body:

1. Heat and energy.
2. Growth and repair.
3. Helps fight disease.

Factors that affect our food choices

- Cost – some foods are too expensive to buy regularly, e.g. fillet steak.
- Foods that are readily available, e.g. potatoes in Ireland.
- Foods in season, e.g. strawberries in summertime.
- Lifestyle, e.g. convenience foods are now more common because of our busy lifestyle.
- Culture and tradition, e.g. pasta dishes in Italy.
- Religious rules, e.g. strict Hindus do not eat meat.
- Nutritional value – some people choose foods because they know they are good for them, e.g. low in fat.
- Personal likes and dislikes.

Malnutrition – what is it?

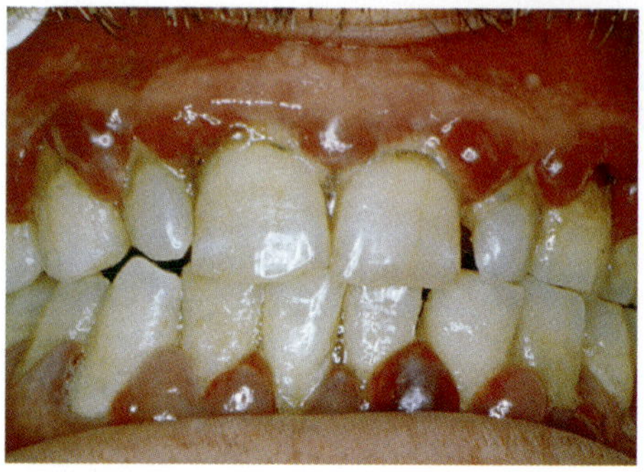

Too little of certain foods, e.g. fruit and vegetables, causes scurvy

Too much of certain foods, e.g. fatty or sugary foods

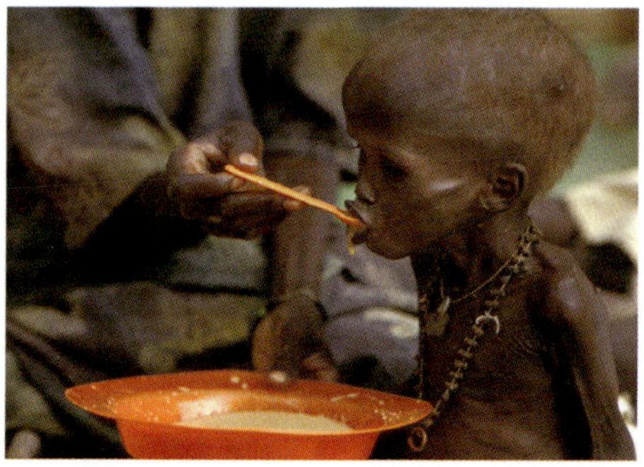

Too little food

Nutrients

All food contains one or more of the six nutrients. The names of the nutrients are:

1. Protein.
2. Fat.
3. Carbohydrate.
4. Minerals.
5. Vitamins.
6. Water.

Each and every one of the six nutrients must be taken in to keep our bodies healthy. Protein, fat and carbohydrate are eaten in large amounts. They must be broken down by the body during digestion and are called **macronutrients**. Minerals and vitamins are needed in smaller amounts and need no digestion. They are called **micronutrients**.

Protein

Composition of protein

Protein is made up of chains of amino acids. Each amino acid is made up of the elements carbon, hydrogen, oxygen and nitrogen (CHON). Of these, nitrogen is the most important, as it is needed for growth of the body.

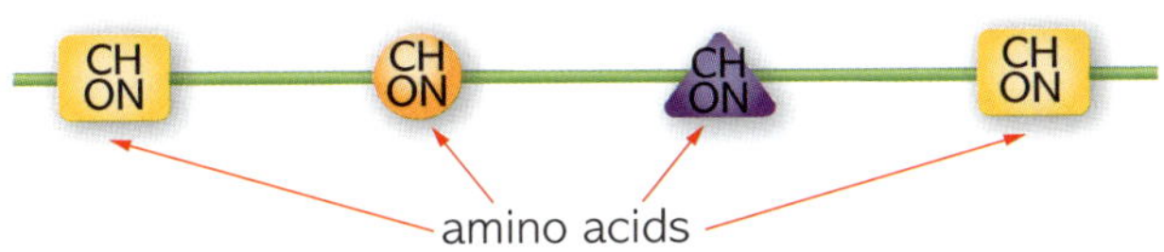

Classification of protein

First-class protein
(Usually from animals)

Sources of animal protein
Meat, fish, eggs, cheese, milk

Second-class protein
(Usually from plants)

Sources of vegetable protein
Peas, beans, lentils, pasta, nuts, brown bread, rice, breakfast cereals

Essential amino acids

You learned earlier that protein is made up of chains of amino acids. While all amino acids are good for the body, some are more important than others. The most important are called **essential amino acids**.

High and low biological value protein

Some protein foods contain most or all of the essential amino acids and are called **first-class** or **high biological value** (HBV) protein foods. These foods usually come from animal sources, such as meat. (The main exceptions are TVP and mycoprotein foods, such as Quorn, which are vegetable proteins with a high biological value.) Other protein foods do not contain all the essential amino acids and are called **second-class** or **low biological value** (LBV) protein foods. These are usually from vegetable or plant sources, such as beans.

Functions: What does protein do in the body?

- Growth of the body.
- Repairs worn-out and damaged cells, e.g. when you cut yourself.
- Makes enzymes, hormones and antibodies.
- Provides heat and energy.

Recommended daily allowance (RDA)

This tells us how much of each of the nutrients we need per day. The table below shows the RDA for some of the nutrients needed by the body.

Nutrient	RDA	Nutrient	RDA
Protein	1g / kg of body weight	Vitamin D	2.5–10mg
Fat	No more than 30% of energy intake	Vitamin A	750–1,200mg
Carbohydrate	Depends on how active the person is	Iron	10–15mg
Fibre	30g	Calcium	500–1,200mg
Vitamin C	30mg	Sodium (salt)	2g

Meat alternatives

There are a number of different high protein meat alternatives on the market today. Textured vegetable protein (TVP) is one made from soya beans. TVP is an excellent food in that it is high in protein and calcium, yet low in fat. It is available in steak, chunk or minced form. Mycoprotein foods (the most common of which is the brand Quorn), which are made from edible fungi, are also available. Quorn is produced both as a cooking ingredient and as a range of ready meals.

Quorn mycoprotein products

Homework Assignment

1 P. 2

Fats

Composition of fats

Fats are made up of fatty acids and glycerol. Each glycerol molecule has three fatty acid molecules attached to it. Fats contain the elements carbon, hydrogen and oxygen (CHO).

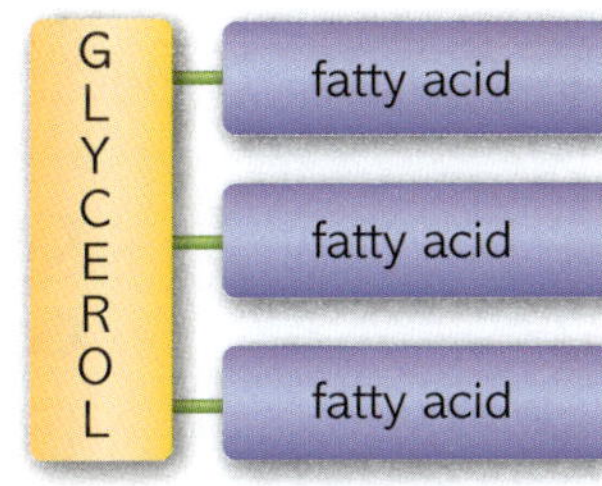

Composition of fat

Classification of fats

Saturated fats

Sometimes called animal fats

Sources of saturated fats

Meat such as rashers, sausages, chops, cream, butter, eggs, milk

Unsaturated fats

Sometimes called vegetable fats

Sources of unsaturated fats

Polyunsaturated margarine such as Flora, beans, nuts, fish, fish liver oils such as cod liver oil, cereals

Functions: What does fat do in the body?

- Gives us lots of heat and energy.
- A layer of fat under the skin called adipose tissue insulates the body (helps keep the body warm).

- Delicate organs such as the heart and kidneys have a layer of fat around them; this layer can protect them from injury.
- Vitamins A, D, E and K dissolve in fat. When we eat fat, we are also eating these vitamins.

Homework Assignment 2 P. 5

How to cut down on fat

- Grill, bake, boil or microwave food instead of frying.
- Use polyunsaturated fats, e.g. Flora, instead of butter.
- Cut fat off meat.
- Cut down on foods like crisps, burgers and chips.
- Use low-fat foods.

Carbohydrates

Composition of carbohydrates

Like fats, carbohydrates are made up of the elements carbon, hydrogen and oxygen (CHO). Fats produce more energy than carbohydrates, as they have more carbon. Carbohydrates are made up of chains of simple sugars.

Composition of carbohydrate

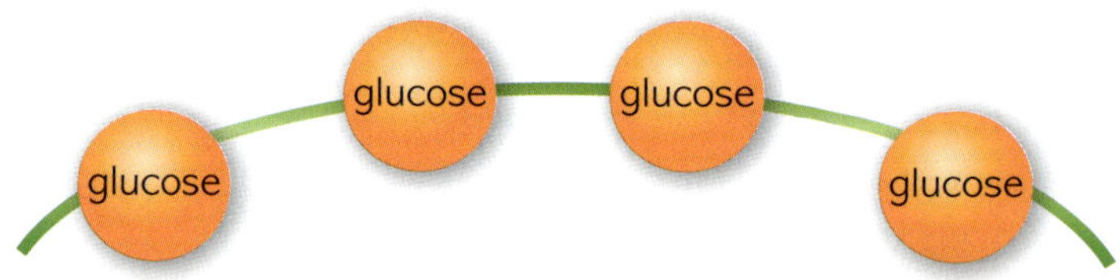

Classification of carbohydrates

Sugars

Sources of sugars

Honey, fruit, ice cream, biscuits, cake, chocolate, sweets

Starches

Sources of starches

Bread, breakfast cereals, potatoes, pasta, vegetables such as carrots and broccoli

Fibre-rich foods

Sources of fibre-rich foods

Brown bread, brown rice, fruits, vegetables, fibre-rich breakfast cereals

Functions: What does carbohydrate do in the body?

- Provides heat and energy.
- Fibre-rich carbohydrates fill you up.
- Fibre helps stop constipation and other bowel problems.

Refined carbohydrates

Fibre

Fibre is very important in the diet because it helps waste pass easily through the intestines. If we do not eat enough fibre, we risk constipation and diseases such as bowel cancer.

It is recommended that we eat 25–30g of fibre per day, yet on average Irish people eat only 15–20g.

Refined or processed foods rarely contain much fibre. To increase fibre intake:

- Eat brown bread and rice instead of white.
- Eat more fresh fruit and vegetables.
- Eat high-fibre breakfast cereals, such as bran flakes.

Empty-calorie foods

Empty-calorie foods

Most of the foods pictured on the right contain lots of sugar but very little goodness. These foods are all high-calorie foods but do not supply any of the other nutrients needed by the body. This is why they are called empty-calorie foods.

Hidden sugar

The foods pictured above are obviously sugary foods. Sometimes, however, foods have hidden sugar: watch out for the words *sucrose*, *glucose*, *maltose*, *fructose* and *dextrose* – these are all types of sugar.

Did you know ketchup is one-quarter sugar?

Homework Assignment
3 P. 7

Vitamins

Vitamins are needed in small amounts by the body. There are two groups of vitamins:

- **Water-soluble:** These dissolve in water (vitamins C and B group).
- **Fat-soluble:** These dissolve in fat (vitamins A, D, E and K).

Fat-soluble vitamins can be stored in the body but water-soluble vitamins cannot and need to be eaten every day.

Water-soluble vitamins

Vitamin	Functions	Sources	RDA	Deficiency diseases
C	• General health. • Healthy skin and gums. • Helps wounds to heal. • Helps absorb iron.	*Fruit:* Blackcurrants, grapefruits, lemons, orange juice, oranges, peppers, strawberries. *Vegetables:* Cabbage, coleslaw, new potatoes, peppers, tomatoes.	• 30mg for adults; more for adolescents.	• Scurvy. • Wounds slow to heal.
B group (6 vitamins)	• Growth. • Healthy nervous system. • Controls the release of energy from food.	Nuts, peas, beans, lentils, yeast bread, brown bread, meat, fish, milk, eggs, cheese.	• Varies with each vitamin.	• Beriberi (nerve disease): May appear with alcoholism. • Pellagra: Sores on the skin and tongue.
NB: Extra folic acid needs to be taken during pregnancy	• Helps prevent neural tube defects, e.g. spina bifida. Usually taken in tablet form for three months before and three months after conception.	Some breakfast cereals are fortified with folic acid.	• 0.4mg daily (one folic acid tablet).	• Increased risk of neural tube defects (spinal) in babies.

Scurvy

Scurvy is a disease caused by a lack of vitamin C. While rare, scurvy still occurs in infants and people living on poor diets that do not contain fresh fruit and vegetables. Babies, especially bottle-fed babies, should be given diluted fruit juice in a cup or from a spoon.

The symptoms of scurvy are:

- Poor healing of wounds.
- Frequent bruising.
- Sore, bleeding mouth and gums.
- Anaemia.

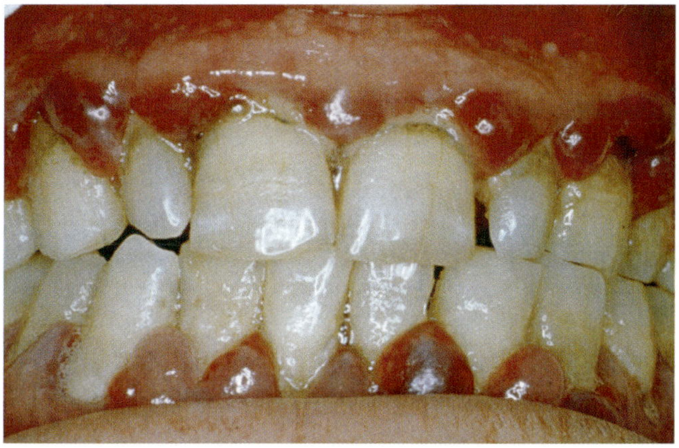

Scurvy

Fresh fruit and vegetables contain vitamin C, which prevents scurvy

Preventing vitamin C loss

Vitamin C is easily destroyed. To help prevent this loss:

- Don't buy wilted vegetables.
- Cook vegetables soon after buying.
- Cook vegetables in a small amount of water, bring to the boil and then simmer.
- Don't overcook vegetables.
- Don't use bread soda when cooking cabbage, as it destroys vitamin C.
- Eat vegetables soon after cooking: vitamin C is lost if they are kept warm for a long time.

Rickets

The disease rickets is caused by a lack of vitamin D. It was first diagnosed in the 1650s and was common in children living in the industrial smog-filled cities at the beginning of the twentieth century. While rare nowadays, rickets does still appear in a small number of infants from low-income families. Some vegetarian children and infants who have been breast-fed for a long time without supplements are also at risk. Because vitamin D is needed to absorb, or use, calcium, and calcium is needed to harden the bones, a child with rickets will have soft, badly formed bones (bow legs) and teeth that are prone to decay.

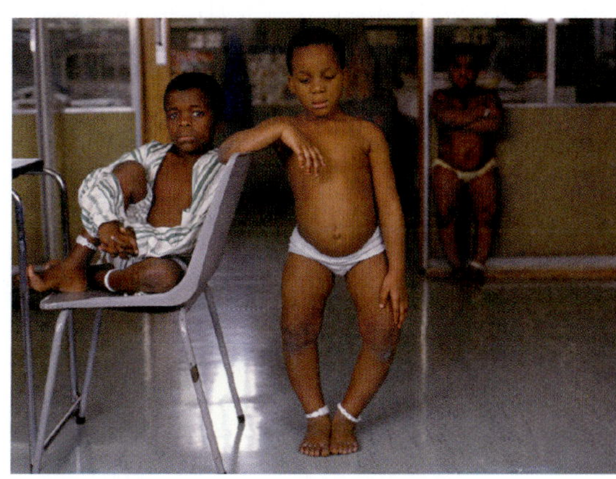

Rickets

Osteomalacia

Osteomalacia is the adult form of rickets. In developing countries, this disease is found in women who have low intakes of vitamin D and calcium. Many of these women have had several closely spaced pregnancies followed by long periods of breastfeeding.

Fat-soluble vitamins

Vitamin	Sources	Functions	Deficiency symptoms
A	*Pure vitamin A:* Eggs, fish liver oils, kidney, liver, margarine, milk, oily fish. *Carotene:* Brightly coloured vegetables, e.g. carrots.	• Growth. • Healthy eyes. • Healthy skin. • Healthy linings of the nose and throat, etc.	• Slowed growth. • Night blindness. • Linings of the nose and throat become dry and irritated.
D	Cheese, eggs, fish liver oils, liver, margarine, oily fish, sunshine.	• Works with calcium for healthy bones and teeth.	• Rickets (children). • Osteoporosis (adults). • Osteomalacia (adults).
K	Made in the bowel, green vegetables, cereals.	• Helps blood to clot.	• Problems with blood clotting.

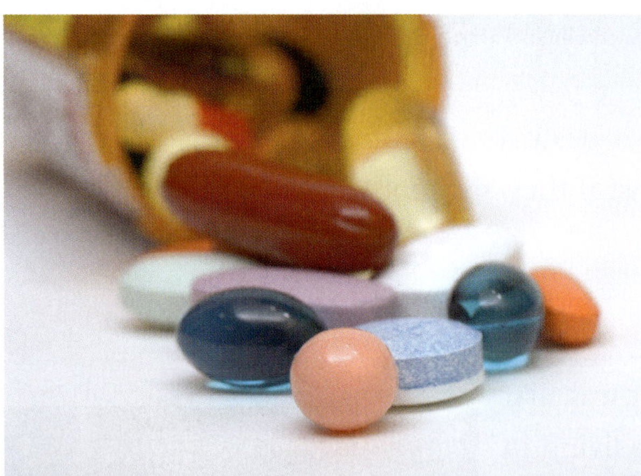

Hypervitaminosis

Because fat-soluble vitamins dissolve in fat, they can be stored in the fatty tissue of the body. Therefore, it is possible to have too much in the diet and a condition called **hypervitaminosis** results. There have been cases of hypervitaminosis A and D in people who eat foods high in vitamin A and D and also take food supplements in tablet form. The effects are dry skin, reduced bone density, hair loss, headaches, skin problems, birth defects and liver problems.

Homework Assignment
4 P. 10

Minerals

Minerals, like vitamins, are needed in small amounts by the body for growth and general good health. Important minerals include:

- Calcium.
- Iron.
- Iodine.
- Fluorine.
- Sodium.
- Phosphorus.

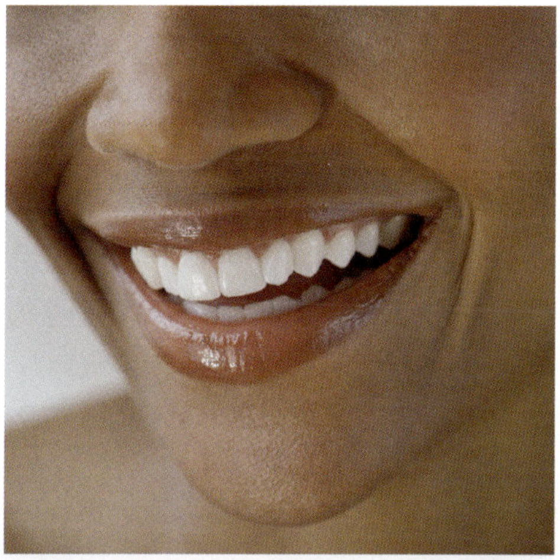

Calcium

Sources: What foods contain calcium?

Cheese, milk, tinned fish, water, yoghurt, beans, bread and cereals.

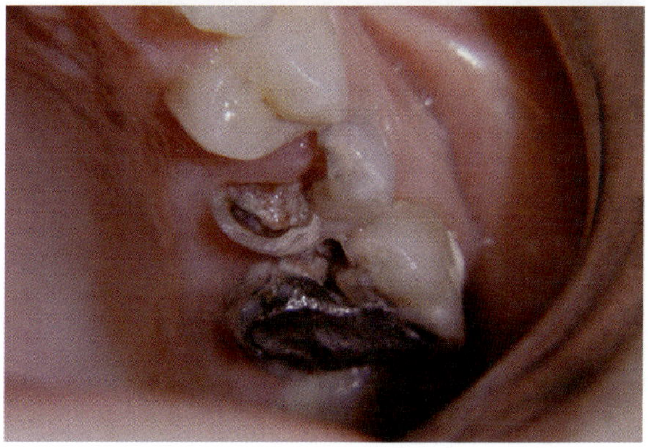

Functions of calcium

Calcium is needed to build strong bones and teeth.

Deficiency symptoms and diseases

If you don't get enough calcium, you risk rickets, osteomalacia (adult rickets), osteoporosis (brittle bones) and tooth decay.

Iron

Sources: What foods contain iron?

Red meat, offal (liver and kidney) and green vegetables.

Functions and deficiency of iron

There is a substance called **haemoglobin** in our blood. Haemoglobin carries oxygen to all our body's cells. Iron is needed to make haemoglobin. If there is not enough iron in our diet, anaemia is the result. The symptoms of **anaemia** are tiredness, paleness, weakness and dizziness. A survey conducted by UCD and UCC in 2008 found that approximately 75 per cent of Irish teenage girls are not getting enough iron.

Other minerals

Vitamin	Sources	Functions	Deficiency symptoms
Iodine	Cereals, milk, sea fish, sea salt, seaweed, vegetables	Needed for a healthy thyroid gland (in the neck)	Goitre (see photo)
Fluorine	Sea fish, tap water, toothpaste	Helps prevent tooth decay	Tooth decay
Sodium (salt)	Salt added to food, bacon, snack and convenience foods	Needed for water balance in the body	Cramps, bloating
Phosphorus	Some is found in most foods, especially high-protein foods	Works with calcium for strong bones and teeth	None known

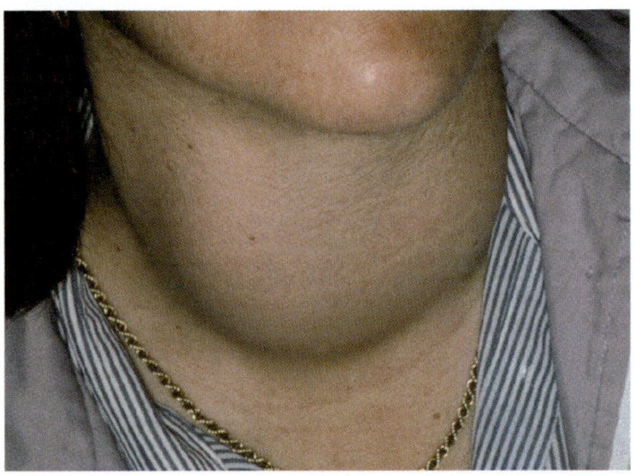

Goitre is a disease of the thyroid gland

Salt

Too much **salt** (sodium) is linked with high blood pressure and strokes.

Vitamin and mineral link

- Vitamin C is needed to absorb iron.
- Vitamin D is needed to absorb calcium.

Homework Assignment 5 P. 13

Fruit and vegetables can consist of up to 90 per cent water

Water

Sources of water

Food

All foods contain water, except solid fats, such as lard, and dried foods, such as cornflakes.

Drinks

Coffee, fruit juice, milk, soft drinks, tea and water.

Properties of water

Pure water is tasteless and has no smell

Water boils at 100°C

Water changes to steam at 100°C

Water freezes at 0°C

Functions: What is water needed for in the body?

- Body fluids, such as blood, are mainly water.
- Water is often a source of calcium and fluoride.
- Water removes waste from the body, e.g. in urine.
- Water helps keep the body at the right temperature; for instance, we sweat water when we are too hot.

Dehydration

Dehydration is when the body loses more than 2 per cent of its normal volume of water. It is particularly dangerous in babies (the main sign of dehydration in babies is a depressed soft spot on the top of their head). Dehydration can occur after a long period of vomiting or diarrhoea or if people consume too much alcohol. The main symptoms of dehydration are bad breath, dark-coloured urine, headaches, cramps, lowered blood pressure, dizziness, dry, itchy skin, constipation, rapid heart rate and tingling in the fingers and toes. To prevent dehydration, eight glasses of water should be drunk every day.

Energy

How energy is produced in the body

Food is burned in the body's cells and energy is produced. Oxygen is needed. This process is called **oxidation**.

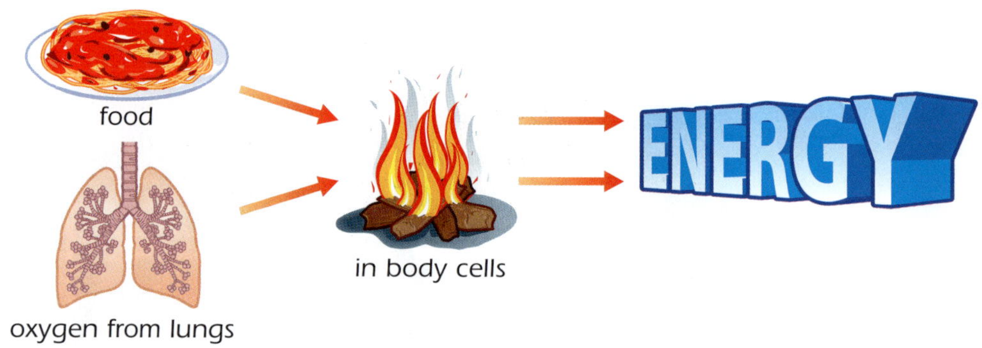

Oxidation

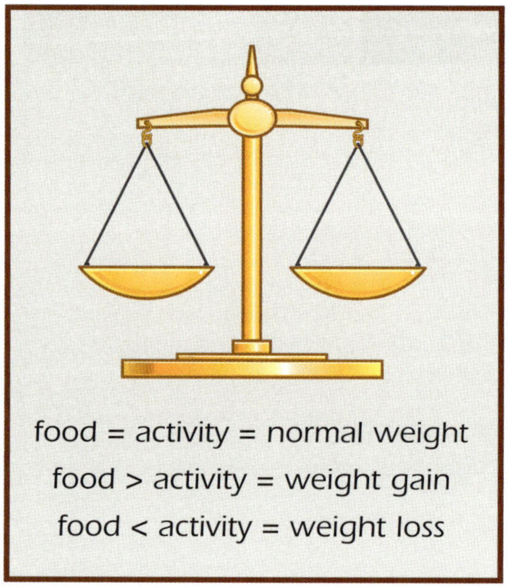

Energy balance

Energy balance, as the name suggests, is all about energy input (food) equalling energy output (BMR + activity).

Note: BMR is explained on p. 15.

Kilocalories and kilojoules

Just as the amount of milk in a carton is measured in litres, the amount of energy provided by food is measured in **kilocalories (kcal)** or kilojoules (kJ). 1 kcal = 4.2 kJ.

Food labels

All foods that contain protein, fat or carbohydrate produce energy and are said to contain calories. Food products must display nutritional information on the package. One piece of information displayed is the food's energy value. Food labels give energy values per 100g of the food. Food labels often give values for a serving of the food as well.

How much energy do I need?

The amount of energy (number of kilocalories or kilojoules) needed by an individual depends on their size, whether they are male or female, their age and how active they are. Pregnant or breastfeeding women and people living in cold climates need extra energy. However, there are **average** recommended daily allowances (RDAs) for energy.

Approximate daily energy requirements (in kilocalories)

Toddler	Child	Adolescent female	Adolescent male	Adult male	Adult female	Adult female
2 years	7–10 years	11–18 years	11–14 years	sedentary	sedentary	pregnancy
1,300	2,000	2,100	2,600	2,600	2,100	2,400
			15–18 years	active	active	lactation
			2,900	3,000	2,300	2,700

Energy output

The body needs a basic amount of energy to stay alive; this is called a person's **basal metabolic rate (BMR)**. Extra energy is needed for activities. Look at the graph below to see the amount of energy (kilocalories) needed for various activities.

Homework Assignment 6 P. 15

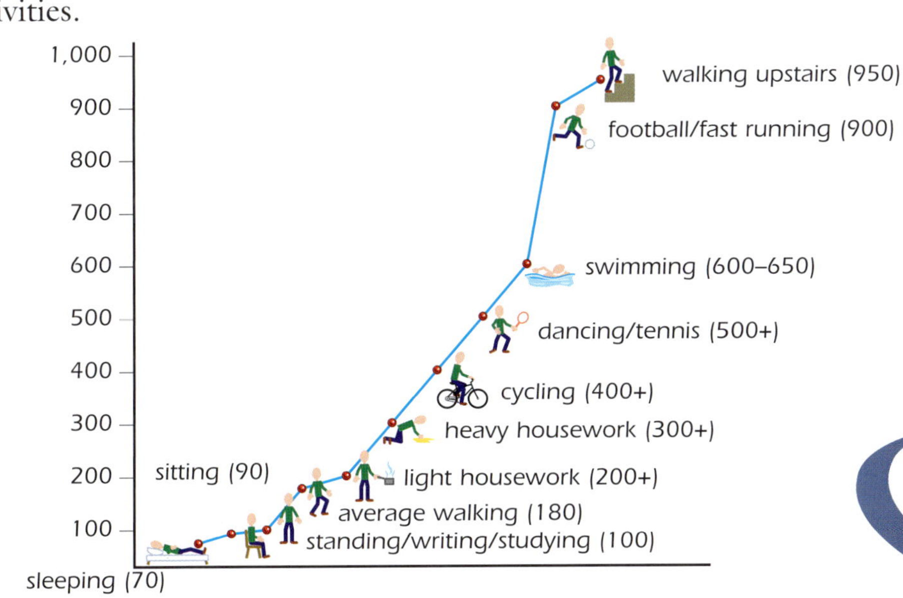

Energy consumption per hour of various activities

CHAPTER 2

Digestion

Teacher's CD-ROM: Slide presentation • Student activity pack – with revision crossword • Class test

Higher Level

As we saw in Chapter 1, food contains the following six nutrients:

- Protein.
- Fat.
- Carbohydrate.
- Minerals.
- Vitamins.
- Water.

Protein, fat and carbohydrate must be **digested**, or broken down, before they can be used by the body. Minerals, vitamins and water, on the other hand, need no digestion and can be used by the body as they are.

Food is **physically** broken down by being chewed in the mouth and churned around in the stomach.

Protein, fat and carbohydrate are **chemically** broken down by **enzymes**.

Digestive enzymes are chemical substances that break down food. Enzymes themselves do not change in the process. Each enzyme can only work on one nutrient. For example, an enzyme that can break down fats would have no effect on protein.

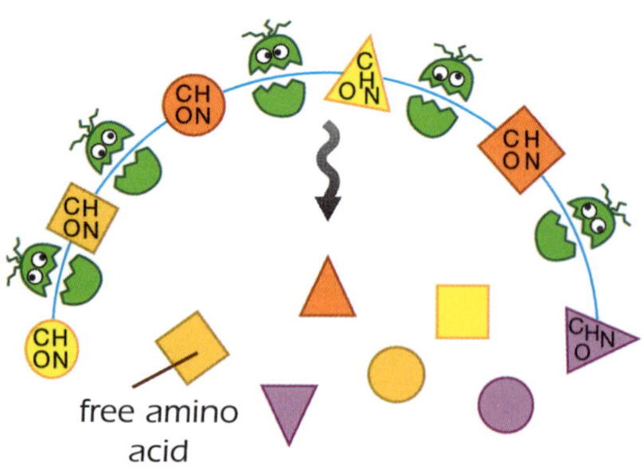

Digestion of protein

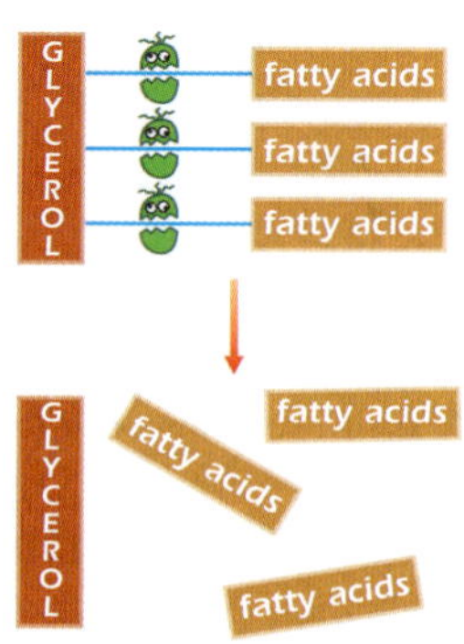

Digestion of fat

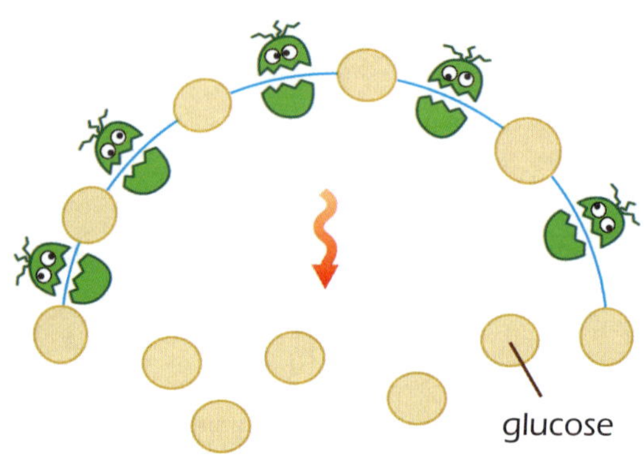

Digestion of carbohydrate

The alimentary canal

Digestion takes place in the alimentary canal. The alimentary canal consists of the:

- Mouth.
- Oesophagus.
- Stomach.
- Small intestine (pancreas and liver).
- Large intestine.
- Rectum.

1. The teeth physically break food down in the mouth. The tongue mixes it with saliva from the **salivary glands**. Saliva contains the enzyme **amylase**. Amylase breaks down long chains of cooked starch, such as bread, into shorter chains called **maltose**.

2. Food is then swallowed and passes into a long tube called the **oesophagus**. The walls of the oesophagus move in and out, squeezing the food along – this is called **peristalsis**.

3. Food then passes into the **stomach**. The stomach can be described as a muscular bag, which lies in the left-hand side of the abdomen under the **diaphragm**. Food is churned about in the stomach until it turns into a liquid called **chyme**. The walls of the stomach produce a juice called **gastric juice**. This juice is made of a strong acid, **hydrochloric acid**, and two enzymes. One of these enzymes is called **pepsin** and it starts to digest protein by breaking the long amino acid chains into shorter ones called **peptides**.

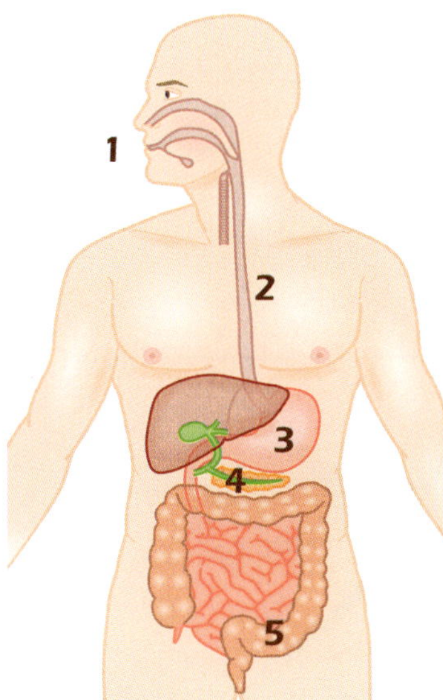

4. Next, food passes into the narrow, but very long, **small intestine**. Again, peristalsis keeps the food moving along. Three digestive juices work here to complete the digestion of our food:

- Pancreatic juice (made by the pancreas).
- Bile (made by the liver; works on fats).
- Intestinal juice (made by the intestine itself).

All three juices work together to change:

- Protein and peptides to free amino acids.
- Carbohydrates to monomers (simple sugars).
- Fats to fatty acids and glycerol.

Digested nutrients are then absorbed into the blood. They travel to our body cells, where they carry out their various functions, such as producing heat and energy.

5. Waste that is not absorbed now passes into the **large intestine** (**colon** or **bowel**). As it passes into the large intestine, the waste is still very liquid. Some of this water passes back through the walls of the intestine into the bloodstream. This causes the waste to become more solid. It is now called **faeces**. Faeces passes out of the body through the rectum and anus.

The small intestine

The walls of the small intestine resemble a very fine carpet. They are covered in a huge number of hair-like projections called **villi.** Each villus has a tiny blood vessel and a lymph vessel. Digested nutrients pass into these vessels.

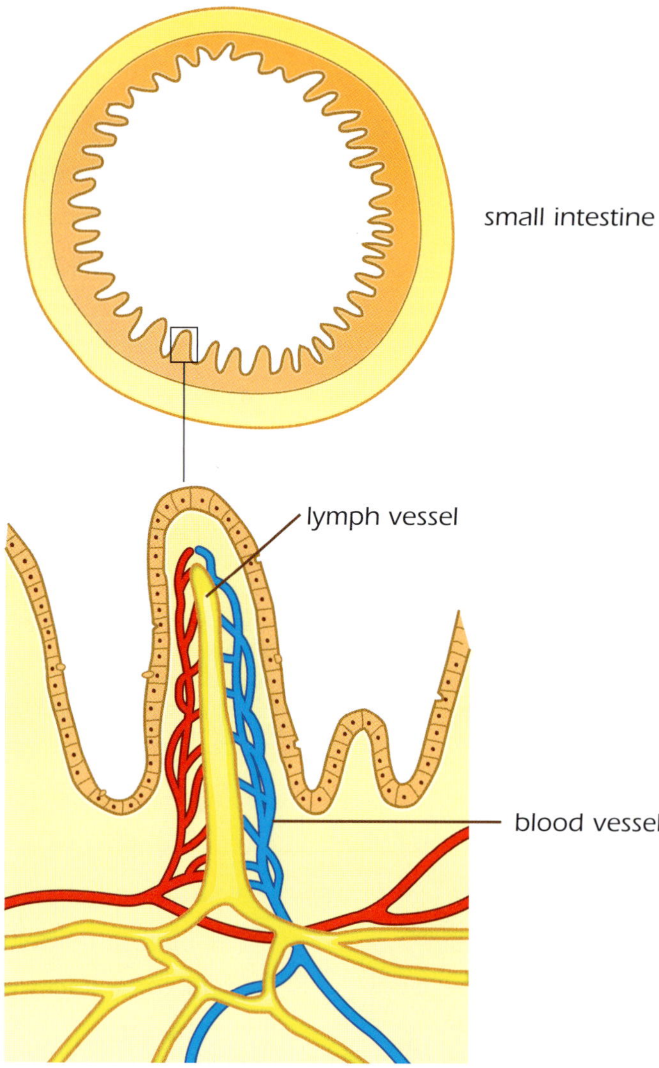

The absorption and transport of protein and carbohydrate is simple:

small intestine → blood vessel of villi → bloodstream → body cells

Fats are more complicated:

small intestine → lymph vessel of villi → lymph system → bloodstream → body cells

Homework Assignment 7 P. 17

Test Yourself eTest.ie

Unit 1 FOOD

CHAPTER 3

A Balanced Diet

Slide presentation • Student activity pack – with revision crossword • Class test

Teacher's CD-ROM

To have a balanced diet, we need to eat the correct amount of each of the six nutrients. The food pyramid pictured here is designed to make planning a healthy, balanced diet easy. It divides food into four groups and then advises us on how much of each group we need per day. The number of servings to be eaten from each group will depend on the individual. For example, a pregnant woman will need extra servings from the meat and milk groups.

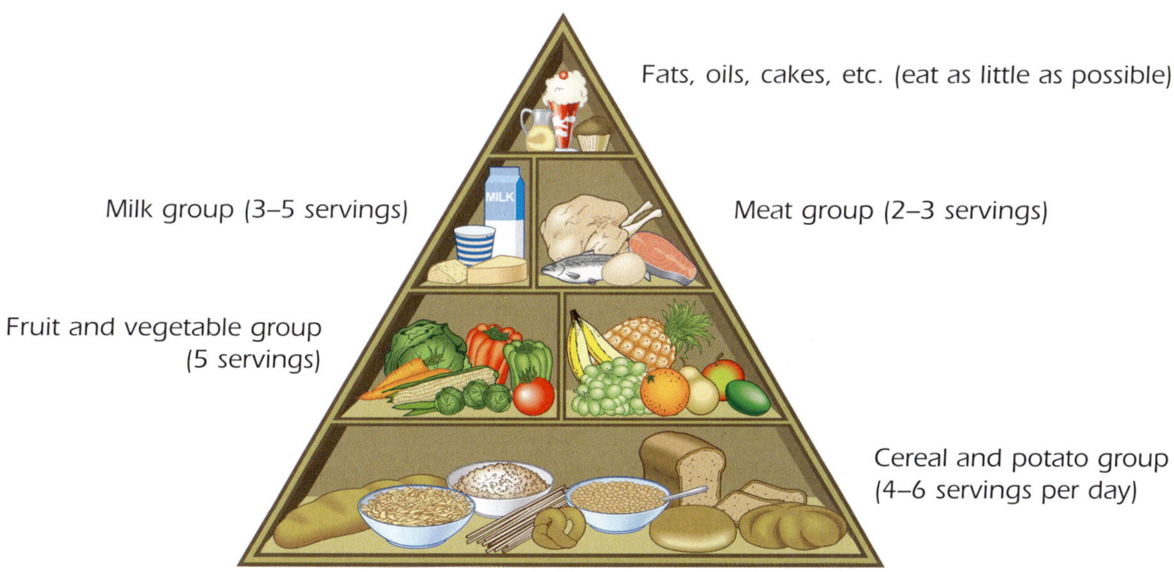

General healthy eating guidelines

- Reduce intake of salt, sugar and saturated fat.
- Increase intake of fibre, fruit and vegetables, water, iron and calcium.

The food groups

	Meat group	Milk group	Fruit and vegetables	Cereal and potato group

Why we need this group	The foods in this group are good sources of protein, needed for growth and repair of the body's cells.	The foods in this group are good sources of calcium and protein. Calcium is needed for strong bones and teeth. Choose low-fat options (except for children under five).	The foods in this group are good sources of some vitamins and minerals. Many contain fibre to prevent constipation.	The foods in this group are needed for energy. Choose wholemeal options, as they contain more fibre to prevent constipation.
A serving is:	50g meat or chicken 50g cheddar-type cheese 75g fish 75g TVP 75g Quorn 75g nuts 2 eggs 8 dessertspoons beans/peas	1 glass milk 1 carton yoghurt 25g cheese	1 small glass fruit juice 4 dessertspoons cooked vegetables 1 bowl homemade soup 1 piece fresh fruit 4 dessertspoons cooked or tinned fruit	1 small bowl cereal 1 slice bread 4 dessertspoons rice or pasta 1 potato
Servings per day from this group	Child **2** Teenager **2** Adult **2** Pregnant woman **3** Breastfeeding mother **3**	Child **3** Teenager **5** Adult **3** Pregnant woman **5** Breastfeeding mother **5**	Child **5** Teenager **5** Adult **5** Pregnant woman **5** Breastfeeding mother **5**	Child **4** Teenager **6** Adult **6** Pregnant woman **6** Breastfeeding mother **6**

A balanced diet for each age group

Babies

1. Breastfeed if possible for the first six months. If bottle feeding, then use a suitable formula milk, as cows' milk should not be given to babies.

2. Do not allow babies and toddlers to sleep with a bottle in their mouth, as this causes 'bottle rot' and they could choke.
3. Wean onto puréed solids at four to six months. Introduce one food at a time. Avoid using convenience baby foods, e.g. jars, as babies become used to their taste and may refuse fresh, home-cooked food (see also weaning on pp. 330–31).
4. Babies need vitamin C. Serve juice in a cup or from a spoon, never from a bottle, as it rots teeth. Stewed, puréed fruit is also a good source of vitamin C.
5. From six months, a baby's natural store of iron runs out. They therefore need iron-rich foods such as dark green vegetables and liver from six months.
6. Do not add salt or sugar to a baby's food.
7. By one year, babies will generally be eating the same foods as the rest of the family. Remove the baby's portion before adding seasonings, especially salt.

Children

1. Have regular meal times.
2. Children need more protein, calcium, vitamin D and iron for their size than adults.
3. Serve small, attractive portions. Each meal should contain a nutrient-dense food. Nutrient-dense foods are foods that contain a number of different nutrients but with little bulk. They are sometimes called superfoods. Examples of nutrient-dense foods are cheese, eggs, chicken and fish.
4. Do not fuss about food refusal; it makes it worse.
5. Serve healthy snacks such as fruit or popcorn.
6. Continue to use whole milk, as it contains vitamin A for growth and vitamin D for healthy bones.
7. Try to serve healthy packed lunches and avoid junk food such as sweets, crisps, etc. Children should be given these foods only very occasionally, especially due to the fact that approximately 10 per cent of Irish children are overweight or obese.
8. Set a good example yourself, as children imitate adults in their eating patterns.

Adolescents/teenagers

1. The growth spurt during the teenage years means teenagers need plenty of protein, calcium and iron.
2. Some very active teenagers will require lots of high-energy foods, though choose foods that provide other nutrients as well, e.g. brown bread, rice and pasta. Inactive teenagers, however, need to monitor their carbohydrate and fat intake to avoid weight gain. The ideal would be that they would introduce an activity, e.g. walking, into their daily routine, even if they are not particularly interested in sport.
3. Girls need to eat iron-rich foods such as red meat and green vegetables to avoid anaemia because of periods (menstruation).
4. For healthy skin, avoid fried foods, chocolate, etc. Eat fruit and vegetables and drink plenty of water (eight glasses per day).
5. Choose healthy snacks such as yoghurt and fruit.

Adults

1. Weight gain becomes more common as people enter adulthood. People with sedentary jobs should cut down on what they eat to avoid weight gain.
2. Many people (especially women) stop taking regular exercise once they leave school. Adults should try to take some form of exercise at least three times per week.
3. Eat plenty of fibre-rich foods such as brown bread, fruit and vegetables, as they prevent bowel disease and are low in calories.

A sedentary worker

A manual worker

4. Do not eat too much salt. It can cause high blood pressure and strokes.
5. Avoid foods that have too much saturated fat, such as butter and sausages. Saturated fats contain cholesterol, which is linked to heart disease.
6. Women in particular should eat calcium-rich foods such as milk, yoghurt and cheese to avoid brittle bones in later life. Also, because of monthly blood loss, all women risk anaemia and so need to eat iron-rich foods such as meat, cereals and green vegetables.
7. Avoid drinking too much alcohol (women maximum 14 units per week, men 21 units).

Note: Vitamin C is also needed to absorb iron.

Pregnant and breastfeeding women

1. Pregnant women are *not* eating for two. Eating empty-calorie foods during pregnancy will cause weight gain, which will be hard to lose afterwards. The average weight gain during pregnancy is 12kg (2 stone). Anything more than this (except with multiple births) is just extra body fat.
2. Avoid smoking, alcohol, strong tea, coffee and spicy foods. Avoid lightly cooked eggs, unpasteurised cheeses and cook-chill foods because of the risk of food poisoning.

3. Eat iron-rich foods such as green vegetables to avoid anaemia. Vitamin C is needed to absorb iron, so fresh fruit and juices should be eaten.
4. Take vitamin D to help absorb calcium. Vitamin D is found in cod liver oil and oily fish such as mackerel, and is made in the body in the presence of sunshine.
5. Eat calcium for healthy bones and teeth. It is found in milk, tinned fish and cheese (pasteurised only).
6. Because of the extra weight bearing down on the bowel, some women experience constipation during pregnancy. To avoid this, eat plenty of fruit and vegetables and fibre-rich cereals such as brown bread, pasta and rice.
7. Breastfeeding women should eat a healthy diet so that they can produce good-quality breast milk. Extra fluids should be taken. Alcohol, smoking and drinking too much caffeine should be avoided, as they all pass into the breast milk.

Folic acid

Approximately 84 babies are born every year in Ireland with serious neural tube defects such as spina bifida. Folic acid helps prevent spina bifida and other conditions and should be taken in tablet form for three months before becoming pregnant and for the first 12 weeks of pregnancy. Some foods, such as breakfast cereals, are fortified with folic acid (this means that folic acid is added artificially by manufacturers).

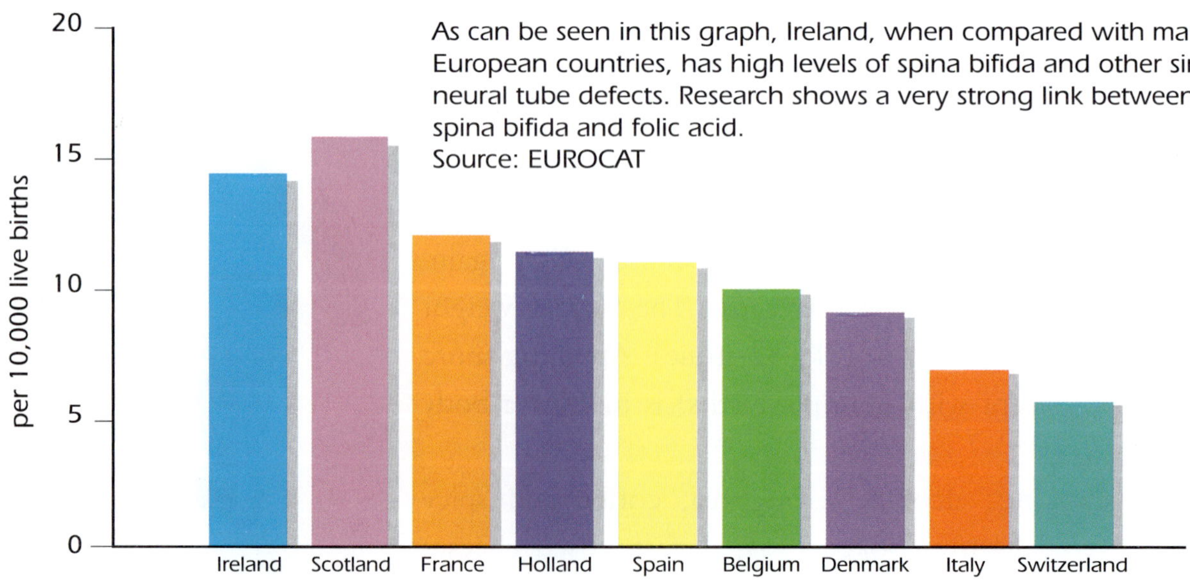

As can be seen in this graph, Ireland, when compared with many European countries, has high levels of spina bifida and other similar neural tube defects. Research shows a very strong link between spina bifida and folic acid.
Source: EUROCAT

Elderly people

1. Some elderly people, especially those living alone, live on nutritionally poor diets. They may have arthritis, making shopping and cooking difficulty. They may have difficulty chewing food or lack the motivation to cook balanced meals. The elderly should try to eat three nourishing meals a day.
2. Choose low-fat cheese, milk and yoghurt, as these foods are high in calcium and low in fat. Calcium prevents osteoporosis (brittle bones).
3. To prevent heart disease, limit high-cholesterol foods such as butter and sausages. Choose polyunsaturated spreads instead, such as Flora.
4. Eat plenty of fruit and vegetables; many elderly people lack vitamin C.
5. Reduce salt, fat and sugar intake.
6. Choose high-fibre foods such as brown bread and fruit, as elderly people can be prone to constipation.
7. Limit intake of processed foods such as tinned foods, white bread and butter.

Invalids and convalescents (those recovering from illness)

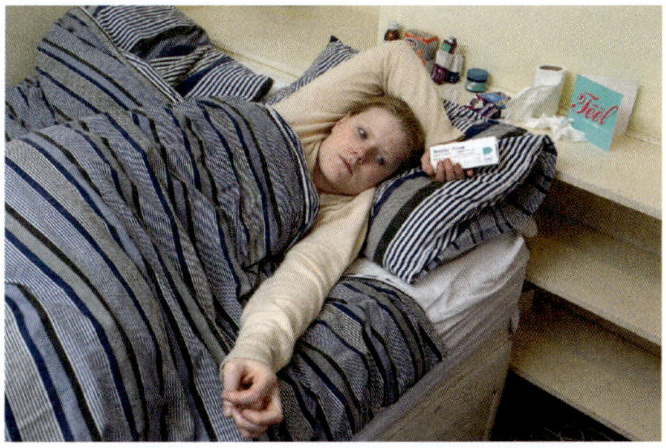

1. Follow the doctor's or hospital dietician's advice.
2. Eat protein-rich foods such as chicken, fish and pulse vegetables for repairing damaged cells.
3. Eat or drink vitamin C-rich foods such as fruit and fruit juices to help fight infection, repair wounds and help absorb iron.
4. Eat iron-rich foods such as offal, green vegetables and brown bread to prevent anaemia if blood has been lost.
5. Foods should be easily digested, such as white fish, chicken, custard, milk, light soups such as broth and fruit juice.
6. Drink plenty of fluids, especially with fever.
7. Boil, bake, grill or steam food. Do not fry, reheat or add spices.
8. Prepare small, attractive portions.
9. Remember: food hygiene is very important.

Homework Assignment

8 P. 19

Test Yourself eTest.ie

CHAPTER 4

Special Diets

Teacher's CD-ROM Slide presentation • Student activity pack – with revision crossword • Class test

People follow special diets for many different reasons. The following diets will be studied in this chapter:

- Vegetarianism.
- Diet-related conditions such as coronary heart disease and obesity and their diet-related treatments, i.e. low-fat, low-salt, low-sugar and high-fibre diets.
- Coeliac disease.
- Diabetes.

Vegetarianism

Vegetarians, for various reasons, do not eat meat or fish. There are two types of vegetarian:

- Lactovegetarians do not eat meat or fish but do eat animal products such as milk, cheese and eggs.
- Vegans, or strict vegetarians, eat only plant foods such as fruit, vegetables, nuts, cereals and soya milk.
- Vegans usually take vitamin B supplements because this vitamin is not found in plant foods at all.

Case Study

Hi, my name is Fiona and I'm a lactovegetarian. I became a vegetarian about three years ago. Some people don't eat meat for religious reasons; my decision was based more on health grounds. I believe it's wrong to kill animals, and also it scares me when I read about all the hormones that are pumped into animals these days.

Being vegetarian has its advantages. My diet is a really healthy one: it's low in fat and high in fibre, which will help prevent bowel disorders and heart disease later in life. It also keeps me at my correct weight. I do have to be careful that I get enough iron and protein, though, so I eat plenty of dark green vegetables and brown bread for iron and foods like cheese, beans, TVP and Quorn for protein.

Generally I find being a vegetarian fine. There are lots of different foods to choose from. I don't feel restricted just because I don't eat meat.

Suitable vegetarian dishes

- Various vegetable soups such as carrot, mushroom or mixed vegetable.
- Vegetarian pizza, quiche, risotto, lasagne, curry.
- Various salads.
- Stir-fries.

Problem diets

Most diet-related problems are linked to the following:

- Eating too much saturated fat (heart disease, obesity and type 2 diabetes).
- Eating too much salt (high blood pressure and strokes).
- Eating too much sugar (obesity and type 2 diabetes).
- Eating too little fibre (bowel diseases such as colon cancer).
- Drinking too much alcohol (heart disease, liver disease, obesity and type 2 diabetes).

Coronary heart disease and strokes

A **heart attack** occurs when an artery becomes totally blocked by the fatty substance known as cholesterol. A **stroke** occurs if the blocked artery is in the brain.

Ireland has the highest death rate from heart disease in people aged under 65 in the EU (see bar chart below).

Most heart attacks happen within a few hours of the symptoms first occurring and before the person reaches hospital. Prevention is therefore vitally important.

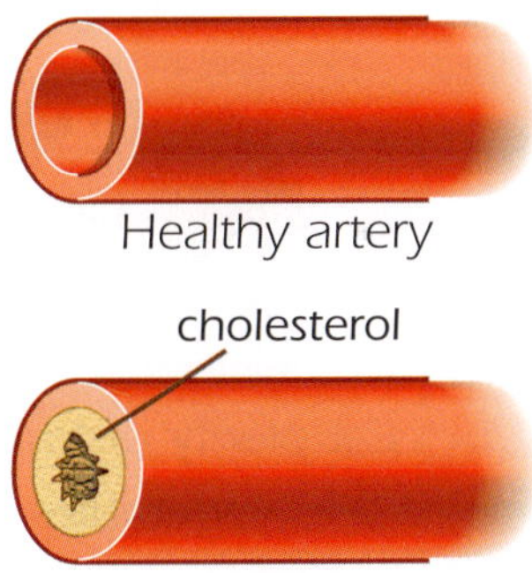

Death rates per 100,000 people from coronary heart disease in the EU (age 0–65)
Source: World Health Organisation

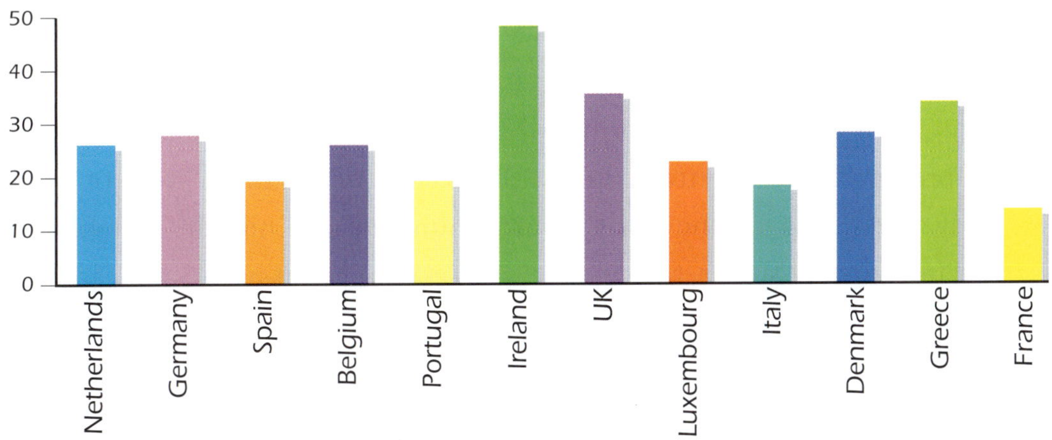

Heart disease is linked to:

- High-fat diet.
- Being overweight.
- Smoking.
- Drinking too much.
- A stressful lifestyle.

Tips for a healthy heart: Low-fat diet

Eat fewer foods from the top of the food pyramid.

Bake, grill, boil, steam or microwave food: avoid frying food.

Use low-fat products.

Use polyunsaturated margarine, e.g. Flora.

Eat plenty of fruit and vegetables.

Drink eight glasses of water per day.

Choose chicken and fish instead of fatty red meats.

Low-salt diet

According to the Irish Heart Foundation, if everyone in Ireland reduced their salt intake by half a teaspoon (3 grams) per day, it would prevent 900 deaths per year from stroke and heart attack.

Salt is the common name for a substance called sodium. Sodium is sometimes represented by the letters Na. Adults need a maximum of 4–6g of sodium per day, according to the Irish Heart Foundation. Children should have less. Many of us, however, take up to 20g. Too much salt in the diet can cause high blood pressure (hypertension), which can lead to heart attacks and strokes.

Reducing salt in the diet:

- Reduce the amount of salt added during cooking or at the table. Use low-sodium alternatives such as LoSalt.
- Flavour dishes with herbs, spices and pepper instead of salt.
- Choose fresh meat and vegetables – these have a naturally low salt content.
- Avoid foods high in salt, e.g. ham, bacon, rashers, sausages, frozen burgers, packet soups and sauces, instant noodles, stock cubes, crisps, popcorn and salted nuts.
- If in doubt, look out for the words *salt*, *sodium* or *Na* on food labels.

Low-sugar diet

Sugar is not needed in the diet. Sugar and sugary food and drinks are often called **empty-calorie foods**. This means that they provide a lot of calories but very little goodness.

Unfortunately, many of us are encouraged to develop a sweet tooth as children, when we are rewarded with sugary foods for being 'good'. Too much sugar in the diet causes weight problems and tooth decay.

Reducing sugar in the diet:

- Avoid fizzy drinks (especially non-diet), sweets, bars, sugary breakfast cereals, cakes, etc.
- Use artificial sweeteners, e.g. Canderel, for cooking.
- Snack on healthy foods such as fresh fruit and unsalted nuts.
- Be careful of 'hidden sugars'. Read labels – glucose, fructose and sucrose are all sugar.

High-fibre diet

Dietary fibre (cellulose) is found in plant foods such as cereals, fruit and vegetables. However, once foods, particularly cereals, are processed, they lose much of their fibre content. Therefore, wholesome, unprocessed foods should be eaten. Having a high-fibre diet has many benefits – it helps prevent constipation, piles and other serious diseases of the bowel, e.g. colon cancer. Fibre absorbs large amounts of water when eaten, creating a feeling of fullness. In addition, it contains no calories, so fibre-rich foods are excellent to include in the diet for anyone trying to lose weight.

Fibre-rich foods include wholegrain breads and breakfast cereals, e.g. All-Bran, brown rice and pasta, fruit and vegetables, nuts and seeds.

Incidence of colon cancer worldwide

Region/countries	Rate per 100,000 population
Australia and New Zealand	45.0
Western Europe, e.g. Austria, Britain, France, Germany, Ireland	36.4
Southern Europe, e.g. Greece, Italy, Malta, Portugal, Spain	29.7
Eastern Europe, e.g. Bulgaria, Latvia, Poland, Romania, Ukraine	25.1
Eastern Asia, e.g. Iran, Saudi Arabia, Syria	25.1
South Central Asia, e.g. India, Nepal, Pakistan	4.1
South Africa	10.1
Northern Africa, e.g. Cameroon, Chad, Ethiopia, Nigeria, Sudan	4.5

What sort of food is traditionally eaten in countries with low/high incidence rates of colon cancer?

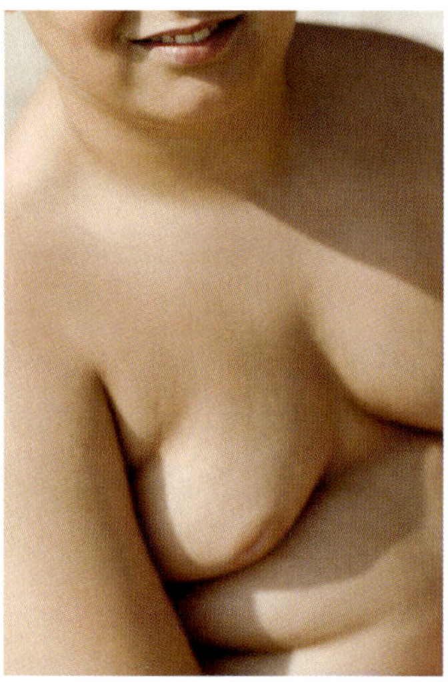

Obesity

Obesity means being 20 per cent or more above the normal weight for your height and build. In Ireland, 20 per cent of men and 16 per cent of women are obese. Obesity levels among Irish children have gone up by almost 70 per cent since 1990, with one in every 10 Irish children now classified as obese.

The thyroid gland in the neck controls the rate at which we burn food. People who are naturally thin burn food quickly, but some people burn food more slowly and are therefore prone to put on weight.

Obesity can be caused by an unhealthy thyroid gland. More often, though, the cause is overeating and lack of exercise.

People who are obese suffer an increased risk of:

- Chest infections.
- Diabetes.
- Fertility problems.
- Heart attacks.
- High blood pressure.
- Low self-esteem.
- Problems when under anaesthetic.
- Strokes.
- Varicose veins.

Body mass index (BMI)

Body mass index (BMI) is a measure of body fat based on height and weight that applies to both **adult** men and women.

$$\text{BMI} = \frac{\text{weight in kg}}{\text{height in m}^2} \quad \text{or} \quad \frac{\text{weight in lb} \times 703}{\text{height in inches}^2}$$

BMI categories:

- Underweight = < 18.5
- Normal weight = 18.5–24.9
- Overweight = 25–29.9
- Obesity = BMI of 30 or greater

Guidelines for sensible weight loss:

1. Avoid crash or fad diets, as they do not work long term.
2. Exercise more – at least three times per week.
3. Plan your meals each day in advance. If you do not do this, you may get hungry and eat unwisely, e.g. buy a takeaway.
4. Always have healthy options easily available, e.g. fruit, if you wish to have a snack between meals.
5. Use a smaller plate and try to eat more slowly. If you eat quickly, you will eat more because your body has not had time to realise it is full.
6. Eat less butter, fatty meats such as sausages and burgers, sugary foods such as biscuits and chocolate and calorie-laden convenience foods such as pizza and garlic bread.
7. If you do buy biscuits, go for low-fat varieties and perhaps individually wrapped portions so you are not tempted to eat more than one or two at a time.
8. Eat more fruit and vegetables, white fish and chicken.
9. Eat bread, potatoes and nuts only in moderation.
10. Drink more water – at least eight glasses per day.

Coeliac disease

Higher Level

During normal digestion, long protein chains are broken down into lots of tiny amino acid units. These single units pass easily through the walls of the small intestine and into the bloodstream.

Gluten is a type of protein found in wheat and some other cereals. A person suffering from coeliac disease cannot break gluten down. The big undigested gluten molecules damage the walls of the intestine as they pass through.

The symptoms of the condition are pains in the abdomen, diarrhoea, failure to thrive and anaemia.

There is only one way of treating coeliac disease: avoid all foods containing gluten.

Foods to avoid:

- All wheat products: biscuits, bread, cakes, pasta, many breakfast cereals.
- Rye and barley.
- Processed meat products such as sausages and fish or anything else in batter or breadcrumbs.
- Packet soups and sauces, many snack foods.

Gluten-free foods and foods very low in gluten:

- Fruit, vegetables, dairy products such as milk and cheese.
- Rice, soya products such as TVP.
- Plain meat and fish.
- Maize products such as cornflakes.
- Specially made gluten-free products such as bread and cakes.

Gluten-free products

Diabetes

Diabetes is a disorder that occurs when the pancreas (a leaf-shaped organ under the stomach) does not produce any/enough insulin to meet the body's needs or stops being able to use insulin, causing abnormally high levels of sugar in the blood.

Normally, when you eat carbohydrates, such as bread, pasta, fruits or vegetables, these foods are broken down into glucose (sugar). This fuel then travels in the bloodstream until it is 'unloaded' into your cells by insulin, which functions like a little team of removal men. With diabetes, however, the body either stops producing any/enough insulin or becomes unable to use it properly. This makes it difficult for the sugar in the blood to get into the cells, so it builds up in the bloodstream. Body cells do not get enough fuel to function properly and literally begin starving to death. If left untreated, diabetes can lead to heart disease, kidney disease, chronic infections or other life-threatening conditions. While there is no cure for diabetes, it can be controlled.

There are two types of diabetes: type 1 and type 2.

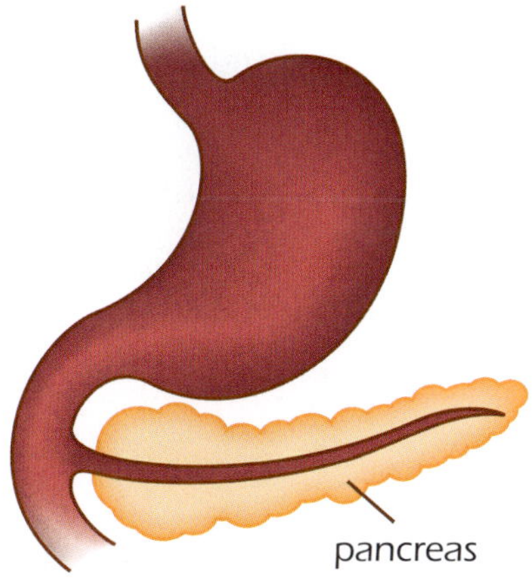

Type 1 diabetes, also called insulin-dependent diabetes, occurs in about 0.5 per cent of the general population. With type 1, the body produces little or no insulin and so insulin injections need to be taken daily. Type 1 may appear at any age but usually begins in childhood or early adulthood, most often among young people with a sibling or parent who also has the disease.

Type 2 diabetes, also called non-insulin-dependent diabetes, occurs in about 2–3 per cent of the general population. You are most likely to develop the disease if you are obese, are over the age of 45 or have a family history of diabetes. While type 2 diabetes used to be practically unheard of in people under 30 (it was actually called adult onset diabetes), now, because of increased obesity levels, it is unfortunately appearing in adolescence and even childhood. Studies show that a hormone produced by fat cells called resistin causes body cells to resist insulin. Thus, the more fat cells, the more resistin and the bigger the likelihood of diabetes. Most people with type 2 diabetes do not have to inject insulin, but some do.

Control of diabetes centres around three things – injections or tablets, diet and exercise.

Dietary guidelines for diabetics:

- Reach and maintain your ideal weight and take plenty of exercise.
- Eat regularly – don't skip meals.
- Keep to a low-sugar diet – some artificial sweeteners, e.g. Canderel, may be used.
- Eat high-fibre carbohydrates such as brown bread and pasta.
- Diabetic foods, such as diabetic chocolate, are available, but is it good to get out of the habit of eating sweet-tasting foods.

Homework Assignment

9 P. 25

Test Yourself eTest.ie

CHAPTER 5

Meal Planning

Teacher's CD-ROM

Slide presentation • Student activity pack • Class test

Factors that affect meal planning

1. Dietary restrictions, e.g. coeliac, diabetes, low-fat.
2. Nutrition: Meals should contain a good number of different nutrients.
3. Amount of time available to shop and cook.
4. Money/equipment available.
5. Climate and the availability of foods in season can also be a factor in meal planning:
   - Cold weather: Hot dishes such as stew.
   - Hot weather: Cold dishes such as salads.
6. Ability of the cook.
7. Occasion: The type of meal, e.g. lunch or dinner, formal or informal.

Meals: Courses

Main meals are usually divided into courses. In medieval times, when banquets lasted for days, meals had as many as 12 courses. In modern times, two to five courses are more common.

Courses

1. Starter or appetiser

This course should be something tasty and not too filling, such as soup, melon, fruit juice or pâté. This course gets the digestive juices flowing.

2. Main course

A meat, fish or vegetarian dish is central to this course. **Accompaniments** are also served, such as:

- Potatoes, pasta or rice.
- Vegetables or salad.
- A sauce or gravy.

3. Dessert or cheese board

- Hot or cold desserts such as trifle, cheesecake or warm apple pie with ice cream.
- A cheese board is a selection of three or four different cheeses served with crackers.
- Tea or coffee.

Menus

There are basically two types of menu:

- Table d'hôte.
- À la carte.

Table d'hôte is a set-price menu, usually cheaper than the à la carte menu, although you pay the full menu price even if you do not have all the courses. Two to five courses are usually on offer, with a limited number of dishes to choose from for each course (see the sample below).

On an à la carte menu, each item is priced separately. The menu may be several pages long, with a separate page with lots to choose from for each course (see the sample on the next page).

Table d'hôte menu

Starters

Pan-fried garlic mushrooms

Bruschetta

Toasted ciabatta bread topped with tomato, basil and olive oil

Deep-fried brie with red onion relish

Main course

Pork medallions

Medallions of pork fillet, pan fried with julienne of onion, peppers and mushroom in a pepper sauce

Poached salmon

Fillet of salmon poached in a light cream sauce

Vegetable risotto

Chicken Piri Piri

Char-grilled corn-fed chicken fillet in a lemon and chilli sauce

Desserts

Meringue nest with fresh fruit

Profiteroles with hot chocolate sauce

Hot apple pie served with fresh cream or ice cream

Tea or coffee

Price €38

À la carte

Starters

Pan-fried garlic mushrooms	€4.50
Home-made roasted winter vegetable soup	€3.75
Bruschetta	
Toasted ciabatta bread topped with tomato, basil and olive oil	€3.75
Tiger prawns in filo pastry	
Tossed in garlic butter and served with a sweet and sour dip	€7.25
Deep-fried brie with red onion relish	€5.25
Greek salad	
Fresh vine tomatoes with peppers, onions, cucumber	
with feta cheese and oregano dressing	€5.25

Rules for writing a menu:

- Write down the centre of the page.
- List courses in the order they are eaten.
- Write the main dish of the course first and then the accompaniments.
- Leave a line or place a motif between courses.
- Describe dishes in some detail: give the cut of meat or fish and the cooking method, such as 'roast loin of pork'.

A buffet table

Buffets

When catering for large numbers, such as a twenty-first birthday party, a buffet is often best. Food should be laid out in a logical way, with drinks served at a separate table.

Hot main course	Salads	Desserts	Other
Beef, vegetable or chicken curry; pizza, quiche, cocktail sausages, chilli con carne, chicken à la king	Cold meat salads, e.g. ham, turkey slices; Waldorf salad, pasta salad, potato salad, rice salad, coleslaw	Cheesecake, fresh fruit flans, mousse, fruit salad and cream, apple and rhubarb crumble or tart	Boiled rice, rolls, bread, salad dressings

Setting the table

- Everything should be spotless: cutlery, glasses, tablemats, tablecloths, etc. They should match if possible.
- Fill clean salt and pepper containers (condiments).
- Keep flower arrangements low.
- Place a jug of iced water on the table just before the meal begins.

Formal table setting

- Cutlery used first is on the outside.
- When serving, serve food to the left of the person eating and clear empty plates from the right.

Planning a meal

Once you have decided what you are going to cook, you now have to shop for the ingredients, store them correctly before use and then prepare the meal using an effective time or work plan.

Shopping for food

1. It is best to shop for food only once a week, as this reduces buying things that you do not really need (impulse buying).
2. When you have planned out your meals for the week or for the special occasion, make out a **shopping list** of all the ingredients you need. Check that you do not have any of them already.
3. Buy food in clean shops with a good variety of goods and a high turnover (this means that fresh foods are being put on shelves regularly).
4. Stick to your shopping list – something is not a bargain if you do not need it.
5. Avoid pre-packed fruit, vegetables and meat, as you cannot examine them for quality.
6. Check use-by dates and that food in supermarket freezer cabinets is stored below –18°C and below the load line (this is usually a red line; food should not be piled up above this mark, as it will not be cold enough).
7. Pack foods away at home as soon as possible after purchase.

Time/work plans

See Chapter 7, pp. 46–7.

Both time and work plans list all the tasks involved in preparing, cooking and serving a meal in the order it makes sense to carry them out. Time plans, unlike work plans (see Chapter 9, p. 65), include specific times. Basically, with both you work out how long it will take to make the various dishes on your menu and begin with the dish that takes the longest to make. For example, if your menu includes prawn cocktail, Irish stew and apple crumble with ice cream, you would start with the stew because it takes the longest to cook, then the crumble and last the prawn cocktail.

A garnished savoury dish

Presenting food

Before we taste food, we see it. How food is presented is very important. All tableware must be **spotlessly clean**. Wipe spills from dishes or plates before bringing them to the table. Garnish or decorate food attractively, but do not overdo it.

Garnishing and decorating food

- Garnish: Savoury foods.
- Decorate: Sweet foods.

Garnishes

Garnishes can either take the form of items placed on or beside food, such as lemon twists, or sauces, such as fillet steak with peppered sauce.

Dish	Suggested garnish
Soup	Parsley, swirl of cream, croutons
Fish	Lemon wedges or twists, tartar sauce, tomato roses
Lamb	Mint sprigs, mint sauce
Turkey	Cranberry sauce
Beef	Horseradish
Pork	Apple sauce
Duck	Orange sauce, orange twists

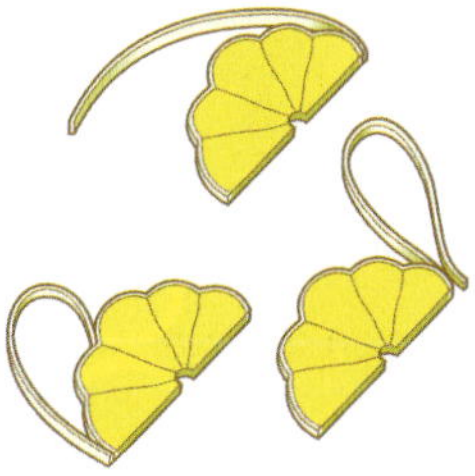

Lemon and lime loops

Spring onion tassel

Lemon/lime twist

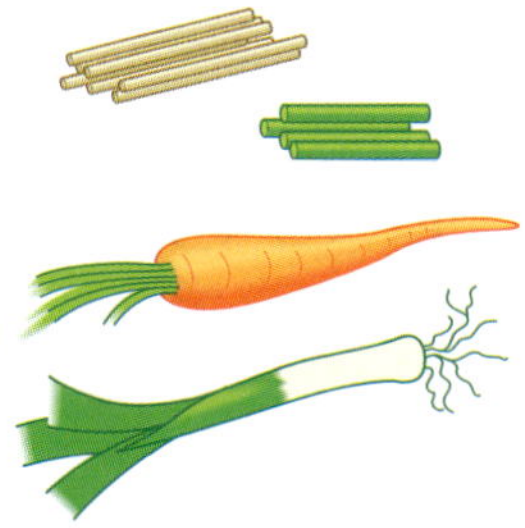

Julienne strips

Herbs

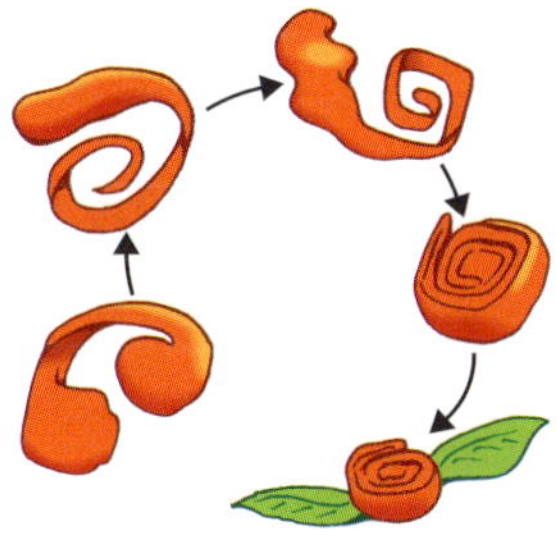

Tomato roses

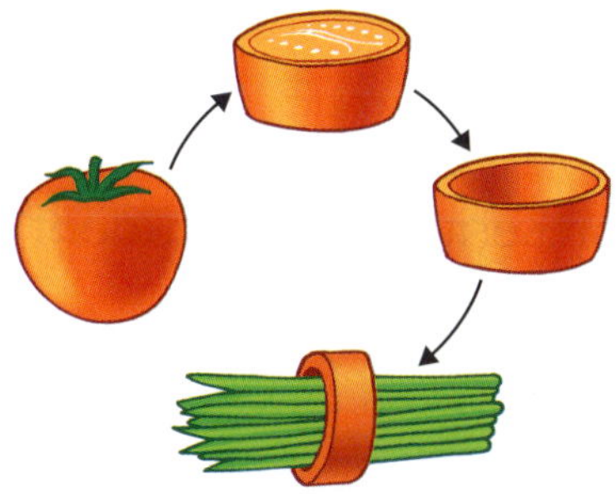

Tomato collar

Sweet dishes are decorated in lots of ways:

- Piped cream.
- Pastry decorations, such as leaves.
- Fruit, such as strawberry fans or slices, cherries, etc.
- Sugar-based decorations, such as angelica, grated chocolate or hundreds and thousands.
- Icing, such as feathered glacé icing, royal icing on Christmas cake, dusting with icing sugar on sponge cake.

Dessert with fruit coulis and sprig of mint

Piped cream

Glacé icing (feathering)

Strawberry fans

Homework Assignment 10 P. 31

CHAPTER 6

Good Food Hygiene and Storage

Teacher's CD-ROM

Slide presentation • Student activity pack – with revision crossword • Class test

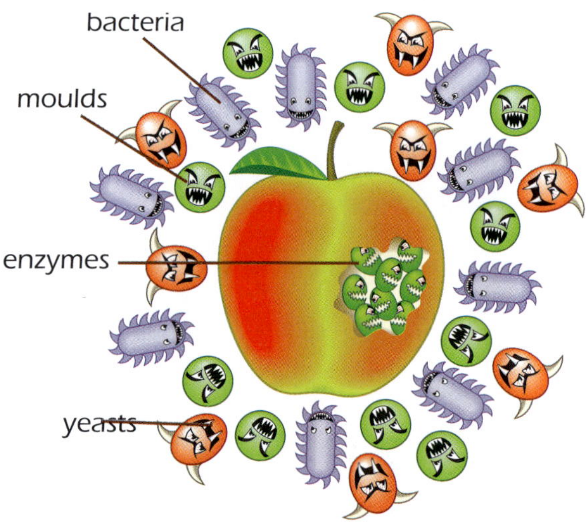

Food spoilage

Food spoilage is when food goes rotten or bad. It is caused by enzymes and micro-organisms (moulds, yeast and bacteria).

- **Enzymes:** Enzymes are naturally present in fruit and vegetables. They cause them to ripen and eventually rot.
- **Moulds:** Moulds cause a fluffy beard to grow on bread, fruit and vegetables. Many moulds are useful, e.g. they are used to make the antibiotic penicillin and blue-veined cheeses such as Cashel Blue.
- **Yeast:** While yeast will attack some foods, such as jam, yeast has a positive use in bread making, brewing and wine making.
- **Bacteria:** Bacteria are everywhere. If they multiply too much, they cause food to go off. They can also cause food poisoning.

Higher Level

Food poisoning

Food poisoning occurs when bacteria multiply to unacceptable levels on food and then the food is eaten. Our bodies respond to this invasion with symptoms such as cramps, nausea, vomiting and diarrhoea.

Some food-poisoning bacteria

Campylobacter

- *Campylobacter* can be found in raw poultry and meat, unpasteurised milk and untreated water. Pets with diarrhoea can also be a source of infection.

- *Campylobacter* is the most commonly identified cause of food poisoning.

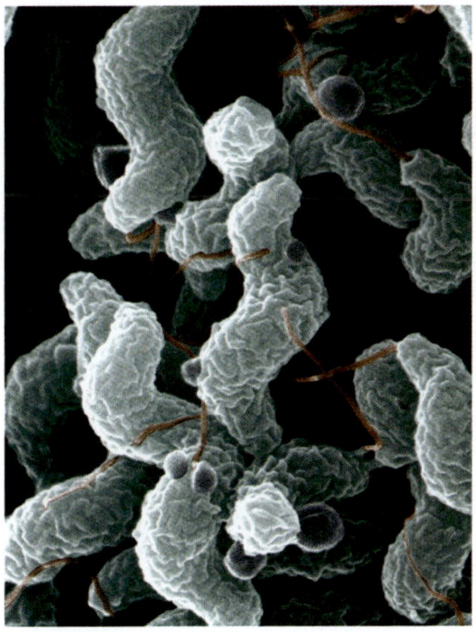
Campylobacter

Salmonella

- *Salmonella* occurs naturally in the intestines of animals and humans. It is found in human and animal faeces.
- It causes no problem until faeces (even tiny amounts) get onto food and food is not cooked, or not cooked enough, to kill the *salmonella*.

Staphylococci

- Often found in the nose, throat and skin of humans, especially on boils and sores.
- When people sneeze or cough over food or handle it with uncovered sores, they risk causing this form of food poisoning.

Listeria

- *Listeria* likes to grow on foods such as soft cheese, pâté and coleslaw.
- It also likes cold temperatures and can multiply even in the fridge.
- Babies, pregnant women and the elderly are most affected; they should avoid the foods mentioned above.

E. coli

E. coli is the name given to a large family of bacteria commonly found in the intestines of humans and animals. Most *E. coli* are harmless, but one in particular, *E. Coli 0157*, can cause serious illness in humans, ranging from diarrhoea to kidney failure and death.

Ireland has one of the highest rates of disease-causing *E. coli* cases in Europe, according to a new report complied by the European Food Safety Authority. The number of *E. coli* cases reported in Ireland is more than four times the EU average. Some 167 such cases were reported in 2007, of which 115 were confirmed. Ireland's average of 2.7 cases per 100,000 inhabitants is exceeded only by Sweden and Denmark. Irish cases have doubled in three years. (*The Irish Times*, 21 January 2009)

Micro-organisms (germs) need five conditions to grow successfully

Conditions for growth of micro-organisms

Food
They like high-protein foods.

Warmth
30°C–45°C is ideal for most micro-organisms.

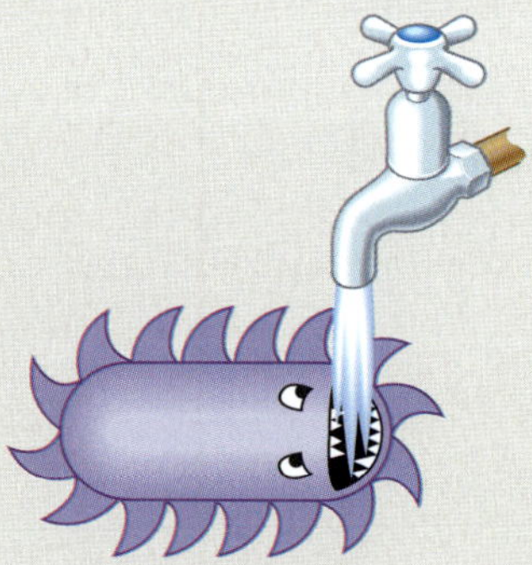

Moisture
Micro-organisms cannot grow well on dried foods such as cornflakes.

Time
Micro-organisms multiply every 20 minutes.

Air
Most need oxygen to survive.

How food is infected by bacteria: four main ways

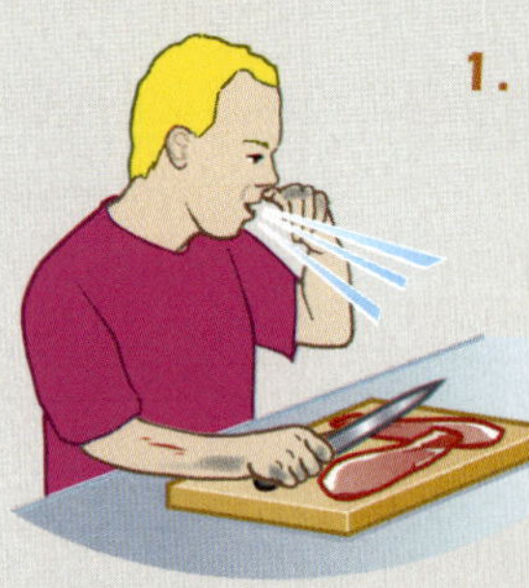

1. Unhygienic people: Not washing hands, especially after using the toilet; not covering cuts; coughing or sneezing over food.

2. Pets, vermin and insects.

3. Dirt and grease: Dirt on surfaces, equipment and cloths provides food for bacteria to multiply.

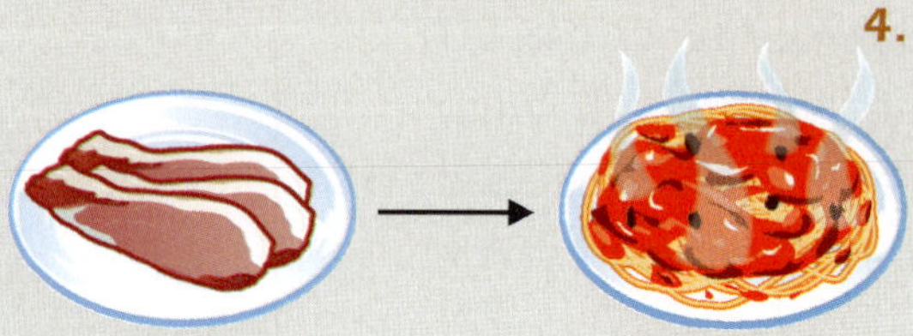

4. Cross-contamination: Preparing or storing raw food, such as chicken, with food that will be eaten without being cooked or cooked again. Bacteria cross from the raw to the cooked food and this now-contaminated food is eaten, resulting in food poisoning.

Food hygiene guidelines

Food hygiene guidelines relate to the food handler, the food itself and to the kitchen in which the food is prepared.

Hygiene in the kitchen: Food handlers

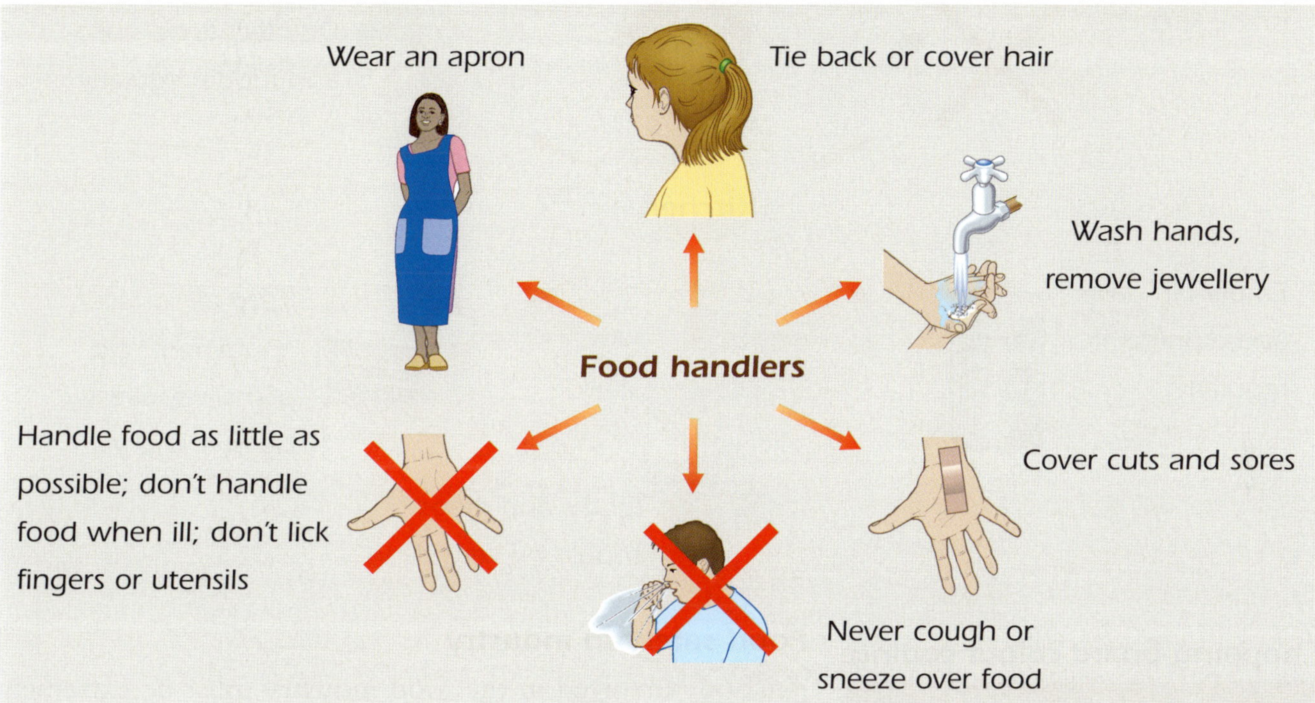

Hygiene in the kitchen: Food

Hygiene in the kitchen: Kitchen

Chopping board colour coding

Chopping board colour coding
Red – Raw meat
Blue – Raw fish
Yellow – Cooked meat
Green – Salad and fruit
Brown – Vegetables
White – Bakery and dairy

Food safety in industry

Anybody involved in the food industry must be extremely conscious of food hygiene and safety. **HACCP** is an international food safety system that is required by law in Ireland for any business selling or providing food to others. HACCP stand for Hazard Analysis Critical Control Points. The HACCP system works by identifying potential risk areas in advance and then putting systems in place to minimise their risk. One example is the use of colour-coded chopping boards to reduce the risk of cross-contamination between raw and cooked foods.

Always follow the instructions on the food label.

Storing food

The **shelf life** of food (how long it remains fit to eat) depends on storing it correctly.

How a food is stored depends on what type of food it is.

- **Perishable:** Food that goes off in three or four days, such as meat, milk, poultry, fish, cream and bread. Store in the fridge or freezer.
- **Semi-perishable:** Food that lasts a week or so, such as fruit, vegetables, cheese, eggs and cakes. Store fruit and vegetables in the fridge or on a

vegetable rack in a cool, dark, ventilated place. Store cheese and eggs in the fridge. Store cakes, etc. in an airtight tin.

- **Non-perishable:** Food that lasts unopened for a month at least, including dried foods such as breakfast cereals, flour, rice, dried fruit, tea and tinned foods. Store in its own package in a clean, dry, wall-mounted press. Once opened, store dried food in an airtight container. Treat tinned food as perishable once opened.
- **Frozen at –18°C or below:** Many perishable and some semi-perishable foods are frozen to prolong their shelf life.

Star markings

Star markings are found on frozen food and on freezers. They tell us how long a food can be stored for.

*	One week
**	One month
***	Three months
****	One year

Packaging: For food cooking and storage

- **Kitchen paper:** Used for mopping up spills and draining grease off fried foods.
- **Aluminium foil** (also commonly but incorrectly called tin foil): Used to cover food in the fridge and for packed lunches. Wrap vegetables, e.g. carrots, in the fridge to prevent wilting.
- **Polythene (plastic) bags:** Used for packed lunches; stronger bags are used for storing frozen food.
- **Clingfilm:** Used for packed lunches and covering food for fridge storage.
- **Plastic boxes and containers:** Used for food storage; old ice cream tubs are useful for frozen food storage.
- **Greaseproof paper:** Used for lining cake tins and wrapping cheese.

Homework Assignment 11 P. 34

Test Yourself eTest.ie

CHAPTER 7

Preparing to Cook

Teacher's CD-ROM: Slide presentation • Student activity pack – with revision crossword • Class test

Kitchen safety

Most household accidents occur in the kitchen. When in the kitchen, take care and be safe.

Kitchen safety guidelines

Kitchen safety

1. Never leave a frying pan or chip pan unattended. If overheated, oil will spontaneously burst into flames.

2. Never touch anything electrical with wet hands.

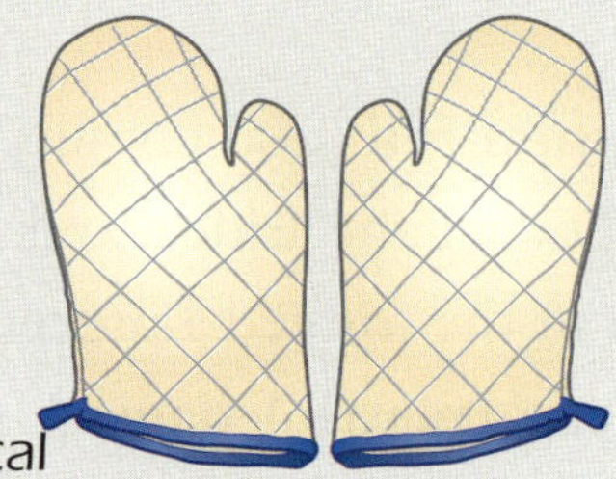

3. Use oven gloves.
4. Keep saucepan handles turned in to the back of the cooker.

5. Curl fingers in when chopping.
6. Never walk around holding a knife or a hot saucepan.

7. Wipe up spills immediately.
8. Never run in the kitchen.

Follow this work routine before you start to cook:

1. You should study the recipe before class. That way, you will know what ingredients you need and the basic steps involved in making the dish.
2. Tie back or cover hair.
3. Wash hands and remove jewellery.

4. Gather all equipment. Is it clean? Set the table (see below).
5. Weigh ingredients accurately.
6. Preheat the oven.
7. Wash as you go.

Ready to go

A recipe has:

- The name of the dish.
- Sometimes a picture of the finished dish.
- A list of ingredients.
- The method (instructions on how to make the dish).
- Serving suggestions.
- Oven temperature and cooking time.

Before starting to cook, read the recipe well.

Weighing (solids) and measuring (liquids)

Solids

Solids are weighed in grams (g). Since a gram is a very small amount, you will rarely see less than 25g written in a recipe. If less than 25g is needed, the recipe will usually say a teaspoon (5g), dessertspoon (10g) or a tablespoon (15g). Recipes mean a level spoon unless otherwise stated.

Note:
1,000g = 1kg

Weighing

Spring scales
Make sure the dial is at 0 after you place the empty bowl on the scales.

Balance scales
Select the weight you need, such as 100g. Add the ingredient to the other side until the scale is level or balanced.

Measuring margarine
Blocks of margarine are usually marked out so that you do not have to use a weighing scales (see photo below).

Measuring
Liquids are measured in millilitres (ml). There are 1,000ml in one litre (L). A measuring jug is used to measure liquid; again, less than 25ml is rare in recipes. Teaspoons (5ml), dessertspoons (10ml) and tablespoons (15ml) can be used to measure liquids also.

Measuring jug

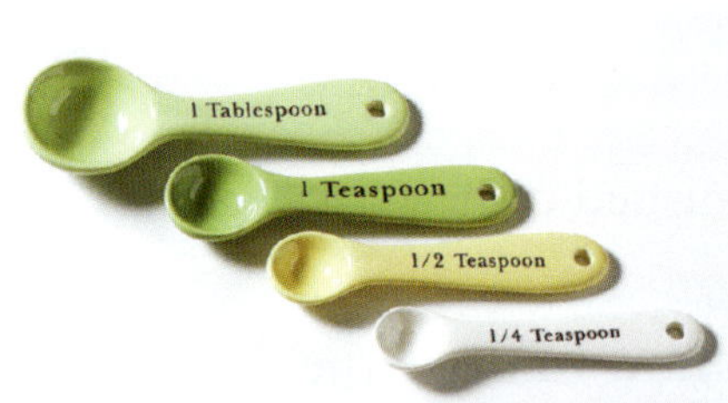

Measuring spoons, while not essential, can be used for small amounts, e.g. baking powder

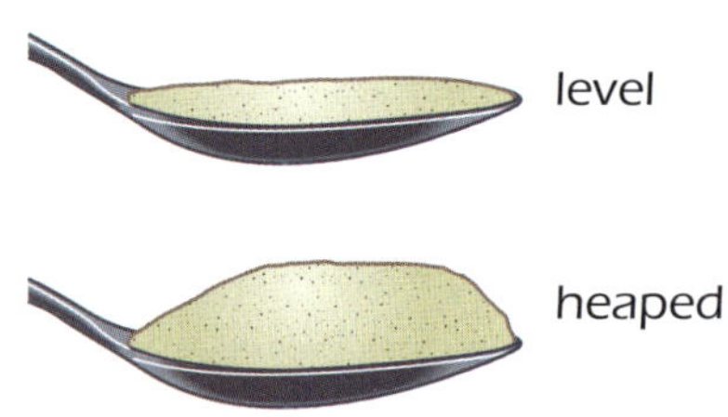

Recipes mean a level teaspoon unless otherwise stated

Recipe modification
Modifying a recipe means changing it in some way.

Possible reasons to modify a recipe
- To make the dish healthier.
- To make it suitable for people with special dietary needs, e.g. vegetarians, coeliacs.

- To increase or reduce the size of the dish.
- To substitute available ingredient(s) for an unavailable one.

Ways to modify a recipe for health reasons

Reduce fat

- Use low-fat milk, cheese, etc. in recipes.
- Use polyunsaturated fats, e.g. Flora, instead of hard fats, e.g. margarine.
- Fry meat in its own fat on a non-stick pan (dry frying).
- Reduce the amount of meat in a recipe and increase the vegetable content.
- Don't use cream in desserts; use low-fat yoghurt instead.
- Use low-fat cooking methods, e.g. steaming and baking, where possible.

Reduce sugar

- Use artificial sweeteners where possible.
- Avoid icing cakes, buns, etc.
- Serve fruit salad in orange juice instead of sugar syrup.

Reduce salt

- Flavour food with herbs instead of salt.
- Don't add salt to baked products, e.g. scones; use salt substitutes if necessary.
- Avoid using commercial stock cubes, as they are high in salt.

Increase fibre

- Leave skins on fruit and vegetables where possible.
- Use brown rice, pasta, bread, etc.
- Add bran and/or seeds to bread and savoury scones.

Equipment

Equipment consists of:

1. Utensils, e.g. cutlery, bowls.
2. Large appliances, e.g. cooker, fridge.
3. Small appliances, e.g. mixer, food processor.

Utensils

Utensils are small pieces of equipment that need to be clean and well cared for.

Some common utensils:

- Bowls
- Cutlery
- Pie dishes
- Saucepans
- Baking tins
- Frying pans
- Casserole dishes
- Chopping board
- Rolling pin
- Wooden spoons
- Sharp knives
- Potato peeler
- Measuring jug

Silicone bake ware (see photo) is becoming very popular. It has many advantages in that it is unbreakable, easy to clean, does not rust and is easily stored. Food does not stick to it easily and it can be used in the freezer, microwave and oven. Many different products are available, from reusable bun cases, muffin tins, loaf tins and roasting tins.

Some less common utensils

Washing dishes and kitchen utensils

- Soak dishes if necessary in cold water to loosen stubborn food.
- Use hot water with a good-quality washing up liquid.
- Scrape dishes off completely before washing.
- Stack all the dirty dishes to one side.
- Wash using a clean dishcloth.
- Drain dishes on the other side of the sink (on a tea towel if there is no double draining board).
- Fill the sink with cold water.
- Rinse all the dishes.
- Dry thoroughly.

To wash metal utensils:

- Never use abrasives, e.g. Brillo pad, on metal utensils or non-stick surfaces, e.g. frying pan, or it will be destroyed.
- Store saucepans when completely dry with the lids off.

To wash wood utensils:

- Scrub with the grain in warm soapy water.
- Do not store away until completely dry or the wood will warp.

Large appliances

- Cooker
- Fridge
- Microwave
- Dishwasher
- Freezer

Using the cooker

Cookers can run on either electricity, gas or solid fuel.

A cooker can consist of:

- A hob.
- A grill (sometimes also a small top oven).
- An oven.

Preheating: Ovens can take 10 minutes to heat up (gas ovens heat up more quickly). With electric ovens, a light usually goes off when the oven has reached the temperature it has been set at. You must preheat the oven for bread and cakes in particular.

Setting the oven: Oven temperature is written in degrees Celsius (°C) or gas mark 1 to 9. Some older ovens may be in degrees Fahrenheit (°F). Each recipe will give an oven temperature and a cooking time.

A conventional oven set at 200°C

Types of oven: There are basically two different types of oven:

- Conventional.
- Fan (fan in oven at the back).

The temperature in a fan oven is the same on every shelf. In a conventional oven, the top shelf is hottest, the middle shelf is as you set it and the bottom shelf is coolest.

Note: Arrange the shelves before you turn the oven on. Never place food on the floor of the oven, as it will burn.

Small appliances

- Liquidiser
- Hand-held electric mixer
- Food processor
- Electric knife

Small appliances

Liquidiser

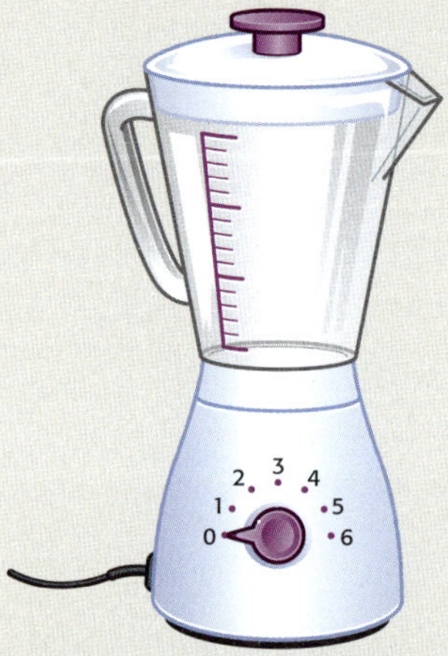

Uses: To blend soups and smoothies, make breadcrumbs, purée cooked fruit and vegetables, no heavy-duty work.

Food mixer

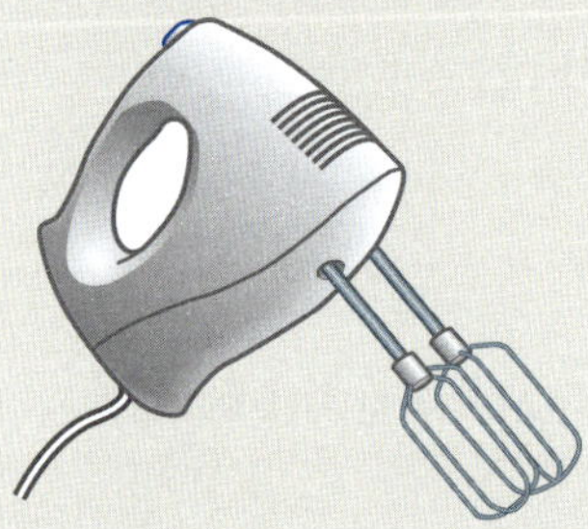

Uses: To cream sugar and margarine, whip cream, whisk egg whites, no heavy-duty work.

Food processor

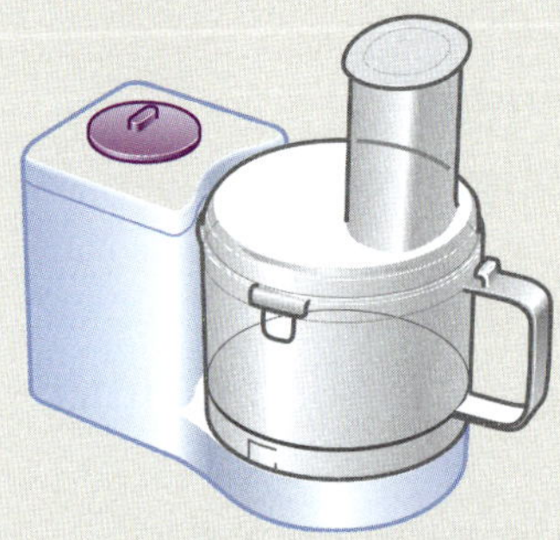

Uses: Can do everything a liquidiser and mixer can do, plus shred, dice, chip raw vegetables and mix stiff doughs and cakes.

Care and cleaning of small motorised appliances

Remove loose parts and wash in hot soapy water. Dry thoroughly and store without putting the appliance back together. Never put the motor in water, just wipe with a damp cloth. Water and electricity are dangerous together.

Glossary of common cookery terms

You will frequently come across these terms in recipes. Read through and learn the list below before completing the crossword in your student activity pack.

Glossary of common cookery terms

Aerate: Introduce air to a mixture (sieving, rubbing in or whisking).

Al dente: Cook food (pasta, vegetables) so they still have bite and are not too soft.

Au gratin: Food cooked in sauce, sprinkled with cheese or breadcrumbs, then browned under the grill or in the oven.

Bake blind: Baking a pastry case before filling it, e.g. for lemon meringue pie.

Baste: Spoon hot fat and meat juices over roasting meat to stop it from drying out.

Bind: Bring a mixture together, e.g. adding beaten egg to minced meat to make burgers.

Blanch: Plunge foods into boiling water, then into cold: this removes skins (tomatoes and almonds) or destroys enzymes (vegetables) before freezing.

Blend: Gently add an ingredient to a mixture.

Bouquet garni: A bunch of herbs (or a commercial sachet) added to flavour soups and stews and later removed.

Brine: Salty water.

Coat: Cover with, for example, batter, breadcrumbs or sauce.

Consistency: Thickness of a mixture.

Cream: Beat foods together until they are soft and creamy.

Croutons: Small cubes of fried bread, used as a garnish for soups.

Dice: To cut into small cubes.

Dredge: To sprinkle sugar or flour, e.g. dredging a table with flour so that pastry does not stick to it while rolling.

Fold: Gently adding an ingredient to a mixture.

Garnish: A decoration for a savoury dish.

Glaze: Brush over bread and cakes before baking to give them a shine when cooked.

Infuse: To give flavour to a liquid by gently heating flavouring ingredients in it, e.g. a vanilla pod in milk.

Knead: To work dough with your hands, e.g. when making bread.

Marinate: Steep foods in flavoured liquid before cooking.

Parboil: Partially cook by boiling (potatoes can be parboiled before oven roasting).

Poach: To cook in gently simmering water, e.g. eggs.

Purée: Mincing up fruit or vegetables.

Raising agent: Produces gas in a mixture (such as bread dough) and causes it to rise.

Roux: A mixture of equal quantities of fat and flour, used as a base for many sauces.

Rub in: To crumble fat into flour using the tips of the fingers – the mixture should resemble breadcrumbs.

Sauté: Fry gently for a short time in hot fat.

Season: Add salt, pepper, herbs or spices to food.

Shortening: Fat added to bread and cakes.

Simmer: Cook gently just below boiling point.

Texture: The feel of something: smooth, lumpy, coarse, crisp, soft, etc.

Whisk: Beat vigorously to introduce air, e.g. egg whites.

Homework Assignment

12 P. 37

Test Yourself eTest.ie

CHAPTER 8

Cooking Food

Teacher's CD-ROM: Slide presentation • Student activity pack – with revision crossword • Class test

Why food is cooked

- Cooking kills harmful bacteria, making food safe to eat. It also has the effect of preserving food. For example, cooked chicken will last longer than raw chicken in the fridge.
- Cooking makes some foods easier to chew and digest, e.g. meat and starchy foods such as potatoes.
- Cooking improves the colour and flavour of many foods.

Effects of cooking on food

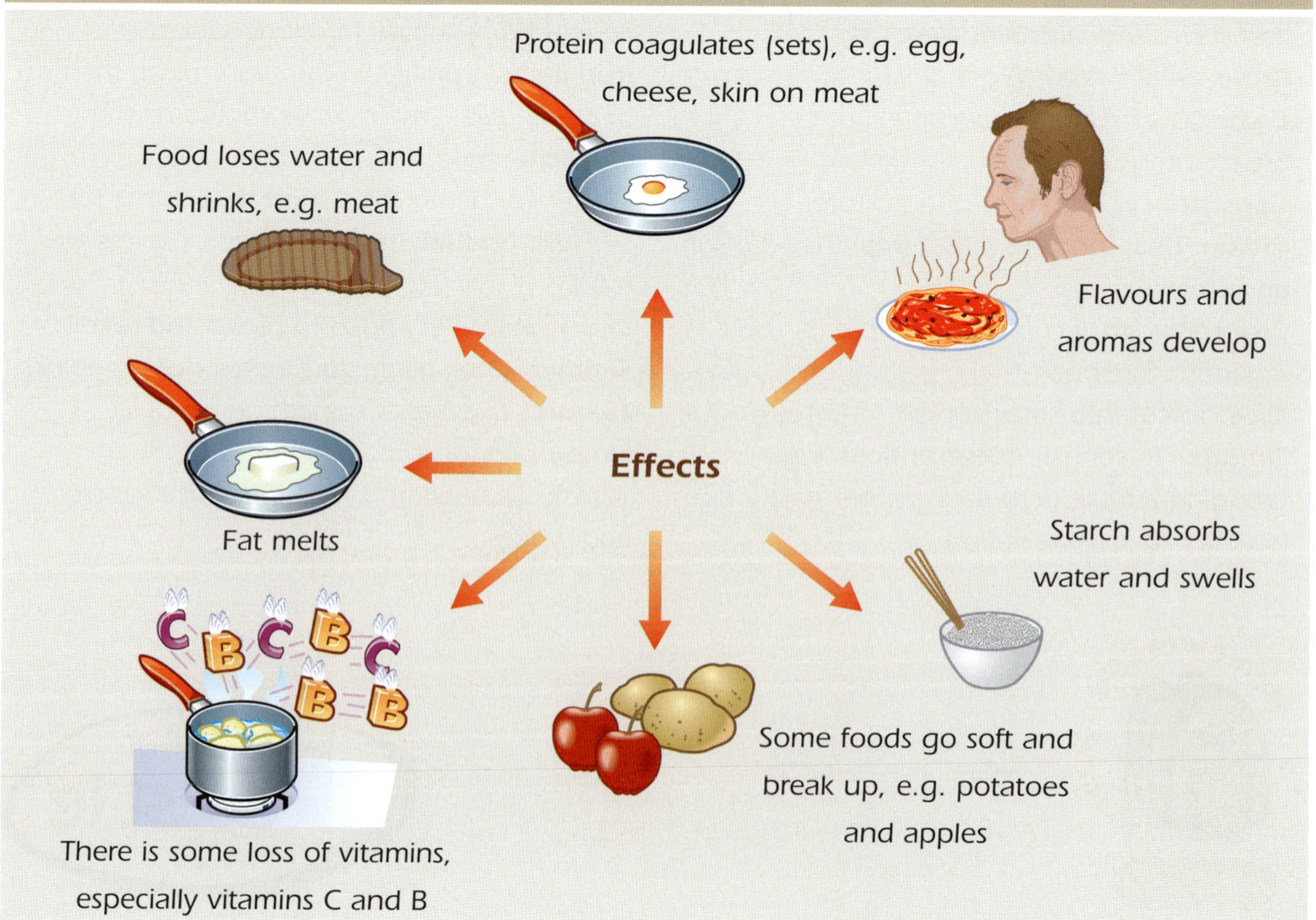

How food is cooked: Methods of heat transfer

Conduction

Example: Frying

Heat travels from molecule to molecule along a solid object. For example, in frying, hot molecules in the cooker ring touch the molecules in the frying pan and cause them to get hot. They in turn touch the food and cause it to get hot, thus cooking it.

Heat travels from the cooker ring to the frying pan to the food by conduction

Convection

Examples: Boiling, deep-fat frying, baking

When liquid and gases are heated, they rise. They are then replaced by cooler gas or liquids. These movements are called convection currents. These currents heat the food by convection.

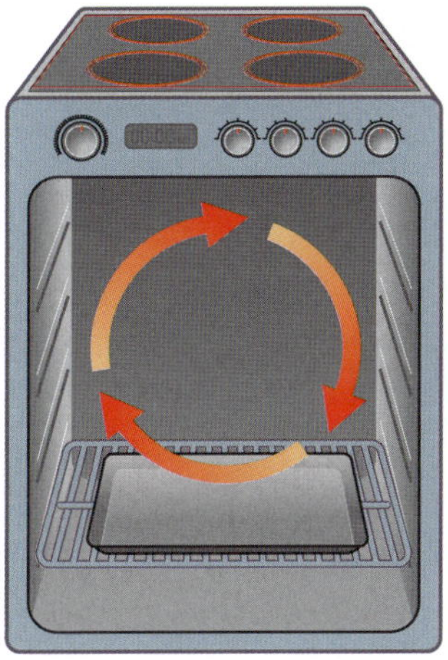

Currents of circulating hot air cook food by convection

Radiation

Example: Grilling

Hot rays from a heat source hit food and heat its surface. The heat then travels into the middle of the food by conduction, thus cooking it through.

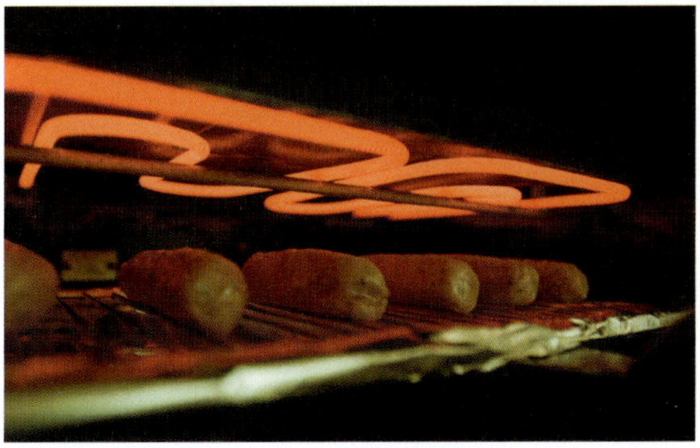

Heat travelling by radiation

Methods of cooking

1. **Moist methods:** Boiling and simmering, stewing, casseroling, poaching, steaming, pressure cooking.
2. **Dry methods:** Grilling, baking.
3. **Methods using fat:** Frying (shallow, deep and stir-frying), roasting.
4. **Other:** Microwave cooking.

Moist methods

Boiling/simmering

- **Description:** Food is cooked in bubbling liquid (100°C). Usually the food is brought to the boil (bubbling rapidly) and then turned down for the rest of the cooking time (bubbling very gently). This is called simmering.
- **Suitable foods:** Meat, vegetables, rice, pasta.
- **Advantages:** Economical, needs little attention, safe for beginners.
- **Disadvantages:** Nutrients are lost into the cooking liquid.
- **Tips:**
  - Use a heavy saucepan with a tight lid.
  - Use cooking liquid for soups and sauces.
  - Once food is bubbling rapidly, reduce to simmer (barely bubbling).

Saucepans should be heavy with tight-fitting lids

Stewing and casseroling

- **Description:** These are slow, moist cooking methods. Food is cooked in liquid in a heavy-lidded saucepan on the hob (stewing) or in a dish in the oven (casseroling). The food and the liquid it has been cooked in are often both eaten.
- **Suitable foods:** Tough cuts of meat, fruit.
- **Advantages:** Economical – a whole meal can be cooked on one ring; tough, cheaper cuts of meat may be used; cooking liquid is consumed, so nutrients are not lost.
- **Disadvantages:** Slow.
- **Tips:**
  - Simmer (don't boil) stew.
  - Keep a tight-fitting lid on so that too much liquid does not evaporate.
  - Use stock as a cooking liquid instead of water, as it adds flavour.

Poaching

- **Description:** Food is cooked gently in water that is barely simmering. A shallow saucepan or poacher is used.
- **Suitable foods:** Eggs, fish.
- **Advantages:** Low-calorie method; food remains digestible (good method for invalid/convalescent cookery).

- **Disadvantages:** Foods can break up; constant attention required.
- **Tips:** Do not let water boil rapidly, or food will break up and be spoiled. When poaching eggs, if you don't have a poacher, break the egg into a small sandwich bag, tie a knot in the top and then poach in simmering water (see photo below).

An egg poacher

Steaming

- **Description:** Food is cooked in rising steam.
- **Suitable foods:** Vegetables, fish, puddings.
- **Advantages/disadvantages:** Steamed food can lack flavour, but is usually easily digestible.
- **Tips:** Flavour foods with herbs and spices, as steamed food can taste a little bland.

Poach eggs in a plastic sandwich bag to prevent them from falling apart during cooking. The sandwich bag may be suspended over the saucepan with a wooden spoon.

A steamer allows you to cook more than one food at once, so they are very economical

Pressure cooking

- **Description:** Food is cooked quickly with steam under pressure.
- **Suitable foods:** Vegetables, tough cuts of meat, puddings.
- **Advantages:** Quick – pressurised steam is very hot and cooks food more quickly than boiling or steaming.
- **Disadvantages:** Can be dangerous if pressure cooker is not used correctly.
- **Tip:** Time cooking carefully; overcooking is common.

Pressure cooker

Dry methods

Grilling

- **Description:** Food is cooked by rays from a hot gas or electric grill.
- **Suitable foods:** Tender meat, e.g. steak, fish, some fruit and vegetables (tomatoes, grapefruit).
- **Advantages:** Quick, not greasy, food has good texture.
- **Disadvantages:** Only expensive meat can be used; needs constant attention.
- **Tip:** Clean the grill pan after each use or old oil will smoke next time.

A deep-fat fryer

Baking

- **Description:** Food is cooked by dry heat in an oven.
- **Suitable foods:** Bread, cakes, tarts, pies, apples, potatoes, puddings, fish.
- **Advantages:** Needs little attention, safe for beginners, adds flavour.
- **Disadvantages:** Expensive if oven is used for one item.
- **Tips:**
  - Batch-bake to make full use of the oven.
  - Always preheat the oven fully.
  - Adjust the shelves before the oven heats up.
  - Do not open the oven door, especially at the start of the cooking time.

A frying pan for shallow frying

A wok for stir-frying

Methods using fat

Frying

- **Description:** Food is cooked in hot fat by deep, shallow or stir-frying.
- **Suitable foods:** Tender meat and chicken, fish, eggs, chips, onion rings, mushrooms.
- **Advantages:** Quick, good flavour.
- **Disadvantages:** Method adds kilocalories, dangerous, greasy, needs constant attention.
- **Tips:**
  - Heat the fat fully before adding the food or it will soak up the fat and become soggy.
  - Fire is a risk with frying: do not leave a frying pan or wok unattended.

- Do not use a chip pan: use a deep-fat fryer with a thermostat instead.
- Drain fried food on kitchen paper to remove some greasiness.

Roasting

- **Description:** Food is cooked in the oven and basted with hot fat (hot fat is spooned over).
- **Suitable foods:** Meat, poultry (chicken, turkey, duck), potatoes and some vegetables, e.g. parsnips.
- **Advantages:** Nice flavours, needs little attention.
- **Disadvantages:** Basting adds kilocalories; food is dry if not basted.
- **Tip:** Covering meat helps prevent drying: uncover 30 minutes before end of cooking to give brown colour.

Microwave cooking

- **Description:** Invisible microwaves bounce around the inside of the oven. The microwaves hit the food and cause the molecules in it to vibrate. This vibrating produces heat, which cooks the food.
- **Suitable foods:** Reheats, thaws and cooks most foods.
- **Advantages:** Quick.
- **Disadvantages:** Does not brown food.
- **Tips:**
  - Do not put metal dishes or dishes with a metal rim in the microwave or sparks will fly!
  - Foods with a skin, e.g. tomatoes, will explode if you do not prick them with a fork first.
  - Allow food to 'stand' after cooking before eating it (standing time).
  - Cover food when reheating to avoid it splattering and dirtying the oven.

Homework Assignment 13 P. 40

Test Yourself eTest.ie

CHAPTER 9

The Practical Cookery Exam

Teacher's CD-ROM

Practical examination template

The practical cookery exam is worth 35 per cent (Higher Level) or 45 per cent (Ordinary Level) of your final Junior Certificate Home Economics mark. It is therefore very important that you prepare well and carry out the task given to you to the best of your ability.

Exam procedure

Approximately two weeks before the exam (exams are usually held in April), you will be asked by your Home Economics teacher to draw one task from a selection of six or seven different tasks. On the day of the exam, you will be given 30 minutes of preparation time and 90 minutes for the actual practical exam.

Sample task

'*Make friends with fish*' is a slogan used to promote the health benefits of including fish in the diet.

Design and set out a two-course dinner menu that includes fresh fish as the main ingredient in the main course. Prepare, cook and serve the complete *main course* of your chosen menu, suitable for at least two adults.

Demonstrate your skills by preparing and presenting an appropriate garnish for this main course using lemon **or** tomato.

Food and Culinary Skills Task, 2008

Before the day of the exam (two weeks)

Once you have drawn your task, you can then:

1. Think about what exactly you have been asked to do.
2. Come up with a number of dishes that would suit the task.
3. Decide on the dish or dishes you are going to cook (solution).

4. Practise your chosen dish or dishes.
5. Complete the paperwork for the exam (see sample).

During preparation time on the day of the exam (30 minutes):

- Collect equipment.
- Weigh ingredients.
- Wash vegetables, but do not peel them.
- Light gas oven but do not set the temperature.
- Check that equipment, e.g. electric mixer/food processor, is working.

The examiner will check your preparation.

During the exam itself (90 minutes):

- Make the dish.
- Serve the dish (the examiner will taste it).
- Taste the dish yourself.
- Wash up (the examiner will check the dishes).
- Tidy away.
- Do your evaluation.

Top tips for the practical exam

When you have read each tip, tick the box.

1. Write your exam number:
   - On all your written work.
   - On a sticker on your apron.
   - On a large A4 sheet of paper taped to your table.

Exam number:	357146
Task number:	4
Dish:	Spaghetti Bolognese
	Garlic bread

☐

2. You must use fresh ingredients where possible. Marks will be lost if you use too many convenience foods, e.g. if you used a bread mix to make brown bread.

☐

3. Make sure you wash your hands, cover cuts, tie back long hair, remove jewellery and have a clean apron on, or else marks will be taken away under 'hygiene'.

☐

4. Take care doing written work for the cookery exam – use the sample below as a guide. Written work makes up 30 per cent of your marks; you could get most of these marks before you even walk in the door, so don't lose out. Use the form provided on the Teacher's CD.

☐

5. Do not waste anything: time, ingredients, water, gas or electricity.
   - **Time:** Know exactly what you have to do so you can work quickly and efficiently. If you have to constantly look at your work plan or recipe to see what has to be done next, you are wasting valuable time and may not get finished. (Marks will be taken off for this.)
   - **Ingredients:** When peeling vegetables, use a peeler; do not take large chunks of skin off with a knife. Try not to have more ingredients than you need. If you have extra, do not throw them out; cover them and place in the fridge.
   - **Water:** Never leave a tap running. Do not wash anything under a running tap.
   - **Gas/electricity:** Turn off cooker rings or the oven immediately after you finish using them.

☐

6. When serving food:
   - Clear the table before serving food. Serve all the food, not just a portion.
   - Garnish or decorate attractively.
   - Wipe any spills off serving dishes with kitchen paper.
   - Have clean cutlery, a side plate and a bowl of hot water ready for the examiner to taste your food.
   - Call the examiner immediately once your food is served.
   - You must taste a little food yourself so you can evaluate the taste of the dish.

☐

7. Wash and dry dishes very carefully. Marks are taken off for badly washed dishes. Do not put your dishes away until the examiner has seen them (see the washing-up guidelines on pp. 50–1).

☐

8. Do not throw out the contents of the bin until you have shown it to the examiner. ☐

9. Evaluate both the dish and how you think you did in the exam (see the sample evaluation). ☐

Case Study

Sarah Byrne has just finished her cookery exam. She had to make either a sweet or a savoury dish from pastry and then cost the dish and compare it to a bought version. She decided to make apple tart. While her tart tasted very nice, it did not look as nice as she would have liked. She had trouble rolling out the pastry, as it kept sticking to the table. This cost her time, and because she was rushing she forgot to glaze the tart with egg and it turned out very pale.

SAMPLE COOKERY EXAM FOLDER

Exam number: 5831563

Task number: 4

> Many factors affect the success of pastry making. List some sweet dishes and savoury dishes that can be made using homemade pastry. Prepare, cook and serve any **one** of the dishes you have listed. Compare the cost of the finished dish with the cost of a similar commercial product.
>
> *Food and Culinary Skills Task, 2008*

Analysis: What have you been asked to do?

I have been asked to list sweet and savoury dishes that can be made using home-made pastry. I must prepare, cook and serve one of the dishes I have listed and then compare the cost of my finished dish with a similar commercial product.

Investigation: List *three* things that you must consider before deciding on what to cook (two must be specific to the task with one general consideration).

1. The dish I pick must be made from home-made pastry (specific consideration).
2. I must be able to find a similar commercial product to compare it to (specific consideration).
3. I must be able to make it in one hour (other half-hour for serving, washing up and evaluation) and it is best if I choose something I have made before and am confident making (general consideration).

List solutions and ideas: *Two* solutions for each part of the task.

Sweet dishes: Apple tart, mince pies.

Savoury dishes: Sausage rolls, steak and kidney pie.

Decision: Choose *one* solution. Give *two* good reasons for your choice of dish(es).

I have chosen to make apple tart.

Reasons for choice:

1. Because it can be made from simple shortcrust pastry in under an hour. I have made shortcrust pastry before in class, so I feel confident I could carry out this task well.
2. Commercially made apple tarts are easy to find, allowing me to carry out my price comparison easily.

Planning and preparation: List all the ingredients and equipment you will need for the task. As you collect them during the half-hour preparation, tick them off on the list.

List of ingredients

Shortcrust pastry	**Cost**
200g plain flour	25c
100g margarine	26c
pinch of salt	1c
cold water	–
Filling	
2 medium cooking apples	128c
3 tablespoons caster sugar	8c
1 teaspoon ground cinnamon	15c
1 egg, to glaze	27c
cost of gas, hot water, etc.	10c
Total	**€2.40**
Bought apple tart	**€3.29**

List of equipment

- apple corer
- chopping board
- dessertspoon
- flour dredger
- knife
- measuring jug
- mixing bowl
- oven gloves
- pastry brush
- rolling pin
- round ovenproof plate
- sharp knife
- sieve
- teaspoon
- vegetable peeler
- weighing scales

Conclusion: The bought apple tart was 89c more expensive.

Note: All prices from Tesco.

Preparation: List everything you are going to do during the half-hour preparation time before the exam.

1. I will collect and weigh my ingredients.
2. I will collect all the equipment I need and set my cookery table.
3. I will check the shelf positions and then light my gas oven but not set the temperature on it.
4. I will wash my cooking apples.

Work plan: List what you have to do during the exam in the correct order. Don't forget evaluation time at the end.

Step 1: Make pastry: sieve flour and salt, add chopped margarine, rub in. Add spoons of water until pastry comes together. Divide pastry in two. Chill in fridge. Wash up.

Step 2: Set gas oven to gas mark 8.

Step 3: Roll out one piece of pastry into a circle slightly larger than plate. Place on plate and trim. Return to fridge.

Step 4: Peel, core and slice apples. Place on pastry and sprinkle with sugar and cinnamon. Brush edges with water.

Step 5: Roll out rest of pastry and place on top of apples. Trim edges. Press well together. Brush with beaten egg. Prick with fork, make cross in centre.

Step 6: Bake for 10 minutes at gas mark 8. Reduce to gas mark 5 and bake for 30 minutes more, until golden. Wash up.

Step 7: Sprinkle with caster sugar.

Step 8: Put out cutlery, plate and bowl of hot water. Call examiner to taste tart.

Step 9: Wash up. Show washing-up and bin to examiner. Put dishes away.

Step 10: Do evaluation.

Note: The evaluation is <u>not</u> a description of the dish.

Colour and presentation: How did you try to make the dish look well? Did you succeed?

The colour of my apple tart was not as good as I would have liked. I forgot to put the egg glaze on it and it therefore turned out too pale, even though it was properly cooked. Apart from this, my apple tart was presented well. No apple leaked out and I sprinkled it with caster sugar to make it look nice.

Texture and taste: Was there more than one texture (contrast)? Was the flavour strong enough/too strong? Would you add anything to improve the texture/flavour?

There was good contrast in texture between the crisp pastry and the soft apples. I thought the tart tasted very nice – not too bitter or not too sweet. I think the cinnamon added a very nice additional flavour.

Cooked/doneness: Was your dish overcooked, undercooked or just right? How did you check if it was cooked properly?

My apple tart was cooked properly. I knew it was cooked because it was in for the correct amount of time, and while it was not as brown as I would have liked because I forgot the egg glaze, it still looked cooked. My tart was on a glass ovenproof plate so I was able to check the bottom of the tart and see that it was brown also.

Did you meet the brief? Did you do everything you were told to do for your task? Explain why you think you did/didn't.

I think I did meet the brief because my apple tart is made from home-made pastry and I did compare its cost with a bought apple tart.

Your overall performance: What did you do well/not so well?

I made the pastry fairly well, although I think it was a little wet. It did not roll out very easily for me, but I did my best by using the flour dredger and moving the pastry often as I rolled it to try to prevent it from sticking to the table. The rolling took a bit longer than expected, and as I was rushing a little, I forgot to glaze the finished tart. This meant that it was a little pale coming out of the oven. I think the tart tasted very well, especially because I added the cinnamon.

Are there any changes you would make?

Yes: I would have put less water in the pastry and glazed the tart with egg before putting it into the oven.

CHAPTER 10

The Food Groups

Teacher's CD-ROM

Slide presentation • Student activity pack – with revision crossword • Class test

There are **four** food groups:

- Protein group.
- Milk and milk products group.
- Cereal and potato group.
- Fruit and vegetable group.

> Questions on the food groups are frequently asked in section B, question 1 (both levels) in the Junior Certificate examination.

Protein group

This group is made up of meat, fish, eggs, meat alternatives and nuts. Eat two to three servings per day from this group.

Meat

The term 'meat' means the edible flesh and often internal organs of cattle, pigs, sheep, poultry (chicken and turkey) and game (wild animals and birds).

Offal is the name given to the edible internal organs, such as liver and kidneys. Offal is cheap, nutritious (particularly high in iron) and cooks quickly, by grilling, baking or frying.

Red meat

Red meat refers to the meat from cattle, pigs and sheep. Red meat is given different names depending on the animal it has come from and whether it has been processed.

Types of red meat

Note:
Percentages are for Higher Level only.

Composition and nutritive value of red meat

Red meat, while a great source of nutrients, especially protein (20–25%), iron and vitamin B, should *not* be eaten every day. This is because it contains large amounts of saturated fat (20%), which is linked to heart disease. Red meat does not contain any carbohydrate (0%), so it is usually eaten with a food high in carbohydrate, such as potatoes.

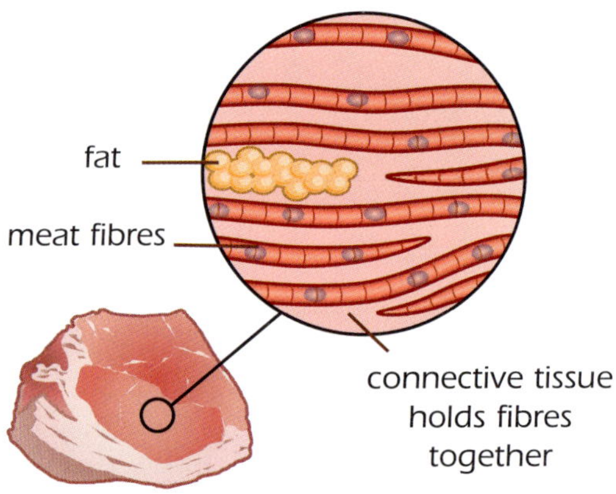

The structure of meat

Under the microscope: The structure of meat

- **Tough meat** has more tough connective tissue and comes from old animals or very active parts of the animal, such as the leg or neck.
- **Tender meat** has less connective tissue and comes from young animals or parts of the animal that do not move much.

Six ways of making meat tender

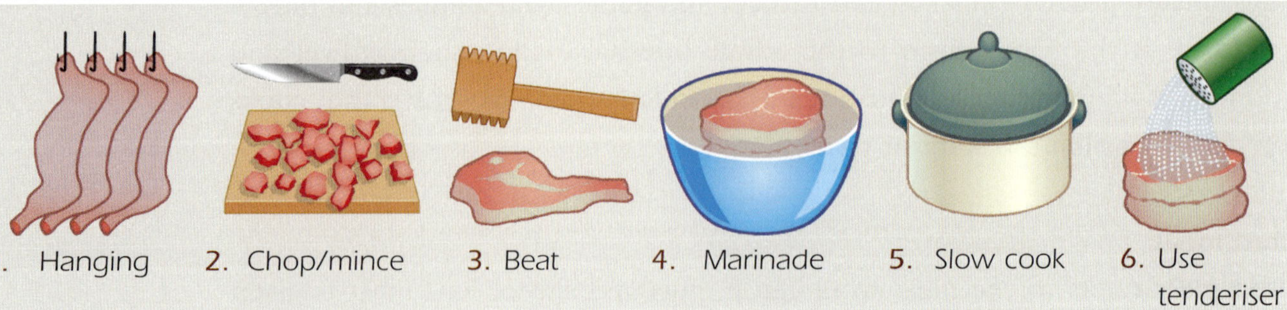

- Hanging at the butcher or meat factory.
- Chop or mince.
- Beat with a steak hammer.

- Marinate (soak in flavoured liquid).
- Slow, moist cook, e.g. stew.
- Sprinkle with tenderisers, e.g. papain.

For some cuts of meat, the more tender the cut, the more expensive it is.

Type of cut	Beef	Lamb	Pork
Tender (frying and grilling)	 Fillet steak	 Cutlets	 Loin chops
Medium (roasting)	 Rolled rib	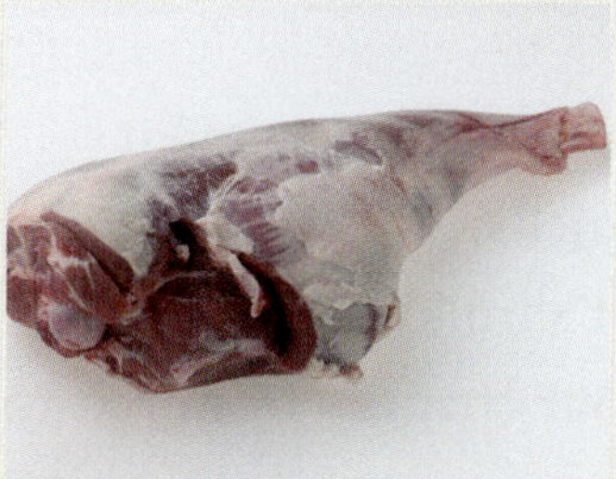 Leg	 Belly
Tough (stewing and mincing)	 Topside	 Gigot	

When buying meat

- Buy from a clean, reliable shop. Meat should be traceable to its farm of origin.
- Meat should have no bad smell.
- Do not buy fatty pieces; ask to have fat trimmed off.
- Check both sides of the meat; if pre-packed, you are taking a chance.
- Buy a cut suited to your cooking method. For example, there is no point in frying tough gigot chops.

Remember: Tough cuts are just as nutritious and tasty as expensive cuts if cooked correctly.

Safe storage of meat

- Meat is a high-protein food, so bacteria like it – use within two days.
- Check best-before dates.
- Store in the fridge on a large plate so it cannot drip; cover loosely with a clean tea towel.

Safe preparation and cooking of meat

- Never prepare or store raw meat and fish near cooked food or food that is eaten raw; food poisoning will result.
- Thaw meat fully before cooking it thoroughly.
- Never refreeze meat.

Effects of cooking on meat

- Fat melts.
- Meat shrinks.
- Colour changes from red to brown.
- Protein coagulates and the surface seals.
- Flavours develop.
- Bacteria are destroyed.

Meat alternatives

There are a number of different products on the market that can be used as high-protein alternatives to meat. The three most common are:

1. Tofu.
2. Textured vegetable protein (TVP).
3. Quorn (made from fungi).

Tofu

Tofu is a white, creamy, high-protein food made by separating soya milk into curds (tofu) and whey and then pressing the curds into cubes or blocks. Tofu can be used in the following ways:

- Tofu can be used much like cheese in vegan pizza or like chunks of chicken in a stir-fry.

- Thread cubes of firm tofu onto skewers with mushrooms, cherry tomatoes and onions. Marinate in soy sauce, brush with olive oil and grill to make tasty kebabs (see photo).
- Whizz tofu with strawberries and honey to make a dairy-free fruit smoothie. Tofu can also be used to make mousse, e.g. strawberry or chocolate.
- Mix with onion, garlic and herbs; form into burgers; coat in flour or egg and breadcrumbs; grill or fry.
- Cream tofu and add flavourings, e.g. garlic, to make tasty, nutritious dips.

Tofu kebabs

TVP (textured vegetable protein)

This protein-rich food is made from soya beans. It is flavoured and shaped to resemble meat (chunks, mince and steaks). TVP is usually bought dried and once reconstituted with water can be used in a huge variety of dishes, e.g. lasagne, spaghetti Bolognese, burgers (see photo), stew or shepherd's pie. Some non-vegetarians use one-third TVP, two-thirds meat in dishes because it is healthier.

TVP burger

Quorn

Quorn is a leading brand of mycoprotein food products. Mycoprotein is a term for protein-rich foodstuffs made from processed edible fungi. Quorn is produced as both a cooking ingredient and as a range of ready meals. Quorn can be used for dishes such as pizza, lasagne and shepherd's pie.

Pulse vegetables

Pulse vegetables (peas, beans and lentils) and nuts are also used as meat substitutes because of their high protein content. Pulses often need soaking before use.

Homework Assignment 14 P. 43

Spaghetti Bolognese made with Quorn

Poultry: Chicken, turkey, duck, goose

Chicken – nutritive value

Chicken is high in protein yet low in saturated fat. However, it is lower in iron than red meat, but can be served with iron-rich foods such as green vegetables. Chicken does also contain vitamin B and small amounts of calcium. Chicken is an easily digested, high-protein food, so it is useful for all age groups.

Buying fresh poultry

- Clean shop.
- Check expiry date.
- No unpleasant smell.
- Flesh should be firm and plump.
- Flesh should not be discoloured.

Buying frozen poultry

- Poultry should be below the load line in . the shop's cabinet.
- Packaging should not be torn.
- It should be frozen solid.
- It should not be discoloured in any way.

Storing fresh and frozen poultry

Fresh

- Remove wrapper and giblets.
- Place on a large plate, cover loosely with a clean tea towel and refrigerate.
- Use within three days.

Frozen

- Place in home freezer as soon as possible after buying it.

Roasting poultry

- Defrost completely.
- Preheat oven to 200°C /fan 190°C/gas 6.
- Remove giblets, wash under cold tap and pat dry with kitchen paper.
- Season inside and out.
- Cook 20 minutes per 500g + 20 minutes extra.
- To test if poultry is cooked, pierce with a skewer – the juices should run clear.

Homework Assignment
15 P. 47

Food safety

To reduce the dangers of food poisoning from harmful *salmonella* bacteria, follow these simple rules:

- Always thaw frozen, whole chicken properly: 24 hours in the fridge or eight hours at room temperature is necessary to defrost it properly.
- Always make sure chicken is cooked right through to the bone. When the thickest part of the flesh is pierced with a skewer, the juices should run clear, not pink.
- After handling chicken, wash your hands and utensils in hot soapy water.
- Prepare and store raw chicken separately from cooked foods or foods eaten raw.

Fish

As a nation, Irish people tend not to eat as much fish as other island nations. We should eat more fish, as it is an easily cooked, nutritious alternative to red meat.

Classification of fish

Fish can be classified according to its nutritive value:

- **White fish**, e.g. plaice, sole, cod, haddock, whiting.
- **Oily fish**, e.g. mackerel, salmon, herring, trout, sardines.
- **Shellfish**, e.g. crab, prawns, lobster, mussels.

Unlike oily fish, which contains up to 20 per cent fat (mostly unsaturated fat), white fish contains no fat. The fat of a white fish is stored in its liver, which is removed before cooking. Shellfish contain some fat (mostly unsaturated).

Fish can be described as either be flat or round.

Flat fish – plaice

Round fish – herring

Composition and nutritive value of fish

- **Protein:** All fish is an excellent source of protein (17–20%). Unlike red meat, it does not contain saturated fat and so will not raise cholesterol levels.
- **Fat:** White fish contains no fat (0%) and is therefore useful for those on weight-reducing diets. Oily fish (13%) and shellfish (2.5%) do contain fat, but it is unsaturated and therefore does not raise cholesterol.
- **Vitamins:** All fish is a good source of vitamin B and oily fish also contains vitamins A and D.

Note:
Percentages are for Higher Level only.

- **Minerals:** All fish contains iodine. Canned fish also contains calcium if the bones are eaten.
- **Carbohydrate:** Fish contains no carbohydrate (0%) and may be served with a carbohydrate-rich food such as potatoes.
- Fish also lacks vitamin C and should therefore be served with a wedge of lemon.

Buying fish

Fresh	Frozen
Buy fish in season from a clean shop. Fish must be very fresh. Look for: • Moist, unbroken scales. • Firm flesh, clear skin and markings. • No bad smell or discolouration. • Bulging, clear eyes. • Gills should be red, not sticky.	• Frozen solid. • Stored below the load line in the freezer. • Wrappings are not torn. • Well within expiry date. • Put fish into your home freezer as soon as possible after buying it.

Storing fish

Fresh	Frozen
• Remove wrapping and rinse in cold water. • Place in a deep container on crushed ice and cover with more ice if possible. • Cover to stop fish flavours from entering other foods. • Place in the refrigerator away from cooked foods. • Use within 24 hours.	• Store in the freezer as soon as possible. • Make sure that coverings are intact to prevent freezer burn. • Use by the expiry date shown on the packaging. • Follow the manufacturer's instructions for thawing and cooking.

How fish is sold

- **Whole:** Small fish, shellfish.
- **Fillet:** Flat or round fish.
- **Cutlets and steaks:** Large round fish – cutlet (taken from head end) or steaks (from tail end).

Preparing round fish

Round fish prepared like this can be stuffed and oven-baked. Round fish can also be filleted: two fillets are removed by paring them away from head to tail; keep the knife as close as possible to the ribcage.

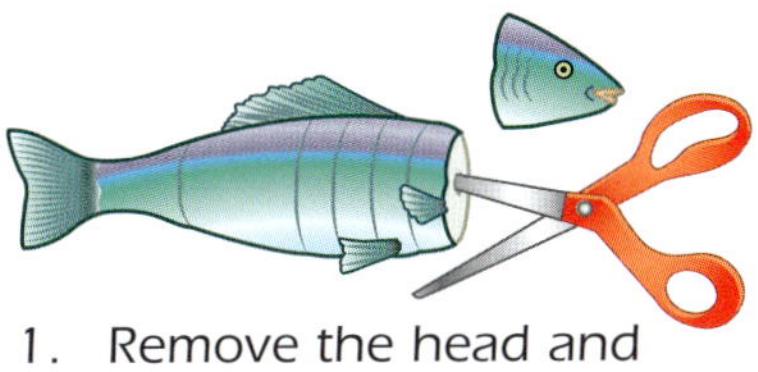

1. Remove the head and slit the underside open.

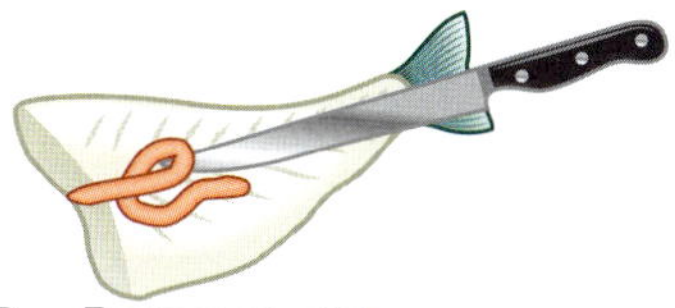

2. Remove gut.

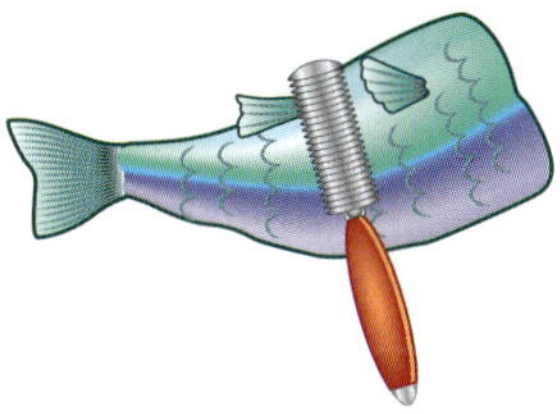

3. Remove scales in the sink, working against the grain from head to tail.

4. Cut the fins off. Remove the black membrane inside the fish by rubbing with salt. Wash fish and dry with kitchen paper.

Preparing round fish

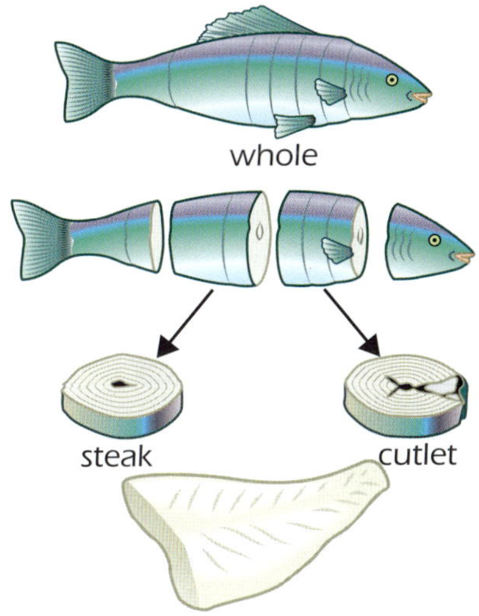

How fish is sold

Preparing flat fish

1. Cut off fins. Make a slit slightly to one side of the back bone.

2. Slice around the head.

3. Using a flexible fish knife, peel off the first fillet, keeping as close to the ribcage as you can.

Preparing flat fish – filleting

Skinning a fish fillet

How to skin fish

A special flexible fish knife makes skinning fish easier.

1. Place fish skin side down, tail towards you on a chopping board.
2. Sprinkle salt on the tail end to give you grip.
3. Slide the knife between the skin and flesh, keeping the knife as close to the skin as possible.

Cooking fish

Fish cooks very quickly; if overcooked, it breaks up. It loses its translucent (see-through) appearance, turning white. Micro-organisms are destroyed and some vitamins and minerals may dissolve into the cooking liquid.

Baked	May be stuffed or baked in a sauce.
Steamed	In a steamer or between two plates. Bland taste, so needs a tasty sauce.
Poached	Make sure liquid is not boiling or fish will break up. Bland taste, so needs a tasty sauce.
Grilled	Very quick method, nutrients retained.
Fried	Fish often coated in batter or egg and crumbs.
Stewed	Firm fish only, e.g. monkfish in a spicy sauce.

Once cooked, fish is usually garnished with a sauce (such as tartar sauce), parsley and a wedge of lemon (see sauces, pp. 104–6, and garnishes, pp. 38–9).

Processed fish

Smoked

- Example: Smoked haddock fillets.
- Smoking preserves fish.

Smoked fish

Frozen

- Nutrients are retained.
- Expensive.
- No waste.
- Coated fish and ready-made dinners available.

Canned/bottled

- In oil or brine.
- Tuna, salmon, sardines and shellfish are often canned or bottled.

Homework Assignment 16 P. 49

Eggs

Uses of eggs in cookery

Coating foods for frying, e.g. in batter or egg and breadcrumbs (fish).

As part of a **main course**, e.g. omelette, quiche.

Glazing: Egg brushed on scones and pastry before cooking gives them a golden colour and a nice shine.

Eggs

On their own, e.g. boiled, scrambled or poached.

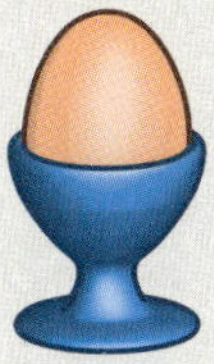

Binding: Egg prevents food from falling apart, e.g. home-made burgers, fish cakes.

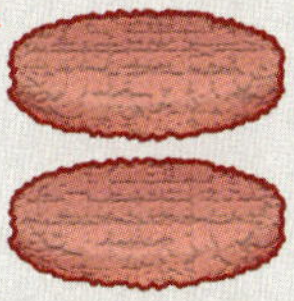

Holding air: Egg white traps air when whisked, e.g. meringue, sponge.

Thickening: Eggs thicken and set mixtures, e.g. custard, quiche.

Note:
Percentages are for Higher Level only.

Composition and nutritive value of eggs

Eggs are a good source of protein (13%) but lack carbohydrate (0%), and so are often served with carbohydrate-rich foods, e.g. boiled egg and toast. Fat (11%) in eggs is easily digested, and contrary to popular belief is mostly unsaturated. Eggs contain vitamins A, D and B and also the minerals calcium, iron and sulphur. Eggs lack vitamin C and so should be served with foods rich in vitamin C, e.g. omelette served with a side salad, or a glass of orange juice served with a boiled egg in the morning.

In the past, people were advised not to eat more than two eggs per week because they contain fat (11%) and were thought to raise cholesterol levels. New research from the British Heart Foundation, however, has found that the fat in eggs does not contribute significantly to raising cholesterol levels (it is predominantly unsaturated – 56%) and therefore need not be as restricted in the diet.

Buying eggs

All the information you need to buy good-quality, fresh eggs must be written on the box they come in. Check that all eggs in the box are unbroken.

1. **Name of the producer:** This must be on the box.
2. **Class:** Eggs are graded A, B, C or Extra. Extra is the best, followed by A and so on.
3. **Size:** Eggs are now graded in four sizes – extra large (XL), large, medium and small. Use large for cooking.
4. **Country of origin.**
5. **Expiry or best-before date:** This is usually three weeks from the day the eggs were laid. Eggs sold loose must have this stamped on each one.
6. **Week number:** Freshness can easily be judged by looking at this number. Eggs are given a number (1–52), week 1 being the first week in January.
7. **Caged or free range:** Whether the eggs came from free-range or caged hens will be written on the box. If caged, then the print is usually very small. Free-range eggs tend to be more expensive.

Free-range hens

Battery or caged hens

Checking if an egg is fresh

If eggs have been removed from their box and placed in the egg compartment of the fridge, you may have no expiry date to tell you whether they are fresh or not. Eggs can be tested for freshness in other ways.

- As an egg gets stale, water evaporates out of the egg through the shell and air passes in. The air sac becomes larger and the egg lighter, so stale eggs float.
- Crack open an egg onto a saucer. It is fresh if the yolk is raised and the white around it is jelly-like. A stale egg has a flat yolk and a runny white.

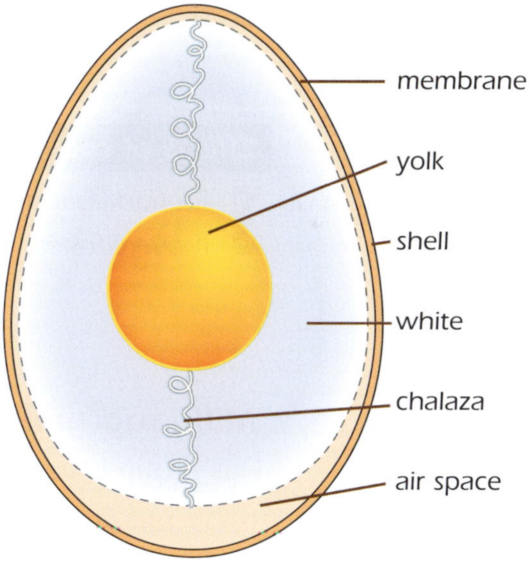

Structure of an egg

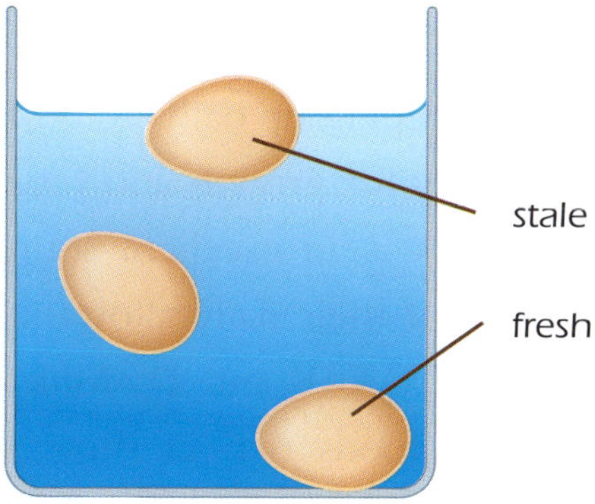

Testing an egg for freshness

Storing eggs

- In the fridge, pointed end down.
- Away from strong-smelling foods.
- If storing yolks separately, place in a bowl of water in the fridge.
- Store whites in an airtight container in the fridge.

Using eggs in cookery

- Bring eggs to room temperature before using.
- Egg whites will not whisk properly if there is yolk present or if the bowl or whisk has even a trace of grease on it.
- To prevent curdling, do not overcook eggs: when adding egg to a hot liquid, e.g. milk for egg custard, cool the liquid somewhat and then add it to the egg, not the other way round.
- Raw or lightly cooked eggs should not be given to babies, toddlers, pregnant women, elderly people or invalids due to the risk of *salmonella* poisoning.

Homework Assignment
17 P. 54

Effects of cooking on eggs

- Protein coagulates (sets) – egg white changes from clear to white.
- If overcooked, they curdle and become less digestible.

Milk and milk products

This group is made up of milk, butter, cream, yoghurt and cheese. Eat three to five servings per day from this group (depends on age group).

Milk

Composition and nutritive value of milk

Note: Percentages are for Higher Level only.

Milk contains 87% water, so is good in terms of keeping up daily fluid intake. Milk is a good source of digestible protein (3.5%) for growth and repair. It contains fat (4%) in an easily digested form. Milk is an excellent source of calcium – one glass provides an adult with half of their daily allowance for healthy bones and teeth. It also contains vitamins A, B and D. Milk lacks vitamin C and iron, so should be served with foods rich in these. Milk contains carbohydrate (4.5%).

Effects of heat on milk	Buying and storing milk
◎ Flavour changes. ◎ Bacteria are destroyed. ◎ Protein coagulates and skin forms. Steam then builds up under the skin and can boil over. ◎ Loss of vitamins C and B.	◎ Check expiry date. ◎ Store in the fridge away from strong-smelling foods, e.g. onions. ◎ Use in order of expiry dates. ◎ Do not mix milks with different expiry dates.

Types of milk

Whole milk: Ordinary milk with 4% fat. Recommended milk for children.

Low-fat milk: Sometimes called semi-skimmed, this has less than half the fat of whole milk.

Skimmed: All but a trace of fat removed. The flavour is altered and vitamins A and D are also removed. Not suitable for children.

Fortified (e.g. Supermilk): A low-fat milk with vitamins A and D and calcium added.

Buttermilk: Acidic, used in baking.

Processed milks

UHT (long-life): Heated to 132°C, UHT milk lasts unopened for months. Available in cartons or small single portions, e.g. hotels.

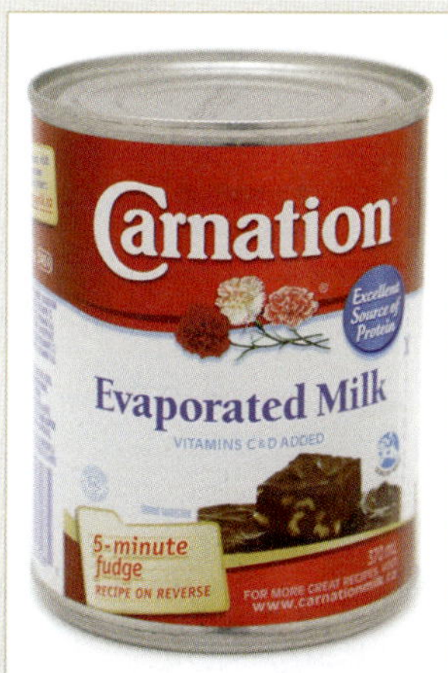

Evaporated milk: Some water is removed and the milk is then canned. Long-lasting; used in dessert-making.

Condensed milk: Similar to evaporated milk but with sugar added.

Dried milk: All water is removed. The milk is made up by adding water. Taste is altered.

Soya milk: Made from soya beans. Suitable for vegans and those with dairy allergies.

Pasteurisation and homogenisation

Pasteurisation kills the bacteria in milk to make it safe without spoiling the taste of the milk. Milk is heated to 72°C for 15 seconds and then cooled quickly. All commercially sold milk is pasteurised.

Homogenisation spreads the cream, or fat, evenly throughout the milk. Most milk is treated in this way.

Uses of milk in the diet and in food preparation

- Milk as a drink is an excellent source of digestible protein and calcium.
- It can be added hot or cold to breakfast cereals, improving their nutritive value.
- It is a main ingredient in many dishes, e.g. quiche, sauces, e.g. white sauce, pancakes and milk puddings, e.g. rice pudding.
- It can be added to soups to give a creamier taste and improve its nutritive value, e.g. cream of mushroom soup.
- It is used in baking, e.g. buttermilk in bread making.

Milk products: Cream and butter

Please note that while cream and butter are milk products, they are not in the milk, yoghurt and cheese group. They belong at the top of the food pyramid and should be avoided or eaten sparingly.

Cream

Cream is the fat that rises to the top of milk and is then removed. Cream is very high in kilocalories.

Types of cream

Type	Description
Standard cream	Carton often states 'fresh cream'; 40% fat.
Double cream	Used in dessert making; 48% fat.
Low-fat cream	Reduced fat, though still contains 30% fat.
Sour cream/crème fraîche	Cream is treated with a lactic acid culture, which pleasantly sours and thickens it. Used for dips, dressings, etc.
Aerosol	Keeps longer, quick and convenient.

Butter

When cream is churned, the fat comes together as **butter**. The liquid that runs off is called **buttermilk**. Butter is usually salted. Butter is very high in fat (80%). **Low-fat** or 'light' butter has half this fat content. **Dairy spreads** such as Dairygold are a mixture of butter and vegetable oil; they contain roughly the same amount of fat but less cholesterol. **Polyunsaturated margarines** such as Flora are very low in cholesterol and are a much healthier option.

Yoghurt

Yoghurt is a milk product made by adding souring lactic acid bacteria (which are harmless) to milk. Yoghurt has all the nutrients of milk. Low-fat varieties are available, while others sometimes have sugar added.

Types of yoghurt

- **Natural yoghurt:** White, unflavoured yoghurt; a good base ingredient for savoury dips, etc.
- **Set yoghurt:** e.g. Petit Filous.
- **Yoghurt drinks:** Milk and flavours are added to plain yoghurt, e.g. Yop.
- **Greek yoghurt:** A thick, creamy, unflavoured yoghurt.
- **Fruit yoghurt:** Either real fruit is added or just fruit juice if a smooth fruit-flavoured yoghurt is required.

Homework Assignment 18 P. 57

Uses of yoghurt

- Healthy alternative to cream.
- Healthy dessert on its own.
- In dips: Natural or Greek with other ingredients added, e.g. chives.
- In salad dressings: Natural or Greek.

Cheese

Classification of cheese

Cheese is classified into hard, semi-hard, soft or processed types.

Hard cheese, e.g. cheddar, Parmesan.

Semi-hard cheeses, e.g. Edam, Cashel Blue.

Soft cheese, e.g. cream cheese, cottage cheese.

Processed cheese, e.g. cheese slices, cheese triangles, cheese strings, cheese spreads.

Note: Percentages are for Higher Level only.

Composition and nutritive value of cheese

- Hard cheese is an excellent source of both calcium (4%), for healthy bones and teeth, and protein (25%), for growth and repair. For this reason, cheese is ideal to include in the diets of children, teenagers, pregnant and breastfeeding women and vegetarians.
- Hard cheese is very high in fat (34%) and cholesterol, so should be eaten in moderation, especially by those on low-fat diets or those with high cholesterol.

- Please note: Cottage cheese is much lower in fat (4%), but is not as good a source of either protein (14%) or calcium (1%).
- Cheese lacks carbohydrate (0%) and is therefore generally served with carbohydrate-rich foods such as bread, pasta or crackers.
- Cheese contains vitamins A and B and varying amounts of water depending on the type of cheese – hard cheeses contain less water than soft or semi-soft.

Uses of cheese in cookery

Effects of cooking on cheese

- **Eat raw** if possible, as cooked cheese is less digestible.
- **Protein coagulates** (sets) and cheese shrinks.
- **Fat melts**. If overcooked, fat separates from cheese and cheese becomes rubbery, oily and indigestible.
- **Mustard** helps make cheese more digestible.

The six stages of cheese making

1. A culture of harmless bacteria is added to pasteurised milk. This gives flavour.
2. Milk is warmed. Rennet is added, which clots the milk.
3. The milk separates into curds (solid) and whey (liquid).

4. Curds are chopped, pressed and salted. Whey is drained off.
5. Curds are put into moulds and pressed – firmly for hard cheeses.
6. Cheese is left to mature. Flavours develop over three to 12 months.

Buying cheese	Storing cheese
◎ Buy in small quantities, as it will go off quickly once opened. ◎ Check the expiry date.	◎ Cover with greaseproof paper, then foil. ◎ Refrigerate. ◎ Remove from fridge one hour before use to let the flavours develop.

Homework Assignment 19 P. 61

Cereal and potato group

Eat four to six servings per day, more if you are very active.

Note: Potatoes are included in the section on vegetables.

Most of the food we eat should come from this food group. All over the world, cereals are eaten because they are cheap, nutritious, filling and are easily prepared.

Cereals

Structure of cereals

This is an illustration of a wheat grain. Other cereals have a similar structure.

- **The bran layer:** This part of the grain contains fibre, iron and vitamin B. It is removed during processing, for instance in making white flour.
- **The endosperm:** Starch and gluten. This is the part of the grain that remains after processing.
- **Germ:** This nutritious part of the grain is also removed during processing. It can be bought on its own as wheat germ. It contains protein, fat and vitamin B.

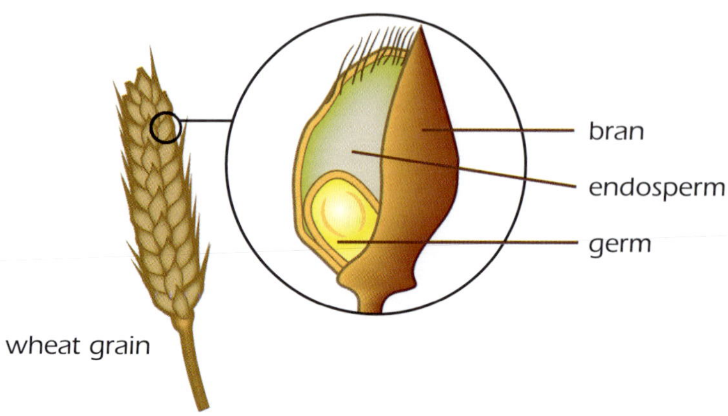

Common cereals and some of their products

Cereal	Wheat	Rice	Maize	Oats	Rye	Barley
Products	Flour, bread, cakes, pasta, breakfast cereals, e.g. Weetabix, noodles and couscous	Brown and white rice, breakfast cereals, e.g. Rice Krispies, rice cakes, rice flour, ground rice	Corn on the cob, sweet corn, breakfast cereals, e.g. cornflakes, corn flour, popcorn, corn oil	Breakfast cereals, e.g. porridge, muesli, Ready Brek	Rye bread (dark colour), rye flour, crispbread, e.g. Ryvita, rye whiskey	Whiskey, beer, pearl barley

Average composition and nutritive value of cereals

- **Carbohydrate** (70%) is the main nutrient found in cereals. Cereals are therefore useful in the diet as a source of heat and energy. Those who lead active lives should eat plenty of carbohydrates (some very active individuals, e.g. athletes, could eat up to 12 servings per day). Those with inactive lifestyles should be careful, though, as cereals such as bread are often accompanied by fatty foods and therefore can cause weight gain.
- Unprocessed cereals, e.g. brown bread and rice, contain fibre, which is essential for a healthy digestive system and should be chosen over processed cereals.
- Cereals also contain **low biological value protein** (13%). **Gluten** is a protein found in some cereals, such as wheat. While gluten gives bread dough its elastic quality and allows it to rise, people with coeliac disease cannot digest gluten and must avoid eating it.
- Cereals do contain a small amount of **fat** (2%), although it is usually what is put on the cereal, e.g. butter or cheese, that increases fat content.
- Cereals contain the minerals **calcium** and **iron** and some **B group vitamins**. If these are removed during processing, they are often put back again. For example, you will see 'fortified with calcium and iron' written on such products.

Note: Percentages are for Higher Level only.

Effect of heat on cereals – starch grains swell, soften and absorb liquid

Effects of cooking on cereals

- Starch grains swell and burst, e.g. popcorn.
- Starch grains, e.g. rice, absorb liquid.
- Starch becomes more digestible, e.g. compare eating a raw and cooked potato.

Flour

Although flour can be made from other cereals, such as corn, wheat flour is the most common in this country. The type of wheat flour produced depends on the type of wheat used and how much processing it undergoes.

Processing flour

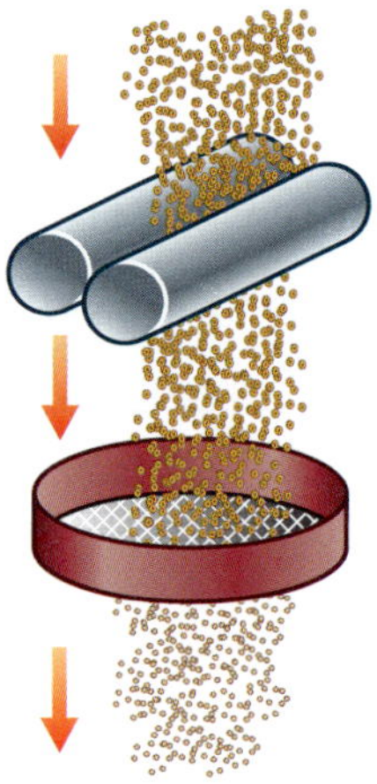

1. Grain is washed, dried and broken open between metal rollers. If processing stops here, wholemeal flour is produced.
2. Grain is sieved and rolled again and again until a white 'refined' product is produced – white flour. Sometimes extra ingredients are added at this stage, such as calcium, or the flour may be bleached.

A **refined cereal product** is a processed product from which much of the bran and the germ have been removed. Examples of refined cereal products are white flour and rice.

Types of flour

Strong flour: Wheat with a high concentration of gluten, used for making yeast bread.

Brown: Similar to wholemeal, but with the coarsest bran and germ removed.

Wholemeal: Coarse brown flour, contains the whole wheat grain.

White or cream flour: Starchy endosperm only.

Self-raising: Brown or white flour with a raising agent such as baking powder added.

Gluten-free: Flour with gluten removed; used to make bread, etc. for coeliacs.

Bread

If the gluten-free symbol appears on a product, it is suitable for coeliacs

Breads from around the world

Bread is one of our staple foods. Nowadays, breads from all over the world are available in our supermarkets. Some of these breads are pictured above.

Pasta comes in many different shapes and often different colours and flavours

Pasta

Special wheat called **durum** wheat is used to make pasta. Flour made from this wheat is mixed with water and egg to make a dough. Sometimes flavouring ingredients such as tomato or spinach are added at this stage. It is then shaped and dried. Fresh pasta is not totally dried and must be used within a few days. Dried pasta is fully dried and keeps for up to a year.

Rice

- **Long-grain rice:** Served with savoury dishes, e.g. curry; cooks in 25 minutes.
- **Medium-grain rice:** Italian rice used for dishes where rice is mixed through, e.g. risotto.
- **Short-grain rice:** Used in sweet puddings and desserts.
- **Whole grain/brown rice:** Brown long-grain rice, high in fibre as bran is not removed; takes 40 minutes to cook.
- **Convenience rice products:** Boil-in-the-bag, non-stick, cooked frozen rice.

20 P. 64

Brown rice should be eaten instead of white rice, as it is higher in fibre, preventing constipation and other bowel disorders.

Fruit and vegetable group

Eat at least five servings of fruit and vegetables per day.

Classification of fruit

Citrus	Berries	Stone	Hard	Dried	Others

Grapefruit	Blackberries	Apricots	Apples	Apricots	Bananas
Lemons	Blackcurrants	Cherries	Pears	Currants	Melon
Limes	Gooseberries	Damsons		Dates	Pineapple
Oranges	Raspberries	Nectarines		Prunes	Rhubarb
Satsumas	Redcurrants	Peaches		Raisins	
Tangerines	Strawberries	Plums		Sultanas	

Note: Percentages are for Higher Level only.

Average composition and nutritive value of fresh fruit

Fresh fruit is very important in the diet for three main reasons:

1. Many fruits are high in vitamin C (up to 200mg/100g for blackcurrants, followed by strawberries with 77mg/100g).
2. Many fruits are high in fibre.
3. Most fruits are low in kilocalories (fruit is up to 90% water).

Also, although less importantly, some fruits contain a little iron and calcium. Highly coloured fruits such as peaches contain **carotene**, which the body changes into vitamin A. Fruit contains carbohydrate (5–20%) in the form of fruit sugar (fructose) and traces of protein. Fruit contains virtually no fat.

Preparing fruit

- Prepare just before cooking or eating to avoid loss of vitamin C.
- **Citrus fruits**, e.g. **lemons:** Wash in warm water if rind is to be grated and eaten.
- **Hard fruits**, e.g. **apples:** Remove core, leave skin on if possible, cut to required size for dish, toss in orange juice to prevent browning (avoid sugar syrup if possible).
- **Soft fruit**, e.g. **strawberries:** Remove damaged fruit, wash gently in a sieve, pat dry with kitchen paper.

Effects of cooking on fruit

- Texture softens.
- Vitamin C is reduced (up to 25%).
- Cellulose breaks down and fruit becomes more digestible.
- Moulds and other micro-organisms are destroyed.

Uses of fruit in the diet

Classification of vegetables

Roots/tubers	Green	Pulses	Fruits

Beetroot	Broccoli	Beans (green	Aubergine
Carrot	Brussels sprout	bean, broad bean,	Courgette
Onion (bulb)	Cabbage	runner bean)	Cucumber
Parsnip	Cauliflower	Dried peas,	Pepper
Potato (tuber)	Curly kale	beans, lentils	Pumpkin
Swede	Lettuce	Peas	Tomato
Turnip (tuber)	Spinach		

Average composition and nutritive value of vegetables

Vegetables are valuable in the diet for five main reasons:

1. Pulse vegetables, that is, peas, beans and lentils, are a good source of **vegetable protein** (up to 7%). For this reason they are very important in the diet, especially of vegetarians.
2. Vegetables are **low in fat** and have a **high water content** (up to 95%). This means that they are low in kilocalories: good news for weight watchers and those at risk from heart disease.
3. Vegetables are a good source of **vitamin C** (peppers have the highest, containing 120mg/100g). Vitamin C is vital for general health and is a vitamin sometimes lacking in the Irish diet.
4. Vegetables, especially green vegetables, are a good source of **iron**. Iron is vital for healthy blood and is another nutrient often lacking in the Irish diet.
5. Vegetables (especially pulse vegetables) are a good source of **fibre** in the diet, which is needed to prevent constipation and other bowel problems.

Note: Percentages are for Higher Level only.

Note: Vegetables also contain **vitamin A** in the form of carotene. Pulses also contain some **B group vitamins**.

Preparing vegetables for cooking

Type	Preparation
Roots/tubers	Scrub, peel if necessary, cut off ends, slice, dice or cut into strips (julienne).
Greens	Remove wilted leaves, separate leaves and wash each leaf under cold running water, chop if necessary with a sharp knife. Do not steep. Do not use bread soda in cooking (it used to be used to preserve colour, but destroys vitamin C).
Pulses	Remove *fresh* pulses from their pod. Soak *dried* pulses overnight in water.
Fruits	Wash in cold water, slice or dice with a sharp knife.

Cooking vegetables

Vegetables can be cooked in a variety of ways.

- **Boiling:** While not the best method of cooking vegetables, it is traditional and still one of the most common ways vegetables are cooked in this country. Greens, roots and tubers and pulses may be cooked in this way.
- **Steaming:** This is an excellent way of cooking vegetables. Because vegetables are not actually sitting in the cooking water, minerals and vitamins are not lost. It is suitable for all vegetable types.
- **Stir-frying:** Chop vegetables for stir-frying just before cooking. Cook in the minimum amount of oil (use oil spray). Vegetables are cooked quickly, so nutrients are not lost. It is suitable for all vegetable types.
- **Roasting:** Vegetables are best if they are par-boiled before roasting (boiled until half cooked). Put a little olive oil in the roasting tin and toss the vegetables in it before roasting in the oven. This method is best suited to roots, tubers and fruits, e.g. peppers.
- **Microwaving:** Prepare vegetables and chop into even-sized pieces. Cover and cook on high for up to 10 minutes (depends on type of vegetable). Allow vegetables to 'stand' for two to three minutes before serving. Suitable for all vegetable types.
- **Grilling:** Used for tomatoes and peppers – sometimes food is brushed with oil.
- Vegetables (mainly roots and tubers) are also cooked in stews and casseroles.

Effects of cooking on vegetables

- Vitamins and minerals dissolve into the cooking liquid.
- Vitamin C is destroyed.
- Fibre softens.
- Starch becomes more digestible, e.g. potatoes.
- Flavour, texture and colour may be lost, especially if overcooked.

Al dente means cooking vegetables until they are soft right through but still have bite.

Preventing nutrient loss when preparing and cooking vegetables

1. Buy good-quality fruit and vegetables. Eat raw where possible.

2. Do not use bread soda when cooking cabbage, as it destroys vitamin C.

3. Use a small amount of water and keep saucepan lids on. Don't overcook – cook al dente.

4. Do not soak vegetables.

5. Cook with the skins on if possible. If peeling, use a peeler, as a knife peels too thickly.

6. Chop with a sharp knife.

Buying fruit and vegetables

- Buy fruit and vegetables in season, when they are the freshest and at their best.
- Buy undamaged fruit and vegetables that feel heavy for their size.
- Buy medium-sized fruits and vegetables, as large ones lack flavour.
- Avoid pre-packed fruit and vegetables, as any damage may not be visible.
- Buy in small quantities, as they go off quickly.

- **In season:** Most fruit and vegetables grow at a certain time of year. This is when they are **in season** and at their best. Fruit and vegetables must be imported when they are **out of season**, and are usually expensive, e.g. strawberries at Christmas.
- **Organically grown** fruit and vegetables are grown naturally, without the use of artificial fertilizers. They are more expensive.

EU grading and regulations

Fruit and vegetables must be:

- Sound and free from chemicals.
- Graded according to size.
- Marked with the country of origin, variety and class.

Classes

- Extra: Excellent quality.
- Class I: Good quality.
- Class II: Marketable but with defects of shape or colour.
- Class III: Marketable but inferior.

Storing fresh fruit and vegetables

- Use as soon as possible after purchase.
- Remove plastic wrappings or bags.
- Store fruits and green vegetables in the fridge if possible.
- Store roots and tubers in a cool, dark, ventilated place on a vegetable rack or basket.
- Bananas should not be stored in the fridge, as they will blacken.

Dried fruit

Processed fruit and vegetables

Fruit and vegetables are generally processed to prolong their shelf life.

Frozen

- No loss of goodness, but can go soft on thawing.

Canned

- Canning involves high temperatures, which destroys vitamins C and B.
- Fruit canned in syrup has a high sugar content.

Dried

- Vitamins C and B are lost.

Homework Assignment 22 P. 72

The examination

As part of section B, question 1 on both the Higher and Ordinary Level paper, you are usually asked to evaluate the nutritive value of a particular food product. Sometimes the product is a single food product, e.g. milk or porridge oats, but other times it is a product that contains a number of the food groups, e.g. a pizza. Below is a sample examination question and answer (the question is from section B, question 1, Higher Level 2008).

Sample question

The following information is displayed on the label of a carton of soup.

(a) Evaluate the nutritive value of the soup.

SOUP TO GO
Chicken and Sweetcorn Soup

NUTRITION INFORMATION

Typical values per cup	
Energy	660kj/158kcal
Protein	4.1g
Carbohydrate	16.0g
(of which sugars)	(4.1g)
Fat	8.6g
(of which saturates)	(0.8g)
Fibre	0.6g
Sodium	0.7g
Salt equivalent	1.9g

Low fat

Ingredients
Water, sweetcorn, onions, chicken, vegetable oil, potatoes, cornflour, peppers, flavouring, skimmed milk, sugar, herbs, sodium, garlic powder, spice extract, beta carotene.

DIETARY INFORMATION
Suitable for a gluten-free diet.
No artificial colours, flavours or preservatives.
A serving contains 1.9g of an adults recommended daily salt intake of 6g.

What you must do here is name each nutrient present in the food product, in this case a soup – protein, fat, carbohydrates, minerals and vitamins. You must state how much of each is present. Comment on each nutrient – state its type (for example, is it animal or vegetable protein, saturated or unsaturated fat) and its function in the body. You could also comment on its energy value (kcal), especially if it is particularly low or high in calories. Comment on nutrients not present. Make a general statement about the food at the end.

Sample answer

This soup contains a number of different nutrients. One cup of this soup contains 4.1g of protein. Because it is chicken soup, it is likely to be animal protein (HBV), which is very useful in the diet for growth and repair of body cells. The soup contains 8.6g of fat per cup, but this fat is almost all unsaturated, which means that this product is low in cholesterol. The soup contains 16g of carbohydrate for heat and energy, 4.1g of which is sugar. It is low in fibre though, containing only 0.6g. The product is very high in the mineral salt, containing 0.7g sodium (salt equivalent 1.9g), so should be avoided by those on a low-salt diet (given that we should consume a maximum of 4–6g of salt per day). It does not contain any other minerals and no vitamins. The soup contains 158kcal per cup, which is quite low. On the whole, while this food is not unhealthy, it is not a very healthy food and should be accompanied by something containing minerals and vitamins, e.g. a fresh salad sandwich.

Homework Assignment 23 P. 77

Test Yourself eTest.ie

CHAPTER 11

Breakfasts, Packed Meals, Soups and Sauces

Teacher's CD-ROM

Slide presentation • Student activity pack • Class test

Breakfasts

A healthy breakfast is an essential start to the day. When you wake up, your blood sugar is low after fasting all night. If you do not eat breakfast, it remains low. Because of this you will be less able to concentrate at school or at work and more likely to eat high-calorie mid-morning snacks such as crisps and fizzy drinks.

Planning a healthy breakfast

- Get up early and do not rush – sit down and enjoy your breakfast.
- Include food from all four food groups – protein group, cereal group, milk, cheese and yoghurt group and fruit and vegetable group.
- It is important to include fluids, e.g. juices, after being without fluids all night.
- Choose high-fibre breakfast cereals and avoid those high in sugar.
- Use polyunsaturated spreads such as Flora instead of butter on bread.
- Grill instead of fry.

Choose foods from each group for a healthy breakfast.

1. Fruit and vegetable group

- Fruit juice (orange, grapefruit, cranberry).
- Grilled grapefruit.
- Fruit segments or whole fruit.
- Stewed fruit, e.g. prunes.
- Grilled mushrooms or tomatoes.
- Fruit smoothies.

2. **Cereal and bread group**
   - Healthy breakfast cereals include muesli, porridge with a sprinkle of All-Bran, cornflakes, bran flakes, Rice Krispies, Weetabix, shredded wheat, Fruit 'n Fibre.
   - Bread (brown, toast, scones, croissants, bagels).

3. **Protein group**
   - Eggs (poached, scrambled, boiled, omelettes).
   - Grilled bacon, sausage, pudding, kidney, liver.
   - Cold meats, e.g. ham.

4. **Milk, cheese and yoghurt group**
   - Milk on cereal or alone.
   - Yoghurt, cheese.
   - Yoghurt in smoothies.

Example of a healthy breakfast: Orange juice, muesli with low-fat milk, boiled egg and toasted brown bread.

Setting a breakfast tray

1. Collect all tableware (it should be spotless).
2. Set tray as shown in the diagram.
3. Cover the cooked main course with another plate to keep it warm.

A breakfast tray

Packed meals, lunches and picnics

Guidelines for a packed meal

- Consider personal likes and dislikes. Perhaps the individual is on a special diet, e.g. gluten free.
- As the individual will usually have had nothing since breakfast and nothing again until evening, it is important that packed meals are both filling and nutritious.
- Try to include all four food groups.
- Try to have variety – the same lunch every day can become boring.
- Avoid empty-calorie foods such as chocolate and include healthier treats such as homemade scones or buns.
- Spread bread thinly with polyunsaturated margarine, e.g. Flora, and use low-fat mayonnaise. A spread provides a waterproof seal on the bread, preventing the sandwich ingredients from soaking into it and making it soggy.
- Use suitable packing materials, e.g. securely sealed plastic boxes and bottles, thermos flasks, foil, lunch bags and cling film.
- Pack heavy items at the bottom of the box, e.g. cartons of juice.
- Include a drink high in vitamin C, e.g. orange juice.
- Do not pack foods that spoil too easily, e.g. banana sandwiches.
- Sometimes it is better to pack ingredients for sandwiches (buttered bread and filling) separately so that they can be easily made up fresh before eating.

Designing a healthy packed meal

Choose foods from each group for a healthy packed meal.

Fruit and vegetable group

Apples, oranges, kiwi fruit, grapes, salads, fruit juices and smoothies, sticks of carrot, celery and cucumber, Branston pickle.

Milk, cheese and yoghurt group

Milk, milkshakes, yoghurt and yoghurt drinks, cheese alone, in crackers or in sandwiches.

Protein group

Sliced cold meats, e.g. chicken, ham, beef, turkey; nuts, sausage rolls, chicken drumsticks, prawn cocktail, tuna, salmon.

Cereal and potato group

Bread: rolls, baps, sliced white or wholemeal, tortilla wraps, bagels, panini, croissants, rice, potato and pasta salad, popcorn.

Sample packed meal

Orange juice
Spiced chicken salad wrap
Low-fat strawberry yoghurt

Sandwiches

Sandwiches need not be boring. They consist of three parts – bread, spread and filling – each of which can be varied. Make sure to use plenty of filling and that it is not too dry.

Sandwich ingredients

Breads	Spreads	Fillings
Wholemeal, soda, brown sliced, white sliced, rolls, baps, pita pockets, bagels, tortilla wraps, panini	Polyunsaturated margarine, low-fat spreads, spreadable butter, low-fat mayonnaise, salad cream, mustard, ketchup, Branston pickle, low-fat cream cheese, chutney	Ham, chicken, beef, turkey, luncheon meats, corned beef, fish, cheese, tuna, salmon, sardines, prawns, eggs, tomatoes, lettuce, scallions, onion, grated carrot, cucumber, peppers, bean sprouts, cress

Types of sandwich

Not only can the bread, spread and filling vary, but also the type of sandwich.

Single: Two slices of bread with spread and filling(s).

Double: Three slices of bread with several fillings.

Club: Four slices of bread, three or more fillings.

Open: Firm bread with a spread and a variety of fillings on top.

Rolls: French stick with a spread and filling(s).

Toasted: Toasted in a sandwich toaster or under the grill – no lettuce.

Pita pockets: Split on one side and filled, e.g. bacon, lettuce tomato and garlic mayonnaise.

Rolled: Thinly sliced crustless bread with a filling, e.g. ham, salmon, cream cheese, rolled and fastened with a cocktail stick – for parties.

Panini: Stick of bread, often ciabatta, filled and toasted on a contact grill, e.g. a George Foreman grill.

Wrap: Tortilla with spread and filling, wrapped tightly and cut in half for eating.

Soups

Soups can be classified into thick soups and thin soups.

Thick soups

- **Puréed:** Thickened by blending the soup's own ingredients using a sieve, liquidiser or food processor, e.g. thick farmhouse vegetable soup.
- **Thickened:** By adding a starch, e.g. flour, cornflour, pasta or potato.

Thin soups

- **Clear soup:** Thin soup made with well-flavoured stock, e.g. consommé.
- **Broth:** Thin clear soup with finely chopped meat, vegetables and a starch such as barley floating in it. For example, chicken broth is made from a thin clear stock, with chicken pieces, vegetables and perhaps barley.

A good soup:

- Is made from a fresh, well-flavoured stock. Soup should be seasoned with pepper and herbs; do not add too much salt – use a salt substitute.
- Tastes of its main ingredient, e.g. tomato soup should have a strong tomato flavour.

Thick soup

Thin soup

- Is piping hot and has no grease floating on the top (note: some soups are meant to be served cold).
- Has a good colour.
- A thick soup should not be too thick and should not have starchy lumps.

Three ways to thicken a soup

1. Blend 25g of flour or cornflour with cold water. Stir this mixture into the soup just before the end of the cooking time. Bring the soup back to the boil and boil for approximately five minutes. Garnish and serve.
2. Begin by gently frying (sautéing) the soup ingredients, e.g. vegetables, in 25g of fat or oil. Add 25g flour and cook for a few minutes. Gradually add the stock. The soup will thicken once it comes to the boil.
3. Add barley, rice or pasta to the soup 20 minutes before the end of the cooking time.

How to garnish a soup

Croutons (cubes of bread fried in oil – use a polyunsaturated fat)

Herbs, e.g. parsley

Swirl of cream, e.g. cream of vegetable soup

Convenience soups

- Instant soups, e.g. Cup-a-Soup, are cheap but are not very nutritious and sometimes contain a lot of salt and flavour enhancers, such as monosodium glutamate (MSG).
- Canned soups just need heating up, so they are very convenient. However, sometimes they taste very artificial, some can be high in salt and some contain flavour enhancers such as MSG.
- Cartons of fresh soup are expensive but convenient, tasty and nutritious. Store in the fridge.

Dried packet soup

Canned soup

Cartons of fresh soup

Sauces

Sauces are well-flavoured liquids and can take many forms. They can be sweet or savoury, hot or cold. Sauces can be used as a garnish or can be part of the dish itself. For instance, cheese sauce is part of a lasagne dish. Sauces can also bind or coat foods and generally add colour and flavour to a dish.

Classification

Type of sauce	Examples
Roux based	White, cheese
Fruit purée	Apple, raspberry coulis, cranberry
Egg based	Egg custard
Cold	Mint
Other	Chocolate, butterscotch, barbecue

Roux-based sauces

A roux-based sauce is made from equal amounts of fat and flour. Different flavourings and amounts of liquid are added to vary the basic sauce.

There are four basic thicknesses of roux sauces. The amounts of fat and flour stay the same for each one; it is the amount of liquid that changes.

Note: If a recipe says, for example, '500ml of coating sauce', it is the amount of liquid that is meant. Thus, the ingredients for 500ml of coating sauce are 50g fat, 50g flour and 500ml liquid.

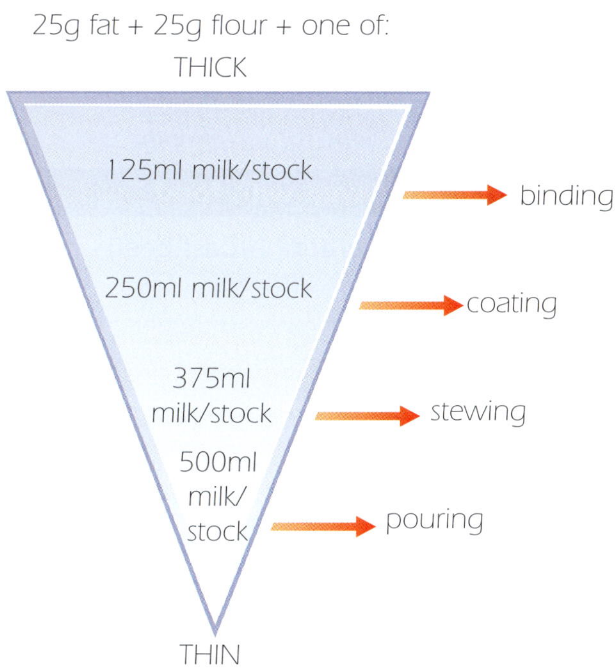

How to make a basic white roux sauce

1. Melt fat. Add flour and seasoning and cook for 1 minute. Do not allow to burn.
2. Take off the heat. Add milk gradually, stirring all the time.
3. Return to the heat. Keep stirring to prevent lumping.
4. Bring to the boil, simmer for 5 minutes, then serve.

Variations on basic pouring sauce (500ml)

Sauce	Extra ingredients	Goes well with
Parsley	Add 2 teaspoons chopped parsley	Bacon, fish
Mustard	Add 1 teaspoon made mustard, 2 teaspoons vinegar	Fish
Cheese	¼ teaspoon mustard (added to roux), 50g grated cheese added at the end and allowed to melt: do not return to heat	Fish, cauliflower
Mushroom	Add 50g sautéed mushrooms after the liquid has been added and then simmer for 5 minutes	Steak, roast beef

Other traditional sauces

Food	Sauce(s) that goes well with food
Beef	Pepper (steaks), horseradish (roast beef)
Pork	Apple
Lamb	Mint
Turkey	Bread sauce or cranberry
Goose	Apple

Fruit coulis

Desserts look good if you decorate them with a simple fruit coulis. To make a coulis, simply purée highly coloured fruits such as strawberries or raspberries, add a little icing sugar and then pour to the side of the dish.

Convenience sauces

Convenience sauces are available in many different forms – canned, bottled, dried, frozen or in cartons. They have **advantages** in that they speed up the preparation and cooking time of some dishes, e.g. buying ready-made sauces for pasta dishes. They are also useful for those with poor cooking skills in that it allows them to cook a greater variety of dishes. Convenience sauces, however, have **disadvantages** in that they can be high in sugar, salt and other additives. They can also sometimes be expensive and often lack flavour.

Herbs and spices

Herbs and spices are used in cookery to add flavour to foods and sometimes make the foods look more appetising. Below is an alphabetical list of common herbs and spices and their uses.

Herb/spice	Uses
Bay leaves	Bouquet garni in soups and stocks
Basil	Added to tomato-based sauces, e.g. Bolognese, pizza
Caraway (seed)	Bread and biscuits as well as in cheese dishes, salads and soups
Cayenne pepper	Add a little to meat, fish, vegetable, egg or cheese dishes
Chives	Salads and dressings, chopped through mashed potatoes, garnish
Cinnamon	Cakes, tarts, biscuits, pickles and chutneys
Cloves	Apple tarts, Christmas puddings, mince pies, with ham and pork
Fennel	Fish dishes, soups and sauces
Garlic (a bulb)	Many savoury dishes
Ginger	Biscuits and cake, Chinese cookery, chutneys
Mint	In a sauce with lamb, as a garnish
Mustard	Many savoury dishes, cheese sauce, with ham and bacon
Nutmeg	Chicken, vegetables, cheese dishes, cakes, custard and milk puddings
Oregano	Italian dishes, e.g. Bolognese, pizza
Paprika	In beef goulash, garnish meat, fish, cheese and egg dishes
Parsley	Used in sauces, most savoury dishes, as a garnish
Pepper	All savoury dishes
Rosemary	Meat (especially lamb), fish and poultry dishes
Sage	Stuffing and casseroles
Thyme	Stuffing, beef, lamb and poultry dishes

Homework Assignment

26 P. 91

Test Yourself eTest.ie

CHAPTER 12

Food Processing and Leftovers

Teacher's CD-ROM: Slide presentation • Student activity pack – with revision crossword • Class test

Food processing

Food processing means treating foods in some way to make them easier to use. Most foods nowadays undergo some degree of processing.

Advantages of food processing

- Processed foods usually last longer than unprocessed foods.
- Requires less preparation – saves time and effort.
- Easier to transport – compare transporting fresh peas with tinned peas.
- Easier to store in shops and at home.
- Seasonal foods are available all year round.

Disadvantages of food processing

- Processed food is expensive.
- Processed food is frequently not as tasty as fresh foods.
- Nutritional value is often reduced, e.g. fibre content.
- Packaging is bad for the environment.

Before processing	After processing
Wheat grains	Flour
Unpasteurised milk	Pasteurised milk
Milk	Cheese
Raw chicken	Chicken curry, TV dinner
Pork	Frozen sausage rolls
Fresh vegetables	Packet of frozen vegetables
Mandarin oranges	Tin of mandarin oranges
Potatoes	Oven chips

Food preservation

Food preservation is a form of food processing that slows down food spoilage (food going bad). Food spoilage is caused by **enzymes**, **moulds**, **yeast** or **bacteria** attacking food. Spoilage of some foods, such as butter, may be caused by oxygen in the air.

Enzymes, moulds, yeast and bacteria need **six conditions** to grow:

Food	Warmth	Moisture
Time	Oxygen (most)	Correct pH

Take one or more of these conditions away *or* add a chemical preservative, such as vinegar (which is acidic and so alters pH), and the food is preserved.

Advantages of preservation

- Prevents waste, so saves money.
- Seasonal foods are available all year round, e.g. strawberries.
- Adds variety to the diet.
- Many preserved foods are easy to prepare, e.g. frozen vegetables.

Methods of preservation

1. Freezing and refrigeration = removing warmth.

2. Pasteurisation, canning and bottling = applying strong heat.

3. Drying = removing moisture.

4. Canning and bottling = removal of air.

5. Adding chemical preservatives, e.g. sugar, vinegar, smoke, salt or other 'E' numbers.

6. Irradiation = passing rays through foods (usually fruit and vegetables). Rays destroy enzymes and bacteria, so food keeps longer. Some scientists question the safety of this method.

Freezing

Food is brought to a temperature of –18°C or below. Enzymes and micro-organisms are not killed at this temperature but become inactive (sleep). Once food is **thawed**, enzymes and micro-organisms become active again.

Guidelines for successful freezing

Frozen food, if frozen properly, is almost as nutritious as fresh food. Because food is usually frozen while at its freshest and most nutritious, it is actually more nutritious than fresh food that has been lying around for a few days.

The first rule of freezing is to turn the freezer to its coldest setting two to three hours before freezing and freeze food *quickly*.

- Freeze food at its freshest.
- Do not freeze too much at a time.
- Cool food before freezing it.
- Choose suitable packaging, e.g. plastic freezer bags, plastic tubs.
- Freeze in useable amounts.
- If there is a 'fast freeze' cabinet, use it to freeze foods.
- Label foods clearly.

Blanching

Blanching destroys enzymes that can reduce the quality of frozen vegetables.

Blanching times	
1 minute	Mushrooms, peas
3 minutes	Beans, broccoli, cauliflower, parsnips, turnips
4 minutes	Brussels sprouts, carrots

Plunge prepared vegetables into boiling water for 1–4 minutes.

Plunge into ice-cold water.

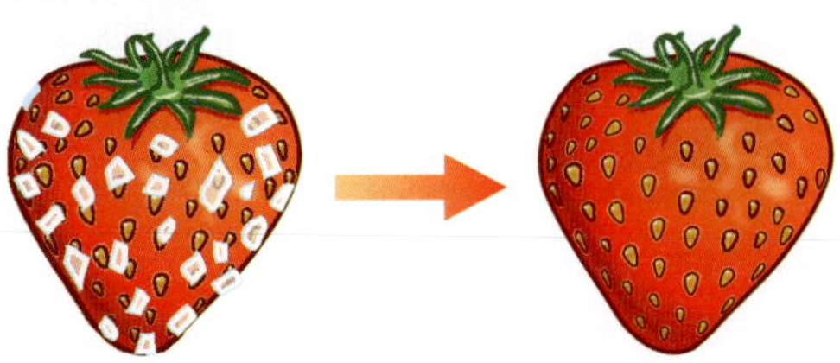

Quick freezing: Small ice crystals are formed. On thawing, cell walls of food are unbroken, food stays firm and keeps its shape.

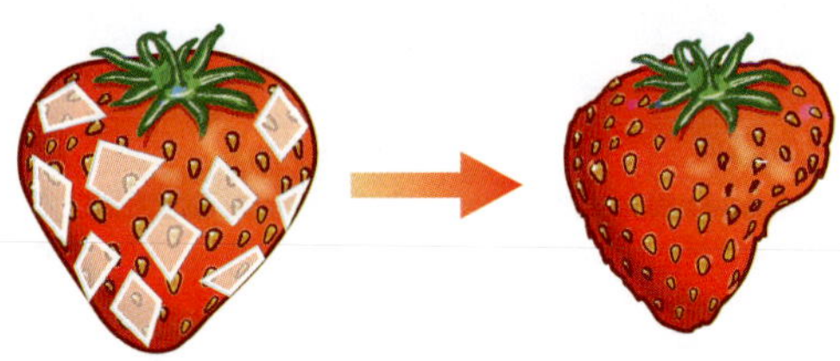

Slow freezing: Large ice crystals are formed. On thawing, food loses its shape and nutrients and becomes soft and mushy.

Open freezing

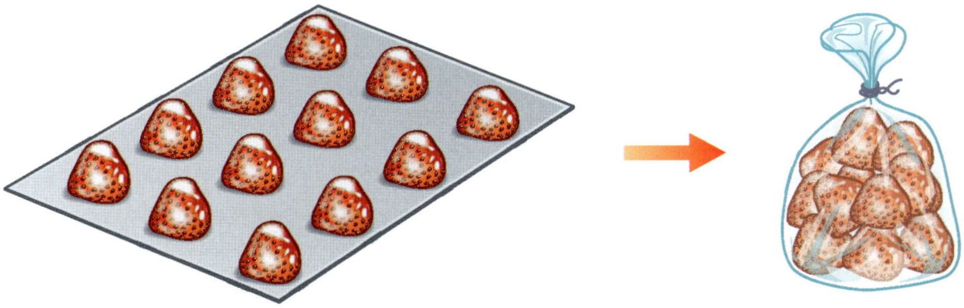

Open freezing: Fruit and vegetables, e.g. berries or peas, that are likely to stick together are open frozen as above and then packed into bags.

Blast freezing

This is a commercial method of freezing. Very cold air (–35°C) is blown over food to freeze it quickly.

Buying frozen foods	Thawing frozen foods
- Packaging should not be torn. - Food should be frozen solid. - The shop's freezer should read –18°C or less. - Check that food is below the load line in open freezers.	- Some foods can be cooked from frozen, e.g. burgers, chips; read the packet instructions. - Thaw meat completely, especially chicken. - Food can be thawed in the microwave or in the fridge overnight. - **Never** refreeze thawed food.

Packaging suitable for freezing

Polythene bags (freezer bags), polythene (plastic) boxes, aluminium foil and containers, waxed cartons with lids. Care should be taken to seal containers well, or **freezer burn** will result and food will be inedible.

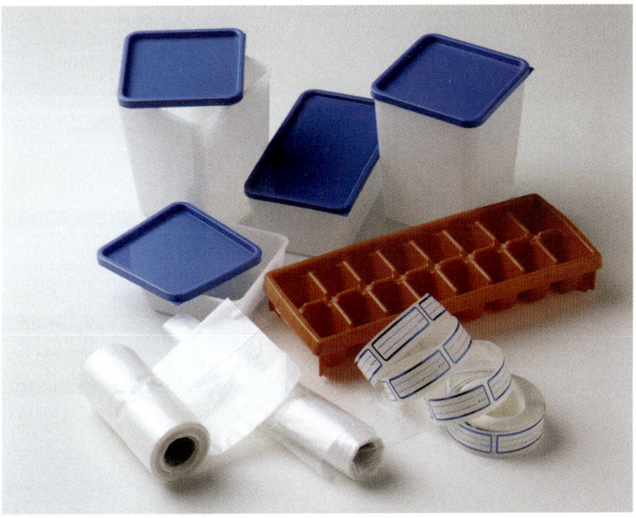

Foods not suitable for freezing

- Vegetables with a high water content, e.g. cucumber or lettuce.
- Bananas and avocados – they go black.

- Whole eggs – they crack (although egg white and yolk can be frozen separately).
- Milk, cream and mayonnaise (the fat and water separate).

Other methods of preservation

Drying	Chemical preservation	Canning and bottling
• Enzymes and micro-organisms need moisture (water) to survive. • Dehydration or drying removes moisture and so preserves the food. • Examples: Breakfast cereals, pasta, rice, raisins (dried grapes), soups.	• Certain chemicals preserve food; many of them are natural and have been used for centuries. • Sugar, e.g. jam. • Vinegar, e.g. pickles. • Salt, e.g. canned fish. • Smoke, e.g. fish. • There are also many artificial preservatives.	• Food is heated to a high temperature (this kills enzymes and micro-organisms). • Food is then sealed in sterile containers. • Food keeps for years. • Vitamins B and C are lost. • Do not buy damaged or bulging cans (they may contain food-poisoning bacteria).

Higher Level

Food labelling

Under EU law, all packaged food must have certain information on the label. These items of information are illustrated below.

- Name of food.
- List of ingredients: product's main ingredient (by weight) listed first, etc.
- Net quantity.
- Use-by/best-before/sell-by date.
- Storage instructions.
- Name and address of manufacturer.
- Country of origin.
- Instructions for use (if necessary).
- Nutritional information (if product is making health claims).

Food additives

In 1984, the EU decided to make it the law for food manufacturers to display lists of ingredients (including all additives) on food packaging. A system of coding additives was also developed and many additives were given an *E number*. There has been much public debate and misunderstanding about E numbers since then. Many people believe all E numbers to be a health risk, causing hyperactivity and allergic reactions. It is because of this bad press that most food labels now list additives by their full names instead of by their E numbers.

What are the facts?

Additives *thought* to be safe by the EU's scientific committee for food are given an E number. Many E numbers are natural healthy substances – for example, vitamin C is E300 and vinegar is E260. There are, however, questions about the safety of some additives still being passed off as safe under EU regulations. Another important issue is that of the '**cocktail effect**'. This means that while individual additives may be quite safe on their own, they may not be so when mixed with others.

Advantages of additives

- They preserve food so that it lasts longer, thus reducing waste.
- They reduce the chance of food poisoning.
- They allow for a wider choice of foods.
- They improve the appearance, texture and flavour of foods.

Disadvantages of additives

- Some people suffer side effects from additives, e.g. rashes, hyperactivity, migraine.
- People get used to the taste of foods containing additives, especially monosodium glutamate (MSG), and may then find healthy, additive-free fresh foods tasteless.
- While individual additives may be safe on their own, it is still unknown what the 'cocktail effect' will be on the body.
- Additives can deceive consumers about food quality, e.g. colourings.

Food additives and their functions

Type of additive	What it does
Colourings (E100–E199)	Make food look more appetising.
Preservatives (E200–E299)	Prevent food from going off, e.g. vinegar preserves pickled onions.
Antioxidants (E300–E399)	These prevent fats, e.g. butter, from reacting with the air and going rancid (off).
Emulsifiers, stabilisers and thickening agents (E400–E499)	Emulsifiers allow oil and water to mix. Stabilisers keep mixtures from separating, e.g. mayonnaise. Thickening agents are used to thicken foods, e.g. sauces, without altering the taste of the product – starch is an example of a thickening agent.
Flavourings (no E number)	Add to the flavour of food, e.g. vanilla essence.
Flavour enhancers (E600+)	Strengthen the flavour of food, e.g. MSG.
Sweeteners	Saccharin.
Nutritional additives (no E number)	These improve the nutritional quality of food or replace nutrients lost in processing.

Convenience foods

Convenience foods are foods that have been processed in some way so as to make them easier and quicker to use. There are a number of different types of convenience foods:

Cook-chill food

1. Foods in cans, bottles and jars, e.g. soups, vegetables, fruits, sauces (such as Bolognese sauce).
2. Frozen foods, e.g. vegetables, fish, meat products, ready meals, pizza.
3. Dried foods, e.g. soups, noodles, sauces, dried fruit.
4. Ready-to-cook foods (foods are prepared for cooking but not cooked), e.g. chicken Kiev, stuffed pork, chicken stir-fry.
5. Cook-chill foods (prepared, cooked and chilled – just need reheating), e.g. lasagne, spaghetti Bolognese, shepherd's pie, mashed potato.

Advantages of convenience foods

- Quick and easy to use, especially for those with busy lifestyles or limited cooking skills.
- Easy to store.
- Some convenience foods, e.g. frozen vegetables, are very nutritious.
- Many last longer and so reduce waste.
- Cook-chill foods often come in individual portion sizes, so are useful for people living alone, e.g. the elderly.

Disadvantages of convenience foods

- Some convenience foods are expensive.
- May contain additives.
- Nutritive value may be reduced during processing, e.g. canned fruit.
- Portion sizes may be very small.
- Cook-chill foods can be a source of food poisoning if not stored properly or reheated thoroughly.

The dangers of cook-chill foods

Cook-chill foods, because they are only reheated and not cooked again at home, can be a source of food poisoning. These foods are safe if they are stored in a fridge or freezer below 4°C and are reheated thoroughly. If a microwave is used to reheat the food, it must be stirred so that all parts of the food reach a high enough temperature.

Leftovers

Good meal planning should ensure that too much food is not cooked for meals. At times, however, there will be food left over. Leftovers may be eaten cold, e.g. roast chicken made into sandwiches, or reheated (réchauffé).

Guidelines for using leftovers

- When food is reheated, its food value decreases, so try to serve leftovers with fresh foods, e.g. leftover chicken with a fresh salad and brown bread.
- Cool leftovers quickly, cover and store in the fridge.
- Use leftovers within two days.
- Reheat leftovers (especially if they contain protein, e.g. meats) thoroughly, as they are a likely source of food poisoning.
- Never reheat leftovers twice.

Homework Assignment 27 P. 95

Dishes using leftovers

- Chicken: Curry, sandwiches, salads.
- Beef: Curry, sandwiches.
- Eggs: Yolks can be used to make mayonnaise or in baking. Whites can be used to make meringues or bread and butter pudding.
- Potatoes: Potato salad, shepherd's pie, cheese and potato pie.
- Bread: Stuffing, French toast, bread and butter pudding.

Test Yourself eTest.ie

CHAPTER 13

Home Baking

Slide presentation • Student activity pack – with revision crossword • Class test

Teacher's CD-ROM

The main advantage of baking your own bread, cakes and biscuits is that you can control exactly what goes into them. Many commercially produced cakes and buns contain a high proportion of fat and sugar. It is possible to bake at home using less fat or unsaturated fat and less sugar too.

Guidelines for home baking

- Collect all ingredients, ensure they are fresh (check expiry dates) and weigh them accurately.
- Collect all equipment and prepare tins (see p. 120).
- Arrange oven shelves, *then* set oven temperature accurately and preheat fully (electric ovens: until light goes off).
- Follow the recipe step by step and take care when adding the liquid to the dry ingredients. Do not over-handle dough and pastry.
- Time cooking accurately and know how to test baked products to see if they are cooked.
- Do not open the oven door unnecessarily.
- Baked products are usually cooled on a wire tray.
- Wash and dry equipment and work surfaces thoroughly. If any food remains on them, they will grow mould, rust if metal and attract vermin to the kitchen.

Baking powder

Yeast

Raising agents

A raising agent is something that makes bread and cakes rise. There are four raising agents:

1. Air.
2. Bread soda.
3. Baking powder.
4. Yeast.

How they work

Air

Air is introduced into the mixture by sieving, rubbing in, creaming or whisking.

Once the mixture is heated, the hot air in the mixture rises, pushing the mixture up. A crust forms on top, which stops the mixture from collapsing when cool.

Bread soda and baking powder

These two raising agents cause a chemical reaction in the mixture.

- **Bread soda** is an alkali; when it is mixed with an acid liquid, such as buttermilk, it produces CO_2.
- **Baking powder** contains both an acid and an alkali. When liquid is added, for example when you add egg, CO_2 is produced.

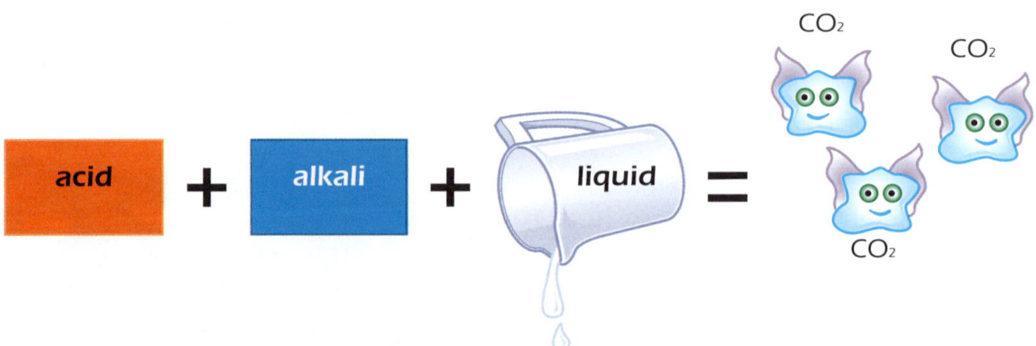

The CO_2 produced works much like the air described above in that it pushes the mixture up. In the oven, a crust forms, which keeps the mixture risen.

Note: Once the acid and the alkali get wet, they begin producing CO_2. It is important to get the mixture into the oven quickly or the CO_2 will escape before the crust forms and the mixture will not rise properly.

Yeast

Yeast are living organisms used in bread making. When they are warm and moist (in bread dough), they produce CO_2. Yeast dough rises before it goes into the oven; a crust then forms in the oven, keeping it in its risen state.

Gluten – its function in bread and cake making

Gluten is a protein found in wheat and other cereals. It has an important role in bread and cake making, although gluten-free products can also be made. When gluten is moistened, it becomes stretchy and elastic. This allows the bread to rise well. Also, in the oven, the gluten sets when heated, forming a crust and keeping the bread risen.

Rubbing in

Methods of making bread and cakes

Rubbing in

Fat is rubbed into the flour with the tips of the fingers until it looks like breadcrumbs. Liquid is then added. Example: Scones.

Creaming

Creaming

Fat and sugar are beaten together until white and creamy. Egg, flour and a raising agent are then added. Example: Queen cakes.

Whisking

Eggs and sugar are whisked until thick and creamy. Flour is then gently folded in. Example: Sponge cake.

Whisking

Melting

All ingredients that melt are melted together, e.g. fat, sugar, syrup. This mixture is then added to the flour and other dry ingredients. Example: Gingerbread.

Melting – a ginger cake made using the melting method

All-in-one

All-in-one

All ingredients are added at once. They are often mixed in a food processor. Example: All-in-one Madeira mix.

Tin preparation

Food	Preparing the tin
Bread, plain scones (no sugar)	Dust lightly with flour
Pastry, small cakes and buns, e.g. coconut buns	Grease lightly
Fatless sponge	Grease lightly and dust with a mixture of caster sugar and flour
Light cakes, e.g. Madeira	Line base only, grease sides
Richer cakes	Line with greaseproof paper (see illustrations below); dabbing some oil on the tin itself will make the greaseproof paper fit more snugly

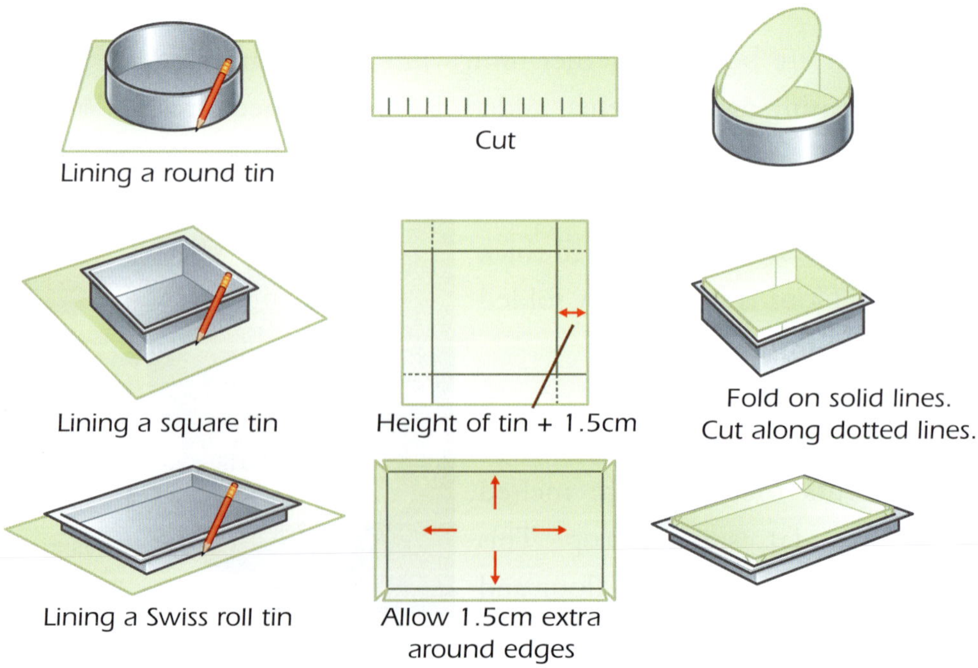

Pastry

Types of pastry and their uses

Type	Uses	Description
Shortcrust and wholemeal shortcrust	Tarts, pies, quiche, sausage rolls	Half the amount of fat to flour; just add water. Add wholemeal flour to make wholemeal pastry; increases fibre content.
Rich shortcrust	Mince pies, sweet flans, pies, e.g. lemon meringue pie	Shortcrust pastry made rich by adding icing sugar and eggs.
Cheese pastry	Quiche	Add grated cheese to shortcrust pastry.
Choux pastry	Éclairs and profiteroles	Melt fat in water, add flour and cook for a few minutes, then gradually beat in egg; spoon or pipe onto tin.
Flaky, puff and rough puff	Vol-au-vents, sausage rolls	Special rolling and folding techniques are used to introduce air into the pastry; high in fat, very time consuming.
Filo	Spring rolls	Very thin Greek pastry.

Pastry-making guidelines

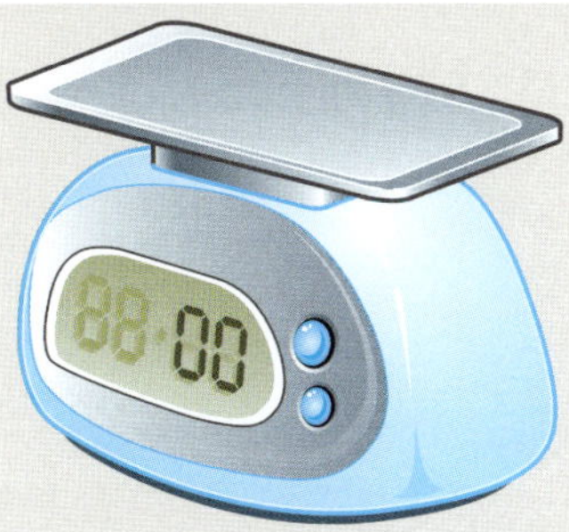

Weigh accurately.

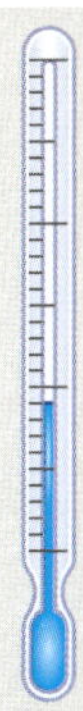

Keep everything cold.

Introduce air, e.g. by sieving, rubbing in, rolling and folding.

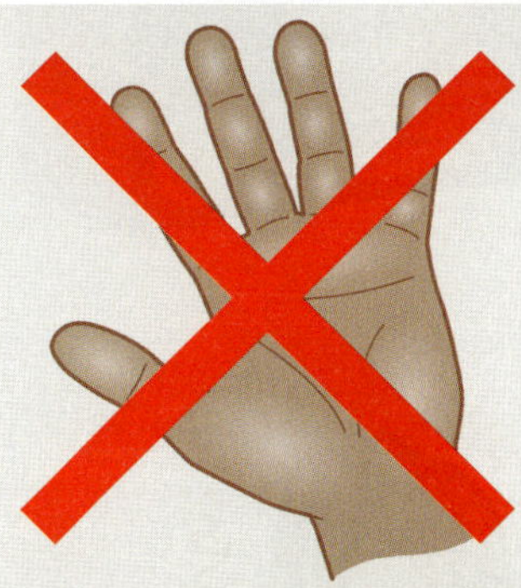

Handle pastry as little as possible.

Pastry-making guidelines

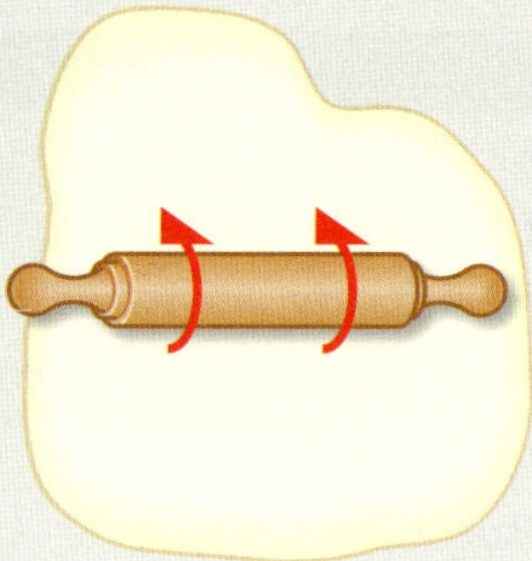

Roll lightly in one direction only on a lightly floured board; turn pastry to prevent sticking; do not stretch pastry.

Allow pastry to relax in the fridge before rolling.

Bake first in a hot preheated oven (220°C/gas 7) then reduce the heat to finish baking.

Commercial cake mixes

Commercial cake mixes contain all the dry ingredients needed to make a cake. To make them up, you usually have to add wet ingredients, e.g. egg, milk or water. Follow the instructions on the packet.

Advantages

- Quick and easy to use.
- Useful for beginners.
- No waste.

Disadvantages

- Expensive.
- Usually do not taste as good as products made from scratch.
- Photo on the front can be deceptive.
- Often high in sugar and salt, low in fibre.
- May contain additives.

Homework Assignment
28 P. 100

Test Yourself eTest.ie

CHAPTER 14

Recipes

Recipe index

Main courses (continued)

Desserts

Pastry

Bread and cakes

Summer berry smoothie

Makes 2 large smoothies

Ingredients

300g frozen fruit (strawberries, raspberries, blackberries)
100g frozen natural yoghurt
500ml cranberry juice, chilled

Method

1 Whiz all ingredients in a food processor until smooth.
2 Serve in a large glass.

Scrambled eggs with cheese and bacon

Serves 2

Ingredients

2 large back rashers
olive oil, to fry
4 large eggs
2 tablespoons milk
salt and pepper
knob butter or margarine
25g cheese, grated
Garnish: sprig of parsley
To serve: toast

Method

1 Chop the rashers into very small pieces and fry in a saucepan with a little olive until brown and a little crispy (do not wash the saucepan, as the oil remaining in it will be used again).
2 Beat the eggs, milk, salt and pepper lightly in a bowl. Mix in the knob of butter and the rashers.
3 Make the toast.
4 Heat the oil remaining in the saucepan from the rashers. Add the egg mixture and cook the eggs, stirring with a wooden spoon until they scramble. **Be careful not to overcook them – scrambled eggs should be thick and creamy, not crumbly and rubbery.**
5 Serve on warm toast. Sprinkle the grated cheese on top and allow it to melt in. Garnish with parsley.

Cheese muffins

Makes approximately 12 medium muffins

Ingredients

150g white flour (or half brown, half white for a healthier option)
50g mature cheddar cheese, grated
1 heaped teaspoon baking powder
½ teaspoon bicarbonate of soda
1 dessertspoon sugar
pinch salt
50g butter, melted
1 small egg
50ml milk
1 dessertspoon grated Parmesan cheese

Special equipment: muffin cases and tin

Method

Preheat the oven to 200°C/fan 190°C/gas 5.

1 Mix the dry ingredients (except the Parmesan) in a bowl.
2 Add the melted butter, egg and milk and mix lightly.
3 Spoon the mixture into 12 muffin cases. Sprinkle some Parmesan cheese on top of each muffin.
4 Bake for 20 minutes. Cool on a wire tray.

Starters

Chilled melon and summer fruits

Serves 2

Ingredients

caster sugar, to decorate wine glass
1 small cantaloupe melon
150g summer fruits, e.g. strawberries, raspberries, blueberries, cranberries, blackberries

Method

1 Decorate the wine glasses first by dipping the rims in water and then in caster sugar.
2 Cut the melon along the equator. Remove the seeds.
3 Using a melon baller, scoop out the flesh.
4 Wash and slice the strawberries (if using). Leave the other berries whole.
5 Place the fruit carefully in wine glasses, chill and then serve the glass on a small plate with a doily.

Apple and walnut stuffed avocado

Serves 4

Ingredients

2 ripe avocados
lemon juice
1 red eating apple
50g walnuts
2 tablespoons low-fat mayonnaise
Garnish: walnut halves
To serve: lettuce, cherry tomatoes, cucumber slices

Method

1. Prepare the avocados:
   - Wash and cut into avocados all round until you reach the stone.
   - Take half the avocado in each hand and twist to separate.
   - Remove the stone by piercing with a knife and twisting.
   - Remove the flesh from the skin in one piece with a dessertspoon.
   - Chop into even-sized pieces. Sprinkle with lemon juice to prevent browning.
2. Wash, core and chop the apple. Chop the walnuts.
3. Mix the avocado, apple and walnuts with the mayonnaise.
4. Fill the avocado shells with the mixture.
5. Garnish with walnut halves. Serve with lettuce leaves, cherry tomatoes and cucumber slices.

Top tip: To make a cucumber look nice, before you slice it, cut into the cucumber by dragging a fork along its length or making little trenches in it with a knife. When you slice it, you will get a nice edge.

cucumber with serrated edge

Prawn cocktail

Serves 4

Ingredients

32 large prawns (double this number if they are small)

1 litre fast-boiling salted water (add 1 tablespoon salt)

Marie Rose sauce:

8 dessertspoons mayonnaise

1–1½ dessertspoons ketchup

1 dessertspoon lemon juice

Salad:

16 cherry or 8 sun-dried tomatoes

4 scallions

1 red pepper, deseeded

bag of mixed baby leaf lettuce, washed

Garnish: paprika, lemon wedges, 4 small parsley sprigs

Note: You can buy some prawns pre-cooked; these just have to be defrosted.

Method

1. Rinse the prawns and add to the fast-boiling salted water. (Prawns do not take long to cook – 1–2 minutes after the water has returned to the boil after adding the prawns). They should be firm and white but not opaque (undercooked) or crumbly (overcooked). Strain off the water through a sieve or colander. Allow to cool.
2. Mix the mayonnaise, ketchup and lemon juice together in a small bowl.
3. To make up the salad, halve the cherry tomatoes or chop the sun-dried tomatoes into small pieces. Chop the scallions and finely slice the red pepper. Arrange on top of the baby leaf lettuce on 4 individual plates.
4. Place one-quarter of the prawns on each plate and spoon over one-quarter of the mayonnaise mixture. Sprinkle paprika on top.
5. Garnish with a lemon wedge and a sprig of parsley.

Bruschetta with olive tapenade and goat's cheese

Serves 4

Ingredients

4 large, thick slices of French bread or ciabatta (see photo)

Olive tapenade (paste):

1 x 30g tin anchovy fillets
100g stoned black olives
1 tablespoon capers
1 teaspoon Dijon mustard
1 teaspoon freshly squeezed lemon juice
3 tablespoons extra virgin olive oil
salt and pepper

Tomato mix:

olive oil, to fry
1 small onion, finely chopped
1 clove garlic, crushed
4 tomatoes, skinned and chopped
1 dessertspoon tomato purée
1 teaspoon chopped marjoram or oregano

Cheese:

100–150g strongly flavoured semi-soft cheese, e.g. goat's cheese or Brie, sliced

Method

Preheat the oven to 200°C/fan 190°C/gas 5.

1. Liquidise all the ingredients for the olive tapenade (paste). It can be left smooth or coarse according to taste. Set aside.
2. For the tomato mix, heat the olive oil in a small saucepan. Fry the onion and garlic until softened but not browned. Add the chopped tomatoes, tomato purée and the marjoram or oregano. Simmer for 5 minutes, until the mixture reduces and becomes fairly thick.
3. Spread each slice of bread thickly, first with the olive tapenade, then with the tomato mix. Lastly, place 1 or 2 slices of cheese (depending on size) on top.
4. Bake for 10 minutes, or until the cheese has melted and has started to brown slightly.
5. Serve with a dressed green salad (see p. 135).

Garlic bread

Makes 1 stick

Ingredients

2 cloves garlic
75g butter or low-fat spread
1 teaspoon chopped parsley
1 French stick
Garnish: sprig of parsley

Method

Preheat the oven to 200°C/fan 190°C/gas 5.

1 Peel and crush the garlic. Mix with the butter and some parsley.
2 Slice the bread as shown. Butter each slice. Put the stick back together and wrap in foil.
3 Bake for 10–15 minutes.
4 Remove the foil. Serve hot, garnished with a sprig of parsley.

Slice of French stick for garlic bread

Soups

Farmhouse vegetable soup

Serves 4

Ingredients

3 medium carrots
1 medium/large potato
1 parsnip
1 medium leek
2 sticks celery
1 onion
1 tablespoon olive oil
1 litre vegetable stock (use 2 stock cubes)
salt and pepper
Garnish: cream, parsley (optional)

Method

1 Wash, peel and dice the carrots, potato and parsnip. Wash and chop the leek, celery and onion. (**Note:** The vegetables will have to be finely and evenly diced/chopped if you do not intend to blend the soup at the end.)
2 Heat the oil in a large, heavy saucepan. Gently fry the onion and the leeks.
3 Add the carrots, celery, potatoes and parsnips. Continue to fry gently for a few minutes.
4 Add the stock, salt and pepper. Bring to the boil. Once boiling, reduce the heat, cover and simmer for 25 minutes. Purée in a blender or food processor if you wish.
5 Serve piping hot in warm bowls. Garnish with a swirl of cream and some chopped parsley.

Cream of roast Mediterranean vegetable soup

Serves 4

Ingredients

6 shallots, peeled (or 1 onion, peeled and cut into quarters, if shallots are not available)
1 red pepper, deseeded and cut into quarters
1 yellow pepper, deseeded and cut into quarters
1 courgette, sliced
½ aubergine, cut into cubes
2 cloves garlic, roughly chopped
olive oil, for frying
1 x 400g tin chopped tomatoes
2 dessertspoons tomato purée
500ml vegetable stock
2 dessertspoons chopped fresh basil or 1 dessertspoon dried basil
salt and black pepper
100ml fresh cream
Garnish: fresh basil

Method

Preheat the oven to 200°C/fan 190°C/gas 5.

1. Toss the shallots, peppers, courgette, aubergine and garlic in 1 tablespoon olive oil in a baking tray. Roast for 15–20 minutes. Halfway through, take the tray out and shake the vegetables so that they roast evenly and brown a little.
2. Transfer to a medium/large saucepan and add the tinned tomatoes, tomato purée, stock, basil, salt and pepper.
3. Bring to the boil and simmer for 5 minutes. Blend in a food processor. Return to the saucepan.
4. If serving straight away, stir in the cream and serve in warmed soup bowls, garnished with a little chopped basil.

Croutons

Ingredients

2 slices thick bread, cubed
1 clove garlic, crushed
¼ teaspoon sea salt
1 tablespoon olive oil

Method

Preheat the oven to 180°C/fan 170°/gas 4.

1. Toss the bread cubes, garlic, salt and oil in a plastic freezer bag.
2. Bake for 15 minutes.

Snacks

Spicy chicken wrap

Serves 2

Ingredients

- 2 chicken breasts
- 2 dessertspoons olive oil
- 2 teaspoons Cajun spices
- 2 large soft flour tortilla wraps
- 2 dessertspoons low-fat mayonnaise
- 2 dessertspoons Ballymaloe (or similar brand) country relish
- baby leaf lettuce
- 6 thin slices cucumber
- 6 cherry tomatoes, halved
- 2 scallions, chopped
- 25g smoked cheddar cheese, grated

Method

1. Toss the chicken breasts in the olive oil and then in the Cajun spices. Grill the chicken on a preheated contact grill, e.g. a George Forman grill, for 8–10 minutes, until the chicken is cooked through. If no contact grill is available, cover the spiced chicken in tin foil and bake at 200°C/fan 190°C/gas 5 for approximately 25 minutes.
2. Dampen the 2 tortilla wraps and heat in the microwave for approximately 30 seconds (depending on wattage of microwave). If no microwave is available, then tortillas can be dampened, wrapped in tin foil and heated at 200°C/fan 190°C/gas 5 for 3–5 minutes in the oven.
3. Spread the mayonnaise and relish on each heated wrap. Place the chicken, salad ingredients and grated cheese on top. Wrap the tortilla as shown in the illustration. Cut in half and serve.

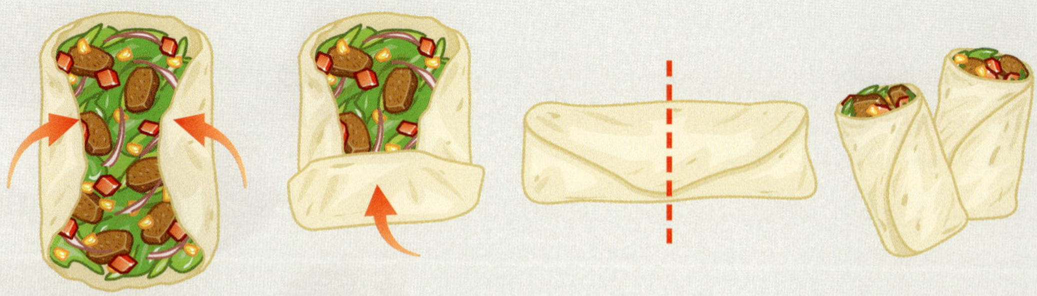

How to wrap up a wrap

French bread pizza

Serves 2

Ingredients

olive oil, for frying
1 small onion, finely chopped
1 large clove garlic, crushed
450g very ripe, fresh tomatoes, skinned and chopped, or 1 x 400g tin chopped tomatoes
1 dessertspoon chopped fresh marjoram or 1 teaspoon dried
black pepper
1 French stick
100g mozzarella cheese, grated
1 dessertspoon finely grated fresh Parmesan
extra toppings can be added, e.g. fried mushrooms, cooked ham, pineapple, etc.
To serve: coleslaw, green salad

Method

Preheat the oven to 200°C/fan 190°C/gas 5.

1 To make the tomato sauce, heat the olive oil in a medium saucepan. Sauté the onion and garlic. Add the tomatoes, marjoram and pepper. Simmer for 5–10 minutes, until the mixture reduces down to a paste.
2 Cut the French stick in half, then cut each piece in half again along the middle. Spread with the tomato sauce and add your chosen toppings. Sprinkle with the mozzarella and Parmesan.
3 Bake for approximately 5–10 minutes, until the cheese has melted.
4 Serve with coleslaw (see p. 135) and a green salad (see p. 135).

Roast Mediterranean vegetable and cheese panini

Makes 4

Ingredients

4 medium part-cooked French sticks or ciabatta
100g mozzarella cheese, sliced

Pesto:

50g fresh basil leaves
50ml extra virgin olive oil
1 dessertspoon pine nuts
1 large clove garlic
25g fresh Parmesan, finely grated

Mediterranean vegetables:

1 red onion, peeled and sliced
1 red pepper, deseeded and sliced
1 yellow pepper, deseeded and sliced
8 mushrooms, washed and sliced
1 clove garlic, crushed
olive oil
To serve: green salad

Method

Preheat the oven to 200°C/fan 190°C/gas 5.

1. To make the pesto, whiz all the ingredients except the Parmesan in the food processor or crush with a pestle and mortar. Stir in the Parmesan.
2. To make the Mediterranean vegetables, toss the prepared vegetables and garlic in a small baking tin with the olive oil. Roast in the oven for 10–15 minutes, until softened and slightly browned.
3. To assemble the panini, cut the bread in half lengthwise. Spread the pesto on the bread first, followed by the vegetables and cheese. Try not to have the cheese too close to the outside edge.
4. Cook the panini on a contact grill or sandwich toaster for approximately 5 minutes, until it has browned and the cheese has melted.
5. Serve with a tossed green salad (see p. 135).

Salads

Green salad

Serves 4

Ingredients

1 small bag baby leaf lettuce, washed
$\frac{1}{2}$ cucumber, thinly sliced
3 scallions, chopped
1 green pepper, deseeded and chopped

Method

1 Mix all the ingredients together in a large bowl. Toss in vinaigrette or balsamic dressing.

Coleslaw

Serves 4

Ingredients

$\frac{1}{4}$ head of white cabbage, very thinly sliced
1 small carrot, peeled and roughly grated
$\frac{1}{4}$ onion, very thinly sliced
1 dessertspoon finely chopped fresh parsley
freshly ground black pepper
3 dessertspoons mayonnaise

Method

1 Mix all the ingredients together in a large bowl, tossing well to combine.

Waldorf salad

Serves 4

Ingredients

1 Pink Lady apple, cored and diced
1 Granny Smith apple, cored and diced
2 sticks celery, sliced
25g coarsely chopped walnuts
50g raisins
3 dessertspoons mayonnaise
1 dessertspoon lemon juice

Method

1 Mix all the ingredients together in a large bowl, tossing well to combine.

Couscous salad

Serves 4

Ingredients

225ml vegetable stock
50g raisins
3 dessertspoons extra virgin olive oil
150g couscous
1 small onion, finely chopped
1 large clove garlic
1 small red pepper, deseeded and chopped
2 dessertspoons red wine vinegar
25g pine nuts, lightly toasted
1 dessertspoon finely chopped fresh parsley
sea salt and freshly ground black pepper

Method

1. Boil the stock, raisins and 1 dessertspoon of olive oil in a saucepan. Stir in the couscous and allow to stand for 5 minutes. Transfer to a bowl and fluff up the couscous with a fork.
2. Heat 1 dessertspoon of olive oil in a saucepan. Sauté the onion, garlic and red pepper until soft but the onion is still pale.
3. In a bowl, combine the couscous mix, 1 dessertspoon of olive oil, the vinegar, pine nuts, onion mix, chopped parsley, salt and black pepper.

Chicken Caesar salad with bacon bits

Serves 4

Ingredients

3 smoked back rashers
2 chicken breasts
olive oil, to fry
1 large head of Cos (Romaine) lettuce, roughly torn
1 portion home-made croutons (see p. 131)
50g freshly grated Parmesan

Dressing:

1 x 30g tin anchovies, drained
2 egg yolks
1 clove garlic, crushed
juice of $\frac{1}{2}$ lemon
$\frac{1}{4}$ teaspoon English mustard powder
1 dessertspoon Worcestershire sauce
1 dessertspoon Tabasco sauce
150ml sunflower oil
50ml extra virgin olive oil
50ml cold water

Method

1 To make the dressing, whiz all the ingredients except the oils and water in a food processor until smooth. Slowly pour in first the oils and then the water, keeping the food processor going all the while.

2 Grill or fry the rashers until crispy. Cut them up small. Toss the chicken in olive oil and then grill on a preheated contact grill, e.g. George Forman, for 8–10 minutes, until the chicken is cooked through. If no contact grill is available, fry the oiled chicken on a frying pan for 2 minutes on each side, then place in tin foil and bake at 200°C/fan 190°C/gas 5 for another 10–15 minutes, until they are cooked through. Cut the chicken into chunks or strips.

3 Pour 1 tablespoon of the dressing per person into a bowl. Toss the lettuce, half the croutons and half the Parmesan in it. Divide into 4 large, deep serving bowls. Spread the remainder of the croutons, chicken and bacon pieces on top. Sprinkle with the remaining Parmesan. (Leftover dressing can be covered and stored in the fridge for 3–4 days.)

Main courses

Beef, pork and lamb

Spaghetti Bolognese

Serves 4

Ingredients

1 onion
1 clove garlic
2 streaky rashers, chopped
75g mushrooms
1 tablespoon olive oil
300g lean minced beef
1 x 400g tin chopped tomatoes or 4 ripe fresh tomatoes, skinned
2 tablespoons tomato purée
1 teaspoon dried oregano
salt and black pepper
To serve: 200g spaghetti, parsley, Parmesan cheese

Method

1 To make the Bolognese sauce, peel and chop the onion. Peel and crush the garlic. Cut the rashers into small pieces with clean scissors. Wash and slice the mushrooms.
2 Heat the olive oil in a medium-sized saucepan. Fry the onion, garlic, rashers and mushrooms gently for 5 minutes.
3 Add the mince and fry until it has lost its red colour.
4 Add the tomatoes, tomato purée, oregano, salt and pepper. Bring to the boil. Turn down the heat and simmer for 20–25 minutes.
5 To cook the spaghetti, boil 2 litres of water in a large saucepan. Add 1 dessertspoon olive oil.
6 When the water is boiling, ease the spaghetti into it. Boil for 10–15 minutes, until the spaghetti is al dente (this means cooked but still has bite).
7 Serve the spaghetti on a warm plate. Spoon Bolognese sauce on top. Garnish with parsley. Serve with freshly grated Parmesan cheese and garlic bread (see p. 130).

Lasagne

Serves 4

Ingredients

1 quantity of Bolognese sauce (see recipe above)
9 sheets lasagne

Cheese sauce:

750ml milk
50g margarine
50g flour
½ teaspoon dry mustard
salt and pepper
150g cheddar cheese
Garnish: parsley
To serve: garlic bread, green salad

Method

Preheat the oven to 190°C/fan 180°C/gas 5.

1 Make the Bolognese sauce as described for spaghetti Bolognese (see recipe above).
2 Grease a large rectangular pie dish.
3 Make the cheese sauce by whisking the milk, margarine, flour, mustard, salt and pepper in a saucepan. Heat until it boils and thickens, stirring with a balloon whisk. Alternatively, make a roux sauce in the traditional way (see p. 105).
4 Add 100g of the cheese to the sauce. Set the other 50g aside.
5 Layer the meat sauce, lasagne sheets and cheese sauce. Finish with a layer of cheese sauce. Sprinkle the remaining cheese on top.
6 Bake for 30 minutes.
7 Garnish with parsley. Serve with garlic bread (see p. 130) and a green salad (see p. 135).

Beef or lamb curry

Serves 4

Ingredients

500g stewing beef or lamb
1 dessertspoon olive oil
1 large onion, chopped
1 clove garlic, crushed
25g flour
2 dessertspoons curry powder (or to taste)
1 litre stock (use 2 beef stock cubes)
1 large cooking apple, peeled and chopped
Garnish: parsley
To serve: rice

Note: Add no extra salt, as there is plenty in stock cubes

Method

1. Remove any fat from the meat. Cut the meat into small pieces.
2. Heat the olive oil in a medium-sized saucepan. Fry the meat, onion and garlic until the meat is brown on all sides.
3. Add the flour and curry powder. Cook for 2–3 minutes.
4. Gradually stir in the stock. Add the apple.
5. Bring to the boil, reduce the heat and simmer for 1–1½ hours, until the meat is tender.
6. Serve on a bed of rice and garnish with parsley.

Carbonnade of pork with mushrooms

Serves 3–4

Ingredients

450g pork fillet
1 tablespoon olive or sunflower oil
1 onion, finely chopped
100ml chicken stock
100g mushrooms, sliced
50g flour
150ml light cream
1 dessertspoon lemon juice
1 dessertspoon chopped parsley
salt and freshly ground pepper
300g uncooked rice (400g cooked)
Garnish: croutons (see p. 131), parsley

Method

1. Cut the pork into very thin strips. Heat a little oil in a saucepan or frying pan and sauté the pork strips a few at a time until brown on all sides. Remove to a plate and keep warm. Do not clean the pan.
2. Heat a little more oil in the pan if necessary and sauté the onion until soft and golden. Add the stock and boil until the mixture reduces by one-quarter. Pour into a jug. Wipe the pan dry.
3. Heat a little more of the oil in the pan and sauté the mushrooms. Return the pork to the pan. Add the flour and cook for 1–2 minutes. Add the cream, lemon juice, most of the parsley and the salt and pepper. Bring to the boil and simmer for a few minutes, especially if the sauce is not thick enough.
4. Serve on a bed of rice. Garnish with croutons and parsley.

Homemade burgers

Serves 4

Ingredients

450g lean minced beef
1 small onion, very finely chopped
2 tablespoons wholemeal breadcrumbs
pinch of mixed herbs
salt and pepper
1 egg, beaten
a little flour
olive oil
To serve: burger bun, lettuce, tomato slices, ketchup and mayonnaise

Method

1 Mix the mince, onion, breadcrumbs, herbs, salt and pepper in a bowl.
2 Bind the mix together with the beaten egg. Divide the mixture into 4 quarters.
3 Shape on a floured board or use a burger press like the one pictured.
4 Brush each burger with a little olive oil.
5 Place the burgers under a preheated hot grill for 5 minutes on each side.
6 Turn again and grill for a further 2 minutes on each side.
7 Serve on a toasted burger bun with lettuce, tomato slices and ketchup or mayonnaise.

Chicken

Warm chicken liver salad

Serves 4

Ingredients

8 very fresh chicken livers
1 tablespoon olive oil
1 tablespoon unsalted butter
2 cloves garlic, crushed
1 teaspoon ginger
Garnish: 1 dessertspoon chopped fresh parsley

Salad:

1 bag of baby leaf lettuce, washed
12 cherry tomatoes, halved
4 scallions, chopped

Dressing:

2 tablespoons olive oil
2 tablespoons walnut oil
1 tablespoon red wine vinegar
2 teaspoons Dijon mustard
sea salt and freshly ground black pepper

Method

1 Prepare the salad by mixing the lettuce, tomatoes and scallions together.
2 Shake the ingredients for the dressing in a screw-top jar to combine them.
3 Wash and dry the chicken livers well and cut each in 4.
4 Melt the oil and butter in a frying pan – do not allow it to get too hot. Add the livers, garlic and ginger and cook for approximately 5 minutes, until nicely brown on the outside and cooked through.
5 Toss the salad in the dressing enough to lightly coat the leaves. Place portions of salad onto 4 large white plates and arrange the chicken livers on top. Sprinkle with parsley.

Chicken curry

Serves 4

Ingredients

2 tablespoons sunflower oil
4 chicken breast fillets, cut in large dice – 6 per fillet
2 large onions, sliced
3 cloves garlic, crushed
3 tablespoons curry powder
1 tablespoon Chinese five-spice mix
1 litre chicken stock
pinch of sugar, salt and black pepper
$1\frac{1}{2}$ tablespoons cornflour, softened with 1 tablespoon water
1 tablespoon chopped fresh coriander
To serve: rice

Method

1 Heat a little sunflower oil in a pan and quickly brown the diced chicken. Remove from the pan and set aside.
2 Add a little more oil to the pan and sauté the onion and garlic until soft, but do not let them colour.

3 Add the curry powder and Chinese five-spice mix and cook for 1–2 minutes, then gradually add in the stock. Bring to the boil. Season with the pinch of sugar, salt and pepper.
4 Thicken with the cornflour, adding it bit by bit.
5 Add the chicken to the sauce and simmer for 8–10 minutes. This will ensure the chicken is cooked through but still moist. Add the coriander and serve on a bed of rice.

Note: Some reduced-fat coconut milk could also be added for extra depth of flavour.

Note: Curries are best eaten the day after they are made, when the flavours have had a chance to develop.

Chicken and bacon risotto

Serves 4

Ingredients

2 tablespoons olive oil
3 streaky rashers, cut into bite-sized pieces
1 medium onion, chopped
1 clove garlic, crushed
6 mushrooms, sliced
1 green pepper, deseeded and chopped
1 red pepper, deseeded and chopped
2 chicken breasts, cut into bite-sized pieces
300g uncooked Arborio rice
approx. 1 litre chicken stock
salt and black pepper
Garnish: parsley

Method

1 Heat 1 tablespoon of oil in a large, heavy saucepan. Fry the rashers and onions until the onions soften and the rashers begin to brown.
2 Add the garlic, mushrooms and peppers. Fry gently for another minute. Remove the rashers and vegetables to a plate.
3 Heat 1 tablespoon of oil in the saucepan. Fry the chicken for 3 minutes. Add the rice and fry for another minute. Add salt and pepper. Return the rashers and vegetables to the saucepan.
4 Add 250ml of the stock, stirring the mixture continuously until the rice has absorbed it. Add another 250ml of stock and stir again. Repeat this process until all the stock has been absorbed and the rice is al dente.
5 Serve on a warm oval plate. Garnish with parsley.

Sweet and sour chicken or pork

Serves 4

Ingredients

2 chicken breasts or 3 pork chops
1 tablespoon olive oil
1 onion, chopped
1 clove garlic, crushed
1 carrot, peeled and cut into strips
1 green pepper, deseeded and diced
½ can (400g) pineapple in own juice
1 dessertspoon cornflour
1 tablespoon vinegar
1 tablespoon soy sauce
1 teaspoon brown sugar
1 teaspoon tomato purée
salt and black pepper
Garnish: parsley
To serve: 300g uncooked/400g cooked rice

Method

1. Wipe the meat, trim the fat and cut into bite-sized pieces.
2. Heat the oil in a medium-sized heavy saucepan. Fry the meat quickly to seal it. Remove from the pan and set aside on a plate.
3. Sauté the onion, garlic, carrot and pepper for 2–3 minutes. Return the meat to the pan.
4. Measure the pineapple juice and make it up to 400ml with water. Blend the cornflour with a little of this juice.
5. Add the pineapple juice, blended cornflour and all the other ingredients except the rice to the saucepan.
6. Bring to the boil, turn down the heat and simmer with the lid on for 30 minutes.
7. Serve on a bed of rice and garnish with parsley.

Fish

Fish pie

Serves 4

Ingredients

4–6 potatoes, depending on size
1 knob butter
1 tablespoon milk
75g margarine
1 small onion, finely chopped
1 large clove garlic, crushed
75g flour
400ml milk
salt and black pepper
75g smoked cheddar cheese, roughly grated
350g mixed smoked fish
To serve: boiled or steamed carrots and broccoli

Method

Preheat the oven to 200°C/fan 190°C/gas 5.

1 Wash, peel and halve the potatoes. Cook in boiling water until soft enough to mash (test with a fork). Mash with a knob of butter and the tablespoon of milk.
2 To make the cheese sauce, melt the margarine in a medium saucepan. Sauté the onion and the garlic. Add the flour to make a roux and cook for 1–2 minutes. Remove from the heat and add the milk bit by bit, stirring all the time. Season with salt and pepper. Put back on the heat and bring to the boil. Cook, stirring all the time, until the sauce thickens. Remove from the heat again. Stir in the cheese and allow it to melt.
3 Mix the smoked fish through the sauce and place into a greased pie dish. Pile the potato on top and spread it over evenly. Score along the top with a fork.
4 Bake for 20–25 minutes. Serve with boiled or steamed carrots and broccoli.

Salmon fishcakes

Serves 4

Ingredients

350g cooked salmon (see method), flaked with a fork
4–6 potatoes, depending on size, cooked and mashed
2 eggs
2 dessertspoons chopped fresh parsley
25g butter, melted
salt and black pepper
50g flour, for dusting
75g breadcrumbs (3 slices of bread)
olive oil, for frying

Method

1 To cook the salmon, wrap in tinfoil and bake at 200°C/fan 190°C/gas 5 for 20 minutes. Set aside to cool.
2 Mix the fish, mashed potatoes, 1 egg, parsley, butter, salt and pepper in a bowl. Leave in the fridge for 30 minutes.
3 Remove from the fridge and roll into a long snake shape on a floured board. Cut the 'snake' into 8 even-sized pieces. Flatten each piece into a round cake.
4 Beat the second egg. Dip each cake in egg and then in breadcrumbs.
5 Fry or grill cakes (grilling is healthier) for 5 minutes on each side, until golden brown on each side and the cake is heated through. Serve with fresh vegetables.

Top tip: In a hurry? Use tinned salmon or tuna.

Smoked salmon and bacon carbonara

Serves 4

Ingredients

300g uncooked (400g cooked) tagliatelle
2 tablespoons olive oil
150g smoked bacon lardoins (small cubes of bacon)
1 small onion, finely chopped
2 cloves garlic, crushed
400ml cream
pinch sea salt
freshly ground black pepper
1 tablespoon finely chopped fresh herbs – use basil, oregano or marjoram
200g smoked salmon, cut into strips
Garnish: chopped fresh parsley

Method

1 Put the tagliatelle on to cook (put 1 tablespoon of olive oil in a large saucepan of boiling water – when boiling, add the tagliatelle and cook until al dente, 10–12 minutes).

2 Heat 1 tablespoon of olive oil in a saucepan or deep frying pan. Fry the bacon lardoins until lightly browned. Add the onion and garlic and sauté gently for a few minutes, until the onion has softened but has not browned. Drain off any excess grease.

3 Add the cream, salt, pepper and herbs. Bring to the boil and simmer, stirring all the time, until the sauce has reduced and thickened a little.

4 Add the smoked salmon and heat right through (smoked salmon is already cooked).

5 Drain the pasta. Divide among 4 deep serving plates. Ladle the sauce evenly over each. Garnish with chopped fresh parsley.

Milk, eggs and cheese

Quiche Lorraine

Serves 4

Ingredients

Shortcrust pastry:

100g flour
pinch salt
50g margarine
cold water

Filling:

4 back rashers
olive oil, to fry
50g grated cheese
1 small onion, finely chopped
2 large eggs
200ml milk
100ml cream
salt and pepper
Garnish: tomato slices, parsley
To serve: green salad

Method

Preheat the oven to 190°C/fan 180°C/gas 4.

1 To make the pastry:
   - Sieve the flour and salt into a bowl.
   - Rub in the chopped margarine until it looks like breadcrumbs.
   - Add the water little by little with a spoon. Stir with a knife until you have a stiff dough.
   - Roll out and line a 20cm flan tin.

2 Fry the rashers in a little olive oil, then chop them up. Place them in the flan tin with half of the grated cheese. Sauté the onion in the fat remaining after frying the rashers until soft but not brown. Spread these on the base as well.

3 Mix together the eggs, milk, cream, salt and pepper. Pour over the rashers. Sprinkle the remaining cheese on top.

4 Bake for 40–45 minutes, until set.

5 Garnish with tomato slices and parsley. Serve with a green salad (see p. 135).

Top tip: Fillings can be varied. Try adding 100g mushrooms: grill or fry the mushrooms, allow to cool, slice and arrange on flan tin with rasher, onion and cheese; continue as stated in recipe.

French savoury omelette

Serves 1

Ingredients

2 large eggs
15g butter or margarine
1 tablespoon water
salt and pepper
mixed herbs
oil, to fry
Garnish: parsley
To serve: toast

Fillings:

choose one or two of the following:
2 cherry tomatoes, quartered
1 grilled rasher, chopped
1 slice ham, chopped
25g grated cheese
50g sautéed mushrooms

Method

1. Lightly beat the eggs, butter, water, seasoning, herbs and filling(s) in a bowl. Do not add cheese at this stage (if using).
2. Heat the oil in a small pan. Pour the egg mixture in. As the egg sets, pull it gently towards the middle of the pan with a palette knife. Tilt the pan and run the uncooked egg into it. Continue until all the egg is just set.
3. Tip the omelette onto a warmed plate. Sprinkle cheese on top and fold the omelette over using a palette knife.
4. Garnish with parsley and serve with toast.

Calzone

Serves 2

Ingredients

For the dough:

100g flour
pinch of salt
25g margarine
1 egg (keep some back for glazing)
a little milk

Filling:

150g mozzarella, roughly grated
1 teaspoon chopped fresh parsley
1 teaspoon dried marjoram
50g cooked ham or crispy bacon
2 tablespoons pesto (see p. 134) or tapenade (see p. 129)
To serve: green salad, coleslaw

Method

Preheat the oven to 190°C/fan 180°C/gas 6.

1. To make the scone base:
   - Sieve the flour and salt into a bowl.
   - Rub in the chopped margarine until the mixture looks like breadcrumbs.
   - Add the egg and enough milk to make a stiff dough.
   - Roll out into a large, thin circle. Place on a greased tin.

2 Mix all the filling ingredients together and place on the base. Do not go too close to the edges or the filling will spill out in the oven.
3 Wet the edges all round and fold the base over on itself. Press sealed with floured fingers. Pierce a few holes in the top with a fork. Glaze with a little beaten egg.
4 Bake on a greased tin for 25–30 minutes. Serve with a green salad (see p. 135) and home-made coleslaw (see p. 135)

Vegetarian

Vegetable stir-fry with rice

Serves 4

Ingredients

400g cooked rice/300g uncooked
1 dessertspoon olive oil

Stir-fry:

½ red onion, chopped
1 clove garlic, crushed
1 carrot, peeled and cut into thin batons
1 red pepper, deseeded and sliced
8 baby sweet corn
8 mushrooms, sliced
1 small courgette, sliced
1 tablespoon olive oil
1 teaspoon cornflour
1 teaspoon Cajun spices
2 tablespoons soy sauce
50g pine nuts

Method

1 Put the rice on to cook in a saucepan of boiling water to which you have added 1 dessertspoon of olive oil. Cook for 15–20 minutes or according to packet instructions.
2 Mix all the vegetables together in a bowl.
3 Heat the oil in a wok or frying pan. Add the vegetables and stir well.
4 Add the cornflour and Cajun spices and stir through. Add the soy sauce and pine nuts. Continue stir-frying for approximately 5 minutes, until the vegetables are cooked but still have bite. Serve with the boiled rice.

Vegetable curry

Serves 4

Ingredients

Curry sauce:

1 dessertspoon olive oil
1 onion, chopped
1 dessertspoon flour
3 dessertspoons curry powder
500ml vegetable stock

Vegetables:

1 carrot, peeled and sliced
1 small courgette, sliced
8 mushrooms, sliced
2 sticks celery, sliced
6 cauliflower florets, broken into bite-sized pieces
6 broccoli florets, broken into bite-sized pieces
1 green or red pepper, deseeded and sliced
1 cooking apple, peeled, cored and chopped
1 dessertspoon coconut
50g sultanas
1 teaspoon lemon juice
1 teaspoon brown sugar
½ x 400g tin pineapple chunks, drained
salt and pepper
Garnish: parsley
To serve: boiled rice

Method

1 Heat the olive oil in a small saucepan. Fry the onion gently for 2–3 minutes. Add the flour and curry powder and gradually stir in 100ml of the stock. This is the curry sauce.

2 Put the rest of the ingredients into a large saucepan. Add 400ml of stock. Bring to the boil, reduce the heat and simmer with the lid on for 10 minutes.

3 Add the curry sauce to the large saucepan. Bring to the boil again, reduce the heat and simmer for a further 10–15 minutes.

4 Serve on a bed of rice and garnish with parsley.

Cheesy vegetable and pasta bake

Serves 4

Ingredients

Vegetable mix:

1 dessertspoon olive oil
1 onion, chopped
1 clove garlic, crushed
1 green pepper, deseeded and chopped
8 mushrooms, sliced
1 x 400g tin chopped tomatoes
1 teaspoon dried basil

Pasta:

200g pasta shapes
1 dessertspoon olive oil

Cheese sauce:

25g margarine
25g flour
500ml milk
50g grated cheese

Topping:

50g brown breadcrumbs
25g grated cheddar cheese
Garnish: parsley
To serve: garlic bread

Method

Preheat the oven to 200°C/fan 190°C/gas 6.

1. Heat the oil in a medium-sized saucepan. Gently fry the onion, garlic, green pepper and mushrooms for 2–3 minutes.
2. Add the tomatoes and basil and bring to the boil. Reduce the heat and simmer with the lid on for 20 minutes.
3. Cook the pasta shapes in boiling water to which the oil has been added for 12–15 minutes. Drain and add to the vegetable mix.
4. To make the cheese sauce:
   - Melt the margarine in a small saucepan, then add the flour. Cook this roux for 1 minute, stirring all the time.
   - Remove from the heat and cool slightly.
   - Add the milk bit by bit, stirring all the time. Return to the heat and bring to the boil. Reduce the heat and cook for 3 minutes.
   - Remove from the heat and stir in the grated cheese. Set aside.
5. Put the vegetables and pasta in a casserole dish and pour on the cheese sauce.
6. Mix the breadcrumbs and grated cheddar together, then spread over the pasta in the casserole dish.
7. Bake for 15 minutes. Serve hot with garlic bread (see p. 130) and garnish with parsley.

Vegetable stew with cheese and pasta

Serves 2

Ingredients

150g uncooked pasta shells (200g cooked)
2 tablespoons olive oil
1 small onion, finely chopped
2 cloves garlic, crushed
8 mushrooms, sliced
1 red pepper, deseeded and sliced
1 yellow pepper, deseeded and sliced
1 x 400g tin plum tomatoes
100ml cream
100g cheddar cheese, grated
1 tablespoon chopped fresh parsley
To serve: garlic bread

Method

1. Put the pasta on to cook in a large saucepan of boiling water to which 1 tablespoon of the oil has been added. Cook until al dente, approximately 10–12 minutes.
2. Meanwhile, heat 1 tablespoon of olive oil in a large saucepan. Gently sauté the onion, garlic and mushrooms until soft but not brown. Add the peppers and continue to fry gently. Stir constantly with a wooden spoon.
3. Add the plum tomatoes with their juice. Break up the tomatoes roughly with a wooden spoon. Bring to the boil and simmer until all the vegetables are softened but not mushy. Remove from the heat and add the cream.
4. Drain the pasta and divide between 2 deep serving plates. Spoon over the vegetable stew. Sprinkle each with grated cheese and chopped fresh parsley.
5. Serve with garlic bread (see p. 130).

Desserts

Fresh fruit salad

Serves 4

Ingredients

1 apple
1 pear
1 orange
6 green seedless grapes
6 black seedless grapes
6 strawberries
2 kiwi fruit
1 banana
200ml orange juice
To serve: low-fat cream, ice cream or yoghurt

Method

1 Prepare the fruit:
   - Core and cut the apple and pear into bite-sized pieces.
   - Remove the pith and skin from the orange. Divide into segments and cut each segment in two.
   - Halve the grapes and strawberries.
   - Peel and slice the kiwi and banana.

2 Arrange the fruit in a bowl. Pour the orange juice over.

3 Serve with low-fat ice cream, cream or natural yogurt (healthier option).

Top tip: Orange juice is a healthy alternative to sugar syrup. It also prevents apples, pears and bananas from browning.

Strawberry and rhubarb crumble

Serves 4

Ingredients

250g rhubarb, sliced
1 x 400g tin strawberries, drained
50g sugar

Crumble:

150g flour
50g margarine, diced
50g brown sugar
1 teaspoon cinnamon
To serve: low-fat cream, ice cream or yoghurt

Method

Preheat the oven to 190°C/fan 180°C/gas 6.

1 Place the rhubarb and strawberries in a greased ovenproof dish. Sprinkle the sugar evenly over the top.

2 To make the crumble:
   - Sieve the flour.
   - Rub in the diced margarine until the mixture looks like breadcrumbs.
   - Add the brown sugar and cinnamon.

3 Spread the crumble evenly over the fruit.

4 Bake for 30 minutes, until golden on top and the fruit is soft.

5 Serve with low-fat cream, ice cream or natural yoghurt (healthier option).

Bread and butter pudding

Serves 4

Ingredients

8 slices of bread
50g butter
50g sultanas
pinch nutmeg
300ml milk
vanilla essence
25g sugar
2 eggs
To serve: low-fat cream, ice cream or yoghurt

Method

Preheat the oven to 190°C/fan 180°C/gas 5.

1. Lightly butter the bread and remove black crusts only. Cut 6 slices into fingers. Cut the remaining 2 slices into triangles.
2. Line the bottom of an ovenproof dish with the bread fingers, butter side down. Sprinkle with the sultanas and a little nutmeg.
3. Repeat until all the bread is used, finishing with a layer of triangular-shaped bread, butter side up.
4. In a saucepan, heat the milk, vanilla essence and sugar until hot – not boiling.
5. Beat the eggs in a bowl. Gradually add the milk to the eggs, stirring constantly.
6. Pour the milk and egg mixture over the bread and sultanas. Sprinkle with nutmeg and a little sugar.
7. Place the dish on a roasting tin. Put some water in the roasting tin: this helps keep the pudding moist.
8. Bake for 30–35 minutes. Serve with low-fat cream, ice cream or natural yogurt (healthier option).

Top tip: Bread and butter pudding can be made in small individual ramekin dishes (grease the ramekin dishes lightly). Tip each one out upside down on a dessert plate. Serve surrounded with hot custard.

Delicious filled crêpes

Makes 6 crêpes

Ingredients

Crêpes:
100g self-raising flour
1 egg
pinch salt
250ml milk
oil, for frying

Fillings (pick one):
ice cream, banana and butterscotch sauce
strawberries and whipped cream
cinnamon-flavoured stewed apple

Method

1 Sieve the flour and salt into a bowl. Make a well in the centre.
2 Drop the egg and half the milk into the well. Using a whisk, beat from the centre out until the mixture is smooth.
3 Add the rest of the milk. Beat for 5 minutes to introduce air.
4 Pour into a jug. Allow to stand in the fridge for 20 minutes if you have time.
5 Heat a little oil in a frying pan. Pour in some batter mixture and tilt to cover the base. Cook until the edges begin to brown. Shake the pan to loosen the crêpe.
6 Turn the crêpe using a fish slice or palette knife. Repeat with the rest of the batter. Keep cooked crêpes warm between two plates over a saucepan of boiling water.
7 Serve 2 crêpes per person on a dessert plate.

To prepare the fillings:

- *Ice cream and banana with butterscotch sauce:* Fill crêpes with 1 scoop of ice cream and half a banana (sliced). Drizzle butterscotch sauce over (see p. 156).
- *Strawberry or apple:* Fill with 4 strawberries (sliced) or 1 dessertspoon apple (stewed with cinnamon). Fold over and serve with whipped cream. Dredge with icing sugar.

Chocolate fudge pudding

Serves 6–8

Ingredients

150g good-quality chocolate
150g margarine or unsalted butter
100g caster sugar
1 teaspoon vanilla essence
150ml warm water
4 eggs
25g self-raising flour
$\frac{1}{4}$ teaspoon cream of tartar
drinking chocolate, to dust
To serve: freshly whipped cream, ice cream or chocolate orange sauce

Method

Preheat the oven to 210°C/fan 200°C/gas 6.

1. Grease one large 1 litre-capacity pie dish or 8 individual ramekins with margarine.
2. Break up the chocolate and melt the butter/margarine in a clean bowl over a saucepan of barely simmering water. When the chocolate is melted, remove from the heat and stir in the sugar, vanilla essence and warm water. Continue to stir until the mixture is smooth, but do not beat.
3. Separate the eggs and whisk the yolks into the chocolate mixture. Fold in the flour.
4. In a spotlessly clean bowl, whisk the egg whites with the cream of tartar until they form stiff peaks. Fold the whites gently into the chocolate mixture and then pour into the dish or ramekins.
5. Place the dish or ramekins on a deep baking tray with hot water in it.
6. To bake:
   - Large dish: Bake for 10 minutes at 210°C/fan 200°C/gas 6, then lower the oven temperature to 170°C/fan 160°C/gas 3 and cook for a further 20–30 minutes, until the pudding is firm on top but still soft and fudge-like underneath.
   - Ramekins: Bake for 15 minutes at 210°C/fan 200°C/gas 6 only.
7. Cool the puddings a little before dusting with drinking chocolate and serving with freshly whipped cream or ice cream and chocolate orange sauce (see p. 156).

Rich chocolate orange sauce

Ingredients

100g plain cooking chocolate
zest of 1 orange
juice of ½ orange
4 tablespoons whipping or double cream

Method

1 Melt the chocolate carefully in a microwave or over a saucepan of barely simmering water.
2 Mix in the zest, juice and cream.
3 Serve.

Top tip: This sauce is very high in calories – serve only a small amount and only very occasionally.

Butterscotch sauce

Ingredients

50g butter
75g brown sugar
50g granulated sugar
4 dessertspoons golden syrup
100ml double cream
½ teaspoon vanilla essence

Method

1 Put the butter, sugars and golden syrup into a heavy saucepan. Melt on a low heat. Simmer for 3–5 minutes, stirring all the time.
2 Remove from the heat and gradually stir in the cream and vanilla essence. Return to the heat for 2 minutes.

Top tip: This sauce is very high in calories – serve only occasionally.

Fruit coulis

Ingredients

100g raspberries (fresh, frozen or tinned)
100g strawberries (fresh, frozen or tinned)
1 tablespoon lemon juice
1 tablespoon icing sugar

Method

1 Wash the fruit. Put all the ingredients in a food processor or liquidiser. Blend until smooth.
2 Put the mixture through a sieve to remove any seeds.

Top tip: A fruit coulis can be served with almost any dessert: rice pudding, ice cream, bread and butter pudding, pancakes, etc.

Pastry

Shortcrust pastry

Ingredients

200g plain flour

pinch salt

100g block margarine, diced

cold water

Method

1 Sieve the flour and salt into a bowl.

2 Rub the diced margarine into the flour with your fingertips until the mixture looks like breadcrumbs.

3 Add the water with a spoon. Mix with a knife until the pastry comes together in a ball. **Do not make it too wet.**

4 Leave to relax in the fridge until needed.

Top tip: Do not handle pastry too much and keep it as cool as possible.

Variations for savoury dishes, e.g. quiche

- *Wholemeal pastry:* Rich in fibre. Use half wholemeal flour and half plain flour.
- *Cheese pastry:* Add 75g grated cheese and $\frac{1}{4}$ teaspoon mustard to the basic shortcrust pastry recipe (add before the water).

Rich shortcrust pastry

Ingredients

200g plain flour

100g margarine, diced

50g icing sugar

1 egg, beaten

2 dessertspoons cold water (approximately)

Method

1 Sieve the flour and salt into a bowl.

2 Rub the diced margarine into the flour with your fingertips until the mixture looks like breadcrumbs. Add the icing sugar.

3 Add the egg and water with a spoon (you may not need all of the water). Mix with a knife until the pastry comes together in a ball. **Do not make it too wet** – you want a firm dough.

4 Leave to relax in the fridge until needed.

Mince pies

Makes 12 pies

Ingredients

200g rich shortcrust pastry (see p. 157)
150g mincemeat
1 egg, beaten
icing sugar, to decorate
To serve: whipped cream, brandy butter

Method

Preheat the oven to 230°C/fan 220°C/gas 8.

1. Make the rich shortcrust pastry (see p. 157).
2. Roll out two-thirds of the pastry thinly. Cut out 12 circles using a large (6cm) cutter. Place each pastry circle in a patty tin. Dampen the edges of the pastry with water.
3. Put 1 teaspoon of mincemeat in each circle.
4. Roll out the rest of the pastry. Use a smaller cutter (5cm) to cut out 12 lids. Put a lid on each pie. Seal with your fingers.
5. Glaze with the egg.
6. Bake for 8–10 minutes, then reduce the heat to 190°C/fan 180°C/gas 5 and cook for a further 10 minutes.
7. To decorate, sprinkle icing sugar over the pies through a sieve.
8. Place on a round plate with a doily. Serve with whipped cream or brandy butter.

Top tip: If a recipe calls for 200g of pastry, this refers to the amount of flour in the recipe.

Top tip: When rolling out pastry, roll lightly in one direction only. Keep turning the pastry to stop it from sticking to the table.

Apple tart

Serves 6

Ingredients

200g shortcrust pastry
2 medium cooking apples, peeled, cored and sliced
3–4 tablespoons granulated sugar
4–5 cloves or 1 heaped teaspoon cinnamon, whichever is to your taste
1 egg, beaten
To serve: ice cream, whipped cream or custard

Method

Preheat the oven to 230°C/fan 220°C/gas 8.

1 Make the shortcrust pastry (see p. 157).
2 Divide the pastry in two. Return one half to the fridge while you roll out the other half to fit the plate/dish. Trim off any excess pastry, cutting away from you all the time.
3 Place the apple slices on top and sprinkle with sugar and cinnamon or cloves. Wet the edges of the pastry with water.
4 Roll out the other pastry half and place on top of the apples. Trim off any excess. Press the pastry firmly together.
5 Brush with the beaten egg and prick a few fork holes on top.
6 Bake for 10 minutes, then reduce the heat to 190°C/fan 180°C/gas 5 for the remainder of the cooking time (approximately 30 minutes).
7 Serve with ice cream, whipped cream or custard.

Bread and cakes

Rubbing-in method

Tea scones

Makes 8–10 scones

Ingredients

200g self-raising flour
pinch salt
50g margarine, diced
25g caster sugar
2 eggs
a little milk

Method

Preheat the oven to 220°C/fan 210°C/gas 7.

1 Sieve the flour and salt into a bowl. Rub in the margarine until the mixture looks like breadcrumbs.
2 Add the sugar. Beat 1 egg and the milk in a bowl. Add to the mixture and mix.
3 Turn the mixture out onto a floured board and knead lightly.
4 Roll out, but not too thinly. Cut out into 8–10 rounds.

5 Place the scones on a greased baking tin. Beat the other egg. Glaze the scones with the egg.
6 Bake for 15 minutes, until golden. Cool on a wire tray.

Variations:

- *Fruit scones*: Add 25g raisins with or instead of sugar.
- *Brown scones*: Use 100g of brown flour and 100g of self-raising flour.

White soda scones

Makes approximately 9 large scones

Ingredients

350g flour
1 teaspoon bread soda
½ teaspoon salt
100g margarine, diced
50g sugar
75g raisins
2 eggs
175ml buttermilk
To serve: butter and jam

Method

Preheat the oven to 220°C/fan 210°C/gas 7.

1 Sieve the flour, bread soda and salt into a bowl. Rub in the margarine until the mixture looks like breadcrumbs. Add the sugar and raisins.
2 Mix in 1 egg and enough buttermilk to make a firm dough, one that is possible to roll out. Knead lightly.
3 Roll or flatten out the scone mix **a little** until it is about 4cm thick. **Do not roll out too thinly.** Using a large scone cutter, cut out 9 or so scones.
4 Place the scones on a lightly greased baking tin. Beat the other egg and brush over the scones to glaze.
5 Bake for approximately 15–20 minutes, until baked through (check that the underside has browned a little) and golden on top.
6 Cool on a wire tray. Serve warm or cold with butter and jam.

Coconut buns

Makes 10 buns

Ingredients

200g flour
pinch salt
1 teaspoon baking powder
50g margarine, diced
50g caster sugar
50g coconut
1 egg
a little milk

To decorate:

2 tablespoons jam
2 heaped tablespoons coconut

Method

Preheat the oven to 200°C/fan 190°C/gas 6.

1. Sieve the flour, salt and baking powder into a bowl.
2. Rub in the diced margarine until the mixture looks like breadcrumbs. Add the sugar and coconut.
3. Add the egg and enough milk to make a stiff dough.
4. Using a spoon and a fork, pile the mixture into 10 heaps on a greased baking tray.
5. Bake for 20 minutes.
6. To decorate, beat the jam in a small bowl to make it soft. Put the coconut onto a plate. Dip the buns first in jam and then in coconut.

Top tip: Never put tins or dishes on the floor of the oven, as the bottom of the food will burn.

Rock buns

Makes 8–10 buns

Ingredients

200g flour
pinch salt
50g margarine, diced
½ teaspoon mixed spice
25g caster sugar
50g dried fruit
25g mixed peel
1 egg
a little milk
granulated sugar, to decorate

Method

Preheat the oven to 200°C/fan 190°C/gas 6.

1. Grease a patty tin.
2. Sieve the flour and salt into a bowl. Rub in the margarine until the mixture looks like breadcrumbs.
3. Add the mixed spice, caster sugar, dried fruit and mixed peel. Mix well.
4. Add the egg and enough milk to make a stiff dough.
5. Pile into the prepared patty tin. The mixture should make 8–10 cakes.
6. Sprinkle each cake with a little granulated sugar.
7. Bake for 20–25 minutes, until golden. Cool on a wire tray.

Creaming method

Chocolate orange queen cakes

Ingredients

100g caster sugar
100g margarine
2 eggs
zest of 1 large orange
150g self-raising flour (or plain flour with 1 level teaspoon baking powder added), sieved
a little milk
100g cooking chocolate

Note: Plain queen cakes can be made by leaving out the orange zest and juice. Add 1 tablespoon of milk and a few drops of vanilla essence instead.

Top tip: A little flour can be added with the egg to stop the egg from curdling. To test if queen cakes are cooked, check the top and bottom of cake: both should be light brown.

Method

Preheat the oven to 200°C/fan 190°C/gas 6.

1. Beat the sugar and margarine until it is white and creamy.
2. Add the eggs and orange zest a little at a time, beating well between additions.
3. Gently fold in the sieved flour. Add a little milk if too dry.
4. Spoon into bun cases in a patty tin. Bake for approximately 15 minutes, until golden. Cool on a wire tray.
5. Break the cooking chocolate into pieces and carefully melt either in the microwave or in a clean bowl over a saucepan of barely simmering water. Make sure no water gets into the chocolate or it will spoil.
6. Dip each bun into the chocolate. Allow the chocolate to set.

Note: This mixture can also be made using the all-in-one method whereby all ingredients are put into a food processor together and mixed at once.

Welsh cheese cakes

Makes 10–12 cakes

Ingredients

Pastry:

100g flour
pinch salt
50g margarine, diced
cold water

Filling:

1–2 tablespoons jam

Madeira mix:

50g caster sugar
50g margarine
1 egg
75g flour, sieved
1 tablespoon milk
1 drop vanilla essence

Method

Preheat the oven to 200°C/fan 190°C/gas 6.

1 Make the shortcrust pastry (see p. 157).
2 Roll out the pastry thinly. Cut into 10–12 circles and place them in a greased patty tin. Put a small amount of jam on each circle.
3 To make the Madeira, beat the sugar and margarine until it is white and creamy.
4 Add the egg a little at a time, beating well between additions.
5 Gently fold in the sieved flour. Mix in the milk and vanilla.
6 Pile 1 large teaspoon of the mix on top of the jam in the patty tin. Smooth out with a wet knife to seal the jam in.
7 Roll out the pastry scraps and cut into thin strips. Lay on top of the Madeira mix in a cross shape.
8 Bake for approximately 15 minutes. Cool on a wire tray.

Chocolate chip cookies

Makes 12 cookies

Ingredients

50g margarine (plus extra for greasing the tin)
50g light brown sugar
1 small egg
1 dessertspoon golden syrup
½ teaspoon vanilla essence
75g plain flour
¼ teaspoon bicarbonate of soda
pinch salt
1 tablespoon boiling water
25g porridge oats
75g plain chocolate chips

Method

Preheat the oven to 190°C/fan 180°C/gas 4.

1 Cream the margarine, sugar, egg, golden syrup and vanilla essence in a large bowl until light and creamy.
2 In a separate bowl, mix together the flour, bicarbonate of soda, salt, boiling water and porridge oats. Add this to the egg mixture and beat together thoroughly.
3 Stir in the chocolate chips.
4 Place approximately 12 rounded teaspoons of the mixture onto a greased baking tray. Make sure that they are well spaced out, as they will expand during cooking. Flatten them out a little.
5 Bake for 10–12 minutes. Remove and cool completely on a wire rack before serving.

All-in-one method

All-in-one chocolate cake

Serves 6

Ingredients

175g margarine, softened
175g self-raising flour
175g caster sugar
3 eggs
2 tablespoons drinking chocolate
1 tablespoon boiling water

Method

Preheat the oven to 180°C/fan 170°C/gas 4.

1 Grease 2 x 18cm sandwich tins. Line the bottom of each with circles of greaseproof paper.
2 Place all the ingredients in a food processor or bowl and beat until smooth.
3 Divide the mixture between the sandwich tins.
4 Bake for 25–30 minutes. Cool on a wire tray.
5 To decorate:
   - Sandwich 2 cakes together with chocolate icing (see below).
   - Spread icing on top of the cake.
   - Score the top of the cake with a fork or pipe roses of icing around edges.

Chocolate butter icing

Ingredients

100g icing sugar
50g margarine, softened
1 tablespoon drinking chocolate
1 tablespoon milk

Method

1 Beat all the ingredients together in a bowl until completely smooth.

Chocolate brownies

Makes 24 brownies

Ingredients

275g margarine, softened
375g caster sugar
4 eggs
75g cocoa powder
100g self-raising flour
100g plain chocolate chips

Method

Preheat the oven to 190°C/fan 180°C/gas 4.

1 Grease a roasting tin (approximately 30 x 23 x 4cm) and line the bottom and sides with greaseproof paper, pushing it neatly into the corners.
2 Mix all the ingredients well in a large bowl.
3 Spoon the mixture into the prepared tin. Spread evenly. Cover with tin foil.
4 Bake for 40–45 minutes, until the brownies have a crusty top and a skewer inserted into the mixture comes out clean.
5 Allow the brownies to cool in the tin before cutting them into 24 squares.

Simple carrot cake

Serves 6

Ingredients

225g self-raising flour
2 teaspoons baking powder
100g grated carrot
150g light brown sugar
2 ripe bananas, mashed
150ml sunflower oil
50g walnut pieces
2 eggs

Topping:

50g icing sugar, sieved
100g cream cheese
3 drops vanilla essence
walnuts, to decorate

Method

Preheat the oven to 190°C/fan 180°C/gas 4.

1 Line the bottom of a 1lb loaf tin with a rectangle of greaseproof paper.
2 Mix all the ingredients for the cake together thoroughly. Pour into the tin. Cover with tin foil.
3 Bake for 50–60 minutes. Cool on a wire tray before decorating.
4 To make the topping, cream the sieved icing sugar, cream cheese and vanilla essence until very smooth. Spread onto the cake. Make lines in it with a fork. Decorate with pieces of walnut.

Brown bread (wet mix)

Makes 1 loaf

Ingredients

250g white flour
250g coarse brown flour
$1\frac{1}{2}$ teaspoons bread soda
375ml buttermilk (approximately)

Method

Preheat the oven to 210°C/fan 200°C/gas 6.

1 Mix the flours with the bread soda in a bowl. Add enough buttermilk to make a wet, sticky dough.
2 Pile into a 1lb loaf tin. Cover with tin foil.
3 Bake for 1 hour. Wrap the bread in a clean tea towel and allow to cool.

Note: Silicone loaf pans are excellent in that the bread will not stick to it.

Banana bread

Makes 1 loaf

Ingredients

250g plain flour
2 teaspoons baking powder
1 teaspoon mixed spice
150g unsalted butter, softened
185g soft brown sugar
2 eggs
2 medium ripe bananas, mashed

Method

Preheat the oven to 190°C/fan 180°C/gas 5.

1 Line a 1lb loaf tin (if you use a silicone tin, you only have to line the bottom).
2 Mix all the ingredients together in a food processor. Pour into the loaf tin.
3 Cover with tin foil.
4 Bake for approximately 45–55 minutes, until golden on top and a skewer pushed into the cake comes away relatively clean.

Whisking method

Fresh strawberry sponge cake

Serves 6

Ingredients

3 eggs
75g caster sugar
75g self-raising flour, sieved
125ml whipped cream
6 strawberries, sliced

Method

Preheat the oven to 190°C/fan 180°C/gas 5.

1 Grease 2 x 18cm sandwich tins. Dust with a mix of caster sugar and flour.
2 Whisk the eggs and sugar until thick and creamy.
3 Fold half of the sieved flour into the mixture, then fold in the other half.
4 Divide between 2 tins and bake for 15–20 minutes (see Top Tips below).
5 Cool on a wire tray. Fill with the whipped cream and sliced strawberries.

Note: To decorate the top of the cake, place a doily on top of the cake and sprinkle icing sugar over through a sieve to make a nice pattern.

Top tip:

1. If whisking the egg and sugar by hand, place the bowl over a saucepan of hot water – the mixture will whisk more easily.
2. To check if a sponge is done, press on it. If it springs back, it is cooked.

Melting method

Ginger snaps

Makes 12–15

Ingredients

100g self-raising flour
1 heaped teaspoon ground ginger
50g margarine
50g granulated sugar
3 dessertspoons golden syrup

Method

Preheat the oven to 180°C/fan 170°C/gas 4.

1. Sieve the flour and ginger into a bowl.
2. Gently melt the margarine, sugar and golden syrup in a saucepan. Do not boil. Mix into the flour.
3. Make 12–15 balls of dough. Flatten into biscuit shapes on a greased tin.
4. Bake for 15 minutes. Cool on the tin.

Gingerbread

Makes 24 squares

Ingredients

100g margarine
50g brown sugar
3 tablespoons treacle
150g plain flour
½ teaspoon mixed spice
2 heaped teaspoons ground ginger
½ teaspoon baking powder
1 egg, beaten
100g stewed apple

Method

Preheat the oven to 180°C/fan 170°C/gas 4.

1. Grease a large baking tray. Line the bottom with greaseproof paper.
2. Gently melt the margarine, sugar and treacle in a saucepan.
3. Sieve the flour, spice, ginger and baking powder into a bowl. Add the melted ingredients and then the beaten egg and apple.
4. Pour the mixture into a baking tray. Bake for 15 minutes.
5. Cut into 24 squares. Remove from the tin and allow to cool on a wire tray.

Unit 2

Consumer Studies

CHAPTER 15

Consumers and Shopping

Slide presentation • Student activity pack – with revision crossword • Class test

What is a consumer?

A consumer is someone who buys or uses goods and services.

Goods and services

Goods: Things

Books, CDs, cigarettes, clothes, computer games, drinks, food, heating, lighting, mobile phones, sweets, toiletries, e.g. shampoo.

Services: People who do something for you

Bin collection, dentists, doctors, education, Gardaí, hairdressers, postal services, public parks, public transport, roads, street lighting, taxis.

Many services provided by the state, e.g. education and the Gardaí, are paid for indirectly through taxation.

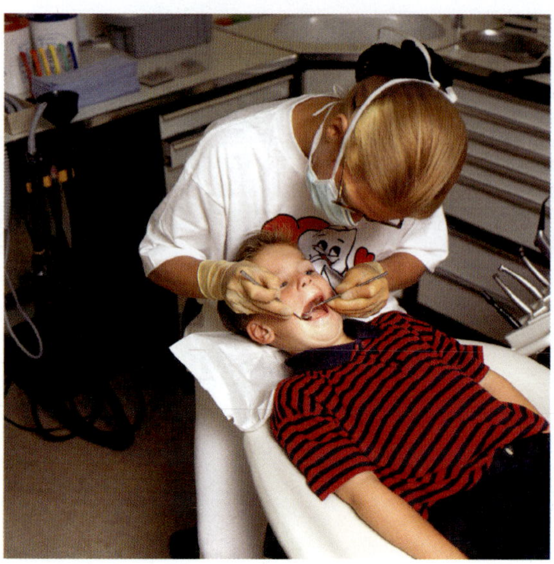

Needs and wants

Needs are *essential* goods and services. Examples of needs are food, clothes, shelter, doctors and dentists.

Wants are *non-essential* goods and services. Examples are takeaways, cars, designer clothes, jewellery, beauticians and hairdressers.

Nowadays, the line between what is a need and what is a want has become blurred. For example, many people would consider having a car a need, yet 40 years ago very few people had cars. Today, in developing countries, a car is most definitely a want.

Whether something is considered a need or a want will depend on the consumer's age, their circumstances (how well off they are) and their values (what is important to them).

In a family where money is tight, debts build up when wants are bought before needs are paid for. For example, buying a wide-screen TV (non-essential) when the electricity bill (essential) has not been paid, or spending money on alcohol and cigarettes (non-essential) when there is no food (essential) in the house.

Shopping

Shopping is part of our lives, something we do to meet our basic needs and wants. What exactly we buy, however, will depend on a number of factors.

Factors that influence consumer decisions

- **Resources (time and money):** During the Celtic Tiger years, Ireland saw a massive increase in consumer spending due to increased money in the economy. People spent little time making consumer decisions because many were cash rich and time poor. More recent times have seen a reversal of this trend – people have less money and more time so are again thinking more before they buy.
- **Peer pressure:** You want what other people your age have.
- **Fashion trends:** For example, UGG boots were fashionable over the past number of years.
- **Advertising:** Advertisements try to make us feel that if we have this product, our life will be better in some way.
- **Personal values:** A golfer who spends €650 on one golf club may be thought of as mad by non-golfers, for example.
- **Culture:** We buy certain things at particular times of year, e.g. Christmas tree.
- **Merchandising:** Retailers have to come up with ways of encouraging you to buy, especially when money is tight, e.g. interest-free credit, discounts – this is merchandising.

Making wise consumer decisions

When we buy things on the spur of the moment without thinking, it is called **impulse buying**. Goods and services bought in this way are often bad buys and ones we often regret. This regret is called **buyer's remorse**. When buying goods and services, it is better to think carefully before we buy. Below are some of the factors that should be considered.

Factors to be considered when choosing a product

1. **Money:** Can I afford it?
2. **Value:** Shop around and compare similar products in different shops.
3. **Quality:** Is the product made from good-quality materials? Does it have any quality symbols on it?
4. **Suitability:** Will it do the job you want it to? Example: Hill-walking boots need to be waterproof.
5. **Durability:** Will it last? Examples: Carpets, shoes.
6. **Design:** Is it nice to look at and well finished?
7. **Safety:** Look for safety symbols, especially on children's toys and electrical goods.
8. **Brand name:** It is often safer to buy well-known, reliable brands. Example: Washing machines.
9. **Environmental impact:** Is the product environmentally friendly?
10. **After-sales service:** Will the shop fix the product if it breaks?
11. **Maintenance:** Is the product easy to look after and keep clean?
12. **Size and comfort:** Are goods such as clothes and shoes well fitting and comfortable?

Sources of consumer information

Sometimes when we buy particular goods or services we are asked where we heard about them. Below are common sources of consumer information about goods and services.

- Newspapers and magazines articles.
- Golden Pages.
- Advertisements.
- Word of mouth.
- Manufacturers' brochures and leaflets.
- In the shop, i.e. salespeople inform us; we also get information about products by looking at them ourselves.
- Internet.

Shopping trends

How we shop has changed dramatically over the past 20 years. There has been:

- A decrease in the number of counter service shopping, e.g. corner shops.
- An increase in self-service shopping, e.g. supermarkets.
- An increase in the number of shopping centres.
- Increased late opening and Sunday shopping (some open 24 hours).
- Better facilities for shoppers, e.g. crèche, parking, cafés.
- Increase internet shopping.

Self-service vs. counter service

Self-service

Advantages	Disadvantages
• Quick. • Products are cheaper, especially own brands, e.g. Euroshopper and St Bernard. • Good choice. • High turnover means fresh goods. • Time is available to study and compare goods to make informed decisions.	• Less personal. • Impulse buying is more likely. • Sometimes crowded with long queues at checkouts. • Often on the outskirts of town, so a car is needed.

Counter service

Advantages	Disadvantages
• Personal, friendly service: this is particularly important for those living alone, e.g. the elderly. • Nearby: Great for those without a car or if you need to pop out for something, e.g. milk. • Some pack and deliver groceries. • Some give credit.	• Can be slow. • Less choice. • Slower turnover: Goods may not be as fresh as supermarket products. • More expensive.

Types of shops

Multiple chain store

These are large self-service shops. Branches are all owned by the same company. Examples include Dunnes Stores, Penneys, Marks & Spencers, Tesco, NEXT, A-wear.

Voluntary chain stores

An individual shop owner can apply and pay to be part of a voluntary chain, e.g. Spar, Centra, Londis, Valuland.

Independent shops

Traditionally family-run shops, usually open till late and on Sundays. Limited choice of goods but personal service.

Specialist shops

Usually sell only one type of product, e.g. shoes, cameras. A boutique specialises in expensive clothes.

Department stores

Very large shops divided into different departments, e.g. household, ladies' fashions, gifts, sportswear, etc. Each department has its own sales staff with good product knowledge, e.g. Clerys, Arnotts, Brown Thomas.

Other

- Shopping online.
- Discount stores: May also be voluntary chains, e.g. Valuland.
- Mail order shopping, e.g. Family Album.
- Markets.
- Auctions.

Grocery shopping guidelines

1. Make a list:
   - Check what is in the house already.
   - Plan meals for the week.
   - Write up a list and be as accurate as possible, e.g. write '4 tomatoes' rather than just 'tomatoes'.
   - Group similar items together, e.g. list all fruit and vegetables together, as these are found together in the supermarket.

2. Stick to the list and avoid impulse buying.
3. Shop around for good value.
4. Try not to shop too often, as you will end up spending more.
5. Bulk buy for items such as washing powder, toilet rolls, etc. as it is cheaper.
6. Check expiry dates for freshness.
7. Avoid shopping when you are tired or hungry.
8. Bring shopping bags.

Shopping technology

Supermarkets today use various types of technology to make their service quicker and more efficient. For example:

- Self-service weighing scales that print the product label.
- Computerised checkouts that scan **barcodes** and then print **itemised receipts**.

Self-service checkouts

Barcodes

A barcode is a series of lines and spaces that are read by a scanner attached to a computerised cash register.

Barcode

TESCO
IRELAND

	€
ISB DOUGHNUTS #	1.00
C/BAGS GOVT LE+	0.22
DISHWASH TABS *	8.79
20 REFUSE SACK *	2.20
ONKEN BIOPOT	1.55
CEREAL BAR *	2.09
ST/FRY SAUCE	1.69
INDIAN SAUCES	1.76
INDIAN SAUCES	1.76
FRESH MILK	0.97
CHIL FRUIT JCE *	2.00
MULLER RICE	0.69
MULLER RICE	0.69
MUSHROOMS 250G	0.99
MUSTARD	2.25
TOTAL	28.65
MAESTRO SALE	28.65

AID : A0000000043060
NUMBER : ************9844 ICC
PAN SEQ NO : 01
AUTH CODE : 299502
MERCHANT : 46358572
EXPIRY : 07/12
Cardholder PIN Verified
CHANGE DUE 0.00

SIGN UP FOR CLUBCARD
You could have earned 28
Clubcard points in this transaction

STORE OPENING HOURS
Monday - Saturday 7:00 - 23:00
Sunday 8:00 - 22:00
Off Licence Open Till 22:30

THANK YOU FOR
SHOPPING AT
RATHMINES 01 4970611

Slán Abhaile

Shop from home today with www.tesco.ie
and have your groceries delivered
right to your door.

6/10/09 17:14 3585 004 1007 0268

An itemised receipt

Advantages and disadvantages of barcodes

- An itemised receipt allows customers to see exactly what was bought.
- Quick stock control: Once an item is scanned, a central stock control computer records that there is one less of that item on the shelves. When stocks of the item get to a certain level, the computer reorders the product automatically.
- Goods are not individually priced.

Customer loyalty cards

Some large chains offer **customer loyalty cards**, e.g. Superclub, Valuecard. The card is swiped every time you shop and you build up points towards various 'gifts'. The advantage for the shop is that they have your name and address together with a complete record of everything you have ever bought in the store. This information can then be used for marketing purposes. For example, a supermarket has a consignment of a particular brand of Bolognese sauce that is not selling well. They see that you buy Bolognese sauce weekly and they send you money-off coupons to encourage you to buy the brand they want to get rid of instead of your normal brand.

Methods of payment

Cash

Cash is still the most common method of payment today. Some large supermarkets have ATM machines in-store for customers to withdraw cash. PASS and BankLink are examples of ATM cards. The main advantage of using cash is that you are less likely to overspend and get into debt. Carrying cash is not very secure, however. If it is lost or stolen, there is nothing you can do about it.

Cheque and cheque card

Customers can write a cheque if they have a cheque guarantee card. The card guarantees the retailer that the cheque will not bounce. Cheque cards usually cover cheques up to €130. This is a secure payment method, but there is a risk of overspending.

Debit card, e.g. Laser

The card is swiped or dipped into the card terminal and the amount is entered. The consumer checks the amount and enters their PIN number. The amount is processed and taken from the cardholder's bank account within a number of days. It is possible to get cash back. Laser cards are secure and convenient, but it is easy to overspend because you are not physically handing over cash.

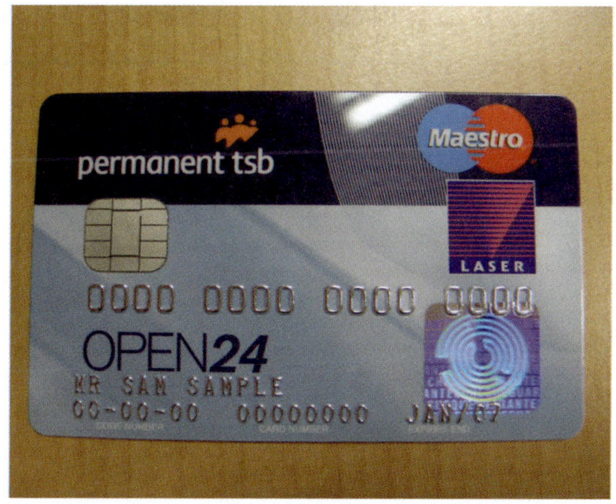

Credit card, e.g. Visa, MasterCard, Access

The card is swiped or dipped into the card terminal and the amount is entered. The consumer checks the amount and enters their PIN number. The amount is processed and it goes onto a bill. The bill can be paid in part or in full every month. No interest is charged if the bill is paid in full. As with laser cards, credit cards are secure and convenient and they can be used for online or over-the-phone purchases, but it is easy to overspend because you are not handling cash – you can forget just how much you have put on a bill and get a nasty surprise at the end of the month.

Shopping terms

- **Loss leader:** These are goods sold off cheaply by the retailer. It is hoped that these will lead you into the shop, where you will buy more.
- **Bulk buying:** You buy a product in large quantities. This is cheaper as long as you use it all.
- **Unit pricing:** Goods are priced per unit, e.g. per kilogram. Meat, fruit and vegetables are often priced in this way. Sometimes the tags on shelves show the unit price of goods, e.g. price of flour, sugar, etc., so that consumers can compare the actual prices of products.
- **Own brands:** Own brands are plainly packaged products, e.g. St Bernard, Euroshopper. They are often good quality and much cheaper than branded products, e.g. Lyons Tea.

Methods used by supermarkets to encourage you to buy

ENTRANCE

Heavy goods such as potatoes are placed at the entrance to encourage you to take a shopping trolley.

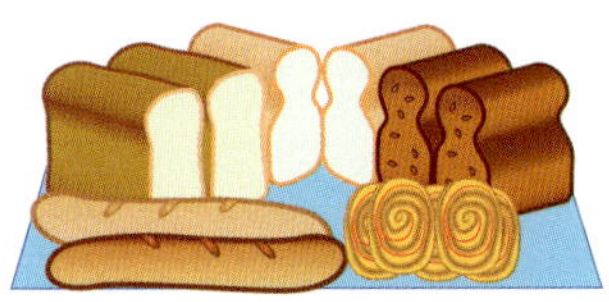

The smell of fresh bread hits you as you enter and makes you feel hungry.

Luxury items are placed at eye level, with essentials lower down.

Essential items such as milk and eggs are placed far from the entrance so that customers must walk through the shop to get them.

Sweets and toiletries are placed at checkouts for impulse buys.

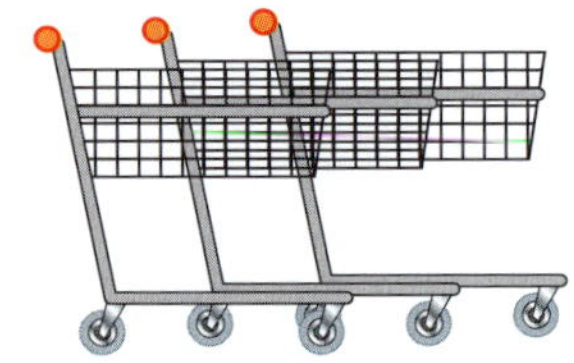

A large trolley is provided for you to fill.

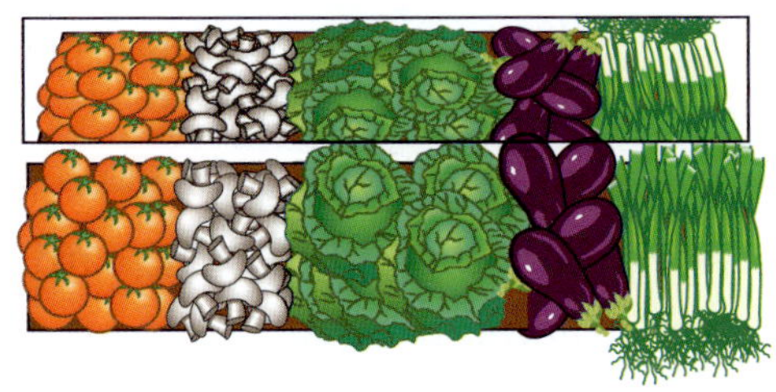

Mirrors, lighting and colour give fruit and vegetables a wholesome, fresh look.

Items that go together are placed together, for example ice cream and wafers, toothpaste and toothbrushes.

Special offers are displayed away from their usual place to give the impression that they are a bargain.

Background music covers up the hustle and bustle, so that shopping seems relaxed. Promotional announcements are made.

CHAPTER 16

Advertising

Teacher's CD-ROM

Slide presentation • Student activity pack • Class test

Advertising is a feature of modern life. We are constantly exposed to it through:

- TV and radio.
- Newspapers and magazines.
- Cinema and DVDs.
- The internet (e-mails and sponsored links on search engines).
- Billboards and bus shelters.
- Buses and trains.
- Sports grounds and sports sponsorship.
- Direct mail and text messaging.
- Carrier bags, logos on clothing, etc.

An effective advertisement must:

- Catch your attention.
- Make you want the product.
- Persuade you to go out and buy the product.

Functions of advertising:

- To introduce a new product to the market.
- To provide information on products, e.g. what they do.
- To increase sales.
- To make people familiar with a brand or logo.

Advertising techniques

There are **seven** basic advertising techniques used by companies to encourage you to buy their products.

Advertising techniques

1. **Humour** catches your attention.

2. **Glamour and romance:** 'If you buy this product, you too can look like this/find romance.'

3. **Traditional, wholesome images:** 'This product is healthy.'

4. **Happy family images:** 'This product will make your family happy and healthy.'

5. **Famous personalities:** Well-known people are used to promote products.

6. **Slogans:** 'Vorsprung durch Technik'.

7. **Statistics:** 'Nine out of 10 cats prefer it.' The Advertising Standards Authority is clamping down on slogans like this, though, as they can be misleading. Colgate has been asked not to use their famous slogan 'eight out of every 10 dentists prefer it' because it is misleading – the reality is that eight out of every 10 dentists recommend Colgate, but not ahead of other brands.

Classified advertisements

Classifieds are ads placed in newspapers and magazines. They are used to sell goods such as cars and furniture, to let and sell property, etc.

PETS

ABANDONED ANIMALS need kind homes for labrador (f) 1 yr. spayed; puppy, 12 weeks (m) house-trained, lovely nature; border Collie (m) 2 yrs; kittens and young adult cats. Tel: 1234567

LOVING HOMES wanted for whippet (m) 4 yrs; black & white Cocker Spaniel (f) 6 yrs; Bloodhound (m) 5 yrs; all dogs very loving with excellent temperaments. Foster homes and fund raisers urgently needed. Tel: 3456789

PET RESCUE urgently need kind homes for Dalmation (m) 7 yrs, owner deceased; pair of gentle Collies (f) 2 yrs; German Shepherd (m) 3 yrs, house-trained; Sable Terrier (f) 1 yr, owner deceased; King Charles Spaniel (f) 10 months, very gentle; Long-haired Lurcher (like Wolfhound) (f) 2-3 yrs; black Setter type (f) 6 mths; tri-coloured Terrier (f) 2 yrs; affectionate and needy cats and kittens - all colours. Tel: 2345678

Advantages and disadvantages of advertising

Advantages	Disadvantages
◎ Provides information. ◎ Creates jobs in advertising. ◎ Creates jobs in factories and shops because of increased sales. ◎ Keeps the cost of TV, newspapers and magazines down.	◎ Heavily advertised goods are often expensive, e.g. Apple iPods. ◎ Encourages people to want only famous brand names. ◎ Encourages overspending. ◎ Sometimes stereotypical images are used, e.g. women really concerned that their whites are white. ◎ Spoils the landscape, e.g. billboards. ◎ Interrupts TV viewing.

Advertising control

Because everyone in our society is exposed to advertising, it must be controlled. Advertising is controlled by the law and the industry itself (voluntary control).

The law

- **The EU Misleading Advertising Regulations:** These can prevent the publication of misleading advertisements.
- **Consumer Information Act 1978:** Advertisements must be truthful.
- **Employment Equality Act:** Protects against discrimination, such as 'single female required for busy restaurant'.

Voluntary control

Advertisers are encouraged by the Advertising Standards Authority to produce ads that are legal, decent, honest and truthful.

Marketing

Homework Assignment 30 P. 109

Nowadays, marketing plays a big part in industry.

Market research means gathering information about consumers' likes, dislikes, wants and needs. Information is gathered by questionnaires, phone interviews and through the use of loyalty cards, etc.

Test Yourself eTest.ie

Case Study

Through market research, Pepsi-Cola found that both males and females were concerned with the high levels of sugar in soft drinks. Males, however, were unwilling to be seen as 'wimps' by drinking diet drinks. Pepsi overcame this by creating a diet drink with a macho image – Pepsi Max.

CHAPTER 17

Consumer Protection and Making a Complaint

Slide presentation • Student activity pack • Class test

Teacher's CD-ROM

Consumer rights

As consumers, we have **five** basic rights. A right is something you are entitled to.

The right to redress

- Repair (item is fixed free of charge).
- Replacement (e.g. a new pair of shoes).
- Refund (money back).

The right to choice

This means having a wide variety of goods and services to choose from. Having choice means that manufacturers must produce high-quality goods or they will not sell.

The right to information

This means that information written on goods or about services must be true. For example, if a chair is labelled 'genuine leather', it must be leather.

The right to quality

Goods must be able to do what they are meant to do and be of good quality. Manufacturers usually test goods for quality before they leave the factory; this is called **quality control**.

The right to safety

Goods and services must be safe for consumers to use. Electrical items, children's clothes and toys must follow strict safety rules. Dangerous goods, e.g. bleach, must carry warning symbols.

A **monopoly** is when only one company provides a good or service, e.g. Iarnród Éireann. What is the disadvantage of monopolies?

Consumer responsibilities

Above are listed your rights as a consumer. As a consumer, you also have **responsibilities**. You should:

- Be well informed about the products you are buying and your consumer rights.
- Examine products and services carefully before you buy.
- Read instructions and labels; heed warnings.
- Shop around for value for money and avoid unnecessary waste.

Consumer law

Consumers are protected in three ways:

1. The law.
2. Government organisations, e.g. the Ombudsman and the National Consumer Agency.
3. Voluntary organisations, e.g. Consumers' Association of Ireland.

Contract

When you buy something in a shop or pay for a service, a **legal contract** is formed between you (the buyer) and the seller, for example the shopkeeper or plumber. The contract **is not** between you and the manufacturer of the goods, for example Tommy Hilfiger.

The two most important consumer laws are:

- The Sale of Goods and Supply of Services Act 1980.
- The Consumer Information Act 1978.

The Sale of Goods and Supply of Services Act 1980

Under this Act, goods must:

- **Be of merchantable quality:** This means they should be fit for sale and not faulty.
- **Be fit for their purpose:** For example, you should be able to walk in a pair of shoes without them falling apart.
- **Be as described:** For example, if a food product is labelled 'gluten free', it should be so.
- **Correspond to (be the same as) samples:** For example, you pick out a particular model of bathroom suite in a shop: the suite delivered to your house should be the same as the sample.

Under this Act, services, such as plumbing and hairdressing, must:

- Be carried out by someone with the necessary skills to do the job properly.
- Be carried out with care.
- Use good-quality materials. For example, a restaurant should use quality ingredients to make the food they serve.

If goods or services are faulty, you are entitled to compensation, that is, a repair, replacement or refund.

Services must be carried out with care and skill

This Act does **not** cover you if:

- The fault was pointed out to you before the sale, for example goods reduced in price and marked as **seconds** or **imperfect**.
- You misuse the goods.
- There is no fault and you simply change your mind (though some shops will exchange goods anyway).

A guarantee

A guarantee is a promise made to you by the manufacturers of the goods you buy. The guarantee, which must be written, usually states that the goods, if faulty, will be replaced or repaired free of charge. There is usually a time limit on the guarantee, for example one year. Guarantees are in addition to, not instead of, your rights under consumer law.

No cash refunds.

Credit notes only.

No exchange on sale items.

No receipt, no refund!

Notices like these are illegal if they refer to the refund or exchange of **faulty goods**. Remember, if you simply change your mind about an item, the shop does not have to refund your money or exchange the item.

The Consumer Information Act 1978

This Act states that information or claims made about goods and services must be true. The Act covers information in advertisements, on packaging, on shop notices and given by shop salespeople. False claims about the prices of goods are also illegal under this Act (this includes present, previous and recommended retail prices).

Examples of claims made about goods and services

WOOLMARK

100% wool

Guaranteed Irish

1-hour photo

Costa del Sol apartment to let, 3 mins from beach

Immaculate 3-year-old Toyota Avensis only 23,000km

Breaches of the Consumer Information Act should be notified to the National Consumer Agency.

Making a complaint

From time to time, we all buy goods that turn out to be faulty. Knowing how to make a complaint effectively makes the experience better and less stressful for all involved.

When you first notice a fault

- Stop using the goods.
- Find your receipt.
- Know your rights.
- Make your complaint to the shop where you bought the goods as soon as possible.

Remember! The shop where you bought the goods and not the manufacturer should deal with your complaint.

At the shop

- Ask for the customer services manager or, in a small shop, the manager.
- Calmly explain what is wrong.
- State exactly what you want done, e.g. a repair, refund or replacement.
- If you get no satisfaction, ask for the name of the managing director of the company, leave the shop and put the complaint in writing.

Remember! No claim if:

- The fault was pointed out at the time of purchase.
- You abused the goods.
- You simply changed your mind and there is no actual fault.

Writing a letter of complaint

Write or type a neat letter to the managing director of the company. Photocopy the letter and keep the copy safe.

Sample letter of complaint

Name and address of managing director of the company

Mr Eoin O'Brien,
O'Brien Sports,
8 Main Street,
Ardee,
Co. Louth

Customer's address

11 Woodland Grove,
Dunleer,
Co. Louth

12 April 2010

Dear Mr O'Brien,

Details of:

- Exactly what you bought (include model number, etc.).
- Where you bought it.
- State you are enclosing a copy of receipt.

I wish to complain about a pair of Nike Shox NZ Girls' Running Shoes I purchased in your shop on Main Street on 25 March. Please find attached a copy of my receipt.

Clear details of complaint.

After wearing the runners on just three occasions, the sole began to separate from the upper and I was unable to wear them. As the runners were not badly treated, the fault is most certainly with them. I returned the shoes to your Ardee branch, but your shop assistant was unable to help me.

Details of action you would like taken.

It is quite clear that there was a fault in the runners when I bought them. I would like a refund for the total amount of €129.

Yours sincerely,

Ruth Monaghan

Wait a couple of weeks for a reply; you could then follow up with a phone call. If you still get no satisfaction, you may wish to go to the small claims court or to one of the following agencies for further advice.

Agencies that provide consumer information and advice

Statutory (government-run) agencies	
Name of agency	**Functions**
The Ombudsman	The Office of the Ombudsman deals with complaints against government-run organisations, e.g. the HSE, An Post. Complain to the organisation itself first and only to the Ombudsman as a last resort.
National Consumer Agency national **consumer** agency gníomhaireacht náisiúnta **tomhaltóirí** putting **consumers** first	The National Consumer Agency (NCA) was established by the government in May 2007 to replace the Office of the Director of Consumer Affairs and Fair Trade. • Enforces consumer laws. • Helps control the advertising industry. • Promotes consumer awareness. • Controls safety and labelling of food and textiles.

Non-statutory (voluntary) agencies	
Name of agency	**Functions**
Consumers' Association of Ireland	• Advises consumers. • Provides consumer information, e.g. teachers' packs, leaflets. • Has an information website. • Produces a monthly consumer magazine called *Consumer Choice*. This magazine gives unbiased information on goods and services currently on the market.
Trade organisations	Some groups of businesspeople, e.g. auctioneers (MIAVI) and publicans (Vintners Association), come together and form a trade organisation. These organisations develop codes of good practice for their members and will deal with complaints.

Homework Assignment 31 P. 111

Small claims court

To make a complaint in the small claims court, you must get and fill in an application form from the small claims registrar in your local district court. The small claims court deals with claims up to the value of €2,000.

CHAPTER 18

Quality

Teacher's CD-ROM

Slide presentation • Student activity pack • Class test

Quality of goods

The term **quality** describes the standard of goods and services. Before goods leave a factory, they are examined and tested to ensure that they reach a certain set standard. This is called **quality control**.

The quality and standard marks below are awarded to goods and services that are of a good quality or standard. These marks will be on the goods themselves or on their box or label.

Quality and standard marks

This **Quality Mark** is awarded to Irish companies for quality goods and services and can be withdrawn if standards drop.

The **Guaranteed Irish** symbol is awarded to high-quality goods made in Ireland.

The **Irish Standards Mark** can be found on any product that has been certified to an Irish standard.

The **European Standards Mark** is awarded by the EU to goods that have reached a high standard of safety. It is found on children's toys, clothes, buggies, electrical goods, etc.

The **BSI Kite Mark** is awarded by the British Standards Institution (BSI) to goods and services, e.g. crash helmets, garage servicing and repairs, to show they have been independently assessed and meet appropriate standards of safety and performance, etc.

Quality of services

A good-quality **service** will have:

- Friendly staff who know what they are doing.
- Clean, well laid-out premises.
- Wheelchair access.
- Little queuing or waiting.
- Clean toilet facilities.

Product labelling

Product labels should give you the following information:

- Quality symbol.
- Warnings about the dangers of misuse.
- Name and address of manufacturer.
- Description of product, what it is made from, weight, colour, number of items, etc.
- Instructions for use, care and cleaning.

Product safety

Product safety is concerned with two things:

- The safety of the user of the product.
- That the product itself is not destroyed by being used, cared for or stored incorrectly.

Product labels carry instructions and also warning and safety symbols. These try to ensure the safe use of the product. The more common ones are shown here.

Instructions

Instructions tell you how to use the product safely. They may come as a separate booklet, which should be kept in a safe place.

Care labels

Care labels tell us how to wash, dry and iron a garment.

Food labels

Food labels
Best before 30.01.12
Date stamping/expiry date

Safety symbols: Show that products have been tested for safety

Flame-resistant mark: Found on furniture, etc. Fabric carrying this symbol does not burn easily.

European Standards mark: Products carrying this symbol, e.g. children's toys and nightwear, have passed strict safety tests.

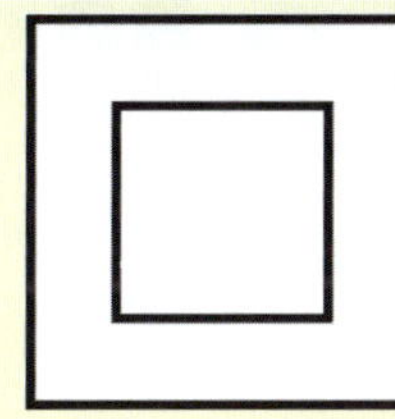

Doubly insulated mark: Found on small electrical appliances.

Warning symbols: Found on potentially dangerous products

Government warnings.

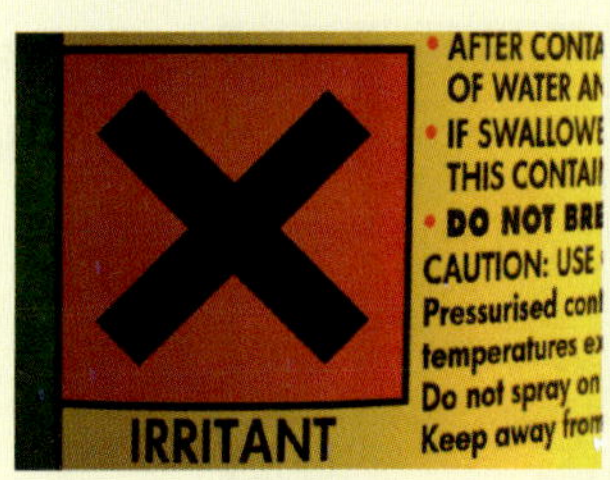

Harmful irritant: This product will damage the skin and eyes, e.g. bleach.

Highly flammable: Will burst into flames easily, e.g. aerosols.

Packaging

With the increase in self-service shopping (such as in supermarkets) and in the use of convenience foods, the amount of packaging has also increased.

Functions of packaging

- Advertises the product.
- Makes it easier to store.
- Protects the product, e.g. food, from contamination.
- Preserves food, e.g. cans.
- Provides essential information, e.g. instructions for use.
- Carries the barcode.

Types of packaging

Plastic

Paper

Glass

Metal

Good packaging is:

- Environmentally friendly.
- Strong.
- Light.
- Easily opened and resealed (if necessary).

Disadvantages of too much packaging

Too much packaging:

- Is bad for the environment.
- Uses up natural resources, e.g. trees.
- Causes litter and pollution, e.g. plastics.
- Is expensive.
- Stops us seeing what we are getting for our money, e.g. ready meals.

Note: See also Chapter 30, Community Services and the Environment.

Homework Assignment 32 P. 115

Test Yourself eTest.ie

Unit 2 CONSUMER STUDIES

CHAPTER 19

Money Management

Teacher's CD-ROM

Slide presentation • Student activity pack – with revision crossword • Class test

Money management is planning our spending wisely so that we have enough for our needs and avoid debt. A **budget** is the actual plan for spending and saving. A good budget balances income (the money we have) with expenditure (what we spend).

Higher Level

The money management process is continual and involves five stages. Budgeting is part of this process.

The money management process

1. **START: Identify goal or aim:** To balance income and spending. →
2. **Identify resources:** Money, energy, time. ↓
3. **Plan:** Balance income and spending on paper (budget). ↓
4. **Action:** Put your budget into action. ←
5. **Evaluate:** Ask yourself if your budget worked. If *yes*, repeat action. If *no*, go back to goal or aim.

Each week or month (or annually if you are self-employed), a person's **gross tax** is calculated. This gross tax is reduced by the **tax credit** due to the person for that week or month to get the net or actual tax payable. Unused credits can be carried to the next week or month.

Gross tax **less** tax credits **equals** net tax (what you actually pay).

Voluntary deductions

Employees can also decide to have **voluntary deductions** taken from their pay. Examples include health insurance payments, savings and pension payments (unless you are a government worker, in which case pension payments are compulsory).

Basic needs such as food must be provided for first

Household expenditure

As stated earlier, the household budget must balance income with household expenditure. The costs of basic needs such as food, clothing and shelter must be met first. Other necessities, such as transport, must then be met before luxury items are purchased.

- Clothes and shoes.
- Crèche payments.
- Educational expenses, e.g. books.
- Food.
- House insurance.
- Household bills, e.g. electricity, gas.
- Housing (rent or mortgage).
- Luxuries, e.g. entertainment, holidays.
- Medical expenses, e.g. doctor, dentist, chemist.
- Medical insurance, e.g. Quinn, VHI, VIVAS.
- Savings.
- Transport (car, bus and train fares).

Advantages of budgeting

- More security – less financial worry.
- Overspending on impulse buys is less likely.
- Areas of overspending become obvious and can be cut down on.
- It sets a good example for children.
- Money can be set aside for major bills and seasonal spending, e.g. Christmas.

Saving and credit

When you decide to buy something that you do not have enough money for, two options are open to you:

- Save for the item.
- Buy it on credit (borrowing).

Saving

Saving for an item and then paying for it in full, in cash, has advantages in that you earn interest rather than pay it, the item costs less in the end than if you borrowed for it and there is no risk of getting into debt. Saving for an item, however, means that you have to wait to get the item, something that we have become less willing to do.

Where can you save?

- Credit union.
- Bank or building society.
- Post office.

Credit Union

Before deciding where to save, find out:

- Who offers the highest rates of interest?
- Do they offer student incentives such as no bank charges?
- How easy is it to lodge and withdraw money?

In banks and building societies, there are two basic types of account:

- Deposit account (savings).
- Current account.

Money left in a deposit account will earn interest. A current account, on the other hand, is designed for everyday use. Money does not stay in it long and earns no interest. Bills can be paid by direct debit from a current account.

Opening a student deposit account

To open a student deposit (savings) account, you must:

- Fill out the bank or building society application form.
- Get a letter from your school saying you are a student there. The letter should also state your name, address and date of birth. Alternatively, you can produce official identification such as your passport.

Buying on credit

Credit buying means **buy now, pay later.** Credit encourages you to buy more than you can afford and has many disadvantages:

- Interest is charged and the item ends up costing much more.
- People run up debts.

On the other hand, if you use credit wisely it does have advantages in that you have the use of the item while paying for it and some very large items could not be bought without credit, such as houses and cars.

Where can you get credit?

1. Credit cards.
2. Bank/building society or credit union loans.
3. Bank overdraft: The bank allows your account to go into the red but charges interest on money owed.
4. Hire purchase: Pay for goods in installments; you don't own the item until it is paid for in full.
5. Catalogues such as Family Album allow customers to pay for goods in installments.

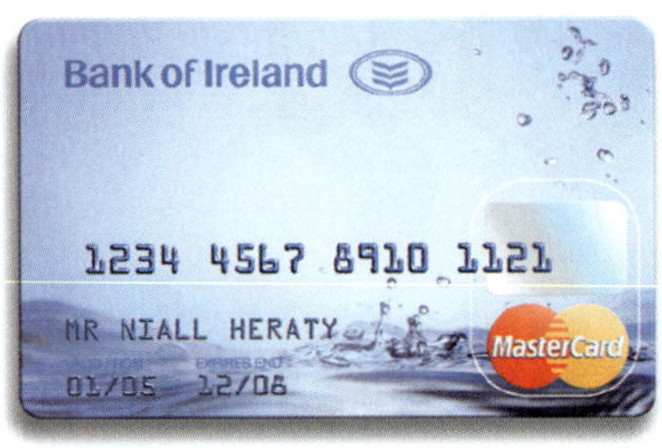

Credit card

Some companies, e.g. car firms, are now offering interest-free loans to allow people to purchase goods. These are an improvement in that you do not pay interest, but they encourage overspending and bills to mount up.

Home filing system

Home filing

A home filing system should contain all the family's important paperwork, e.g. bills, receipts, school reports, guarantees, bank statements, etc. Keeping a household filing system has many **advantages**:

- Bills are not mislaid and can therefore be paid on time.
- Time is not wasted searching for paperwork, since it is all in one place.
- Guarantees and receipts are at hand should you have a problem with goods purchased.
- Past and present bills can be compared.
- School progress can be monitored from year to year.

Homework Assignment 33 P. 118

There are many simple yet effective home files on the market; generally they cost from about €30 upwards.

Unit 3

Social Studies

CHAPTER 20

The Family

Teacher's CD-ROM: Slide presentation • Student activity pack – with revision crossword • Class test

The family

Types of family

- **Nuclear family:** Father, mother, child or children living in the same house.
- **Extended family:** Includes grandparents, uncles, aunts and cousins all living together or near each other.
- **One-parent family:** A family headed by a parent who may be unmarried, separated, divorced or widowed.
- **Blended family:** When parents and their children from previous relationships form a new family. Parents may also have children together.

Changes to the family

- **Increased one-parent families:** In the past in Ireland, the only type of one-parent family seen as acceptable was where a parent had died. Today, as a result of divorce, increased marital separation and an acceptance of single unmarried parents, one in six families in Ireland is headed by one parent.
- **Increased cohabiting couples:** For various reasons, many couples decide not to marry but live together and rear their children. As of the 2006 census, 11.6 per cent of all family units in Ireland are headed by cohabiting couples.
- **Increased blended families:** Because of increased levels of divorce and separation, an increasing number of children are growing up in blended families, whereby they live with their parent's new partner and their children. (Although as of 2007, Ireland still had the lowest divorce rate in Europe at seven per 1,000 marriages – the European average is 21 per 1,000).

- **Increased isolation:** Nowadays, many couples move away from their extended family to find work, etc. Childrearing can be more difficult as there are no family members nearby to help out.

Functions of the family

A **functional** family will provide us with our physical, social and emotional needs. A **dysfunctional** family will only provide some of them.

- **Physical needs:** Food, clothing, shelter.
- **Emotional needs:** Love, security, support.
- **Social needs:** Healthy, respectful relationships, guidance on what is right and wrong, boundaries.

Rights of children

- Love and security.
- Care.
- Education.
- Protection from neglect or abuse.

Children can be neglected as a result of parents being too busy

Roles and responsibilities within the family

Every family member has rights, but each also has responsibilities. **A responsibility is something that is expected of us.** What responsibilities a family member has will depend on their role in the family. **Roles** include that of child, adolescent, parent or grandparent.

Child	Adolescent	Adult
• To respect household boundaries (rules). • To show respect for all family members. • To participate well in school. • To help out in the home.	• To respect household boundaries (rules). • To show respect for all family members. • To help out in the running of the home. • To behave in an acceptable way in society.	• To provide for the family's needs. • To set reasonable boundaries (rules) for members of the household. • To show respect for all family members. • To behave in an acceptable way in society, setting a good example.

Conflict in the family

Relationships between family members will generally be good if each person fulfils the responsibilities connected to their role. There is often conflict between adolescent family members (teenagers) and their parents because of **role confusion**, with each side seeing the same situation differently. For example, a parent feels they have a responsibility to ensure that their teenage son or daughter is safe so asks them to be home by 10 p.m. The teenage son or daughter feels they are old enough to make decisions for themselves about when they return home (see also Dealing with Conflict on p. 206).

'Supermum'

Homework Assignment
34 P. 122

Gender roles

Gender means being either male or female. In the past, males and females had very different **gender roles**, meaning they were expected to behave very differently from each other. For example, many men were expected to go out to work and do very little housework or childrearing. Women were expected not to work outside the home and to do all the housework and childrearing.

Stereotyping

Stereotyping means having an oversimplified, fixed and often wrong idea about a group of people, e.g. 'all Americans are loud'.

Gender stereotyping means having a fixed and often wrong idea about men's and women's personalities and life expectations. Examples of gender stereotyping:

- Personalities: Women are emotional; men are not.
- Life expectations: Women want to find a husband and have children; men want a career.

Gender-role stereotyping means having a fixed and often wrong idea about how men and women should behave in society, e.g. 'Women should do the childrearing and housework and men should go out to work.' In Irish society today, more than 50 per cent of women work outside the home, yet many are expected to carry on their traditional roles as well, resulting in many women feeling burned out.

Gender equality means treating men and women equally. Both can be who and what they want to be without being judged or discriminated against. Are men and women treated equally in Irish society?

Test Yourself eTest.ie

CHAPTER 21

Growth and Development

Slide presentation • Student activity pack – with revision crossword • Class test

Growth and development

Our growth and development as human beings are influenced by two things:

- **Heredity:** What has been passed on by our parents.
- **Environment:** How we are brought up; our surroundings.

During our lives, we go through four stages of development:

- Childhood.
- Adolescence.
- Adulthood.
- Old age.

As human beings, there are also five different **areas** of development.

Type of development and what it means

Physical

- Growth of the body, e.g. getting taller.
- Increased co-ordination and ability to do things, e.g. ride a bike.

Mental

- Development of memory, understanding, imagination and creativity.

Language

- Development of speech, reading, writing.

Type of development and what it means

Emotional

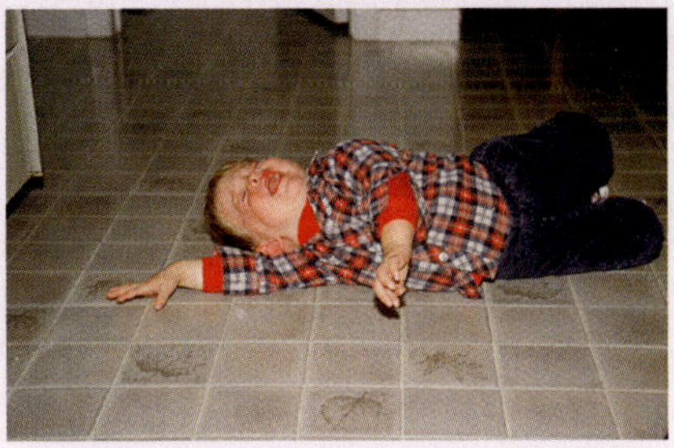

- Learning to handle your emotions, e.g. anger, fear.
- Development of self-esteem (how you feel about yourself).

Social and moral

- Learning what behaviours are acceptable in society, e.g. to use a tissue.
- Developing friendships and relationships with others.
- Knowing right from wrong

For development during childhood, see Chapter 37, pp. 320–43.

Development during adolescence

Adolescence (age 11–18), like early childhood, is a time of rapid development.

Physical development

- Co-ordination improves, i.e. the ability to dance, to play sports and to complete skilled tasks increases.
- Physical and sexual development takes place during puberty, caused by sex hormones (see illustrations below). Puberty is occurring earlier nowadays than in the past. This is due to the fact that children are heavier than in the past and many have better nutrition.

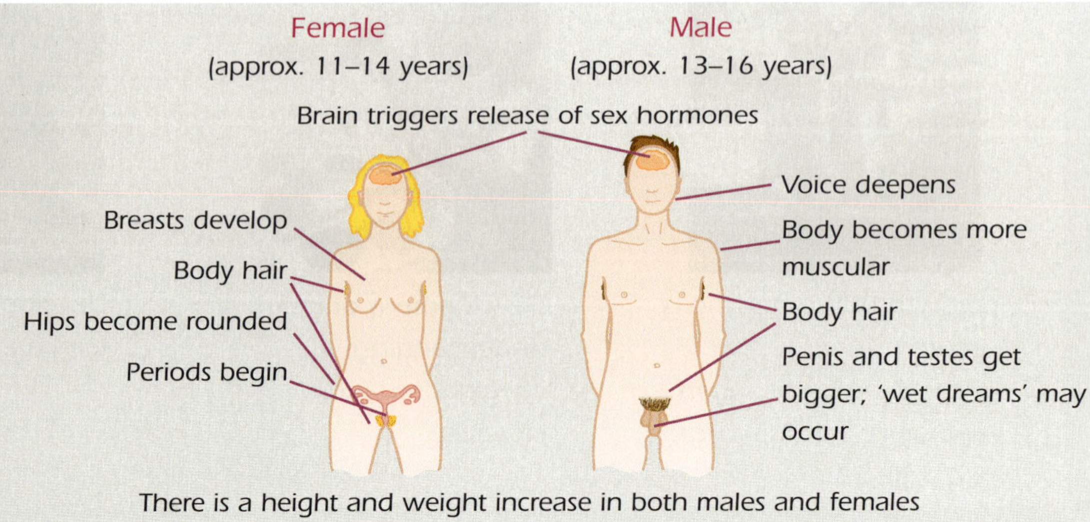

Mental development

During adolescence, most young people become capable of more complex thought. Younger children tend to think more in the here and now, about what they can now see, hear, smell or touch. They do not think about the past and the future as much. Most adolescents, on the other hand, become able to plan, understand abstract concepts such as justice and democracy and think about or carry out more than one thing at a time. A stimulating environment is important for mental development.

The psychologist David Elkind believed that adolescents think differently to adults in three basic ways and that these differences influence adolescents' behaviour.

- **Imaginary audience:** The belief that others are watching you and are as concerned with your behaviour and appearance as you are yourself. This results in adolescents being influenced by fashion trends and being easily mortified or embarrassed by events.
- **Personal fable:** The belief that their experiences are unique, e.g. everyone else is allowed out except me.
- **Invincibility:** While adolescents are aware of the dangers of risky behaviours, there is a stronger sense at this time that 'it will not happen to me'. This results in, for example, adolescents driving or sitting in cars that are being driven too fast.

Emotional development

During adolescence:

- Sexual feelings develop.
- Adolescents are often very concerned about how others see them (see imaginary audience above). The advertising industry uses these insecurities to sell their goods.
- Conflict increases.

Conflict is a normal part of development for many adolescents. Conflict is usually about housework, money, appearance, substance use or abuse (such as drinking), schoolwork, curfew, boy/girlfriends and sexual behaviour. Adolescents usually want more independence than their parents will allow. This is frequently the cause of conflict.

Dealing with conflict

If you are fighting with a parent or someone else:

- **Do not** get aggressive or blame them.
- **Do not** ignore the problem – it will not go away.
- **Do** listen and calmly discuss the issue and try to work out a solution.

Social development

During adolescence, the **peer group** becomes very important. Your peer group is people your own age who share similar interests. Adolescents usually spend less and less time with their family and more with their peer group. **Peer pressure** is when your peer group puts pressure on you to do something, e.g. to smoke. **Peer pressure is not always bad.** Can you think of an example of positive peer pressure in your life?

Moral development

Moral development occurs in two stages. Some people never reach stage two.

- **Stage 1:** Actions are driven by a desire for rewards or a fear of punishment, e.g. 'I won't steal from my mother's purse because if she notices, she will kill me.' Some adults remain at this stage, e.g. career criminals.
- **Stage 2:** Actions are led by your own sense of right and wrong, e.g. 'I won't steal from my mother's purse because I feel it is wrong to steal.'

Higher Level

Norms

Our sense of right and wrong is often influenced by the norms of the society and home we live in. Norms are acceptable ways of behaving, such as putting rubbish in the bin, not damaging other people's property, etc. People's understanding of norms are developed in early childhood, which is why it is difficult to change attitudes later in life, e.g. towards littering.

Homework Assignment 35 P. 125

Test Yourself eTest.ie

CHAPTER 22

New Life

Unit 3 SOCIAL STUDIES

Slide presentation • Student activity pack – with revision crossword • Class test

Teacher's CD-ROM

The menstrual cycle (menstruation – periods)

Certain changes occur in a woman's body every month. These changes are referred to as the **menstrual cycle**, which begins at puberty and continues until **menopause** (which normally occurs between 45 and 55 years of age, when periods stop).

During menstruation:

1. An egg, or **ovum**, is released from one of the female's ovaries. This is called **ovulation**.
2. The egg goes into the **fallopian tube** nearby and waits to be **fertilised** by the male sperm.
3. If the egg is not fertilised, it travels down into the womb and out of the body. The girl or woman then has her monthly period.
4. If the woman has sex, sperm comes up to the fallopian tube and may join with the egg: this is called **fertilisation** or **conception**.
5. The egg makes its way to the **uterus** (womb) and attaches itself to the womb wall. The woman is then pregnant.
6. The female hormones **progesterone** and **oestrogen** cause:
   - Ovulation.
   - Changes during puberty, e.g. breasts develop, growth of pubic hair.
   - Changes during pregnancy.

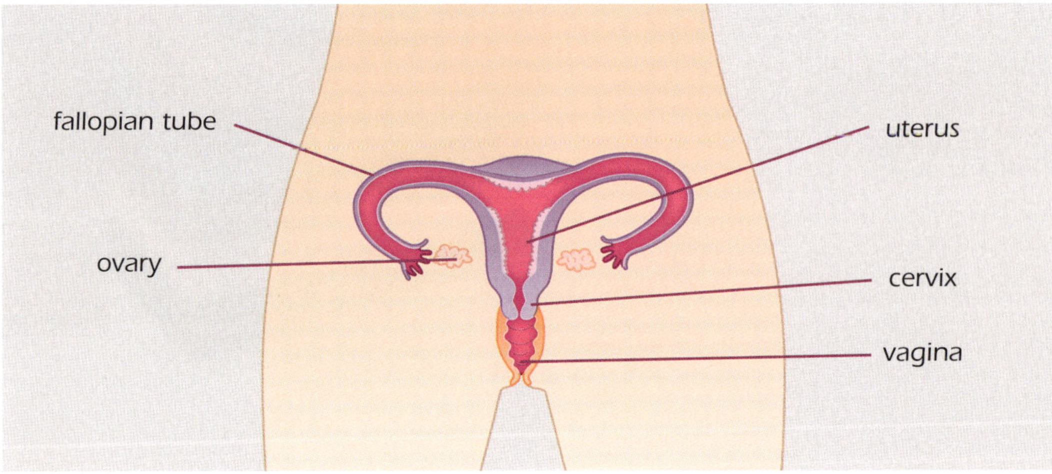

Hygiene during menstruation

- Change pads or tampon every 3–4 hours.
- Wash your pubic area well every day.
- Wash your hands before and after changing a pad or tampon.
- Wear tight-fitting underwear with pads to prevent leaking.
- Buy dark-coloured underwear to wear during periods.

The male reproductive system

1. From puberty onwards, the male **testes** produce **sperm**. The testes lie outside the body in a sac called the **scrotum**.
2. During sexual intercourse, the blood vessels of the penis fill with blood and it becomes stiff and erect. This allows the man to insert his penis into the woman's vagina. When the man reaches orgasm, sperm travel quickly through two sperm ducts and spurt out through the penis into the woman's body. While travelling to the penis, the sperm mix with fluids that nourish the sperm and allow them to swim. This mixture is called **semen**.

The moment of conception

3. At the moment of **ejaculation**, many thousands of sperm are released near the woman's cervix. They begin swimming towards the fallopian tubes in an effort to fertilise an egg which may or may not be there. In the end, only one sperm fertilises the egg.
4. The male hormone **testosterone** is made in the testes and causes:
   - Sperm production.
   - Other changes during puberty, e.g. facial hair.

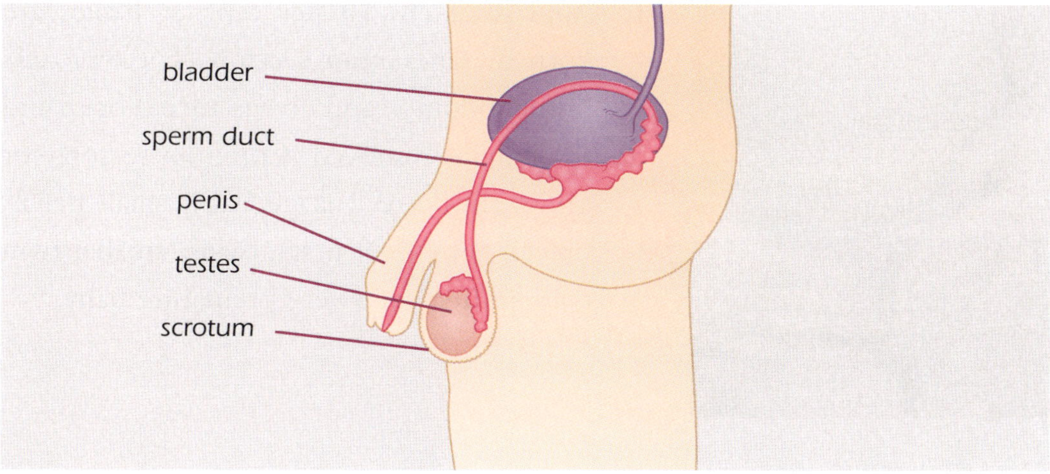

Pregnancy

1. A few days after conception, the egg travels along the fallopian tube to the womb, where it attaches itself to the womb wall. It is now called an **embryo**. At eight weeks it is called a **foetus**.
2. Sometimes the egg does not remain implanted and an early miscarriage occurs.
3. The **placenta** forms where the embryo is attached. The **umbilical cord** then forms, joining the placenta to the baby. The umbilical cord is the baby's lifeline, supplying food and oxygen.
4. Unfortunately, harmful viruses, e.g. rubella and HIV, and harmful substances such as alcohol, nicotine and other drugs can also pass to the baby.
5. A baby's due date is calculated as 40 weeks from the first day of the woman's last period.
6. From about 32 weeks, the baby's head will face downwards. When the baby is about to be born, the waters usually break and contractions start. This is called **labour**. As labour progresses, contractions will become stronger and more frequent. Some women decide to have an epidural, which is an anaesthetic injected into the spine for pain relief.
7. Sometimes labour is **induced**. This involves giving the woman hormones to start labour.
8. During birth, the head is delivered first. (Babies coming feet first are described as being in the breech position. Because of the risk of suffocation, they are usually delivered by Caesarean section.)
9. Often a cut is made in the vagina to make the opening bigger and to stop tearing; this is called an **episiotomy**.
10. Once the head is out, the rest of the body and the **afterbirth** are delivered.

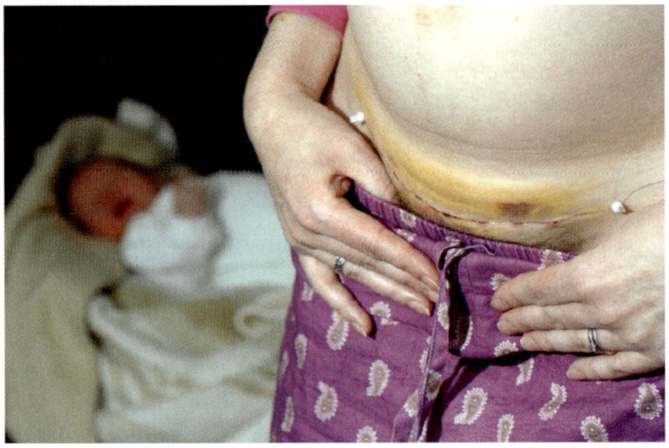

A Caesarean scar

11. Approximately 10 per cent of babies are born by **Caesarean section**. The woman's lower abdomen and uterus are cut open and the baby is removed. Common reasons for a C-section are a large baby, small pelvis, breech baby (feet first), twins (smaller twin coming first) or a very premature baby.

Responsible sexual behaviour

In 2007, almost 2,500 teenagers gave birth in Ireland. Studies show that many teenagers (especially teenage girls) have sex because of various pressures rather than because they really want to. Most people believe that sex is best kept for close, long-term relationships and that casual sex can be damaging for the individual.

Casual sex can lead to:

- Unplanned pregnancy.
- Feelings of being used.
- Sexually transmitted infections (STIs), e.g. genital warts, herpes, AIDS.
- While any woman can develop cervical cancer, there is an increased incidence of cervical cancer in women who were sexually active before the age of 18.

Alcohol or other drugs are often involved when people make risky decisions about sexual activity.

Homework Assignment 36 P. 128

Test Yourself eTest.ie

CHAPTER 23

The Human Body

Slide presentation • Student activity pack – with revision crossword • Class test

Teacher's CD-ROM

The human body

In this chapter, you will study:

- The teeth.
- The skin and personal hygiene.
- The respiratory system.
- The circulatory system (Higher Level only).

The teeth

Healthy teeth are very important. They are attractive and allow you to speak properly and chew food.

A baby's 20 milk teeth generally appear by age two and a half and fall out from age seven. An adult, on the other hand, has 32 permanent teeth. The four wisdom teeth are the last to appear, in the mid to late teens.

Types of adult teeth

There are four different types of teeth, each with a different function.

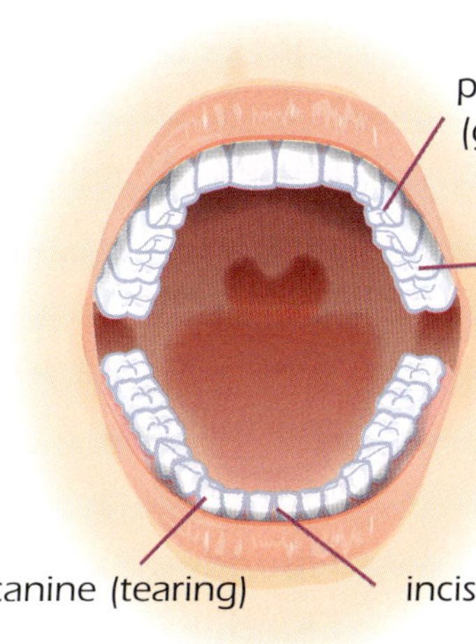

Structure of the tooth

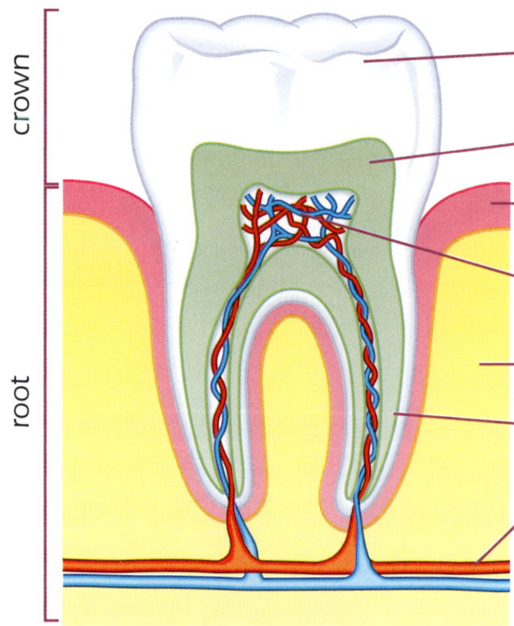

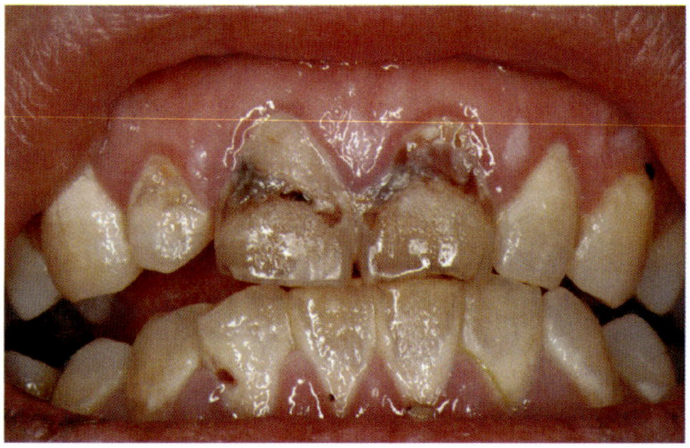

Tooth decay and gum disease

Unhealthy teeth are unattractive and can cause the person to become very self-conscious, have bad breath and suffer from gum and stomach infections.

Plaque

Plaque is the yellowish coating that forms on teeth between brushings. Plaque contains food and bacteria. If teeth are not brushed, the bacteria begin digesting the food and **acid** is produced. This acid burns into the tooth and causes it to decay or rot. A toothache is not felt until the acid has burned through to the pulp cavity. Why?

Gum disease

Gum disease occurs when acid attacks the gums, leaving them infected, sore and swollen.

Fluoride

Fluoride is a substance often added to water supplies and toothpaste. Fluoride strengthens teeth and helps prevent decay.

Brushing teeth

Teeth have four surfaces – outer, inner, chewing surface and between teeth. All four surfaces should be cleaned thoroughly by brushing and flossing.

Dental products

- Use dental floss to clean between the teeth safely. Floss before brushing and never use metal objects to do this: it damages the enamel.
- Mouthwash helps kill the acid-producing bacteria in plaque. Use after brushing.
- The good circular action of an electric toothbrush does not damage gums.

Caring for the teeth and gums

There are five basic rules for caring for the teeth and gums

1. Eat calcium-rich foods and raw fruit and vegetables.
2. Avoid sugary food and drinks.
3. Brush after meals with a soft toothbrush. Replace your brush regularly.
4. Have a dental check-up every six months. Never use your teeth to open bottles, etc., as this damages the enamel.
5. Do not brush teeth too aggressively, as this will cause gums to recede or pull back from the teeth.

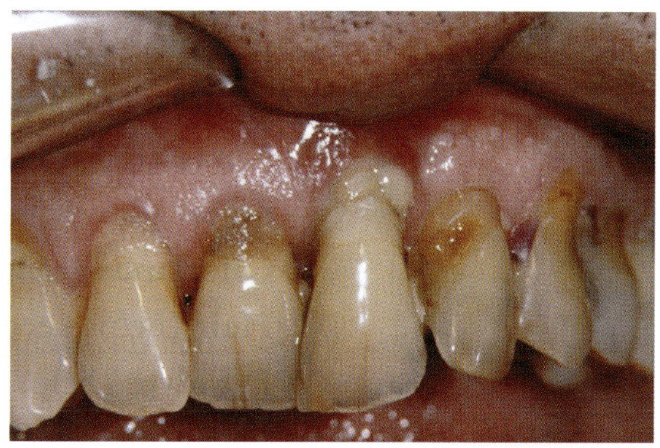

Receding gums

The skin and personal hygiene

Homework Assignment 37 P. 132

The skin is a very important organ in the body. It is an **excretory** organ, meaning that it gets rid of waste products from the body such as water and salts (sweat).

Structure of the skin

The skin has two layers:

- **Epidermis** (the surface you can see).
- **Dermis** (under the surface).

The epidermis is the outermost layer of the skin. As you can see in the illustration on the next page, the top layer of the epidermis consists of **flat, dead cells**. These cells are constantly brushed off and replaced from beneath. The **Malpighian layer** lies further into the epidermis. This layer contains a

Promoting healthy skin

- Have a good skincare routine – cleanse, tone and moisturise the face every day.
- Never sleep with make-up on.
- Wash the rest of the body daily and use a body moisturiser.
- Eat a healthy diet with plenty of fresh fruit and vegetables.
- Drink at least eight glasses of water per day.
- Take exercise daily and get enough sleep.
- Avoid smoking and alcohol.
- Wear sun cream on your face every day.

Skin cancer

Skin cancer is the most common cancer in Ireland. Due to our skin type, Ireland has one of the highest rates for skin cancer in Europe, affecting one in every eight men and one in every 10 women. Yet 90 per cent of skin cancers can be avoided by:

- Avoiding too much sun – just because you are wearing sun factor does not mean you can stay out indefinitely in the sun, especially if abroad.
- Wearing sun cream **daily** (factor 25, even in Ireland).
- Never using sun beds.

Children's skin is easily damaged; they must wear a high-factor sun cream.

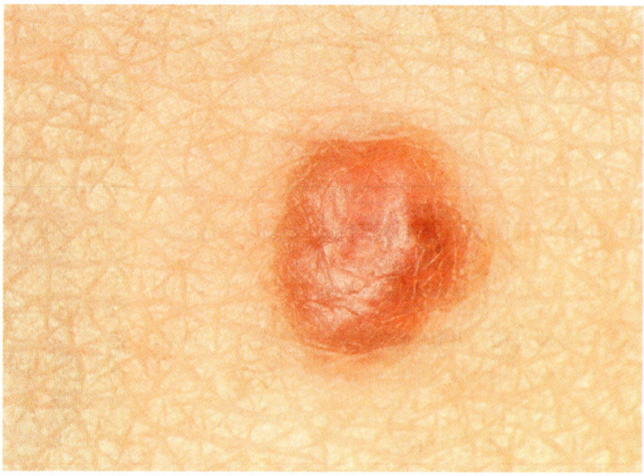

Sunbathing = skin cancer and wrinkles

Care of the hair, hands and feet

Care of the hair

- Wash hair at least once a week.
- Use conditioner on the ends.
- Rinse well to prevent dandruff.
- Avoid too many hair treatments or blow-drying.
- Trim hair every six weeks.

Care of the hands

- Wash hands, especially after using the toilet.
- Keep nails clean and filed.
- Use hand cream.
- Use rubber gloves when doing the washing up.

Care of the feet

- Wash daily and dry well between the toes.
- Wear good supportive footwear.
- Cut nails straight across.
- Change socks daily.

Homework Assignment 38 P. 135

Respiratory system

The respiratory system takes oxygen from the air when we breathe in and brings it to the cells of the body to make energy. This is called **oxidation**. **Carbon dioxide** is produced as waste and is removed by the respiratory system when we breathe out. The respiratory tract (below) is part of this system.

Nose → Pharynx → Larynx → Trachea → Bronchus → Bronchioles → Alveoli

1. Air passes through the mouth and nose, where it is warmed. Some dust is filtered by the hairs in the nose.
2. Air then passes by the **pharynx** and **larynx** (voice box) and **epiglottis**. The epiglottis is a flap of skin that covers the windpipe when we swallow to stop food from going down the windpipe.
3. Air then passes into the **trachea**, or windpipe. The trachea divides into branches called **bronchi**. Each bronchus divides again and again to form tiny **bronchioles**.
4. At the end of each tiny bronchiole is an **air sac**, or **alveolus** (plural: **alveoli**). Here oxygen and carbon dioxide are exchanged.

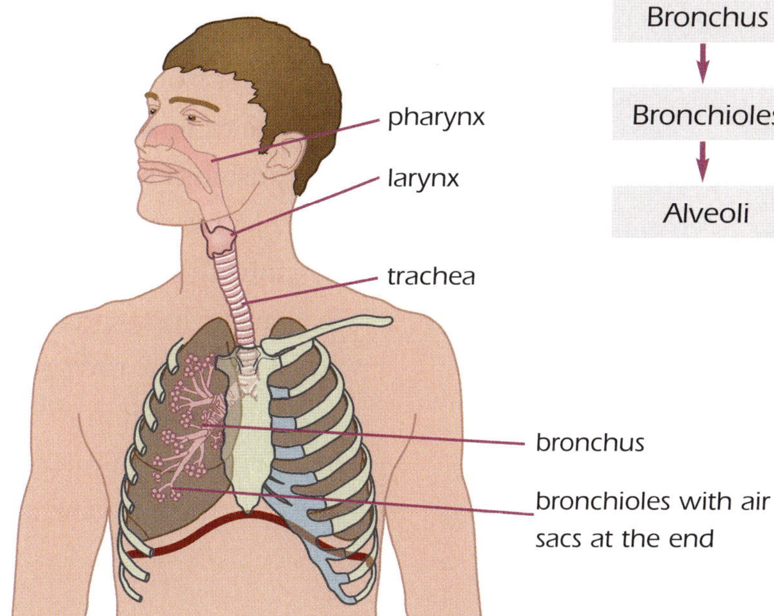

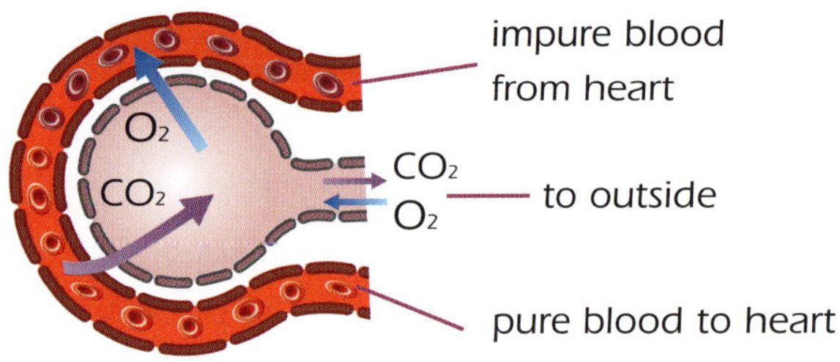

Exchange of gases

The exchange of gases happens in the air sacs (alveoli) of the lungs. The air sacs are surrounded by capillaries. Carbon dioxide is removed from the blood in the capillaries and oxygen is added in its place. This oxygen-rich blood then returns to the heart and is pumped around the body.

Homework Assignment

39 P. 139

Functions of the lungs

- Take in oxygen.
- Remove carbon dioxide and water vapour (see also diseases of the lungs in the section on smoking, pp. 225–6).

Higher Level

Circulatory system

The circulatory system consists of the heart, the blood vessels and the blood. The circulatory system's job is to carry blood full of oxygen and nutrients around the body and then to collect waste products, such as carbon dioxide.

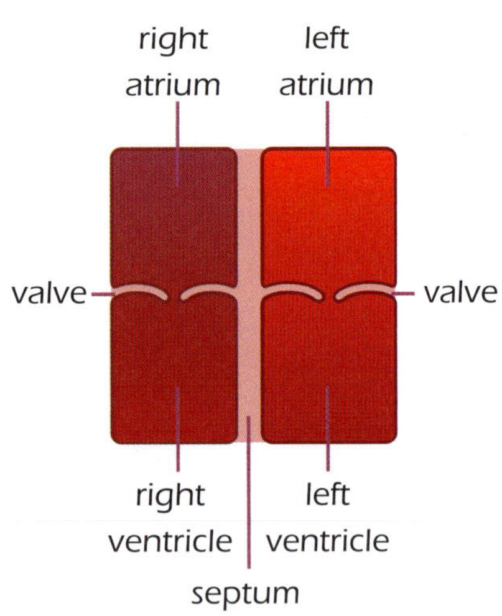

The four chambers of the heart

The heart

The heart is a strong muscular organ that pumps blood either to the lungs (to get oxygen) or around the body. It lies between the lungs in the middle of the chest and is about the size of your fist. The heart has four chambers with a wall called the septum dividing the left and right sides.

Blood flow through the heart

1. Impure blood (full of carbon dioxide) comes into the heart from the rest of the body through the vena cava into the right atrium. The right atrium contracts (squeezes in), pushing the blood through valves into the right ventricle.
2. The blood is then pushed out of the heart through a valve into the pulmonary artery and to the lungs.
3. In the lungs, carbon dioxide is exchanged for oxygen.
4. The blood then returns through the pulmonary veins to the left atrium.
5. The left atrium contracts, pushing blood through a valve into the left ventricle.

6. The left ventricle then contracts, pushing blood through a valve into the aorta.
7. The aorta brings the oxygen-rich blood around the body.
8. The body uses this oxygen and produces carbon dioxide. This carbon dioxide is brought back to the vena cava and the cycle begins again.

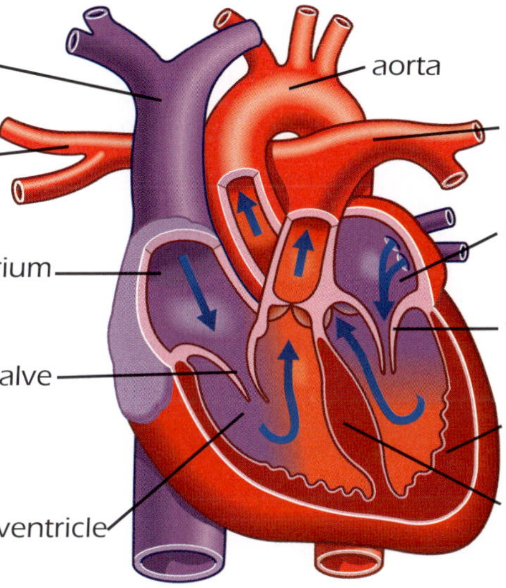

Pulse

The heartbeat is the sound of the valves in the heart opening and closing. Each time the heart beats, blood is forced into the arteries; this can be felt as a pulse. The average pulse is 72 beats per minute. It is usually taken by placing the first two fingertips on the wrist, as shown in the photograph, and counting.

Taking a pulse

Blood vessels

Blood vessels are tubes that carry blood around the body. There are three types:

1. **Artery:** Arteries carry blood away from the heart under pressure. They have thick elastic walls.
2. **Vein:** Veins carry blood to the heart. The blood is not under much pressure, so valves are needed to stop it from flowing backwards. They have thin walls.
3. **Capillary:** Capillaries join arteries and veins. Their walls are only one cell thick. This allows oxygen and nutrients to pass through into the body cells.

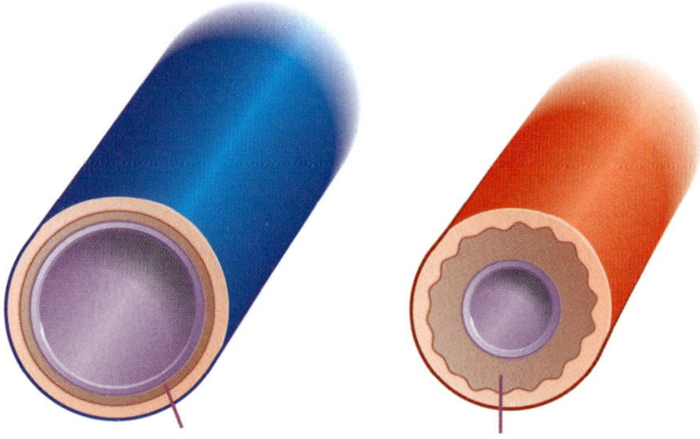

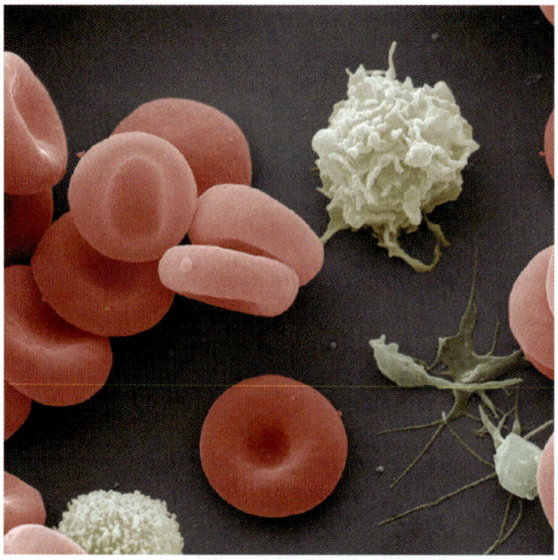
Red blood cells, white blood cells and platelets

Fast food is generally very high in cholesterol

The blood

An adult has approximately 5 litres of blood in their body.

Composition

- **Plasma:** A yellowish liquid in which the blood cells float.
- **Red blood cells:** These disc-shaped cells contain haemoglobin, which carries oxygen around the body. Iron is needed to make haemoglobin.
- **White blood cells:** These fight infection. They surround the germs causing the infection and destroy them. Puss is the result of white blood cells and germs fighting each other.
- **Platelets:** Small cells that clot blood when we get a cut to form a scab.

Functions of the blood

- Transports oxygen, carbon dioxide, nutrients, hormones, enzymes and waste around the body.
- Fights infection (white blood cells).

Coronary heart disease

Sometimes the arteries of the heart become blocked by cholesterol. If this happens, a heart attack occurs and the person's life is at risk. The risk of coronary heart disease can be reduced by decreasing the amount of animal fat in the diet.

Homework Assignment 40 P. 141

CHAPTER 24

Health Education

Teacher's CD-ROM

Slide presentation • Student activity pack – with revision crossword • Class test

In this chapter, you will study:

- Good health.
- Health hazards.

Health

The World Health Organization (WHO) describes health as **a complete state of physical, mental and social well-being and not simply the absence of disease or infirmity**. With this definition in mind, we can list seven general guidelines to good health.

Good health guide

1. Eat a balanced diet.

2. Get enough rest and sleep.

3. Avoid cigarettes, drugs and alcohol.

4. Have good personal hygiene.

5. Take regular exercise.

6. Treat those around you with respect – you in turn will be treated with respect.

7. Think positively about yourself and your experiences (mental well-being).

Healthy diet

Try to follow a balanced diet. Remember the healthy eating guidelines (see Chapter 3):

- Eat less food that is high in fat, salt or sugar, e.g. crisps, cakes, highly processed foods.
- Increase fibre: Eat more fruit, vegetables, brown bread, rice, etc.
- Drink plenty of water.

Exercise

Exercise is vital to good health. Most children do not need to be told to take exercise; they just do it automatically.

Unfortunately, during the late teens and early twenties, many people give up sport and regular exercise. This results in unfitness and weight gain. Habits formed during this time can stay for life.

Benefits of exercise

Relaxation and sleep

Getting enough sleep is vital to good health. For a good night's sleep, avoid having large meals, tea or coffee late in the evening. Stop doing homework or studying at least one hour before bedtime, as your body and mind need to be relaxed for you to sleep well.

Stress is the most common cause of sleeplessness. It is better to treat the stress itself rather than the sleeplessness alone (for example, with sleeping pills, which can be habit-forming).

Leisure time

Leisure time is time spent away from work, school or study. Some people waste their leisure time and then complain about being bored. They say things like, 'There is absolutely nothing to do in this area or town.' This is rarely true. Sometimes leisure facilities are there but people either do not know about them or are unwilling to use them.

Aerobic exercise, such as jogging, step aerobics or playing active sports, works the heart and lungs, making them stronger and healthier.

Mental health

A mentally healthy person generally:

- Feels positive about themselves (positive self-image or high self-esteem).
- Feels positive about the people and world around them.
- Is able to cope with life most of the time.

Mental health guidelines

1. Look after your physical health (good diet, exercise, relaxation and sleep).
2. Do not smoke or use drugs; keep alcohol within healthy limits.
3. Think positively about yourself (see the self-esteem section below).
4. Form a few close, trusting friendships. Do not neglect these friendships, for instance if you have a new boyfriend or girlfriend.
5. Discuss problems and feelings with a trusted friend.
6. Have a good routine in your life, including regular sleep and meals.
7. Make good use of leisure time.
8. Avoid too much stress.

Mental and physical health rely on each other: neglect one and the other suffers

Self-esteem

People who like themselves and have confidence in their abilities have **high self-esteem**. Those who do not think much of themselves or their abilities have **low self-esteem**.

Why do some people have low self-esteem?

During childhood, how others treat us plays an important part in the development of self-esteem. Children who are neglected, abused, criticised or live with family problems such as alcohol abuse or poverty are more likely to have low self-esteem. In adulthood, how we treat **ourselves** has a lot to do with our self-esteem.

The issues below are sometimes linked with low self-esteem.

- Alcohol or drug abuse
- Being very critical of others
- Bullying (bullies usually have low self-esteem)
- Leaving school early
- Mental illness, e.g. depression
- Overeating
- Possessiveness
- Smoking
- Staying in abusive relationships
- Teen pregnancy

Stress

Stress is a normal reaction to difficulties in our lives. Some stress is healthy or else we would become bored. It is when we experience too much stress that problems occur.

Common effects of stress on the mind and body	
Body	**Mind**
Short term:	Anger
Faster breathing	Anxiety
Increased heartbeat	Being easily irritated
Indigestion	Feeling depressed
Sweating	Feeling unable to cope
	Forgetfulness
Long term:	Frustration
Backache	Low self-esteem
Frequent headaches	Tearfulness
High blood pressure	Tension
Prone to infection	Tiredness
Skin problems, e.g. eczema	
Stomach ulcers	

Coping with stress

There are two basic ways of coping with stress:

1. Get rid of the cause of the stress, e.g. reduce your workload.
2. Do something to relieve the symptoms:
   - Eat well.
   - Take physical exercise.
   - Take time to relax.
   - Get enough sleep.
   - Talk over your problems with someone you trust.

Health hazards

Every year in Ireland, thousands of people die prematurely because they expose themselves to health hazards such as smoking, excessive alcohol and illegal drugs use.

Smoking

Effects of smoking

Emphysema

Emphysema is a serious, incurable disease of the lungs. Ninety per cent of people with the disease are smokers. Someone with emphysema has great difficulty in breathing or doing anything that needs energy, such as climbing stairs.

Passive smoking

Passive smoking means inhaling other people's smoke. Frequent passive smokers run the same health risks as smokers.

Smoking during pregnancy

If you smoke, your baby smokes too.

- There is an increased risk of the baby miscarrying or being stillborn.
- Babies of smokers are smaller and more likely to be premature. While even very premature babies often live nowadays, they can be left with permanent problems such as cerebral palsy, blindness, deafness and lung problems.
- Smoking near a baby either before or after it is born increases the risk of cot death.
- The children of smokers are more likely to smoke themselves.

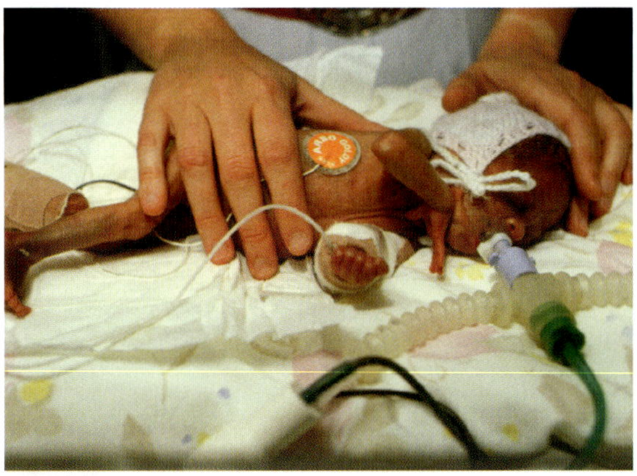

Babies of smokers are more likely to be born premature

It is widely believed that giving up smoking is as difficult as giving up heroin. So why do so many young people start each year? Curiosity? Image? Peer pressure? What do you think?

Alcohol

When taken in moderation, alcohol can be a positive social substance. Historically, however, the Irish have had a very unusual relationship with alcohol. We have tended to either not drink at all or else drink to excess. In fact, it is estimated that one in 10 Irish adults are problem drinkers (previously termed alcoholics).

A person is considered to be a problem drinker when alcohol is causing a problem in their home, at school, in their social life or at work, e.g. missing a day from work because of a hangover.

Moderate social drinking

Safe alcohol limits spread over the week

Fully grown men: 21 units per week

Fully grown women: 14 units per week

One unit = half a pint of beer or lager, a small measure of spirits or a glass of wine

Effects of alcohol abuse on the mind and body

Short term:

- Face turns red.
- Loss of inhibitions, e.g. has unprotected sex.
- Mood alters: drinker may become aggressive, sad, etc.
- Vomiting.
- Lack of co-ordination, e.g. staggering.
- Poor driving skills: A 17-year-old male driver is 40 times more likely to have an accident after one and a half to two units of alcohol.

Long term:

- Addiction.
- Brain damage.
- Mental illness, e.g. depression.
- Heart disease.
- Liver disease (cirrhosis).
- Cancer of the mouth or stomach.
- Foetal alcohol syndrome (birth defects caused by drinking during pregnancy).

Effects of alcohol abuse on the family

- General unhappiness and uncertainty in the family: 'Will he/she be drunk tonight?'
- Separation and divorce.
- Violence in the home.
- Financial problems.

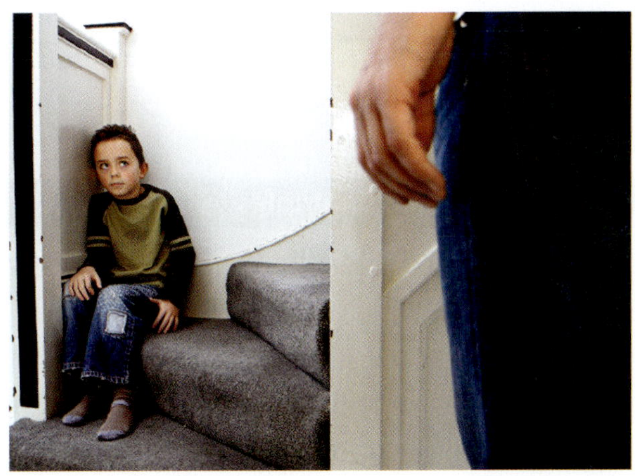

Alcohol is often a factor in child abuse cases

Effects of alcohol abuse on society

- Road accidents: In 2003, alcohol was a factor in almost 40 per cent of fatal road accidents, killing 123 people.
- Crime: Some people become violent when drunk.
- Cost of treating people for alcohol-related health problems.
- Absenteeism: People not turning up for work because of alcohol abuse.

Help for those affected by alcohol abuse

- Alcoholics Anonymous (help for the problem drinker themselves): (01) 842 0700; www.alcoholicsanonymous.ie.
- Al Anon (help for families and friends of problem drinkers): (01) 873 2699; www.al-anon-ireland.org.
- Al Ateen (help for the teenage children of problem drinkers): (01) 873 2699; www.al-anon-ireland.org.

Note: These are all central numbers/websites; they will direct you to local services.

Drugs

Classification

Drugs can be classified in two ways: according to their effect on the body (see table below) or their legal status.

Legal status

Drugs can be legal, e.g. caffeine, nicotine and alcohol; illegal, e.g. cannabis, cocaine; or restricted, e.g. Valium, which is only available through a prescription.

Type	Examples	Effects
Depressants	Alcohol	Slows down the nervous system, making the person relaxed but uncoordinated.
Hallucinogens	LSD, magic mushrooms, solvents, ecstasy, cannabis	Causes changes in mood and thought patterns, may hear and see things in a different way to reality.
Sedatives	Sleeping tablets, cannabis, tranquillisers, e.g. Valium	Relief of tension/anxiety, causes sleep, physical and psychological dependence.
Opiates	Heroin, methadone, morphine	Feelings of euphoria (intense pleasure) but highly addictive.
Stimulants	Caffeine, nicotine, ecstasy, cocaine	Increases heart rate and breathing, prevents sleep. Feelings of intense well-being and energy (ecstasy and cocaine).

Effects of drug abuse on the individual and their families

- Health problems, e.g. HIV, from sharing dirty needles, weight loss, cancer if drug is smoked.
- Physical, psychological and social addiction makes it difficult for the addict to cope with life without the drug.
- Loss of self-respect: An addict will do anything to get the drug.
- Loss of ambition: For example, regular cannabis use can have a huge effect on a young person's desire to do well at school, in sport, etc.
- Mental illness, e.g. depression, paranoia.
- Families and children of addicts may suffer poverty, worry, neglect and abuse.

Effects of drug abuse on society

- Crime: Many addicts steal to support their habits.
- Cost to the taxpayer.
- Addicts strain an already stretched health care system.
- Welfare payments for addicts unfit to work.

Health Education

Unit 4
RESOURCE MANAGEMENT AND HOME STUDIES

CHAPTER 25

Home Management

Teacher's CD-ROM

Slide presentation • Student activity pack • Class test

The tasks involved in running the home include:

- Budgeting
- Child care
- Cleaning and maintenance
- Cooking
- Gardening
- Laundry
- Shopping

Well, someone's got to do it, dear.

Some of these tasks need to be done daily, others weekly or less often. In order to make sure they get done, planning is needed. **Home management is the efficient running of the home.** When a home is run efficiently, money is not wasted, the home is kept clean and tidy, laundry is done and the family tends to eat more healthily. Because of today's busy lifestyles, efficient home management is even more important. **All family members should be involved in the running of the home.** Good home management means using **resources** wisely to achieve **goals**.

Resources

Resources are what we use to carry out the tasks listed above. There are four basic resources.

Basic resources

1. Time.

2. Human energy.

3. Skill.

4. Money (and what money can buy).

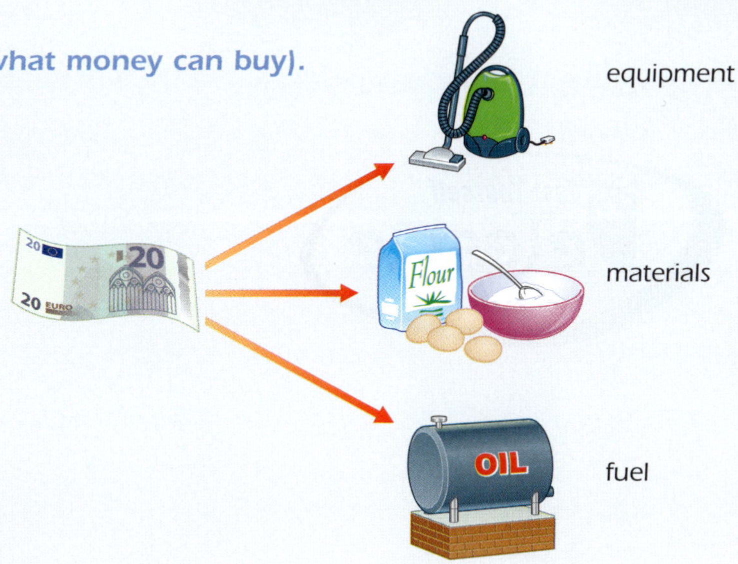

A good management system

A good management system allows you to achieve what you set out to achieve and involves five steps:

1. **Goals:** Decide what it is you want to achieve, e.g. provide healthy family meals for the week.
2. **Resources:** Think about everything you need to carry out for the tasks involved, e.g. time, food, equipment, etc.
3. **Plan:** For example, make out menus for the week, make out a shopping list, etc.
4. **Action:** Carry out the action, e.g. make out a shopping list, buy the food, cook the food.
5. **Evaluate:** How well did you achieve your goals? If they were not achieved, why not? What could you do better next time?

Weekly cleaning roster/work routine

1. List all the jobs that need to be done and divide them up according to how often they have to be done.
   - Daily, e.g. dishes, make beds.
   - Weekly, e.g. vacuum stairs, change beds.
   - Occasionally, e.g. wash windows.
2. Divide the jobs according to how much free time the person has and how old they are (for example, a young child cannot be expected to cook dinner).
3. Make sure two or three weekly jobs are done every day and that one occasional job is done every week.
4. Try out the roster and change if necessary.

Homework Assignment 42 P. 150

Test Yourself eTest.ie

CHAPTER 26

Home Design and Room Planning

Teacher's CD-ROM

Slide presentation • Student activity pack • Class test

Shelter is a basic human need. Even though house prices in Ireland remain relatively high, a large percentage of Irish people are homeowners.

Types of accommodation

- **Houses:** Bungalow, two to three storeys, detached, semi-detached, terraced.
- **Apartments:** Purpose-built or a large house divided into flats or bedsits (one room).
- **Institutions:** Convents, hostels (such as Homeless Aid), boarding schools, nursing homes.
- **Sheltered housing:** A number of small housing units built together, for example for elderly or disabled people; there is a warden and sometimes a doctor or nurse on call.
- **Caravan, mobile home:** Used by the Irish Travelling community. Young people sometimes live in mobile homes on site while their house is being built to save spending money on rent.

Sheltered housing

Making a house a home

A house simply provides shelter; a home also contains people and their unique possessions. It provides for other needs as well.

- **Physical needs:** Shelter, warmth and protection.
- **Emotional needs:** Safety, security, love, privacy (curtains are one of the first things people buy for a new home).

- **Social needs:** It is at home that we learn our basic social skills, e.g. table manners, as children. People feel comfortable and can be themselves at home.

Choosing a home

Choice of housing is usually influenced by:

- **Cost:** Is it within my price range?
- **Location:** Is it close to work, family, etc.?
- **Size:** Is it big enough for my needs, e.g. a growing family?
- **Style of house:** Do I like the overall style of the house, how it is laid out, etc.?

Design

Good design is when something is safe, functional, attractive to look at and hard-wearing.

Features of design include:

- Function.
- Form (shape and line).
- Colour.
- Pattern.
- Texture.

What shapes do you see in this modern kitchen?

Function

Products that are well designed do what they are meant to do or serve their function. For example, a vegetable peeler must be able to peel vegetables, a lunchbox must stay closed in a schoolbag.

Form (shape and line)

Shape

Most objects in the home, rooms and even houses themselves use four basic shapes: square, rectangle, triangle and circle.

Line

Lines in rooms, houses, furniture, clothing or objects can be vertical, horizontal or curved. Each creates a different effect.

Vertical lines cause the eye to look up and down. They make things look taller and narrower. For example, if you wanted to make the ceiling in a room look higher, you could use vertically striped wallpaper.

Horizontal lines make things look shorter and wider. For example, if you wanted to make the ceiling in a room look lower in order to make the room look cosier, then you could use horizontal striped wallpaper.

Curved lines appear soft and feminine.

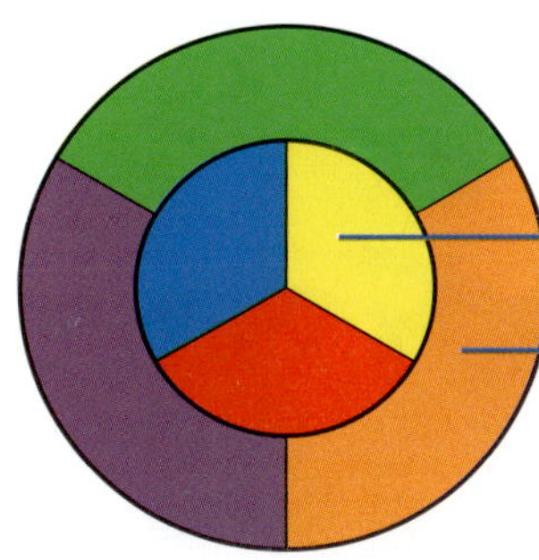

The colour wheel

Colour

Colour is an important element of design, especially interior design. Paint a room white and you will create a feeling of light and space. Paint that same room plum and it will feel smaller and cosier.

The colour wheel

- **Primary colours:** Blue, yellow, red.
- **Secondary colours:** Two primary colours mixed.
- **Tertiary colours:** One primary colour and one secondary colour mixed, e.g. blue + green = turquoise.

Warm colour adds interest to pastels and neutrals

Describing colours

Colours can be described as being warm, cool, neutral or pastel. Each of these can be used to create a different effect in the home.

Warm colours: Vibrant warm colours such as reds, oranges, pinks and purples are very rich. When used alone they make a room look much smaller than it is. They are best used in small amounts with neutrals or pastels. For example, paint three walls white with one wall a rich, warm colour.

Cool colours like blue and green create an atmosphere that is cool and restful. Best used in warm, sunny rooms.

Pastels like light blue, green, pink and yellow are also restful and are ideal for bedrooms.

Neutral colours: Black, white, cream and beige are often called neutral colours. Interest can be added to neutral colours by adding splashes of strong colour.

Cool colours

Pastels

Neutral colours

- **A shade:** Black is added to a colour to darken it.
- **A tint:** White is added to a colour to lighten it.

Pattern

Pattern can add interest to a room. Too much pattern makes a room look crowded and untidy. It is possible, however, to have several different patterns in a room if you keep their colour the same.

Texture

Texture describes how an object feels: rough, smooth, warm or cool.

- Smooth texture, e.g. the texture of tiles and painted surfaces, gives a cool, clean, hygienic feel.
- Rough texture, e.g. the texture of carpets and curtains, absorbs sound and gives a warm, cosy feel.

Good use of pattern

Smooth texture – clean and hygienic.

Rough textures add warmth and interest

Higher Level

There are four important elements in design. These apply well to interior design.

- **Proportion:** This relates to the size of objects. Pieces of furniture in a room should be *in proportion* to each other and to the room. For example, a large antique table would be *out of proportion* in a small apartment.
- **Emphasis:** When the eye is drawn towards something in the room. This is called the *focal point*, e.g. a fireplace.

- **Balance:** When there is an equal spread of colour, pattern and texture in a room.
- **Rhythm:** This is where a colour, shape or pattern links or ties a room together. Look at the room in the photo.

An example of rhythm. What colour is tying this room together?

Room planning

When planning or redecorating any room, consider each of the following.

- **Likes and dislikes** of the person planning or living with the room.
- **Money available** for decoration.
- **Function:** Which room are you planning? If it is a sitting room, it needs to be comfortable and relaxing. A kitchen, on the other hand, needs to be hygienic and easy to work in.
- **Existing fixtures and fittings:** Doors, windows, fireplaces and radiators cannot easily be moved and need to be considered in a plan.
- **Heating and lighting:** This must be decided upon early, as rewiring, etc. may need to be done.
- **Storage:** A room with little storage will be difficult to keep tidy. Plan plenty of storage space.
- **Traffic flow:** Furniture should be placed so that people can walk around the room without bumping into it. Do not put too much furniture into a room.
- **Colour:** The colour you choose for a room will often depend on its aspect, that is, whether it is north or south facing. North-facing rooms tend to get less sun, so warm colours are often used. South-facing rooms get lots of sun, so cool colours can be used.
- **Pattern and texture:** The use of pattern and texture can add interest to a room.

Floor plan

When planning a room, it is wise to make a floor plan. The room outline should be drawn **to scale** on graph paper. Fixtures such as doors and windows are then drawn in. Furniture can be drawn to scale, cut out and then moved around on the floor plan until the best arrangement is achieved.

Kitchen design

A kitchen must:

- Be hygienic and easy to keep clean.
- Be efficient – not too much walking between the fridge, sink and cooker.
- Have enough storage space.
- Be bright and well ventilated.
- Be safe to work in.

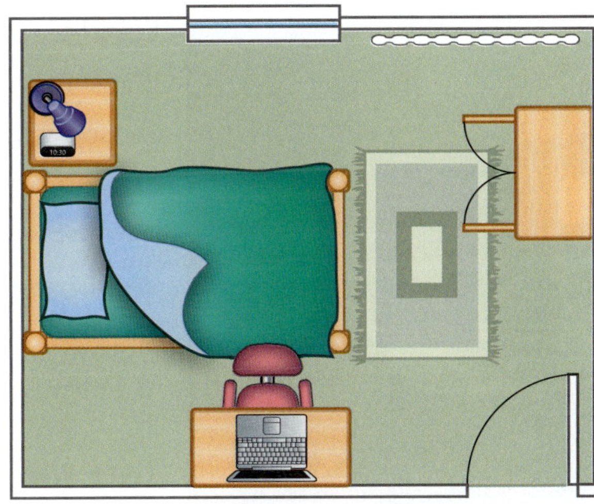

A floor plan

Ergonomics

Higher Level

Ergonomics is the study of how efficiently people work. Design has a lot to do with ergonomics. In a badly designed workplace, frequently used pieces of equipment will not be conveniently located.

The work triangle

The fridge, sink and cooker are the three pieces of equipment used most in the kitchen. It makes sense to locate them near each other in an invisible triangle. There should be work surfaces in between.

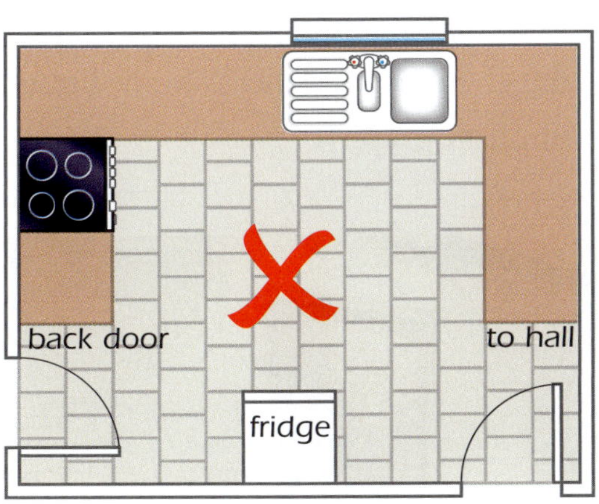

Too much walking between the fridge, sink and cooker

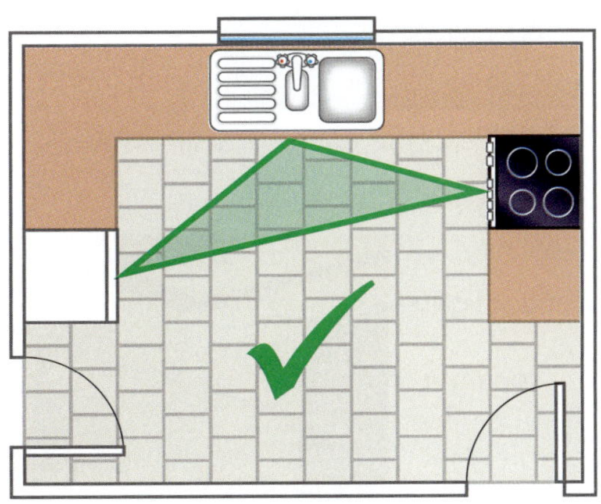

A well-designed kitchen – note the work triangle

Flooring

There is a wide variety of types of flooring on the market. The type you choose will depend on the type of room it is being used for, personal taste and money available. Common floor coverings include carpets, wooden floors and laminates, tiles and vinyl.

A room with a richly papered feature wall

Walls

Walls may be painted, papered or tiled. What wall covering is chosen will usually depend on the type of room being decorated, the condition of the walls, personal taste, fashion trends and cost. Because so much of a room is taken up with wall space, care should be taken when choosing colours for walls. Avoid using paper or paint that is too overpowering. Sometimes a rich paper or paint can be used on one **feature wall**.

Soft furnishings

Soft furnishings can be used in every room in the house and include curtains, blinds, cushions, rugs, duvet covers, pillows and throws, lampshades, soft covers on chairs, tablecloths and table runners. Soft furnishings create interest in a room and also make the room appear warmer and cosier.

A bed dressed with soft furnishings

Lighting

Good lighting is needed to prevent eyestrain and accidents in the home. Lighting is also a great interior design tool and can add a special atmosphere to a room. Most rooms have a large central light. This light can be supported by other, smaller ones, such as table lamps, standard lamps, wall lights, spotlights, etc. (see photograph).

Homework Assignment

43 P. 151

CHAPTER 27

Services to the Home

Teacher's CD-ROM

Slide presentation • Student activity pack • Class test

Electricity

Electricity is a form of energy produced and/or supplied in Ireland by the Electricity Supply Board (ESB) and, more recently, Airtricity and Bord Gáis. Electricity is produced by the movement of either wind or water or by burning fuels such as gas, turf, oil or coal.

When the electricity leaves the power station, it travels in huge **service cables** to a **main fuse** on the outside of our homes. Electricity enters the house through the **fuse box** and then goes to all the light fittings and sockets in the house.

The amount of electricity used is recorded by an **electricity meter**. Sometimes there are two meters, one for cheaper **Night Saver** electricity (night-time) and one for the daytime. Households are sent a bill every two months.

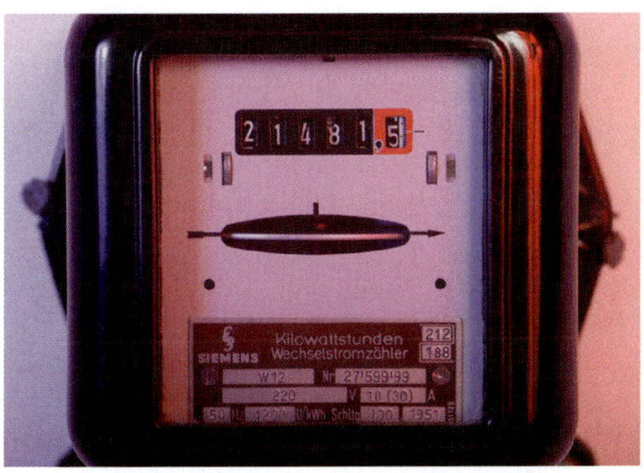

Electricity meter

Modern fuse box

Modern fuse boxes do not contain actual fuses. Instead, they contain switches called **circuit breakers**. These switches click off if there is a fault. They are easily switched on again when the fault is corrected.

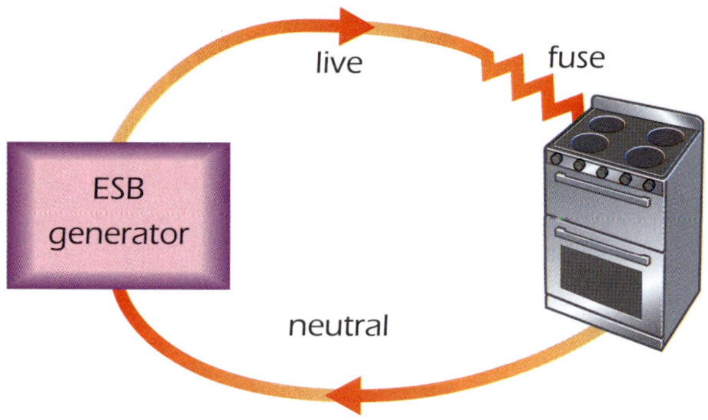

Electrical circuit

Electrical circuit

Electricity always travels in a circuit, or circle. A **fuse** or **circuit breaker** is a deliberate weak link in this circuit. If anything goes wrong, the fuse will blow or the switch will flick off on the circuit breaker and the circuit will break. This stops the electricity flowing. Circuit breakers can be found in the main fuse box of the house and in fuses in electric plugs.

All electrical appliances must have at least two wires:

- Live (brown).
- Neutral (blue).

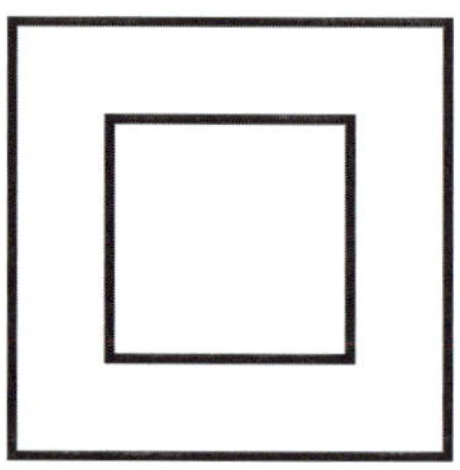
Doubly insulated

The **live** wire brings electricity to the appliances in our homes and the **neutral** wire returns to the ESB/Bord Gáis generator. A third wire called the **earth** wire (yellow and green) is for safety. If something goes wrong, electricity will flow to the ground through this earth wire and not through the person using the appliance. Appliances with no earth wire should be doubly insulated and carry this symbol.

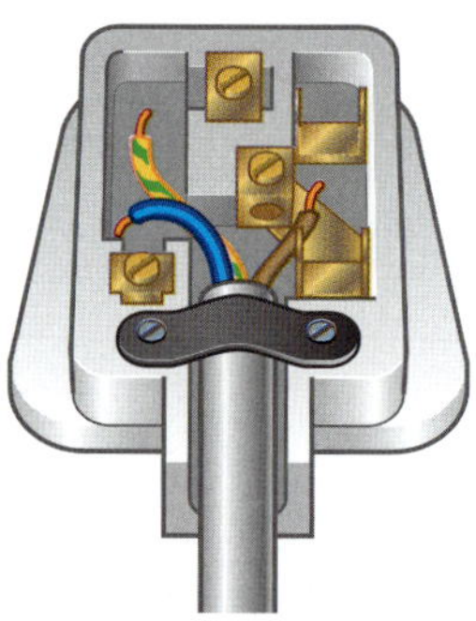

Wiring a plug

- Open the plug top.
- Clamp the wire into the plug top.
- Trim three small wires to size.
- Screw each wire into the correct place.
- Replace the fuse and top of plug.

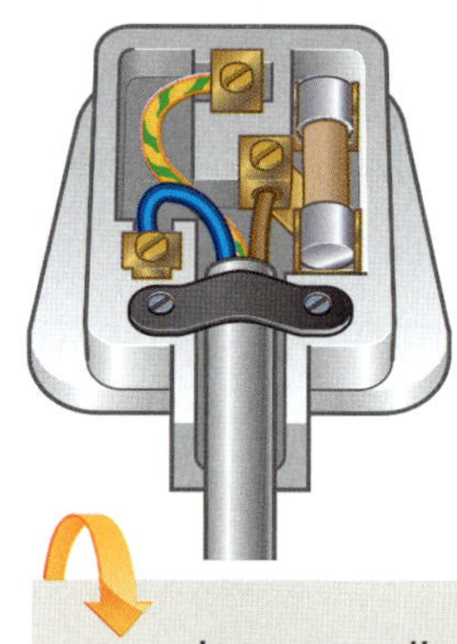

brown = live
blue = neutral
green and yellow = earth

Domestic wind turbine

Domestic wind turbines

With rising fuel costs, an increasing number of households are producing their own electricity. One way of doing this is by having a domestic wind turbine like the one pictured. Turbines supply the household with electricity and excess energy produced can be sold to the national grid. At times when there is no wind, electricity can be bought from the ESB, Bord Gáis or Airtricity in the normal way. Some systems have huge batteries that allow for energy storage at times when there is no wind. Turbines are expensive to buy but pay for themselves within a few years.

Electrical safety

Never touch anything electrical with wet hands.

Never bring portable electrical appliances (except a razor) into the bathroom.

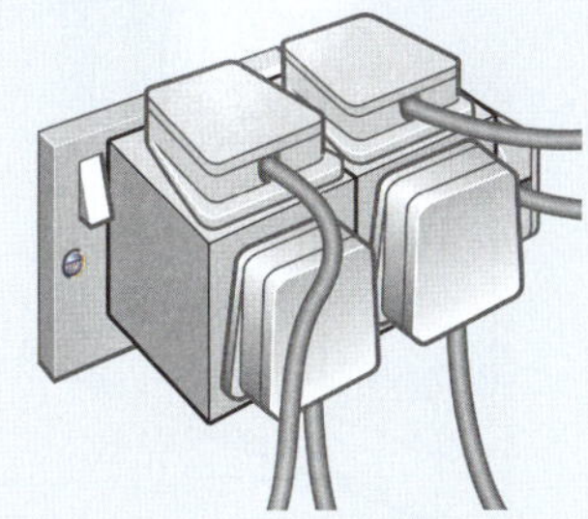

Don't overload sockets.

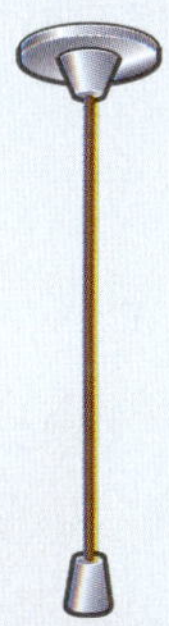

The bathroom light switch must be outside the door or on a pull cord.

Replace damaged flexes; do not try to repair them.

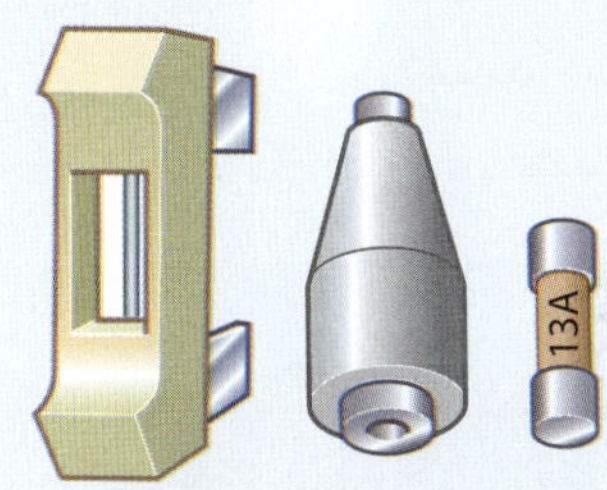

Use the correct size of fuse.

Gas

There are two types of gas available in Ireland.

1. **Natural gas:** Natural gas is piped ashore in gas pipelines from under the seabed. These large gas pipelines branch off and a smaller line enters the house through a meter control valve. This records how much gas is used and also is where the gas can be turned off if necessary.
2. **Bottled gas:** Available in tanks or cylinders.

A natural gas fire is clean and attractive but not very warm

Gas safety

- Gas can be dangerous: appliances should be fitted only by a qualified person and serviced regularly.
- Gas needs proper ventilation. Gas used in a badly ventilated room can, and does, kill. Never block wall vents.

If you smell gas, act quickly

Do open doors and windows.

Do check if the flame has gone out on an appliance and the gas has been left on.

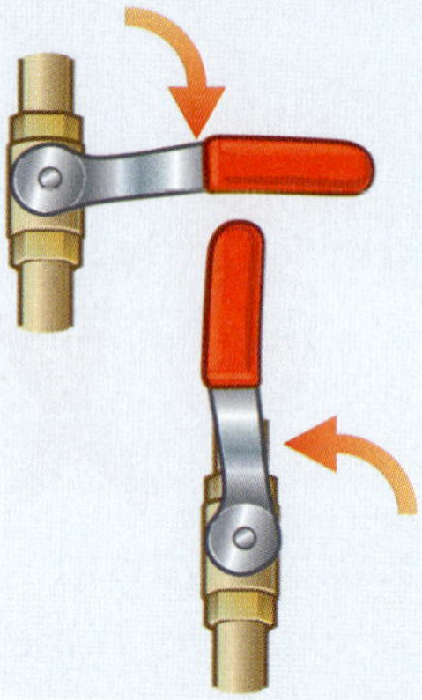

If not, turn the gas off at the meter valve.

Do call the gas company from a neighbour's house or from your mobile phone once you are out of the house.

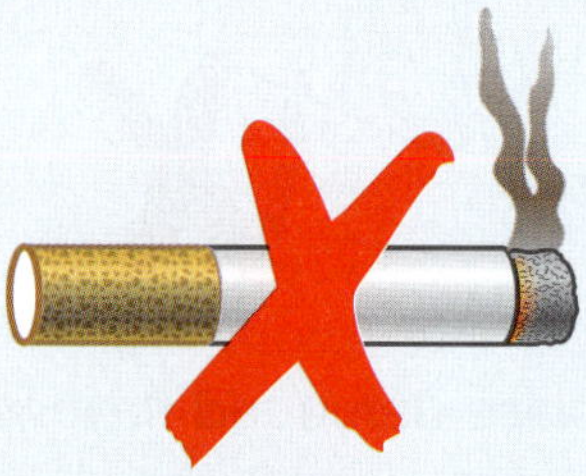

Don't smoke or light matches. Never use a lighted flame to look for gas leaks – it is explosive.

Don't use anything electrical – even a light switch or mobile phone – inside, as they can give off a tiny spark and cause the gas to ignite.

Water

Water is the most basic service to our homes. Fresh water is supplied to our homes by the corporation (urban), county council (rural) or by private water schemes (rural). Water is collected in a lake or a man-made reservoir and from there it goes to a treatment plant to be cleaned.

Note: Individual households not on any of these schemes will have to dig their own well when building their house.

Water treatment

1. Filtered to remove impurities.
2. Chlorine added to kill bacteria.
3. Fluoride added for strong bones and teeth.

Clean water travels in a **mains pipe** to the houses of the area. Water enters each individual house through a **service pipe**. There is a valve on this pipe that can turn the water off.

Fresh water goes directly to the kitchen sink and also fills the tank in the attic. Water from this tank supplies the toilet, cold taps in the bathroom and the cylinder in the hot press.

Water may be heated in the house in a number of ways:

- Immersion heater in the tank in the hot press.
- Instantaneous water heaters, e.g. electric showers.
- Back boiler behind an open fire or stove.
- Central heating system that also heats the water.
- Solar panels.

The kitchen sink

The kitchen sink is usually placed under a window. There are several reasons for this:

- Light.
- Ventilation.
- Easily plumbed.
- It is nice to look out the window while working.

A ceramic Belfast sink

Kitchen sinks are usually made from stainless steel (Belfast sinks are ceramic) because it is hygienic, durable and does not stain. All sinks have an S- or U-bend. The S- or U-bend stops germs and smells from coming back up the plughole. Sinks can become blocked by substances, especially grease.

Unblocking a sink

1. Cover overflow with a cloth. Place a plunger over the plughole and plunge up and down. If this does not work, try step 2
2. Put washing soda in the plughole and rinse down with boiling water; plunge again. If this does not work, try step 3.
3. Place a basin under the U-bend, unscrew it and remove whatever is blocking the sink with a piece of wire clothes hanger. Flush out and replace the U-bend.

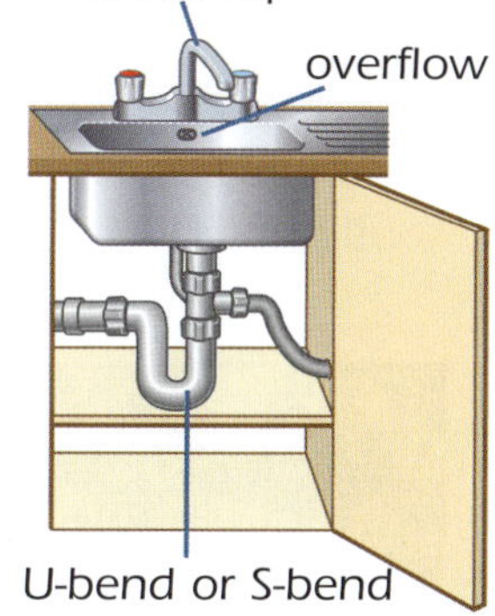

Burst pipes

Pipes may freeze in cold weather. Water expands when frozen and in this way cracks the pipes. It is not until the pipes thaw again and flooding occurs that we notice a problem.

What to do:

- Turn off the water at the mains.
- Run cold taps to clear the pipes.
- Turn off heating.
- Call a plumber.

The sun

Lighting

Types of lighting

Filament bulb

1. The sun.
2. Tungsten filament bulbs will be a thing of the past from 2010. They shall be replaced by other, more energy-efficient light bulbs.
3. Halogen bulbs are a variation on the tungsten filament bulb in that they have a tungsten filament but are also filled with halogen gas, which makes them more efficient. Halogen bulbs give off a good light, but are expensive and heat up, so care must be taken with regard to where they are placed.

A modern kitchen with halogen spotlights

4. Fluorescent tubes are glass tubes 0.5–2.5m long. They last for approximately 3,000 hours but give off a cold, clinical light.
5. Compact fluorescent lamps (CFLs) are expensive to buy but last approximately 8,000 hours. They are cheap to run (they use 80 per cent less electricity than tungsten) but give a cold, clinical light.
6. Light-emitting diodes (LED) are bulbs without a filament. They are very economical and long lasting and they do not heat up like halogen bulbs, but are not very bright.

Fluorescent tube

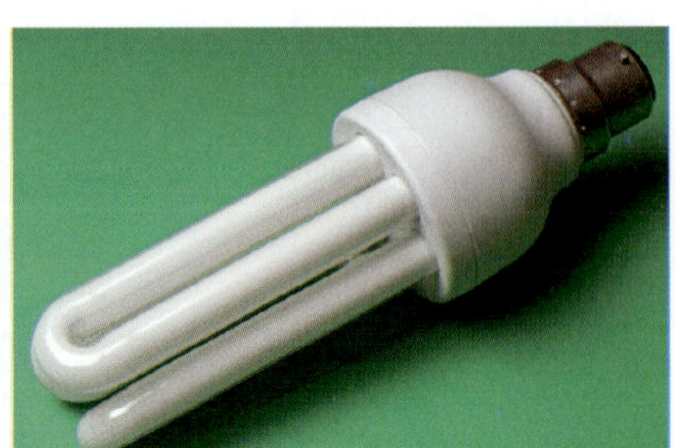
CFL

LED bulb

Heating and insulation

Methods of heat transfer

Heat can be transferred from a heat source such as a fire to a person in three ways:

1. **Conduction** (heat travels along something solid and the entire object becomes hot). A **storage heater** heats by conduction. Heat travels through bricks in the heater, the bricks become hot and begin giving off heat (by convection).
2. **Convection** (air or water is heated, rises and is replaced by cool air or water – the cycle continues). A **fan heater** heats by convection. It takes cold air in at the bottom, the element inside warms the air and gives off hot air at the top.
3. **Radiation** (heat rays heat the object or person they shine on). A **bar fire** heats by radiation. It heats whatever it shines on, not the air in between.

Storage heater

Fan heater

Ways a home can be heated

1. **Central heating:** A boiler or stove (fuelled by gas, oil, wood, wood pellets, etc.) is connected by metal pipes to radiators in each room or to a network of rods under the floor (under-floor heating). Water heated by the boiler or stove runs to the radiators or the under-floor pipes, heating each room as it goes. The main **advantage** of central heating is that it keeps the whole house at a comfortably warm temperature and it is cheaper than heating each room with individual heaters.
2. **Individual heaters:** Storage heaters use off-peak electricity and can be left on. Others are used for shorter periods of time, such as gas 'supersers', open fires and stand-alone stoves. Individual heaters are expensive if they are used as the only source of heat in a house but can be useful as an extra source of heat on particularly cold nights or as a feature or focal point, e.g. open fire.

Bar heater

A wood-burning stove can also heat water and radiators

Fuels

There is a wide variety of fuels available to households. Each has both advantages and disadvantages.

Fuel	Advantages	Disadvantages
Oil	Convenient and easily available Gives off a strong heat	Cost variable, dependant on world oil prices It's a fossil fuel – not good for environment Storage tank is unsightly and oil can be stolen from it
Gas	Clean and efficient Can be used for both heating and cooking Natural gas on the mains, so it won't run out Sourced in Ireland	Natural gas is not available in all parts of the country Gas cylinders are awkward and can run out Dangerous if leaks occur or if used in unventilated rooms
Coal and slack	Widely available Gives off a strong heat Little waste, can be bought in quantities required	Dirty to use and store It's a fossil fuel – not good for environment Hassle cleaning out the fire after use Can't be lit on its own
Wood	Cheap and freely available Environmentally friendly if wood is sourced from renewable forests Visually attractive	Burns quickly and doesn't give off as much heat as other fuels Bulky, difficult to store Environmental impact if wood is not sourced from renewable forests
Wood pellets	Cheaper than oil or gas Give off a strong heat Environmentally friendly if wood waste or wood from renewable source is used	Not widely available If bought in bulk, storage can be a problem
Briquettes and turf	Cheap and widely available Sourced in Ireland Light easily	Burn quickly and don't give off as much heat as other fuels

Wood pellets

Thermostats and timers

Digital room thermostat

Thermostats and timers control when your heating system is switched on and off.

Thermostats can be set for a certain temperature, such as 21°C in a living room. Once that temperature is reached, the thermostat switches the heating system off.

Thermostats can be on:

- The central heating boiler itself.
- Each radiator.
- The wall in each room (these can be dial or digital).

Radiator thermostat

Timers can be set to switch the heating on or off at various times during the day or night. For example, the heating can be set to come on two hours before you return home in the evening.

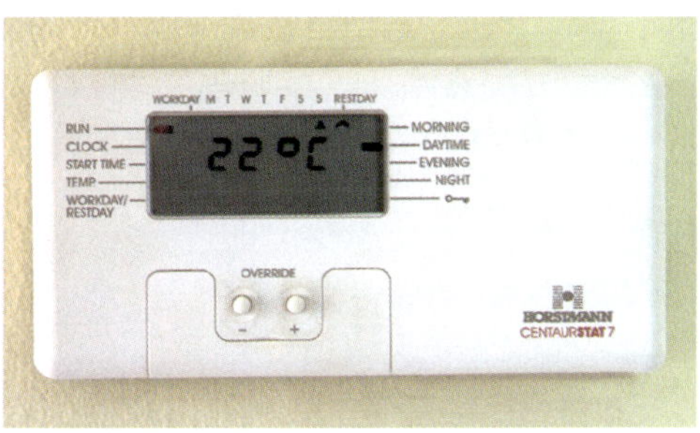

Digital central heating timer

Insulation

Insulation means trapping heat in the house. A house with poor insulation loses up to 75 per cent of its heat and will be cold, draughty and expensive to run. Windows, roofs, walls, floors and doors should all be insulated with materials that are *bad conductors of heat*. Bad conductors do not let heat pass through them easily. Examples of bad conductors are air, fabric, fibreglass and polystyrene.

Heat loss from an uninsulated house

Attic

Fibreglass, wool, condensed foam or foam pellets are laid on the floor of the attic to prevent heat loss through the roof.

An insulated attic

Cavity wall insulation

Walls

Modern houses have cavity walls. This means that there are two rows of blocks or bricks (or one row and a timber frame) with a gap between them. Trapped air, along with other insulation materials, stops heat from escaping from the house through the walls.

Floors

Carpet and carpet underlay are both bad conductors/good insulators.

Draft excluders

Windows

Double-glazed windows help insulate the house because there is air trapped between the panes of glass. Air is a bad conductor/good insulator.

Double-glazed window

Draughts

Heavy curtains or draught excluders can prevent heat loss through windows, doors and letterboxes.

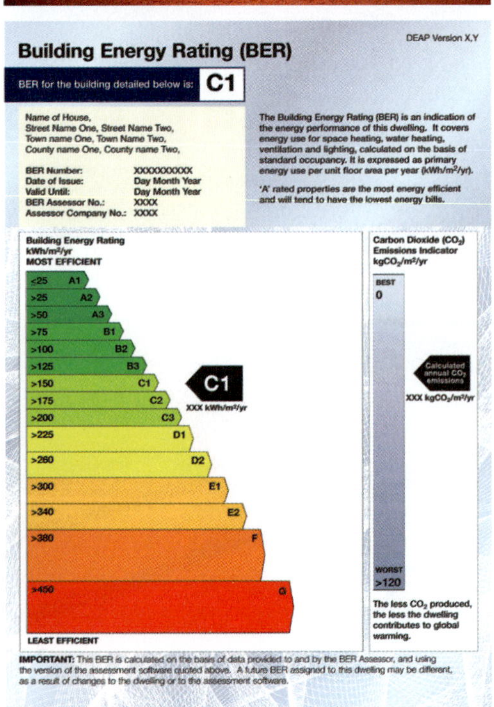

BER certificate

Building Energy Rating

A Building Energy Rating (BER) is similar to the energy label on your fridge, with a scale of A to G. A-rated homes are the most energy efficient, while G is the least efficient. Since 1 January 2009, a BER certificate is compulsory for all homes being sold or rented. So if you wish to sell or rent a house, you will have to have your house assessed by a registered BER assessor in order to get your certificate. The assessor will also advise you on how you can improve the energy rating of your home.

Ventilation and condensation

Ventilation

A good ventilation system replaces stale air with fresh air without causing a draught. Ventilation is needed to:

- Provide fresh air (rich in oxygen).
- Remove stale air (high in carbon dioxide).
- Control humidity (the amount of moisture in the air).
- Prevent condensation.
- Prevent the room from getting too warm and stuffy.

Methods of ventilation include doors, windows, fireplace, wall vents, extractor fans (kitchen and bathrooms) and cooker hoods.

Condensation

Condensation occurs when warm, humid air (full of water vapour) comes in contact with a cold surface, e.g. a window. If a room frequently has a lot of condensation, then dampness can result. This will cause wallpaper and paints to mould, metals to rust and wood to rot. It will also cause the room to smell musty and unpleasant.

Condensation can be controlled by good ventilation, good insulation and a good heating system.

Mould caused by condensation

Conserving resources in the home

- Choose appliances with a good energy efficiency rating (A or B).
- Fit the hot water cylinder with a lagging jacket (new cylinders come ready insulated).
- Have showers instead of baths – they use less water.
- Fit thermostats and timers and only heat rooms if they are in use.
- Use CFL bulbs and switch off lights when not in use.
- Don't leave TVs, computers, DVDs and computer games on standby, as they use electricity in this mode – switch them off.
- Wait until there is a full load before using the dishwasher or washing machine. Where possible, dry clothes outside.
- Only boil the amount of water you need in the kettle.
- Insulate the home well and exclude draughts.

Homework Assignment
44 P. 156

Test Yourself eTest.ie

CHAPTER 28

Technology in the Home

Teacher's CD-ROM

Slide presentation • Student activity pack • Class test

Advances in technology have made running the home very different than it was even 30 or 40 years ago.

- Washing and caring for clothes have been made much easier by automatic washing machines, tumble dryers and electric steam irons.
- Dishwashers and vacuum cleaners (including central vacuum systems) allow us to wash dishes and clean carpets and floors more efficiently.
- Food preparation and storage are aided by equipment such as freezers, refrigerators, microwaves, food processors, modern cookers, etc.
- The internet can be used for shopping, gathering information, booking holidays, banking online, sending e-mail, etc.

Modern household appliances

There are three basic types of household appliance:

1. Appliances with a motor (noisy), e.g. vacuum cleaner, electric knife, food processor.
2. Appliances with a heating element, e.g. toaster, heater, kettle, cooker.
3. Appliances with both a motor and an element (may not be a heating element), e.g. washing machine, dishwasher, fridge and freezer.

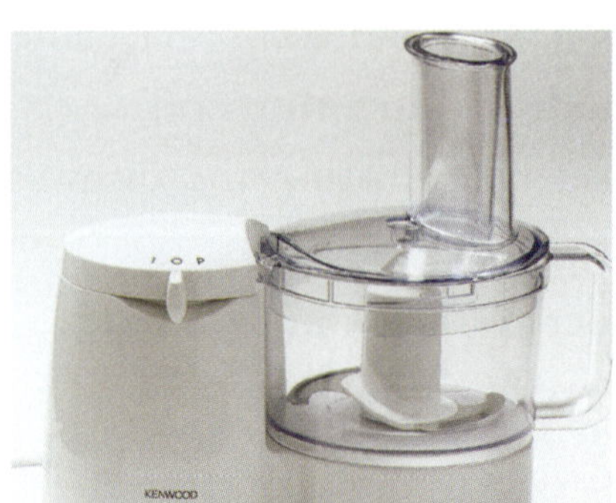

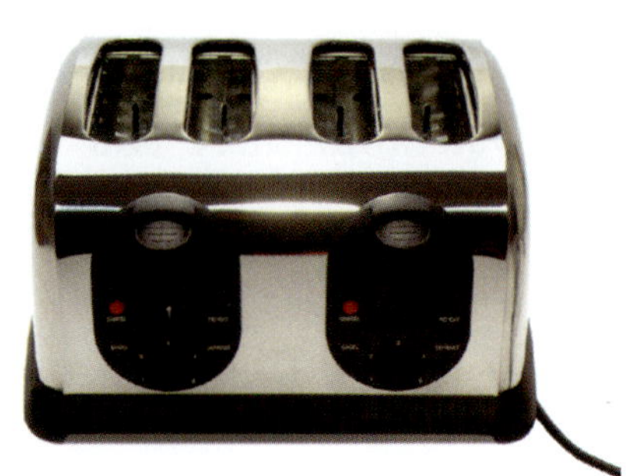

Buying electrical appliances

- **Cost:** Compare different models and the same models in different shops.
- **Safety:** Buy from a reliable shop; check for safety labels.
- **Energy efficiency label:** The appliance should ideally have an A or B rating.
- **Size:** Will the appliance fit in the space you have for it?
- **Special features:** Do not spend money on appliances with lots of special features if you will never use them.
- **Demonstration:** If necessary, ask to have a demonstration on how to use the appliance.
- **Check the guarantee:** It should be for at least one year.
- **After-sales service:** Ask about this.

QUALITY
I.S. EN ISO 9001:2008
NSAI Certified

Irish Standards mark

European Standards mark

Doubly insulated

The microwave

See also microwave cooking, p. 59.

The microwave oven produces energy waves called microwaves. These waves hit food and cause the molecules in it to vibrate. This produces heat, which cooks the food. Some microwave ovens are more powerful than others. They range from 600 watts to 1,200 watts (1,200 watts is the most powerful). Cooking time decreases as wattage increases. Food continues to cook for a few minutes after it has been removed from the microwave, so it should not be eaten for a few minutes. This is called **standing time**.

Microwave oven

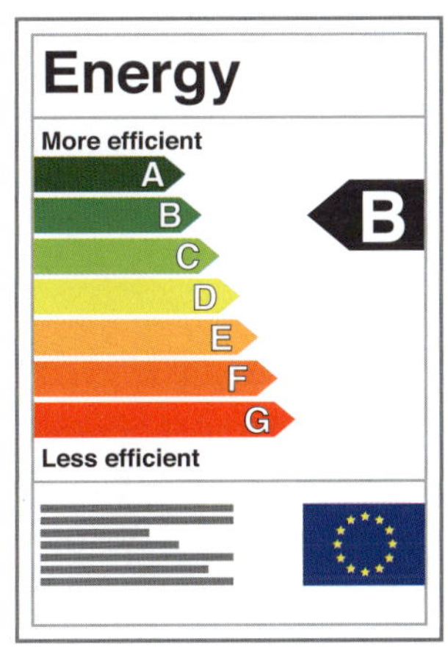

Energy efficiency label

Advantages of microwave ovens

- Cooks food very quickly; suits today's busy lifestyle.
- It is a healthy cooking method:
  - No extra fat is added.
  - Fast cooking – little loss of nutrients.

- Thaws food quickly; suits today's busy lifestyle.
- Can reheat food quickly and thoroughly.
- Small, convenient appliance that uses little fuel.

Disadvantages of microwave ovens

- Does not brown food (unless a browning dish is used).
- Not suitable for all foods, e.g. large joints of meat.
- It does not make meat tender.
- Foods that have an uneven thickness are not suitable, as the thin parts overcook while the thicker parts remain undercooked.
- Foods with large amounts of sugar and fat tend to burn.
- Special microwave recipes are needed, as many conventional recipes will not work in the microwave.

Uses of microwave ovens

- Cooks, thaws and reheats most foods (except if browning is needed).
- Melts jam, chocolate, jelly, etc. quickly, but be careful not to overheat.
- Ripens avocados, bananas or tomatoes (on low heat; pierce skin).

Safe use of the microwave

- Do not put anything metallic into the microwave. Use glass, china or heat-resistant plastic instead.
- Prick anything with a skin, e.g. tomatoes, potatoes, sausages, before cooking to prevent bursting.
- Cover foods with a plate so that they do not spatter the oven.
- Be careful to mix foods thoroughly before eating: food may be cool on the outside and red hot in the middle.
- Leave to stand for a few minutes before eating, as food continues to cook during this time.
- Wipe up spills immediately, as they will be more difficult to remove later.
- Do not switch on when empty, as this can cause damage.

Buying a microwave

Read the general guidelines on p. 255 for buying electrical appliances. Also, consider these special features that may be available in a microwave:

- Does the oven have a turntable? (This helps ensure even cooking.)
- What is its wattage? (The higher the wattage, the more powerful the oven.)

- Many modern microwave ovens have a host of special features, e.g. temperature probes, automatic programming facilities and a browning element. Do not spend money on a complicated microwave if you are unlikely to make use of its features.

Cleaning a microwave

- Prevent food spills and spatters in the first place by using a big enough container and by covering food loosely while it cooks.
- Wipe up spills as soon as they occur, as they will be removed much more easily.
- Remove the turntable and wash in warm soapy water.
- Wash the inside of the microwave with warm soapy water and a cloth. Using harsh abrasives or scrubs will scratch the metal interior and should not be used.
- Polish the exterior of the oven with a soft cloth and glass cleaner, e.g. Windolene.

Solid fuel cooker

The cooker

Types of cooker

- Gas cooker.
- Electric cooker with gas hob.
- Split level: Hob can be built into the worktop and the oven at waist level; one can be gas and the other electric.
- Solid fuel cookers, e.g. Aga, often heat water and radiators as well as cook, but they are very expensive to buy.

Ceramic hob

Modern features

- **Fan ovens:** A fan oven blows hot air around the oven, which cooks food more quickly (set the cooking temperature 10°C lower than what the recipe calls for).
- **Top oven:** Grill can also be used as a small oven.
- **Ceramic hob:** Easy-to-clean, heat-resistant glass surface (see photo).
- **Dual rings:** Can be set so that only the middle part of the ring heats, e.g. for small saucepans (see illustration).
- **Induction hob:** Electric hob, heats and cools instantly. Need to use cast iron or specific stainless steel saucepans.

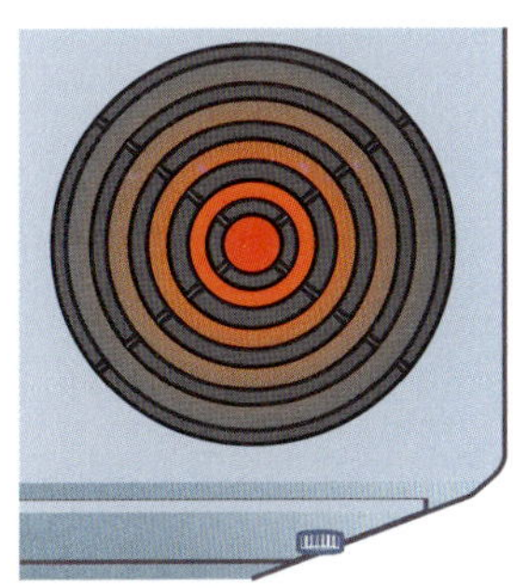

Dual ring

- **Dual grill:** Full grill or one side only heats up for small amounts of food.
- **Self-cleaning ovens:** Door locks; oven reaches very high temperatures; food burns off; ash can then be swept out.
- **Autotimers:** Three clocks, may be digital (see below).
  - Set clock 1 for the time you want the oven to come on at, e.g. 3 p.m.
  - Set clock 2 for the time you want the oven to switch off at.
  - Set clock 3 at the present time, e.g. 7.30 a.m.
- **Timers** are less complex. You set the timer for a certain amount of time, e.g. one hour; the oven switches on there and then (it cannot be set for later in the day, like autotimers). It switches off when the time is up.

Clock 1 Clock 2 Clock 3

Autotimer

Buying a cooker

1. See the general guidelines for buying electrical appliances (p. 255).
2. Should you buy a gas or electric cooker? If your house does not have natural gas, you may wish to choose an electric one, as bottled gas can be inconvenient. Gas cookers, on the other hand, heat up quickly and are easily controlled.
3. Do not pay for a cooker with extra features if you are unlikely to use them.

Care and cleaning of cookers

- Wipe up spills straightaway. (Why?)
- Wash the grill pan after each use. (Why?)
- Never drag saucepans over a ceramic hob; they will scratch it. Use a special ceramic hob cleaner.

When cleaning a cooker:

- Protect your hands, clothes and surroundings.
- Remove all removable parts, washing and drying them in warm soapy water.
- Use a special oven cleaner to dissolve burnt-on food in the oven itself.
- Wash out, rinse and dry the oven.
- Wash, dry and polish the exterior of the cooker and replace all removable parts.

Positioning a cooker

- The cooker needs to be positioned within the work triangle (see p. 241).
- Position close to electrical or gas connections.
- Position away from refrigerators or freezers.
- Position gas cookers away from draughts to avoid the risk of fire.

The refrigerator

Types of refrigerator

Fridge with icebox

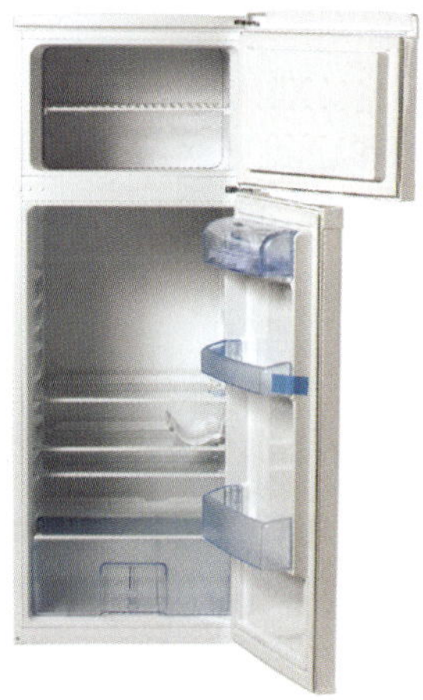

Fridge-freezer

Integrated fridge

Features of a modern refrigerator

- Thermostatically controlled.
- Door of fridge can be made to match kitchen units (see photo of integrated fridge above).
- Cold drinks dispenser and ice maker.
- Moulded door storage and moveable plastic-coated shelves.
- Automatic defrost: The fridge or fridge-freezer switches itself off every now and then; ice does not build up, so the icebox or freezer is kept defrosted.
- Salad drawers.

Choosing a refrigerator

See the general guidelines for buying electrical appliances (p. 255).

Rules for using a refrigerator

1. Do not position the fridge near the cooker or a radiator, as its motor will have to work harder to keep the fridge cool.
2. Never put hot food in the fridge.
3. Cover food before putting it in the fridge. This stops it from drying out and absorbing strong smells such as onions.
4. Do not over-pack the fridge and make sure to clean the fridge out regularly, throwing out anything that is out of date.
5. Put meat (especially raw meat) on a plate so it does not drip onto other food. Store it in the coldest part of the fridge, near the icebox.
6. Close the door immediately after use.
7. Defrost the freezer compartment regularly.
8. If a fridge is not in use, e.g. you are going on holiday, clean it thoroughly and leave the door open.

Care and cleaning

Defrosting the icebox

1. Choose a time when the icebox or freezer is fairly empty.
2. Some models have an automatic defrost (see p. 259). If not:
   - Remove all food and wrap in a good insulator, e.g. newspaper.
   - Allow ice to melt into the drip tray, then empty the drip tray.
   - When all the ice is gone, wash out with warm water and bread soda, then dry the icebox or freezer.
   - Plug the refrigerator back in and return the food items.
   - Never use a knife to remove ice.

Cleaning the refrigerator

1. Choose a time when the fridge is fairly empty.
2. Remove all food and wrap in a good insulator, e.g. newspaper.
3. Remove all moveable shelves and parts.
4. Clean the fridge with a solution of 2 tablespoons bread soda mixed with 1 litre of water.
5. Rinse with plain warm water. Dry. Replace shelves and food.
6. Wash the outside with warm water and washing up liquid. Dry well.

Disposal of electrical appliances

Under European law (EU Directive on Waste Electrical and Electronic Equipment 2005; better known as the WEEE Directive), electrical appliances can no longer be disposed of in landfill sites by owners themselves. For environmental reasons, appliances must be brought to special collection points (most large electrical outlets have a collection point), where they will be collected and recycled in an environmentally friendly way. In order to cover the cost of this, customers must now pay a white goods disposal charge when purchasing a new appliance. The charge depends on the size and type of appliance. For example, a large American-style fridge carries a disposal charge of €30, whereas a smaller under-the-counter fridge carries a charge of €10 (2010 figures).

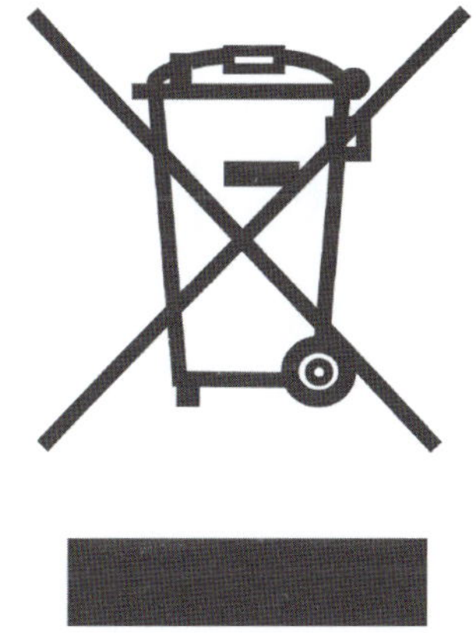

Homework Assignment 45 P. 161

CHAPTER 29

Home Hygiene, Safety and First Aid

Teacher's CD-ROM: Slide presentation • Student activity pack • Class test

Home hygiene

A good standard of hygiene in the home is essential for good health. Bacteria thrive in damp, dirty conditions and cause food poisoning and disease.

General guidelines for good hygiene in the home

1. Ensure good ventilation – bacteria love stuffy, damp conditions.
2. Keep the house warm and dry.
3. Open curtains and windows daily – sunlight and fresh air help destroy bacteria.
4. Kitchens and bathrooms should have smooth, easy-to-clean surfaces such as tiles.
5. Empty kitchen bins daily and large dustbin weekly; wash and disinfect regularly.

Hygiene in the kitchen and bathroom is most important

6. Keep toilets and sinks spotless; disinfect once a week.
7. Carpets and floors should be vacuumed or washed at least once a week – more often if necessary.
8. Bed sheets and pillowcases should be washed at as high a temperature as the fabric will allow and changed weekly.

Cleaning agents

Nowadays there is a huge number of different cleaning agents on the market. Many are poisonous, so:

1. Store only in their original containers – dangerous products will often have a childproof container.
2. Keep out of the reach of children (do not store under the sink).
3. Store in a dry place.
4. Follow directions carefully.
5. Wear gloves and protective clothing while using.
6. Rinse away all traces of the cleaning agent after use.

Cleaning agent	Examples	Use
Water	—	Warm (washing), cold (soaking)
Detergents	Washing powder, soap, washing-up liquid, dishwasher powder	Washing clothes and dishes
Abrasives	Cream cleaners, e.g. Cif, Brillo pads	Stubborn stains on scratch-resistant surfaces, e.g. ceramic bathroom sinks, metal saucepans (not non-stick)
Multipurpose cleaners	Cillit Bang, Flash liquid	Used on most work surfaces and floors
Window cleaners	Windolene	Cleans windows without streaking
Polish	Pledge, Mr. Sheen (sprays), solid wax	Polishing furniture
Metal polishes	Brasso, Silvo, silver cloths	Polishing metal – brass and silver
Bleaches	Parazone, Domestos	Kill germs, remove stains
Disinfectants	Dettol, Savlon	Kill germs
Alternative products	White vinegar	Removes lime scale from around taps, cleans windows
	Bread soda (with water)	Cleaning fridges and toilets
	Lemon juice	Removes blood and grass stains, also bleaches whites
	Cola and denture tablets	Both (separately) remove stains from toilets (leave overnight)

Do not use bleaches and toilet cleaners, e.g. Harpic, together, as a poisonous gas is given off when they are mixed.

Accidents in the home

Causes

- Carelessness or curiosity (children especially).
- Badly designed homes, e.g. hidden steps, poor lighting.
- Faulty equipment.
- Incorrect storage of dangerous substances.

Accident prevention

Childproof cover

Electricity

- Electricity and water do not mix – never touch anything electrical with wet hands.
- Wire electrical appliances correctly with the correct size of fuse.
- Check for safety symbols on appliances.
- Never take anything electrical, such as a heater or hairdryer, into the bathroom.
- Never overload sockets or repair flexes with tape.
- Fit childproof covers on electric sockets.

Fire

Have an exit plan and make sure everyone knows how best to get out of the house in the event of a fire.

- Never leave matches or cigarette lighters where children can get them.
- Fit a full fireguard.
- Do not hang a mirror over the fireplace. (Why?)
- Use an electric deep-fat fryer, not a chip pan.
- Stub cigarettes out completely and never smoke in bed.
- Check that nightwear is fire-resistant (especially children's).
- Unplug electrical appliances before going to bed.
- Close doors at night – this stops a fire from spreading.

Fire safety equipment

Smoke alarm: Check the battery on the same day each week

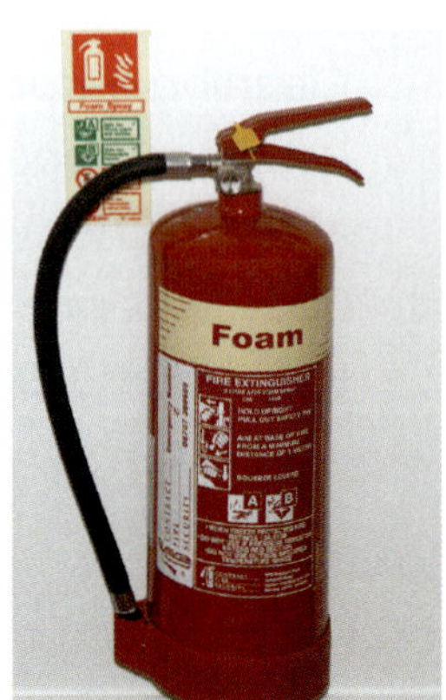

Fire extinguisher: Aim at the base of the fire

Fire blanket: Keep in the kitchen; throw over a small fire to smother it

Fire drill

Few people realise how quickly a house fire spreads until they witness one. Fire drills are therefore vital so that all occupants know what to do in the event of fire.

Small fire

1. Use a fire extinguisher or a fire blanket to put out the fire.
2. Never put water on burning oil or an electrical appliance.
3. If a chip pan catches on fire, do not bring it outside – the oxygen will feed the fire. Try to put the lid on to smother the flames.
4. Call the fire brigade if necessary.

Large fire

1. Get out, following your exit plan. Crawl along the floor, as there is more oxygen low down.
2. Call the fire brigade.
3. Do not re-enter the house.

Falls

- Have a light switch at the top and the bottom of stairs. Make sure the carpet is not loose. Never leave objects, such as toys, on the stairs.
- Avoid frayed carpets and over-polished floors.
- Have grips on the sides of baths and showers. The bottom of the shower or bath should have a non-slip surface (especially for elderly people).
- Be careful on newly washed floors; wipe up spills immediately.

Children

Accidents are the biggest cause of injury and death of children in this country. Each year, approximately one in five children has an accident at home that is serious enough to need treatment by a doctor or in hospital.

All children have accidents, no matter how safe the home or how careful the parents. Nevertheless, parents can reduce the risk of accidents by taking the following precautions:

- **Never** leave a young child unsupervised in the house.
- **Only** buy equipment and toys with safety symbols attached.

Type of accident	How to prevent it
Choking and suffocation 	◎ Keep plastic bags and small, hard objects out of reach of children. ◎ Never leave a baby or a young child alone while feeding. ◎ Be careful with curtain cords, etc.
Scalds 	◎ Have a short safety flex on kettles. ◎ Do not use table cloths. (Why?) ◎ Keep hot drinks away from the edges of tables. ◎ Never drink tea or coffee with a child in your lap. ◎ Turn saucepan handles inwards on the hob. ◎ Put cold water into the bath first.
Falls 	◎ Fit window locks. ◎ Fit stair gates. ◎ Do not allow children onto balconies alone. ◎ Strap babies into buggies and high chairs.
Poisoning 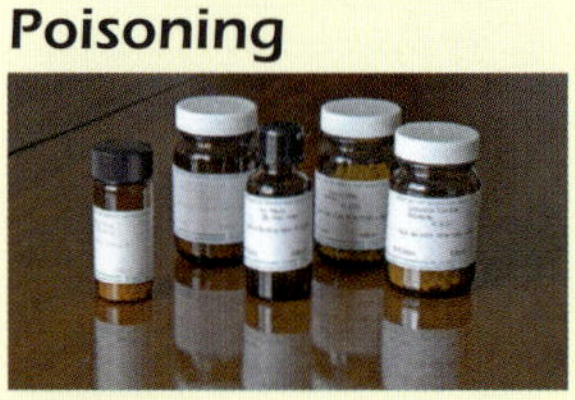	◎ Keep medicines locked away. ◎ Medicines should be stored in childproof containers. ◎ Lock other dangerous substances away, e.g. alcohol, bleach, weed killer, rat poison.
Burns 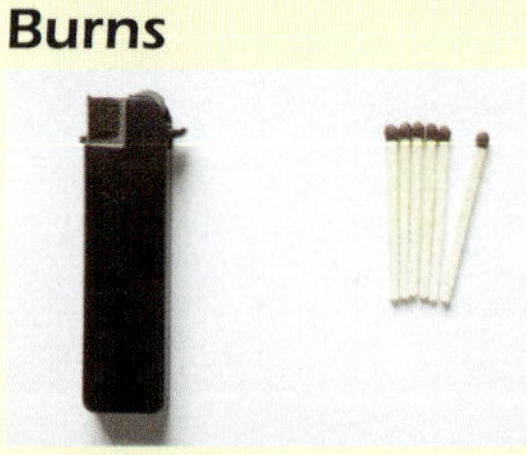	◎ Fit a fire guard. ◎ Never leave matches, lighters or petrol within reach. ◎ Be careful using an iron; do not allow the flex to dangle. ◎ Be sure nightwear is flame-resistant.
Drowning 	◎ Never leave a child alone in the bath or anywhere there is water.

First aid

Aims of first aid

- To **preserve** life, e.g. give mouth-to-mouth resuscitation (see below).
- To **prevent** the condition getting worse, e.g. stop the bleeding (see below).
- To **promote** recovery, e.g. put in the recovery position (see p. 269).

A serious accident

1. Do not move the patient unless absolutely necessary.
2. Check for a pulse (inside of wrist or under earlobe).
3. If patient is not breathing, start mouth-to-mouth resuscitation.
4. Do not give the patient anything to eat or drink (they may need to fast for an anaesthetic later).
5. Ring 999 and give clear directions to the accident scene.

The ABCs of resuscitation

A is for AIRWAY

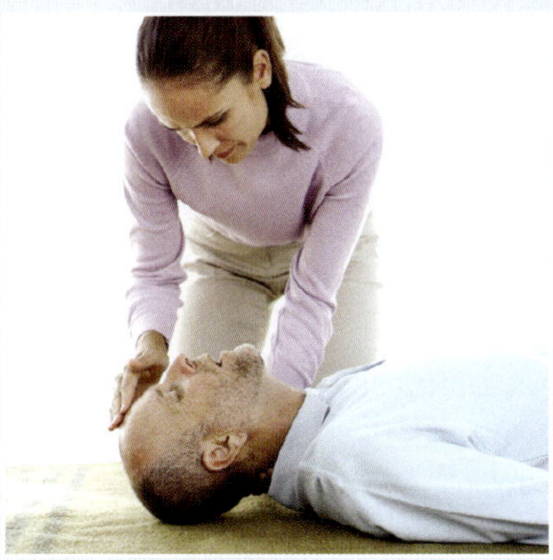

Tilt the casualty's head back and lift the chin. This will open the airway.

B is for BREATHING

If the casualty is not breathing, breathe for them. Cover their mouth with yours and blow air into their lungs.

C is for CIRCULATION

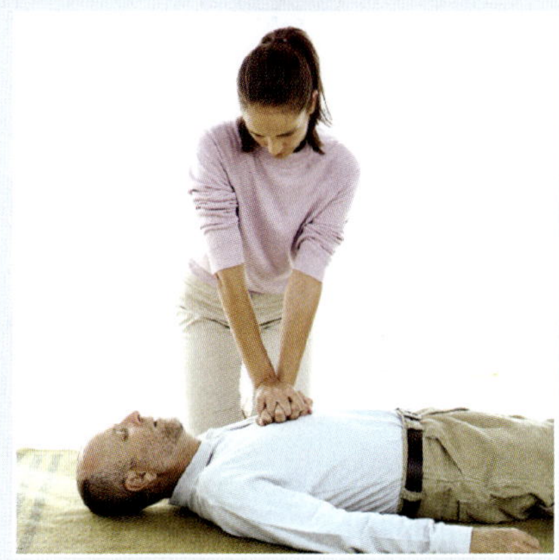

If the heart stops (no pulse), you can apply chest compressions. Two breaths – fifteen compressions, two breaths – fifteen compressions, and so on.

Why not do a basic first aid course?

Contact The Irish Red Cross Society, 16 Merrion Square, Dublin 2. Telephone: (01) 676 5135; www.redcross.ie; e-mail: redcross@iol.ie. They will put you in touch with your local branch.

First aid kit

Every home should have a well-stocked first aid kit. It should contain the following items.

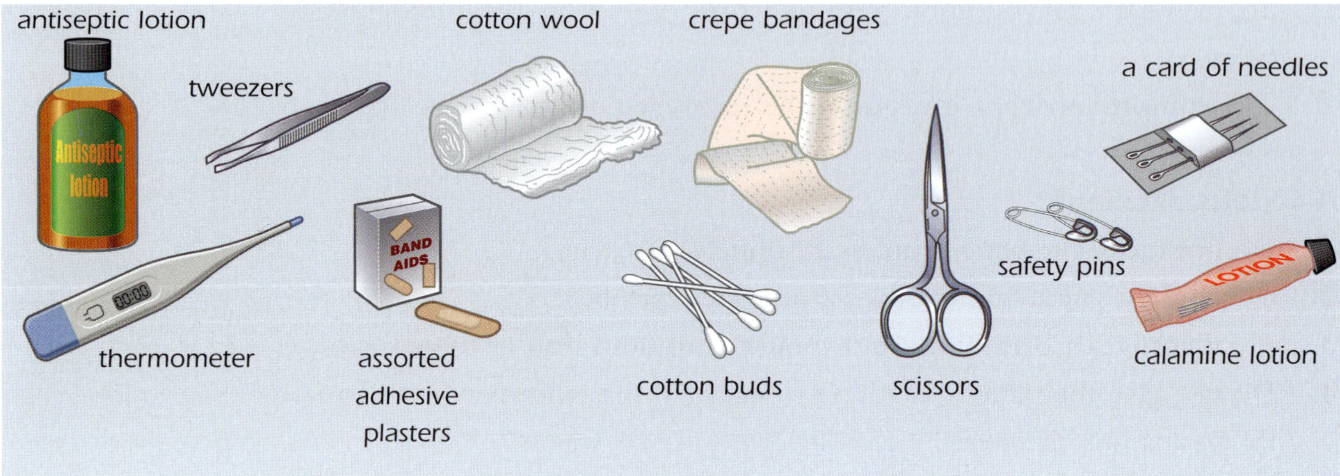

Basic first aid treatments

Burns and scalds

Minor (not serious)

1. Stop the burning – pour cold water on the burn for 10 minutes.
2. Gently remove rings, watches, belts, etc. before the area swells.
3. Reduce the risk of infection – cover with a clean, non-fluffy dressing.
4. Do not put any creams on the burn.

Major (serious)

1. Put out the fire by wrapping the victim in a blanket or coat or by rolling them on the ground.
2. Call an ambulance.
3. Pour cold water on the burn.
4. Resuscitate if necessary.
5. Do not remove any clothing stuck to the burn.
6. Gently remove rings, watches, etc. before the area begins to swell.

Bleeding

1. Try to stop the bleeding by applying pressure to the wound with your fingers for 10 minutes.
2. If there is glass or something else in the wound, press on either side of it.
3. If it is a limb, raise it up to help stop the bleeding.
4. Wrap in a bandage.
5. Call an ambulance if bleeding is severe.

Choking

- **A child:** Place face down on your lap with the head lower than body. Slap sharply between the shoulder blades.
- **An adult:** Slap sharply between the shoulder blades. If this does not work, try the Heimlich manoeuvre (see photo).

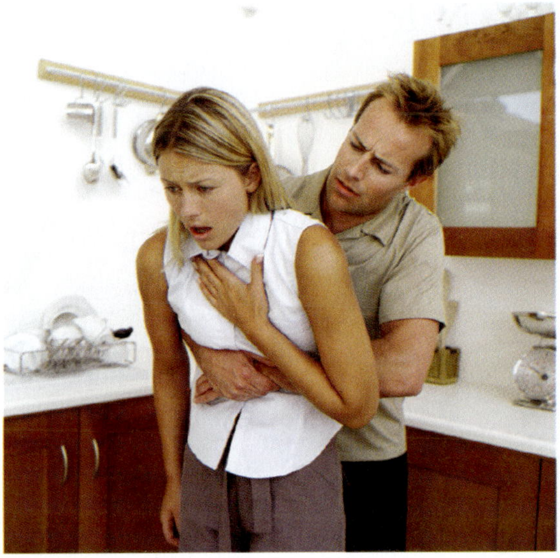

Shock

Shock in this sense does not mean emotional shock. Physical shock usually occurs when there has been a heart attack, a severe loss of blood or a loss of body fluids through severe diarrhoea or vomiting.

Symptoms

Pale, clammy skin, rapid shallow breathing, sweating but cold, nausea, thirst, weak pulse, dizziness and fainting.

Treatment

1. Treat the cause of shock, e.g. bleeding.
2. Lay the patient down with legs raised.
3. Loosen clothing; cover with a coat or blanket.
4. Do not give anything to eat or drink.

The recovery position is the safest position for the casualty

Poisoning

Approximately 170 people die each year in Ireland from poisoning.

1. Call an ambulance or take the patient immediately to casualty.
2. Find out what the patient has taken and bring the container to the hospital.
3. Do not try to make the patient vomit.
4. Resuscitate if necessary – put in the recovery position.

Homework Assignment
46 P. 167

Test Yourself eTest.ie

CHAPTER 30

Community Services and the Environment

Teacher's CD-ROM

Slide presentation • Student activity pack – with revision crossword • Class test

'We don't have to stop using the earth's resources, but we do have to stop wasting them.' (ENFO)

Environmental pollution

Environmental pollution is the term used to describe the ways in which the waste products of human activity harm the natural environment. Environmental pollution is one of the most serious problems facing mankind and all other animals and plants on earth today.

Most people, when asked, say they would like to see pollution reduced. Unfortunately, most of the pollution that threatens our health and the health of the planet comes from products people want and are unwilling to do without, e.g. unnecessarily large cars and houses, foreign travel, etc.

Important environmental issues

Air pollution

According to the World Health Organization, about one-fifth of the world's people are exposed to dangerous levels of air pollution. Air pollution occurs when factories and vehicles, etc. release large amounts of gas, smoke and dirt into the air. The burning of rubbish in incineration plants can release smoke and heavy metals such as mercury into the atmosphere.

Effects of air pollution

Air pollution causes:

- Lung problems such as asthma, bronchitis and cancer.
- Smog.
- Decrease in ozone layer.
- Acid rain (see below).
- Climate change (see p. 272).

Smog

Smog is one of the most common types of air pollution. Smog is a brown, hazy mixture of gases and smoke. Smog forms when these gases react with sunlight; this reaction then creates hundreds of harmful chemicals which make up smog. Smog is still a problem in many cities today. It causes many health problems – increased lung infections, asthma, irritation of linings of the eyes, nose and throat and it also decreases the body's ability to fight infection and disease. Dublin had a smog problem in the 1980s, which prompted the government to allow only smokeless fuels to be burned in Irish cities and large towns. This action led to a 70 per cent reduction in smog levels in Ireland.

Acid rain

Acid rain is rain or snow that is unusually acidic. It has harmful effects on plants, aquatic animals, buildings and human health (cancer). Acid rain is mostly caused by human emissions of sulphur and nitrogen (as a result of burning fossil fuels), which react in the atmosphere to produce acids.

Effects of acid rain on forestry

Climate change

Climate change is any long-term significant change in expected **average weather patterns**. The main reason for climate change is **global warming**. Global warming occurs because we are producing increasing amounts of **greenhouse gases** such as carbon dioxide. These gases trap heat on the earth's surface, raising the temperature (global warming).

Causes of increased greenhouse gas production

- **Increased CO_2 emissions:** There are more cars and trucks on the roads, burning of fossil fuels such as oil by households and industry.

Community Services and the Environment

- **Deforestation:** Because plants use CO_2 and give off oxygen, cutting down large areas of forest increases the amount of CO_2 in the atmosphere.
- **Burning waste:** Large incineration plants.
- **Large power plants burning fossil fuels** to produce electricity, e.g. ESB.
- **Intensive livestock rearing** produces methane, a greenhouse gas.

Effects of climate change

- Flooding (because the icecaps in Antarctica are melting).
- More stormy, wet weather.
- Appearance of insects such as mosquitoes in countries like Ireland, which increases the risk of disease in these countries.
- Previously fertile land becoming dry and barren, resulting in extreme poverty and starvation.

Flooding and drought are both effects of climate change

Ozone layer

The ozone layer is a layer of gas (O_3) found nine to 18 miles above the earth's surface. Ozone is important in that it shields us from the sun's harmful (cancer-causing) UV rays. During the 1970s, scientists discovered that holes were forming in the ozone layer, mainly as a result of two groups of substances – CFCs and halons. CFCs were found in aerosol sprays, fridges and freezers, fast food cartons and air conditioning systems, while halons were in some types of fire extinguishers. Nowadays, as a result of the Montreal Protocol (an international agreement) that came into force in 1989, there is a ban on CFCs and halons in most countries in the world, and the ozone layer is now repairing itself. Experts believe that it will recover fully by 2050.

Water pollution

Water pollution is the contamination of water by substances such as human sewage, agricultural runoff and chemical waste from industrial plants.

According to the World Heath Organization, approximately 5 million people die every year from drinking polluted water – that is more than the population of Ireland. The main effects of water pollution on humans are diseases such as cholera, dysentery and *E. coli* poisoning (see p. 41). Water pollution also causes the death of fish and damage to birds, plants and other wildlife.

Waste disposal

One of the biggest problems facing society is waste disposal. Waste products can be:

- **Organic or biodegradable:** This means that they can be easily broken down by nature, e.g. paper, vegetable peels, etc.
- **Inorganic:** This means that the waste cannot be easily broken down and is harmful to the environment, e.g. plastic, glass, metal. However, while some inorganic waste does not break down easily, it can be **recycled**.

If waste is not recycled, then it must be disposed of in one of two ways: dumped and buried in landfill sites or burned in incinerators. Both of these methods can be damaging to us and the environment.

We therefore need to remember the three Rs with regard to waste management:

- **Reduce** the amount of waste produced.
- **Reuse** goods where possible, e.g. shopping bags, old clothes as polishing cloths.
- **Recycle** both organic, e.g. compost bin, and inorganic waste, e.g. bottle bank.

Protecting the environment

What can you do to help protect the environment?

1. Be an eco-friendly shopper:
   - Avoid over-packaged goods, e.g. buy fruit, vegetables and meat loose rather than pre-packaged.
   - If goods are packaged, ensure packaging is recycled or recyclable.
   - Look for the EU Ecolabel (this shows that the product is environmentally friendly and does not harm the environment).
   - Bring a shopping bag.

EU Ecolabel www.ecolabel.eu

The EU Ecolabel

Recycling symbol

Compost bin

2. Recycle:
   - Bottles, cans, paper, plastic, batteries, mobile phones – there is probably a recycling centre near you, it just takes a little effort.
   - Recycle clothes by donating them to charity shops.
   - Recycle organic waste, such as vegetable peels, by having a compost bin or compost heap (some local authorities are supplying compost bins at a reduced price).
3. Don't litter and don't tolerate those who do.
4. Use less water:
   - Showers use less than half the water baths do.
   - Fix dripping taps.
   - Do not turn on the dishwasher or washing machine for small amounts. Use half-load or economy wash if you must wash less than a full load or if the load is not very dirty.
5. Walk or cycle to school where possible.
6. Use less energy:
   - Do not over-heat the home.
   - Turn off lights when not in use.
   - Use energy-saving bulbs (CFLs).
7. When choosing electrical appliances, choose energy-efficient models: A or B labels (see p. 255).

Government action

- **Plastic bag levy.**
- **Car tax based on carbon emissions:** All new cars registered since July 2008 are now taxed based on their rates of carbon emissions rather than engine size. Cars are graded A to G (A is best, having the lowest carbon emissions). Grade A cars are taxed at €104 per year, whereas owners of grade G cars must pay €2,100 in car tax annually (figures as of 2010). Most cars fall somewhere in between these two figures.

- **Sustainable Energy Ireland:** This is a government organisation set up in 2002 to promote and assist in the development of sustainable energy in Ireland. For example, they administer grants for people wishing to improve the energy efficiency of their home, e.g. install better insulation.
- **Recycling centres:** Over the past number of years, the government has improved recycling facilities throughout the country. In general, nowadays people do not have to travel far to a centre.
- **Government-sponsored websites:** These provide useful information on the environment and what you can do to help. Sites include:
  - www.change.ie
  - www.enfo.ie
  - www.sei.ie
- What other measures do you think the government could introduce to help us help the environment?

Organisations involved with environmental protection

- Environment Protection Agency
- Friends of the Earth
- Greenpeace
- The Green Party

Community services

When people live together in urban (city or town) or rural (country) areas, they form a **community**. Most communities have a number of **services** and **amenities**.

Services

Statutory (government-run)

- Education (schools, some pre-schools)
- Gardaí
- Health (hospitals, health centres)
- Libraries
- Local authority housing (council or corporation)
- Postal services
- Public transport
- Social welfare

Voluntary services

- GAA, soccer and rugby clubs
- Homeless Aid
- ISPCC
- Meals on Wheels
- Neighbourhood Watch
- REHAB Foundation
- Samaritans
- Society of St Vincent de Paul
- Youth clubs

Homework Assignment 47 P. 172

The GAA is a voluntary service

Amenities

An **amenity** is another word for a leisure facility. Amenities can be **natural** – rivers, lakes, beaches, etc. – or **man-made** – parks, playgrounds, sports pitches, cinemas, museums, fitness centres, swimming pools, etc.

Test Yourself eTest.ie

Unit 5

Textile Studies

Unit 5 TEXTILE STUDIES

CHAPTER 31

Textiles in the Home

Teacher's CD-ROM

Slide presentation • Student activity pack • Class test

What are textiles?

A textile is a fabric or cloth. The clothes we wear and many of the items in our homes are made from textiles.

Textiles can be used to make a room warm and cosy

Uses of textiles in the home

- **Soft furnishings:** These are items other than furniture that are used to decorate a room and make it more comfortable. Examples include curtains and blinds, cushions, rugs, wall hangings and lampshades.
- **Upholstery:** This is the name given to the covering fabrics and fillings that are used in furniture such as sofas, armchairs, mattresses and chair seats.
- **Carpets:** A variety of different types of carpets are available. Some are very hardwearing, while others are cheaper and less so.
- **Bed linen:** This includes sheets and pillowcases, duvets and duvet covers, blankets, bedspreads and throws.
- **Table linen and towels:** This includes tablecloths, napkins, table runners, placemats, dishcloths, tea towels, hand towels and bath towels.

Higher Level

Properties of textiles

A property is a characteristic or quality of a textile. When choosing a textile for a particular purpose, e.g. towels, the properties of the textile you choose are important. Imagine buying towels made from a non-absorbent, rough, dry-clean-only textile. **Desirable properties** are those that are most important. For example, desirable properties for a face towel would be absorbent, soft and washable.

Examples of properties

Cool, soft, warm, absorbent, waterproof, washable, colour-fast (won't run), soft, shiny, rough, smooth, delicate, light, heavy, hardwearing, breathable, non-absorbent, crease-resistant, flame-resistant, resilient (bounces back into shape), stretchy, insulating, stain-resistant, transparent (lets light through).

Choosing fabrics for household items

Points to consider:

- Cost: Some fabrics, e.g. silk, are very expensive.
- Desirable properties, e.g. durable and stain resistant.
- Colour, pattern and style should fit in with the décor already there.

Soft furnishings

Soft furnishings include curtains and blinds, cushions, rugs, wall hangings and lampshades.

Functions:

- Curtains and blinds give us privacy.
- Curtains insulate the room and help to keep draughts out.
- Soft furnishings such as rugs and cushions make the room more comfortable.
- All soft furnishings absorb sound and so reduce noise in the room.
- They finish off a room, making it more attractive.
- They allow us to express our personal taste.

Curtains

Measuring curtains

- **Length:** From rail to 5cm below windowsill (for short curtains); from rail to 2cm off the floor (for long curtains).
- **Width:** 2.5 times the width of the window or rail.
- **Suitable fabrics:** Cotton, linen, velvet, dralon (best lined).

Curtains insulate and decorate

Higher Level

Properties

Curtains should:

- Hang well.
- Be fade resistant.
- Be washable or dry cleanable.
- Be fire resistant.
- Be pre-shrunk.
- Have a close weave.

A cheap non-woven carpet with low pile density

An expensive woven carpet with high pile density

Carpets

Carpets can be one of the most expensive purchases for the home, so should be chosen wisely. Carpets can be:

- Woven (expensive).
- Non-woven (less expensive).

With woven carpets, tufts of carpet fibres are woven into a heavy cloth backing. Non-woven carpet tufts, on the other hand, are glued into or onto a rubber or cloth backing.

The **pile** of a carpet describes the tufts on the surface of the carpet. The pile can be long or short, twisted or straight, dense (tightly packed) or loose. The density of the pile is very important. If the pile is dense (a lot of tufts per square centimetre), then the carpet will be soft and luxurious. However, it will also be expensive.

Classification or grading of carpets

Carpets are graded according to how hardwearing (durable) they are.

- **Light domestic:** Suitable for bedrooms.
- **General domestic:** Suitable for living rooms.
- **Heavy domestic:** Suitable for halls, stairs and living rooms.

What type of carpet you buy will depend on which room it is for and how much money you have to spend. Ideally a room with a lot of traffic, such as a living room, hall or stairs, should have a quality carpet. A less expensive carpet, on the other hand, would be fine for a bedroom.

Properties

A good carpet will be:

- Resilient (bounce back after being walked upon).
- Warm.
- Hardwearing.
- Stain resistant.

Higher Level

Carpets are generally made from:

- **Wool** because it is warm and resilient.
- **Nylon and acrylic** because they are hardwearing and cheap.

The best carpets (although they are the most expensive) are made from a mix of wool (80 per cent) and nylon (20 per cent).

Bed linen

Household item	Made from	Points to remember
Sheets, pillowcases, duvet covers	Cotton, polycotton, polyester	Need to be washable, easily dried and absorbent.
Bedspreads and duvets (a bedspread is like a duvet except it is not covered with a separate cover – it is made from decorative fabric)	Covering: cotton, polyester or polycotton; filling: polyester or duck down	The warmth of a duvet or bedspread is measured by a tog rating – 4.5 to 15 tog (warmest). Duvets and bedspreads need to be warm, light and washable.
Blankets	Wool, wool and nylon or acrylic mixed, acrylic	Wool blankets are warm but expensive; wool mixed with acrylic or nylon is hardwearing as well; acrylic on its own is cheaper but not as warm.
Throws, cushions	Cotton, wool, satin, acrylic, silk	Usually compliment the rest of the bed linen.

An attractively dressed bed

Upholstered furniture

Upholstery

Covering and filling on sofas, armchairs, mattresses, chair seats, mattresses.

- **Desirable properties:** Durable, stain resistant, closely woven, easy to clean, fire resistant.
- **Suitable fabrics:** Heavy cotton, linen, wool, leather, velvet and dralon (like velvet).

Homework Assignment

48 P. 178

Test Yourself eTest.ie

CHAPTER 32

Clothing, Fashion and Design

Teacher's CD-ROM

Slide presentation • Student activity pack • Class test

Clothing

One of the most important uses of textiles is clothing. Natural fabrics such as cotton, wool and linen are used together with man-made fabrics such as nylon, polyester and acrylic.

Functions of clothing

There are six basic functions of clothing.

Functions of clothing

1. Protection from the weather.

2. Safety.

3. Modesty: Levels of modesty vary between cultures and also situations.

4. Self-expression.

5. Identification – uniforms.

6. Creating an image or impression.

Skinny jeans are now back in fashion, though five years ago you would not have dreamed of wearing them

Fashion and design

Fashion is a word used to describe clothes or other items that are trendy or popular at any given time. Fashion changes constantly. **Fashion trends** are changes in fashion. Most people also see that fashion trends form cycles of fashion. For example, 1980s drainpipe jeans and batwing tops have returned in an almost identical form almost 30 years later as skinny jeans and batwing. **Fashion fads** are short-term fashion trends, e.g. wearing leg warmers.

Fashion trends are influenced by:

1. The fashion industry.
2. Famous people and the media.
3. Historical events and the economy.
4. Technology.

The fashion industry

It is in the interest of the fashion industry that fashion is ever changing. Otherwise, how would the industry continue to make money? Twice every year, fashion shows are held in Paris, London, New York and Milan. Here the world's top fashion designers show off their new designs. These **haute couture** clothes are hand made, one of a kind and *very* expensive. For example, you could pay in excess of €25,000 for a suit.

Top designers such as Prada, Versace and Christian Dior also produce less expensive machine-made clothes. These ranges, called **prêt-à-porter** (ready-to-wear) clothes, are still expensive and only available in designer boutiques.

Chain stores such as Sasha, NEXT, Cocoon and Dunnes Stores then buy or recreate these looks and sell them cheaply as **off-the-peg clothes**.

Haute couture – high fashion

Famous people

Pop stars, sports stars, models, actors and actresses all influence current fashion trends through the media.

Historical events and the economy

- During World War II, fabric was scarce, so skirts became straight and shorter.
- During times of economic recession, aggressive, anti-establishment fashions become more popular, e.g. punk, Goth.

Famous people influence fashion trends

In 1950s fashion, pencil skirts became fashionable due to a scarcity of fabric

Technology

As new fabrics are developed, they influence fashion.

Buying clothes

What influences your choice?

- **Age:** As you get older, your idea of what is nice changes.
- **Cost:** How much money you have influences where you shop and what type of clothes you buy.
- **Fashion:** Fashion trends often influence our likes and dislikes. For example, low-rise jeans are in fashion for teenage girls today, so most teenagers like low-rise and dislike jeans that sit high on the waist.

- **What suits you:** Sometimes people follow fashion trends even when they do not suit them, e.g. low-rise or skinny jeans do not suit someone who is overweight, yet many will still wear them because they are in fashion.
- **Peer pressure:** You may be influenced by what your peers are wearing.
- **Lifestyle and occupation:** A student would be likely to dress differently to a bank manager, for example.
- **Culture:** Some cultures have a dress code, e.g. Muslims.

Factors to consider when buying clothing

- Cost: Can I afford it? Is it good value for money?
- Need: Do I need it?
- Does it suit my figure, hair colour, skin colour?
- Fit: Does it fit me well? Is it comfortable?
- Quality: Is it good quality?
- Is it washable or will it have to be dry cleaned (expensive)?
- Does it suit the occasion, e.g. a job interview?

Accessories are worn with an outfit to complete it. Examples include jewellery, belts, hats, shoes, bags, etc. Some accessories also have a function – for example, a bag is used to carry things.

Accessories

Designing clothes

When designing clothes, there are two basic aims. The item must:

- Function as it should.
- Look good.

As with interior design (see p. 236), certain design guidelines or factors, when followed, can achieve these aims.

Design guidelines or factors

1. **Function:** The properties of the fabric you choose should allow the finished product to function as it should. What properties would be important in fabric for an apron?
2. **Colour:** Choose colours that suit your hair, skin and eye colour. For example, bright red may not suit a person with red hair. Some colours never go out of fashion, such as black, white, navy and denim.
3. **Pattern:** Avoid too much, especially large patterns.
4. **Texture:** Texture is the feel of a fabric. Can you name a clothing fabric with a smooth or a rough texture?
5. **Line:** Horizontal lines (stripes) make a person look wider. Vertical lines make a person look taller and slimmer. Curved lines, such as those in a flowing dress, are feminine.
6. **Shape:** The shape or outline of a garment. A well-cut garment can flatter any figure.

The same principles of proportion, emphasis, balance and rhythm also apply to clothing and textile design (see interior design, pp. 239–40).

The outfit pictured here will function well as a work suit. It will not date, as black and white are colours that do not go out of fashion. The suit has a well-cut, rectangular shape that flatters the figure. It is nicely accessorised with a necklace and belt.

Homework Assignment
49 P. 181

Test Yourself eTest.ie

CHAPTER 33

Fibres and Fabrics

Teacher's CD-ROM

Slide presentation • Student activity pack • Class test

Fibres are tiny hair-like threads. They are twisted together into **yarn** and the yarn is then made into **fabric**.

fibres → yarn → fabric

Classification of fibres

Fibres can be divided or classified into two groups: natural fibres and man-made fibres. Each group can be divided again.

Natural fibres	Man-made fibres
Animal: Wool, silk. Plant: Cotton, linen.	Synthetic: Polyester, nylon, acrylic. Regenerated: Viscose, acetate.

Natural fibres (animal)

Wool

Source and production

1. Sheep are sheared (also goats, camels, rabbits).
2. Fleece is graded, washed and dried.
3. Wool is brushed (carded) and combed.
4. Strands are spun into yarn: long strands (worsted) and short strands.

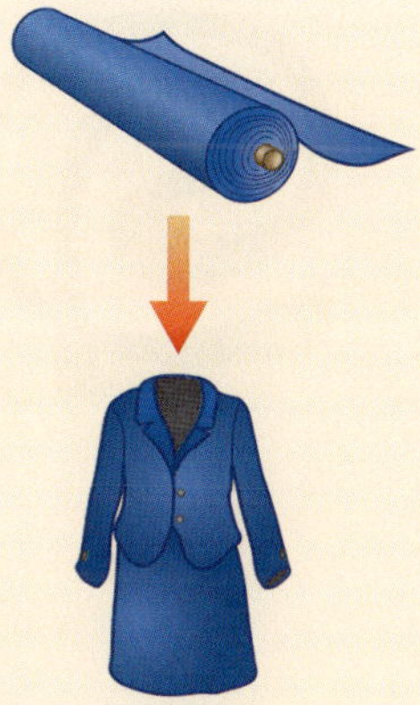

Long strands (worsted) are used to make wool fabric

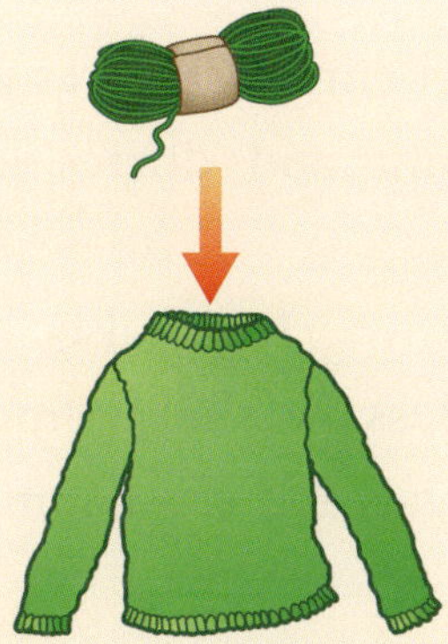

Short strands are used for knitting wool

WOOLMARK®

100% wool

WOOL BLEND®

Wool blend (wool + another fibre)

A suit made from wool

Properties

☺ **Good:** Wool is a warm, absorbent fabric that does not burn easily. Wool carpets are hardwearing and resilient (do not stay flattened when walked on).

☹ **Bad:** Untreated wool shrinks if washed at too high a temperature or if tumble dried. Coarse qualities, in common with most other fibres, can irritate the skin.

- **Uses of wool (short fibres):** Jumpers, blankets, carpets.
- **Uses of wool (long fibres):** Long worsted fibres are used to make different types of wool fabric, e.g. gabardine, tweed and crepe.

Silk

Source and production

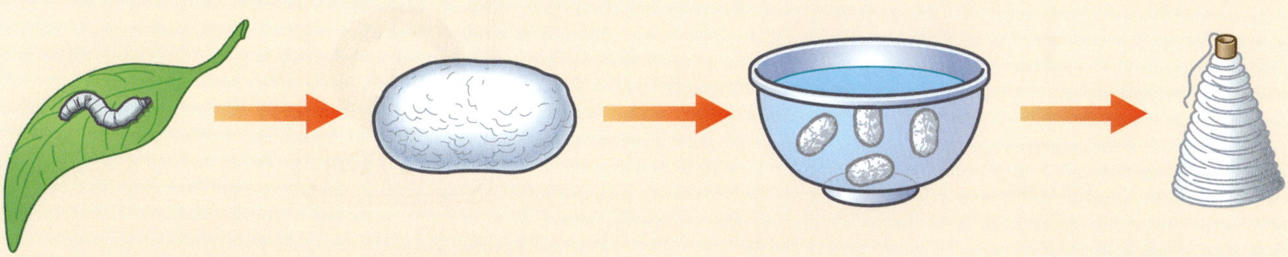

1. Silkworm feeds on mulberry leaves.
2. Silkworm spins a cocoon of silk around itself.
3. Cocoons are soaked in water.
4. Silk threads are unwound from cocoons onto reels.
5. Several of these thin silk threads are spun or twisted together to make thicker thread. These are then woven into fabric.

Silk evening dresses

Properties

☺ **Good:** Silk is absorbent, crease resistant, strong, smooth, light and drapes (falls) well.

☹ **Bad:** Silk is expensive. It is also easily damaged by careless washing, moths, sunshine and chemicals and it is flammable (burns easily).

Silk symbol

Uses of silk

Silk is a luxury fabric and is used for shirts, evening dresses, etc. In the home, silk can be used for paintings, cushion covers and curtains (line them; why?).

Types of silk

Chiffon (very light), taffeta, wild silk, satin.

Source and production

Cotton bolls

↓

picked
cleaned
graded
combed
spun

↓

Yarn

Natural fibres (plant)

Cotton

Properties

☺ **Good:** Cotton is absorbent, cool, strong, washes and dries well and is easy to dye and bleach.

☹ **Bad:** Cotton creases, shrinks and burns easily. It can be damaged by mildew (mould).

100% cotton symbol

Uses of cotton

Clothes, towels, sheets and curtains.

Types of cotton

- Flannelette (fluffy sheets).
- Denim.
- Towelling (towels).
- Muslin (a light, see-through fabric).

Denim is one of the most popular types of cotton

Linen

Flax plants

Linen symbol

Source and production

1. Flax plants are grown in wet countries like Ireland.
2. Flax stems are soaked until the woody part rots (retting).
3. Fibres are separated from the woody stem. They are then bleached and spun into yarn.

Properties

☺ **Good:** Linen is absorbent, cool, strong and washes well.

☹ **Bad:** Linen is expensive, creases and shrinks easily. It is difficult to dye and is damaged by mildew.

Linen shirt

Uses and types of linen

Irish linen is famous the world over. Linen products range from heavy damask tablecloths and sheets to finer lawn and cambric clothing.

Man-made fibres

Man-made fibres can be either **regenerated** or **synthetic**.

Regenerated

Viscose, rayon, acetate.

Source and production – regenerated

1. Cellulose from spruce trees or cotton waste is pulped (mashed).
2. Chemicals are added.
3. Heat is applied.
4. Liquid is forced through a spinneret.
5. Yarn is formed.
6. Yarn can be left (i) in long filaments and used to make smooth, silky fabrics or (ii) twisted and cut to make soft 'wooly' fabrics.

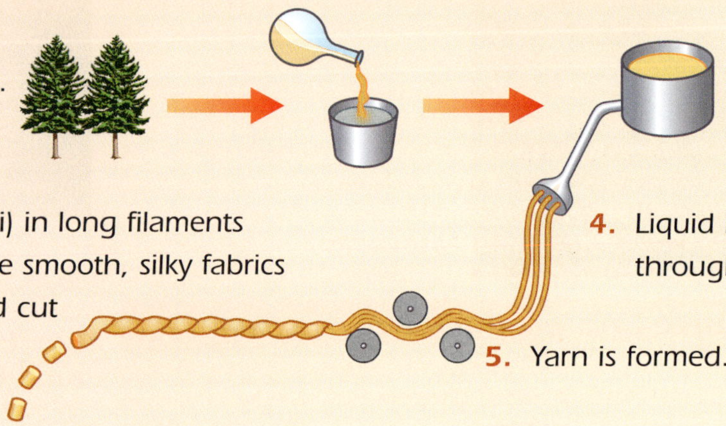

Uses

Fabrics made from regenerated fibres, such as rayon and viscose, are used to make silky blouses, dresses, etc. (see the photograph).

Properties

☺ **Good:** Regenerated fabrics are absorbent and cool to wear.

☹ **Bad:** They are not hardwearing and tear easily after a lot of washing.

Synthetic

Nylon, polyester, acrylic, elastane (Lycra).

Acrylic jumper

Source and production – synthetic

1. Synthetic fabrics are made from oil, coal, etc.
2. Other chemicals, air and water are added.
3. The mixture is forced through a spinneret to form long, continuous filaments.
4. Continuous filaments can be made into smooth, silky fabrics.
5. Or continuous filaments can be chopped and twisted to make soft 'woolly' yarn (for jumpers, etc.).

Uses of synthetic fibres

- **Acrylic:** Jumpers, fake fur, dresses, carpets.
- **Nylon:** Umbrellas, swimsuits, tents, raincoats, tights, blended with wool for carpets.
- **Polyester:** Usually blended with cotton in trousers, blouses, shirts; used to make the filling in duvets and coats.
- **PVC:** Fake leather goods.
- **Elastane (Lycra):** Added to other fabrics to make a garment stretchy, e.g. swimwear.

Properties

- ☺ **Good:** Synthetic fabrics are all strong and hardwearing. Acrylic and polyester are warm (acrylic jumpers, polyester filling in duvets and coats). Nylon repels water, so is good for tents, rain gear, etc.
- ☹ **Bad:** All synthetics are flammable. Some, such as nylon, cling and are clammy in summer, as they don't absorb moisture.

Making fibres into fabrics

Yarn

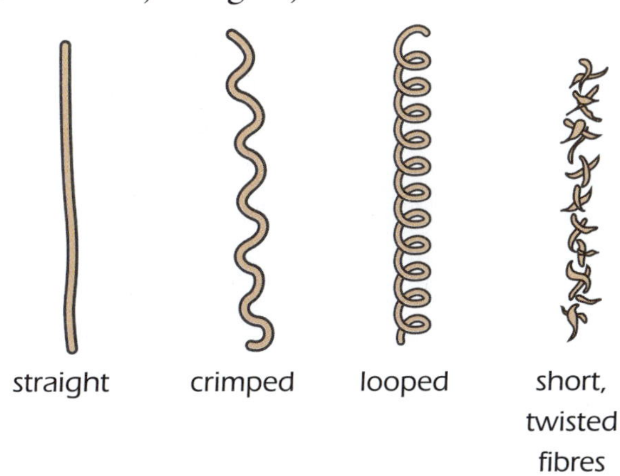

Fibres such as cotton, linen, polyester and wool are twisted into **yarn**. Yarn can be straight (makes smooth fabric) or crimped, looped or short fibres

9 denier tights – barely visible

twisted together (makes textured fabrics) – see the illustration. Yarn is then either woven or knitted to make fabric. (**Bonded** fabrics are made from fibres that have not been spun into yarn.)

Denier refers to the thickness of man-made fibres. The lower the denier, the finer or thinner the yarn.

Ply refers to the number of yarns twisted together. It usually applies to knitting wool. Wool can be anything from single ply to 20 ply, which is very chunky.

Yarn to fabric

Weaving

Most weaving is done on a loom. Warp threads (vertical) are put onto the loom first and weft threads are then woven through them. The selvedge is the edge that the weft threads make; it doesn't fray.

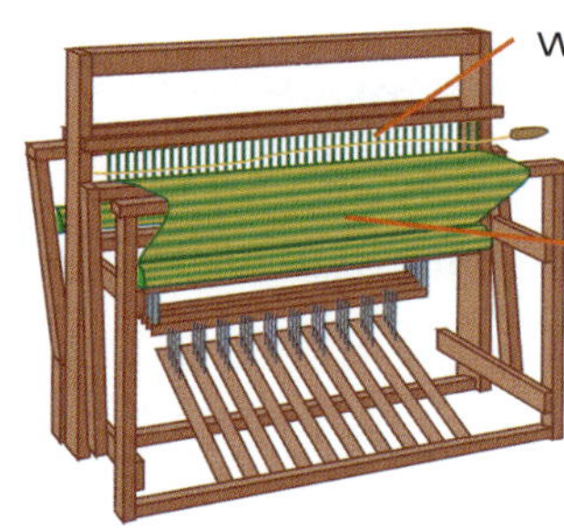

Knitting

Knitting can be done by hand or by machine. Most people, when they think of knitting, think only of jumpers, hats and scarves. Many fabrics are also knitted, as you can see if you look closely at them. All knitted fabrics are stretchy. Tracksuits, T-shirts, jumpers and tights are all made from knitted fabrics.

Bonded fabrics

Bonded fabrics are made from fibres that have **not** been spun into yarn. They are made by sticking fibres together, by applying moisture, pressure and heat.

Examples: Felt (snooker tables, hats), wadding (filling inside duvets, coats, carpet underlay), disposable fabrics (J-cloths, hospital gowns).

Fabric finishes

Finish (trade name)	Function	Use
Waterproofing (Scotch Guard)	Stops water from soaking through	Anoraks, waterproof sportswear, e.g. golf jackets, tents
Water repellent (Scotch Guard)	Makes fabric shower proof	Shower-proof coats, jackets
Stain repellent (Scotch Guard)	Stops stains from soaking into fabric	Clothes, carpets and upholstery
Flame resistant	Fabric won't catch on fire easily	Children's nightwear, upholstery fabrics, e.g. on sofas
Brushing	Makes fabric feel warmer and softer	Flannelette sheets
Crease resistant	Reduces creasing, no need to iron	Shirts, trousers, sheets, curtains
Permanent pleating	Pleats won't fall out	Skirts and trousers
Stretch (Lycra)	Woven into fabric to give stretch	Swimwear, trousers, cycle shorts, underwear
Non-shrink	Stops shrinking	Clothing, furnishing fabrics
Moth proofing	Stops moths attacking fabrics and making holes	Wool and silk
Anti-static	Stops clothes from clinging	Synthetic underwear, clothing and carpets
Polishing (mercerising)	Makes fabric smooth and strong	Cotton thread and fabric
Stiffening	Gives a sharp, crisp finish	Cuffs and collars

Adding colour and pattern to fabric

- **Weaving:** Different coloured yarns are woven together on the loom to create different effects, e.g. checks and tartans.

Pattern woven into fabric

Batik

- **Dyeing:** In the past, natural products such as berries and leaves were used to dye fabric. Today, chemical dyes are used. Chemical dyes, unlike natural dyes, are **colourfast**, meaning they do not run. Dye can be used to create pattern in **batik** and **tie-dye**.
- **Printing:** Printing applies colour to one side of the fabric using a block, screen or roller.

Printed fabric

Fibre and fabric identification – burning tests

Burning tests are used to identify fibres and fabrics. Observe the following:

1. How the test fibres or fabrics burn.
2. The odour given off.
3. The residue (what is left after burning).

Fibre	Odour	How it burns	Residue
Wool or silk	Burning hair	Slowly	Dark ash
Cotton, linen, viscose	Burning paper	Quickly	Paper-like ash
Nylon	Celery	Melts	Hard bead

Homework Assignment 50 P. 183

Test Yourself eTest.ie

CHAPTER 34

Fabric Care

Slide presentation • Student activity pack • Class test

Caring for clothes

Before storing:

- Mend.
- Remove stains, wash or dry clean.
- Fold knitwear and store flat in a drawer.
- Close zips and buttons; hang on shaped or padded hangers.

Care labelling

Care labels found sewn into clothing and household textiles carry five basic symbols.

Care labels				
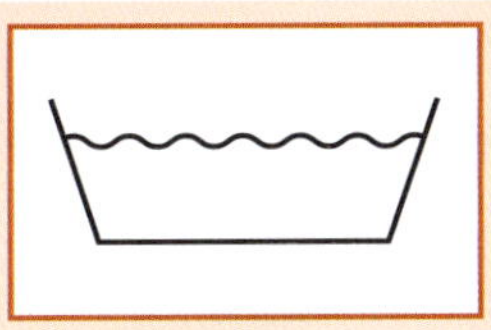	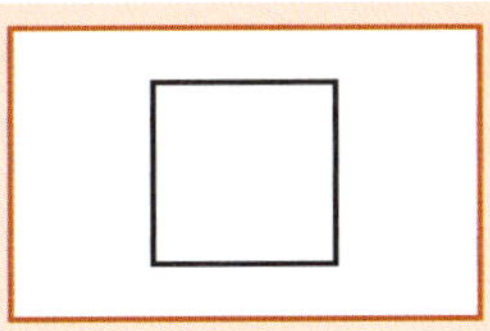			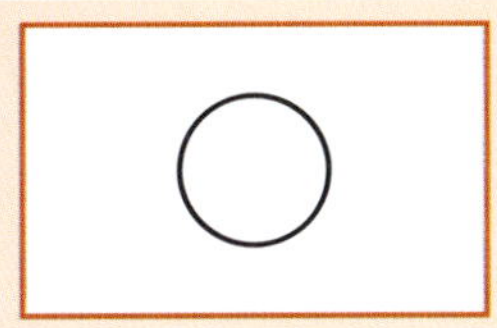
Washing instructions	Drying instructions	Ironing instructions	Bleaching instructions	Dry cleaning instructions

Washing instructions

There are three basic factors to consider when machine washing:

1. Water temperature.
2. Wash action: How fast the machine moves the clothes around during the cycle.
3. Spin length: Spin (full) or short spin.

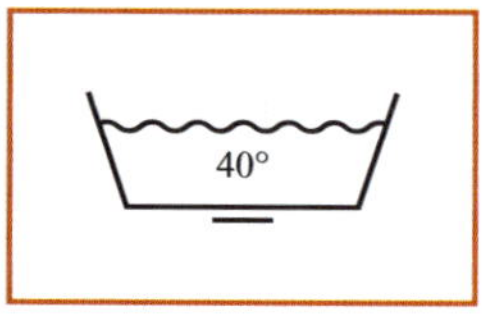

Water temperature is written inside the washtub symbol.

The bar symbol under the washtub tells you the correct wash action and spin length for the item you are washing.

Bar symbols

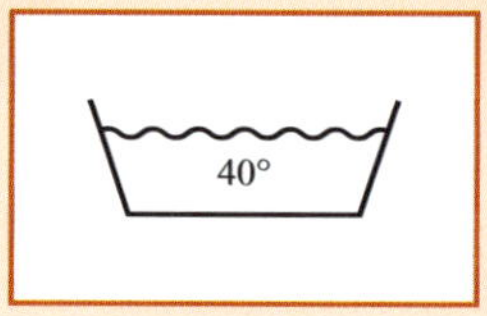

No bar:
Maximum/normal washing action and normal spin.

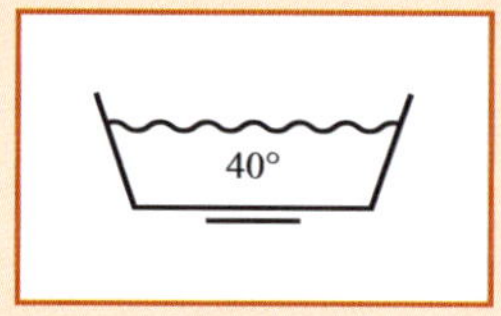

Single bar:
Medium/reduced washing action and short spin.

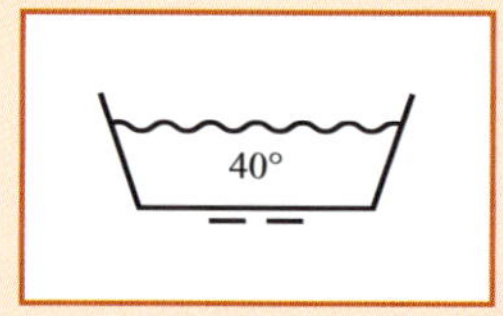

Broken bar:
Minimum washing action and wool cycle spin.

Tables like this one are found on washing detergent packets. They explain how fabrics can be washed and spun.

Textile/machine code	Machine wash	Hand wash	Fabric
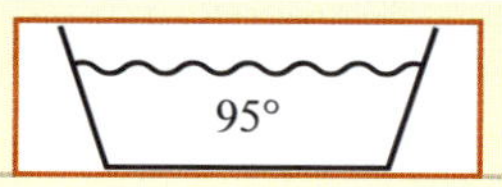	Maximum wash in cotton cycle	Hand-hot or boil, spin or wring	White cotton, linen; no special finishes
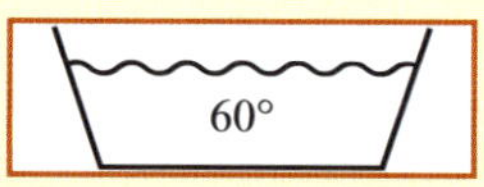	Maximum wash in cotton cycle	Hand-hot or boil, spin or wring	Cotton, linen, viscose; no special finishes; colours fast at 60°C
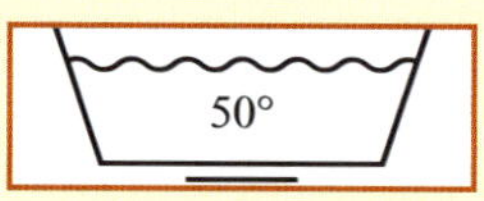	Medium wash in synthetic cycle	Hand-hot, cold rinse, short spin	Polyester-cotton mixes, nylon, polyester, cotton, viscose articles with special finishes, cotton-acrylic mixes
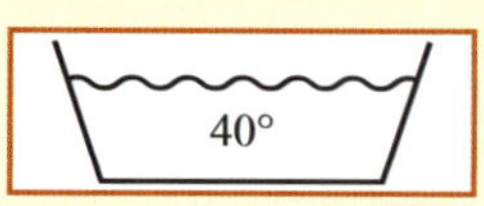	Maximum wash in cotton cycle	Warm, spin or wring	Cotton, linen, viscose where colours are not fast at 60°C
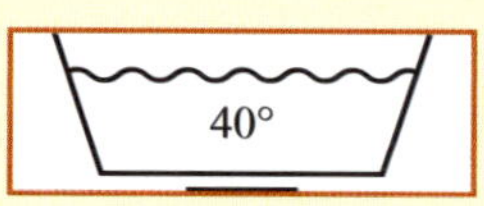	Medium wash in synthetic cycle	Warm, do not rub; spin, do not wring	Acrylics, acetate and triacetate, including mixes with wool; polyester-wool blends
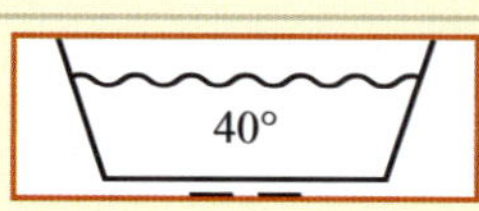	Minimum wash in wool cycle	Warm, do not rub; spin, do not wring	Wool, wool mixes, silk

Textile/machine code	Machine wash	Hand wash	Fabric
	Hand wash only	See individual care label	Some pleated fabrics
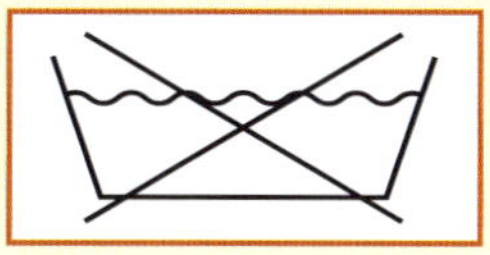	Do not wash	Do not wash	See individual care label

Drying instructions

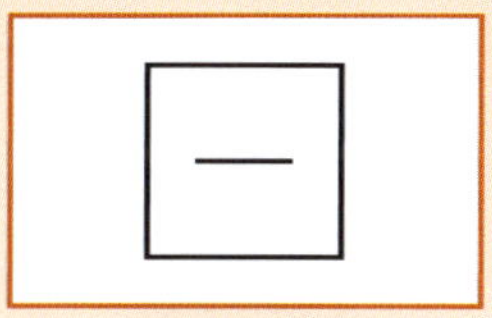

Dry flat (wool)

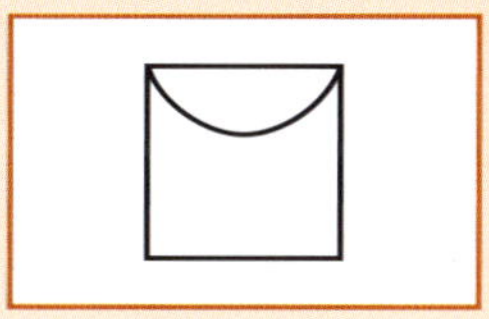

Line dry

Drip dry

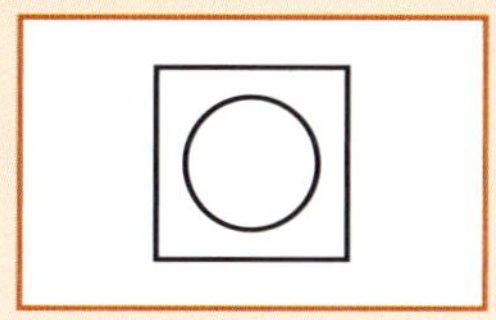

Tumble dry

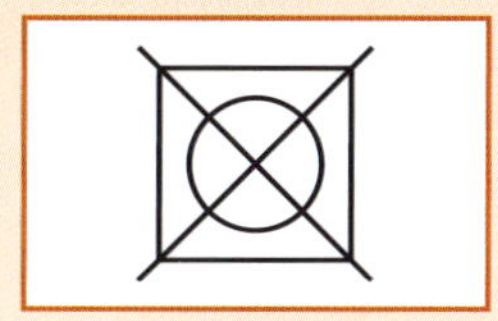

Do not tumble dry

Ironing instructions

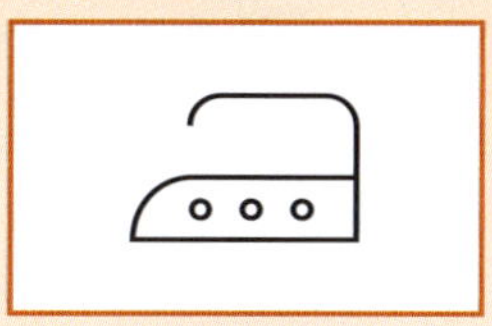

Hot iron (cotton, linen)

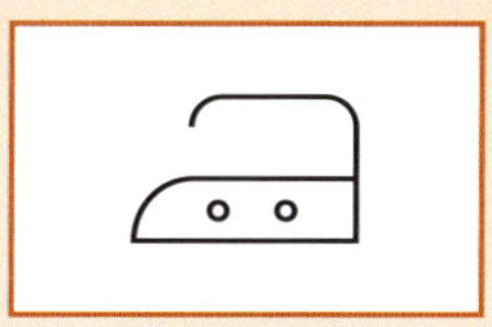

Warm iron (wool, polyester, silk)

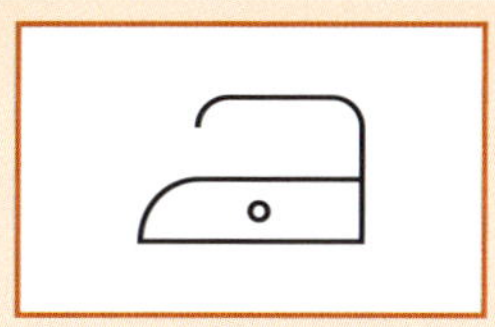

Cool iron (nylon, viscose, acrylic)

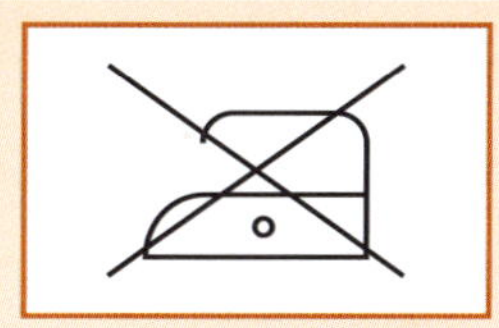

Do not iron

Dry cleaning instructions

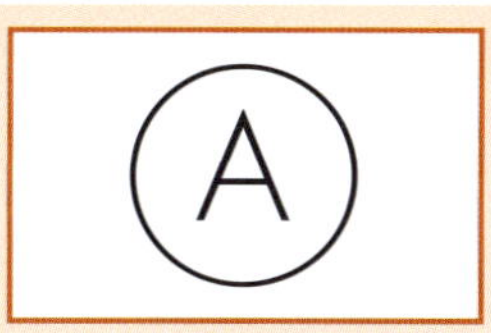

The letters tell the dry cleaner which chemicals to use

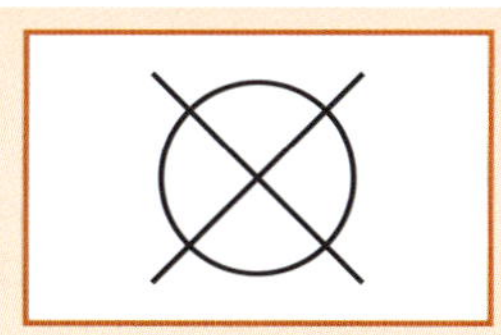

Do not dry clean

Bleaching

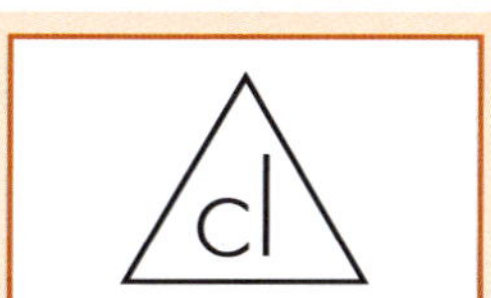

Bleach can be used

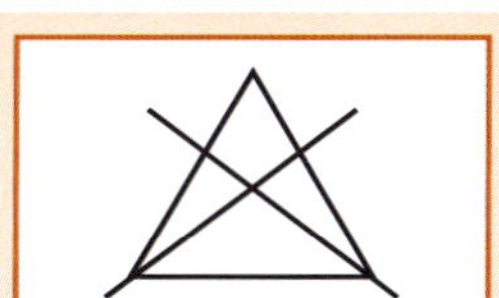

Do not bleach

Preparing a wash

- Empty pockets.
- Repair any clothes that need mending.
- Remove stubborn stains before washing.
- Close zips and buttons.
- Sort clothes according to their colour and their care labels – the colour in some clothes is **colourfast**, meaning it will not run. Other clothing has colours that are **non-colourfast**. These clothes need to be washed separately, as their colour will run into other clothing in the wash.

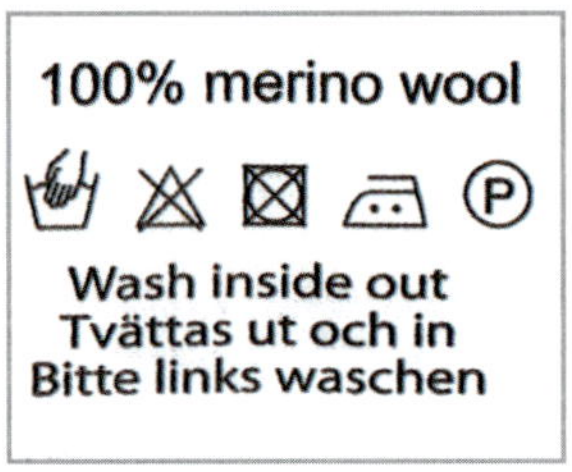

Care label. What sort of garment do you think this was attached to?

Delicate fabrics – wool and silk

- Wash by hand.
- Use a mild detergent.
- Rinse twice.
- Squeeze to remove excess water.
- Roll in a towel to remove water.
- Drip or dry flat.

Stain removal

- Act quickly or the stain will set.
- Do not rub the stain into the fabric – blot or scrape off as much as you can.
- Use the mildest treatment first, e.g. soaking in cold water.
- If you have to use a chemical stain remover, first test it somewhere on the garment that will not be seen.
- Remove stains before washing.

Commercial stain removers

There is a wide variety of stain removers on the market today. For example, some Stain Devils are specific to a certain type of stain, e.g. grass, while others are more general, e.g. Vanish products.

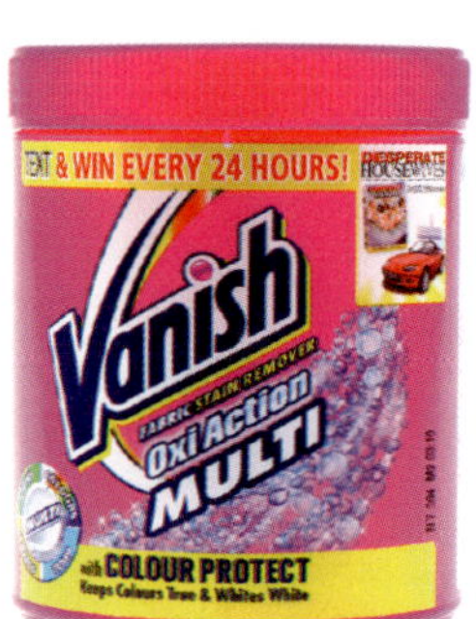

Colour catcher and colour run remover products

Colour catchers try to prevent strong colours from running into lighter colours in the wash by trapping the excess colour on a fabric sheet. Colour run removers try to remove unwanted colour from light-coloured clothing.

Stain	How to remove it
Protein stains: blood, egg, gravy	If stain is fresh, soak in cold water, then wash. If stain is older, soak in warm water with an enzyme (biological) detergent, then wash.
Chewing gum	Freeze, then pick off. You may have to use a grease solvent, e.g. Benzene, or a Stain Devil.
Ink, grass	Dab with methylated spirits and wash.
Chocolate	Dab with glycerine and wash in hot water.
Tea, coffee, perspiration (sweat)	Soak in warm water with an enzyme (biological) detergent, then wash.
Grease and oil	Wash in hot water and dab with a grease solvent, e.g. Benzene, if necessary.
Mildew (grey spots on cotton and linen)	Whites: Soak in a mild bleach solution. Colours: Treat with hydrogen peroxide.

Detergents

Detergents such as Persil and Ariel help remove dirt and stains from clothes. Detergents contain a range of ingredients, each with its own job to do.

- **Emulsifiers:** Attach themselves to the dirt at one end and to the water at the other. This takes dirt off clothes and into the washing water.
- **Bleach:** Helps to remove stains and keep whites whiter.
- **Enzymes:** Removes protein-based stains, e.g. blood.
- **Water softener:** Softens hard water, allowing the detergent to work more effectively.
- **Perfume:** Gives clothes a nice scent.

Types of detergent

- Powder, tablet or liquid detergents.
- Hand washing (for delicates, e.g. Woolite).
- Low-foaming (automatic powders for modern washing machines).
- Biological (contain enzymes which break protein stains down at under 40°C; powder washes at other temperatures also).
- Eco-friendly detergents.

Detergents

Fabric conditioners

Fabric conditioners

These are added during the final rinse. They soften clothes, reduce static cling and reduce wrinkling. Some liquid detergents also contain conditioner.

The washing machine

Guidelines for use

- If you can, wait for a full load before using the machine.
- Use a low-foaming (automatic) detergent.
- Use the economy button if clothes are not very dirty.
- Know which programmes are suited to which fabrics.

Drying

Clothes may be line dried, dried indoors on a clotheshorse or tumble dried.

Be careful when tumble drying, as some clothes will shrink (wool) or discolour (synthetic underwear) if tumble dried. Tumble drying, while quick and great for removing creases, is expensive.

Ironing

Most modern irons are steam irons. They contain a heating element, water tank and thermostat that controls how hot the iron gets.

Guidelines for use

1. Store iron sitting upright.
2. Unplug to fill the water tank and empty after use.
3. Use pre-boiled water in hard water areas to prevent lime scale build-up.
4. Set iron to correct temperature (look at care label).
5. Iron on the wrong side unless you want a shine, e.g. linen tablecloths.

Homework Assignment 51 P. 191

Cotton fabric treated with a chemical resin stops non-iron shirts and blouses from wrinkling. All you need to do is hang them up after washing.

CHAPTER 35

Needlework Skills

Teacher's CD-ROM

Slide presentation • Student activity pack • Class test

Hand sewing guidelines

1. Use a single thread, not too long.
2. Pin and tack if necessary.
3. Start and finish with a secure stitch.
4. Small, even stitches are strongest.
5. A thimble can be used for tough fabrics such as denim.

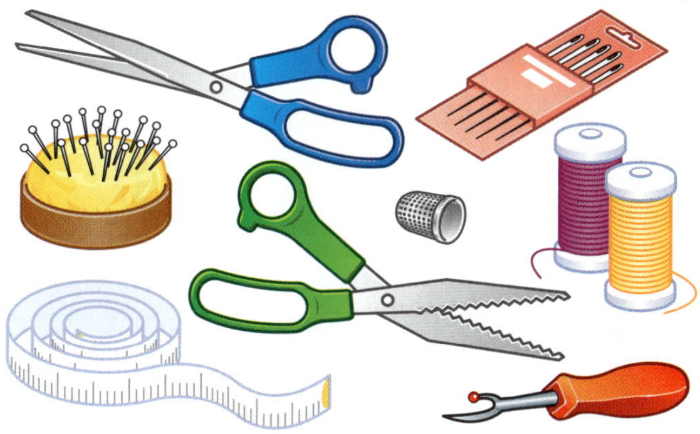

Essential sewing equipment: Scissors, measuring tape, thread, pins, needles, stitch ripper, thimble, pinking shears (not essential).

Common stitches

The best way to learn how to hand sew is to:

- Ask for a demonstration.
- Study some samples of the stitches you want to learn.
- Practise.

Tacking

Uses

Tacking is a *temporary* stitch. It is used to:

- Hold pieces of fabric together for permanent stitching.
- Help keep machine stitching straight.
- Hold a garment together for fitting.

Finish tacking with a backstitch, that is, two or three stitches on top of each other.

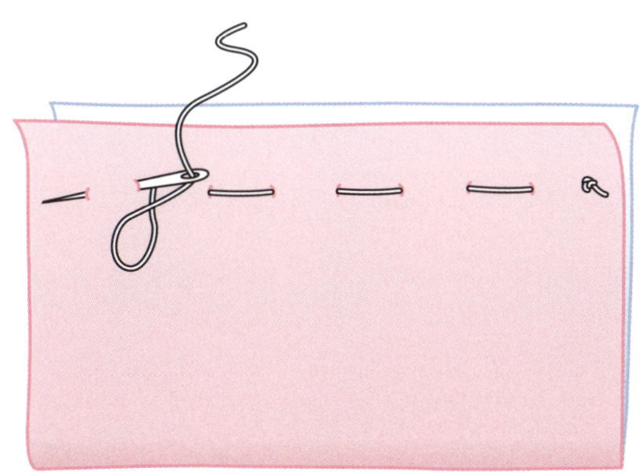

Tacking

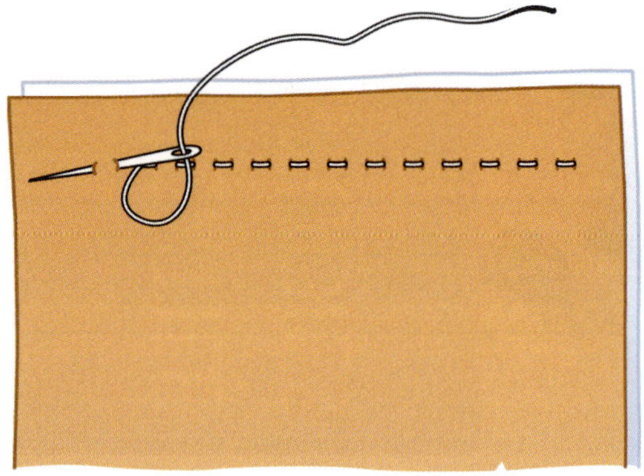

Running

Running

Running is like small tacking. Begin with a backstitch.

Uses

Two rows of running stitch are used to gather fabric if you have no machine.

Gathering is used when you wish to join a wide piece of fabric to a narrower one, e.g. fabric into the waistband of a skirt.

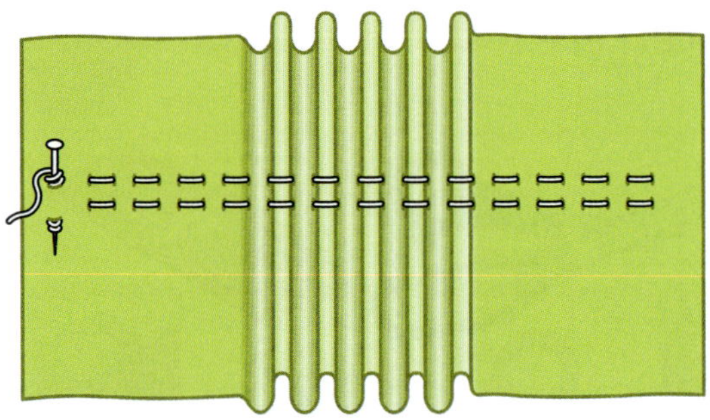

Gathering

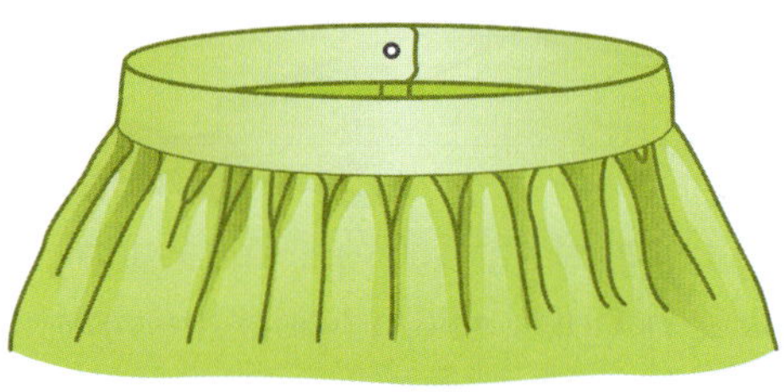

Gathered waistband

Gathering (machine or running)

1. Loosen machine tension.
2. Machine or run two rows 1cm from the top of the fabric to be gathered; leave threads.
3. Gently pull the gathering threads until you get the correct size; secure with a pin (see illustration).

Backstitching

Uses

Backstitching is a strong stitch used for seams instead of machining. Start with a backstitch. Put the needle in at the end of the last stitch and out 2mm in front. Repeat. There is little or no gap between stitches.

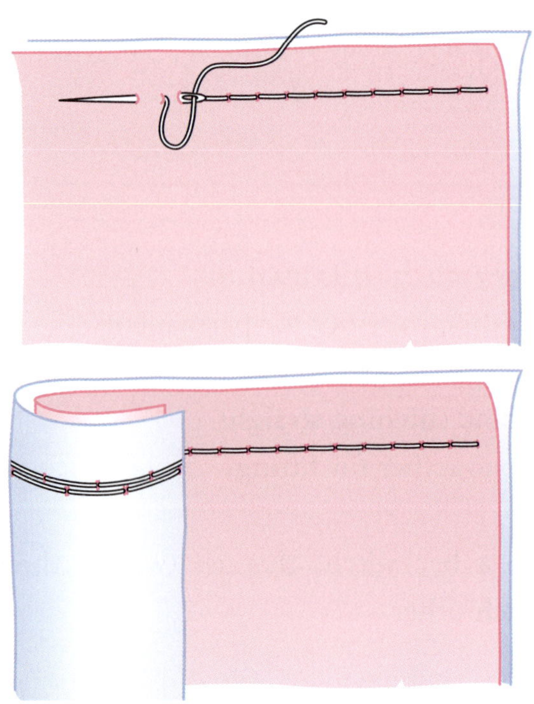

Backstitching

Hemming

Uses

Hemming is a strong slanted stitch used for stitching down collars and waistbands.

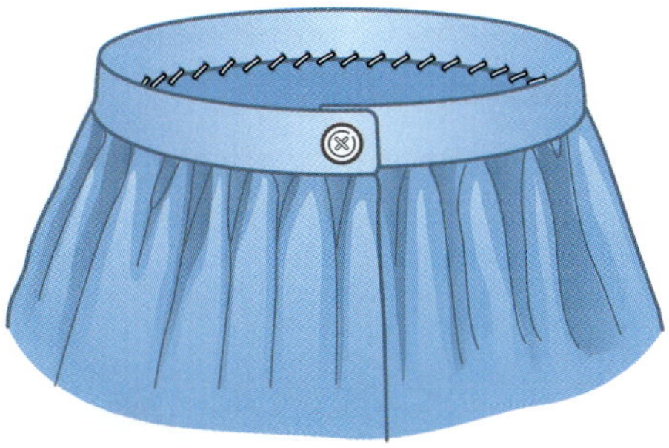

Use of hemming – stitching down collars and waistbands

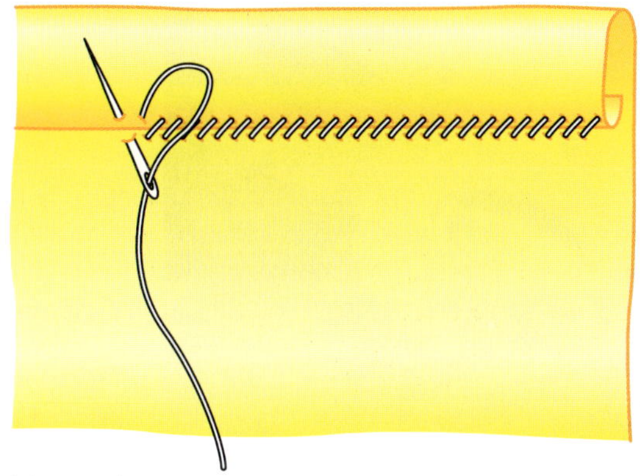

Hemming

Slip hemming

Uses

Slip hemming is used to sew up hems on skirts, trousers and dresses. If well done, it is almost invisible on the right side.

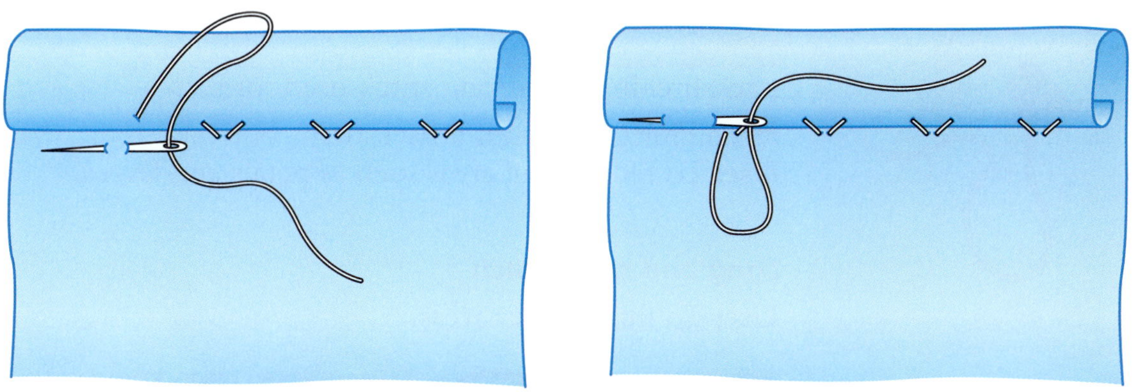

Two stages of slip hemming

Tailor tacking

Uses

Tailor tacking is used to transfer markings from paper patterns to fabric.

Tailor tacking

Embroidery

Embroidery is used to decorate fabrics.

- Embroidery thread is made up of six strands; use three strands at a time.
- Use **crewel** needles (large eye).

Hand embroidery

- Start with a few running stitches along the line to be embroidered. These secure the stitching and are covered as you work embroidery stitches over them.
- Finish by weaving thread through stitches at the back.

Common embroidery stitches

Again, the best way to learn embroidery stitches is to:

- Ask for a demonstration.
- Examine samples.
- Practise.

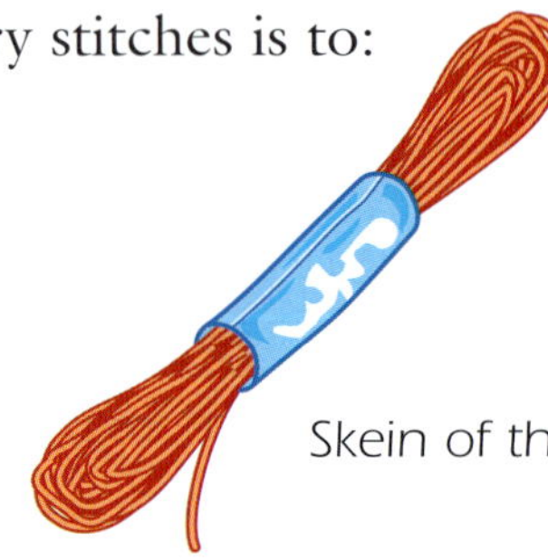

Skein of thread

Stem stitch

Use: Outline stems, etc.

Stem stitch.

Satin stitch

Satin stitch

Use: To fill in small areas such as petals and leaves.

Long and short stitch

Use: To fill in larger areas.

Long and short stitch

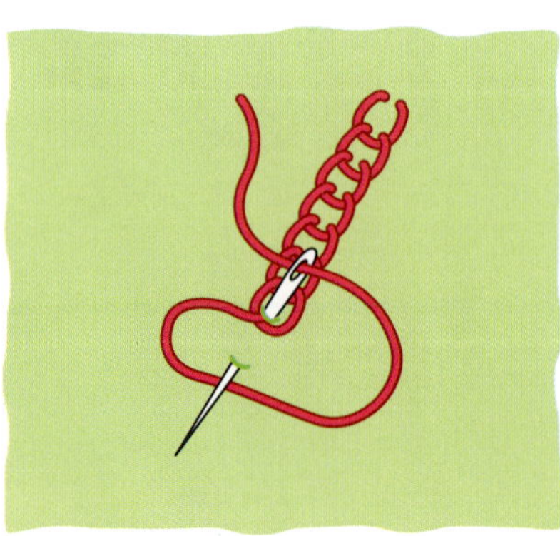

Chain stitch

Chain stitch

Use: Usually to outline.

The sewing machine

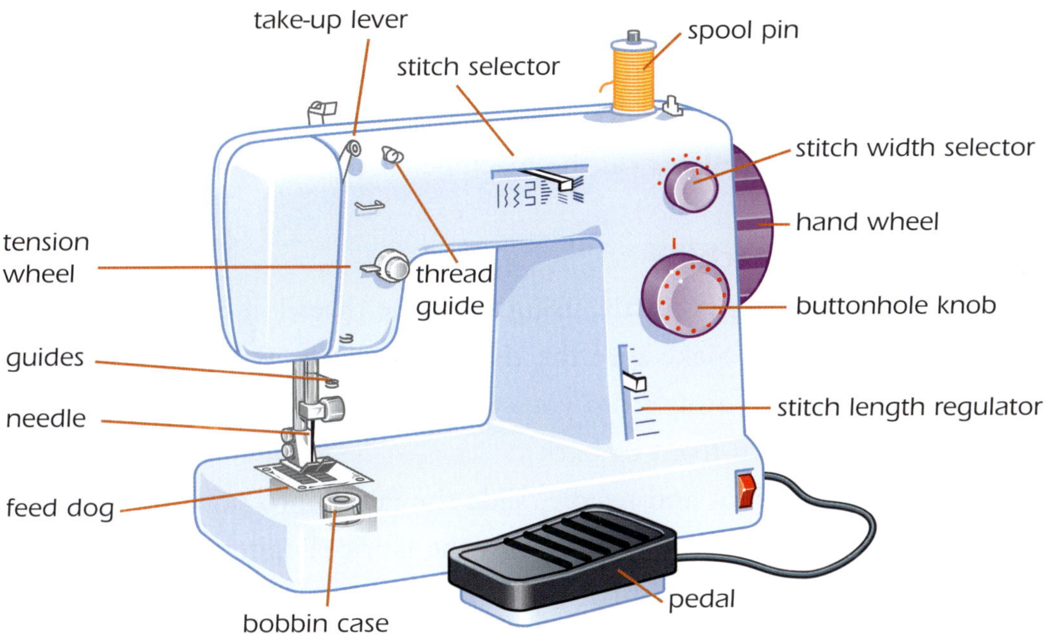

Sewing machine

Threading

This varies from machine to machine (read user instructions), but generally:

- Have thread coming from the back of the spool to the thread guide (1).
- Around tension wheel (2) to take-up lever (3).
- Through thread guides (4) and through needle (5), usually from the front to back, although can be from left to right depending on the machine.
- Thread the bobbin and insert; bobbin thread will be brought up by turning the hand wheel.

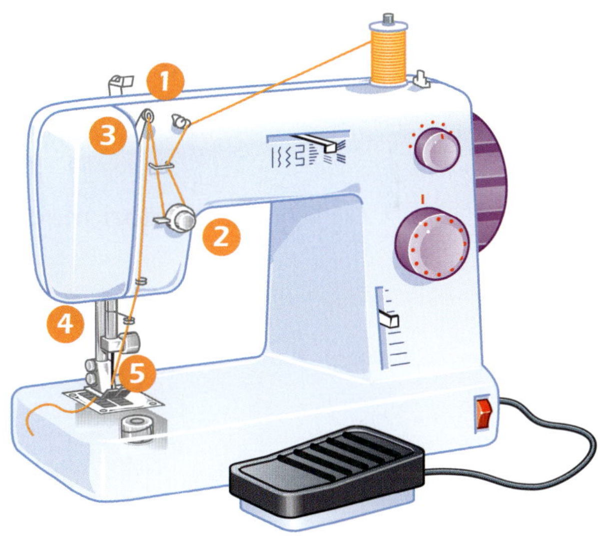

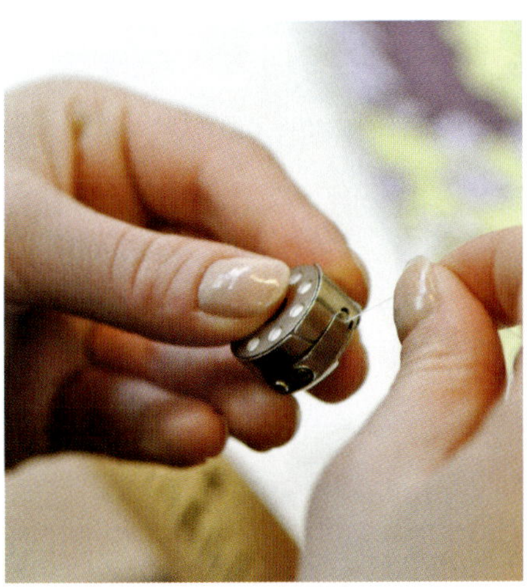

Bobbin and bobbin case

Stitch tension

Two threads form a machine stitch: one from the top spool and the other from the bobbin. Tension (the tightness of the thread) must be equal between both threads. If tension is too tight, it causes the fabric to pucker. If it is too loose, it will cause the thread to loop. The tension can be adjusted by twisting the tension wheel or regulator on the machine.

Using the sewing machine

1. Thread the machine correctly, using the same thread in both the bobbin and the top spool. Make sure the thread is not too thick for the fabric. Bring both threads away from you, towards the back of the machine (if needle threads from front to back).
2. Raise the presser foot and needle, slide the fabric into position and then lower the presser foot and needle into the fabric. Begin machining.
3. Do not push or pull the fabric, just gently guide it.
4. If you must stop in the middle of a line or to turn a corner, lower the needle into the fabric (you can then start again exactly where you left off).
5. When you finish, you can secure stitching by reversing back a few stitches or by hand sewing a few backstitches.

Common machine stitches

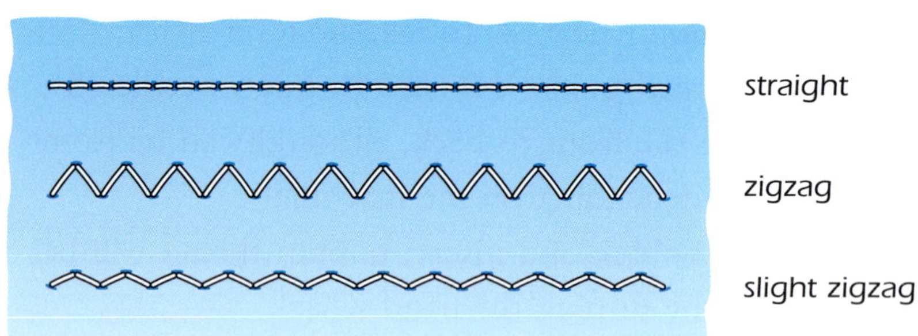

- **Straight stitch:** Used for seams and hems.
- **Zigzag:** Mainly used for seam finishing; a slight zigzag can be used for seams and hems on stretchy fabric.
- **Buttonhole stitch:** Machine buttonholes.
- **Machine embroidery:** To decorate.

Choosing a sewing machine	Care of the sewing machine
◎ Cost: Compare models; compare the same models in different shops. ◎ Buy a reliable brand from a reliable shop. ◎ Buy an elaborate machine only if you intend to use its special features. ◎ Check guarantee and after-sales service. ◎ Ask for a demonstration.	◎ Carefully read the care instructions that come with the machine. ◎ Cover machine when not in use. ◎ Clean dust from moving parts with the small brush provided with the machine. ◎ Oil occasionally (see care instructions for where to oil). ◎ Have the machine serviced and repaired by a sewing machine mechanic occasionally.

Machine faults: Possible causes

Fault	Possible causes
Needle breaking	◎ Needle has been put in back to front. ◎ Needle is blunt and cannot get through fabric properly. ◎ Fabric is too thick; sewing over zips or pins. ◎ Presser foot loose, needle is hitting it.
Thread breaking	◎ Machine is not threaded properly. ◎ Thread is too fine or of poor quality. ◎ Faulty needle or needle in back to front.
Looped stitches (underneath) 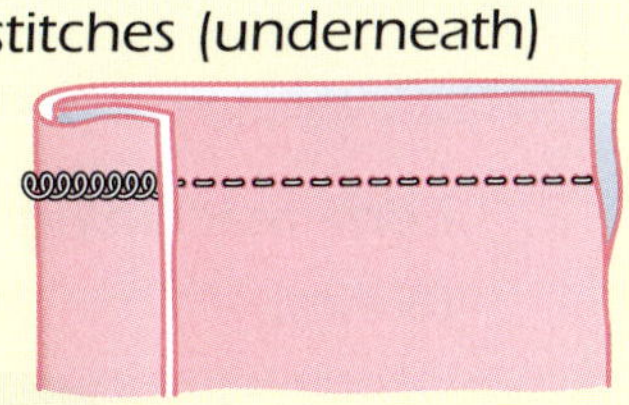	◎ Top tension too loose. ◎ Top and bobbin threads not the same. ◎ Presser foot not down. ◎ Machine not threaded correctly.
Slipped stitches 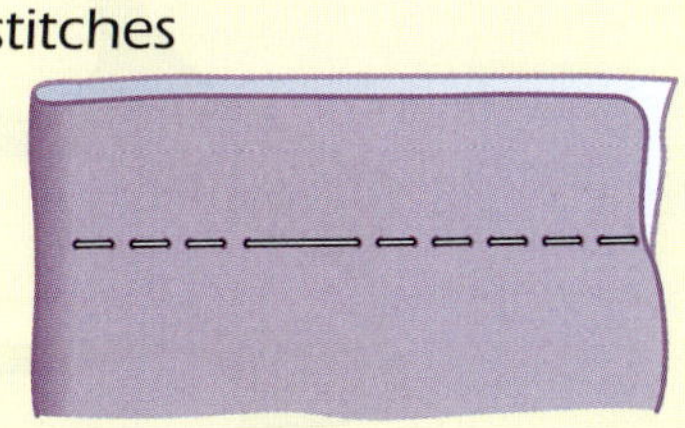	◎ Blunt needle. ◎ Needle in back to front. ◎ Needle is the wrong size for the fabric.
Puckered seam 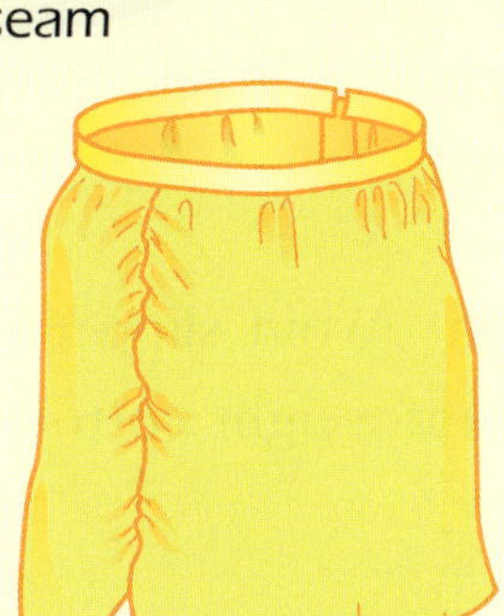	◎ Tension (top or bobbin) too tight. ◎ Blunt needle. ◎ Top and bottom threads are different. ◎ Stitch too long (fine fabrics, e.g. satin, need shorter stitch).

Seams

Seams are used to join pieces of fabric together to make clothing and other textile items. The flat seam pictured here is the most common type.

Flat seam

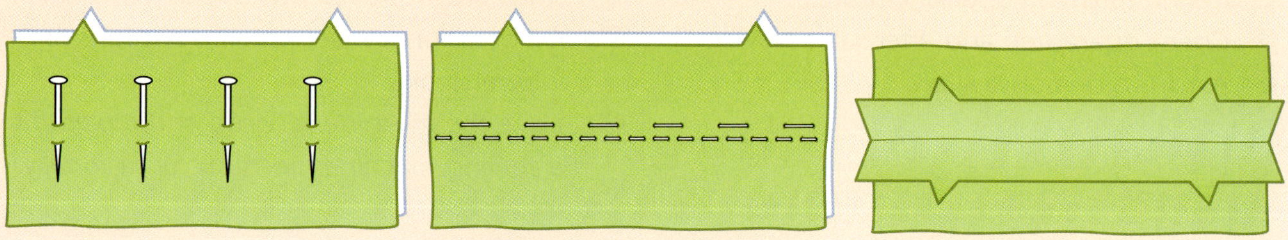

1. Pin right sides together, match notches.
2. Tack, sew 1.5cm from edge.
3. Press flat.

Seam finishes

Raw edges may be finished in one of the three ways pictured here. This prevents fraying.

Seam finishes

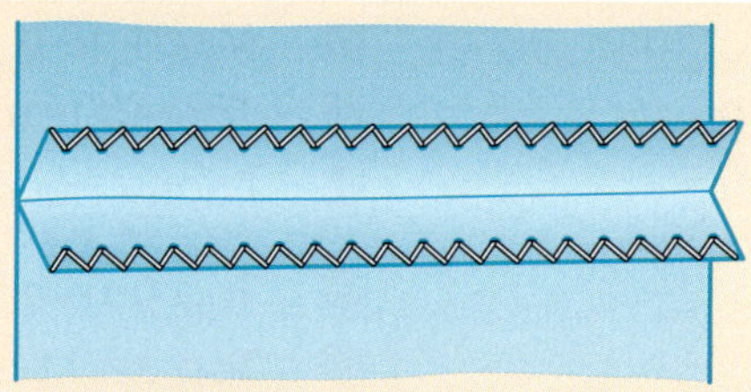

1. Zigzag.

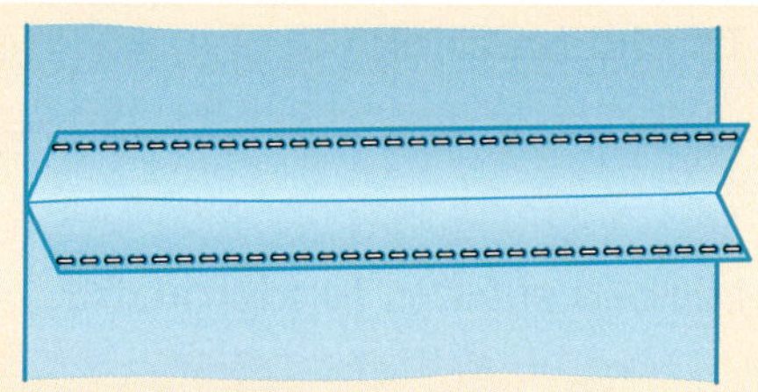

2. Edge machining (fine fabrics).

3. Pinking shears (closely woven fabrics).

Choosing a fabric for home sewing

1. Choose a fabric that is easy to work with. Avoid slippery or stretchy fabrics, as these are difficult to sew. Medium-weight cotton is good for beginners.

2. Fabrics that have a nap, e.g. velvet, or a one-way design are more difficult to cut out properly and need more fabric.
3. Fabrics are sold in different widths. The wider the fabric you buy, the less of it you will need.
4. Calculate the amount of fabric you will need using the grid on the back of your pattern envelope.
5. Check wash-care instructions on the fabric roll.
6. Buy anything else you need: a list of requirements or notions (matching thread, zip, buttons, etc.) will be given on your pattern envelope.

Note: Nap fabrics are smooth when brushed one way and rough when brushed the other, e.g. velvet.

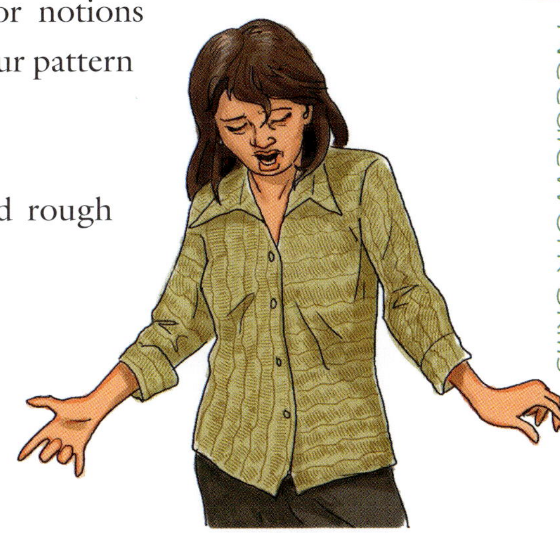

Beginners should avoid fabrics with a nap or one-way design

Selvedge

Selvedge threads, also called warp threads, are strong threads that run up and down the length of the fabric. When cutting out pattern pieces, it is important that the selvedge runs down the length of the piece. This allows the finished garment to hang well.

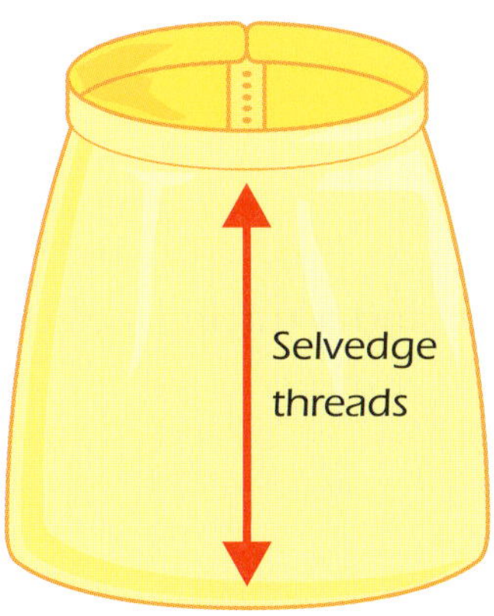

Bias: If fabric is cut on the bias (see illustration), it is stretchy. Strips of bias binding can be used to neaten armholes, necklines or for piping.

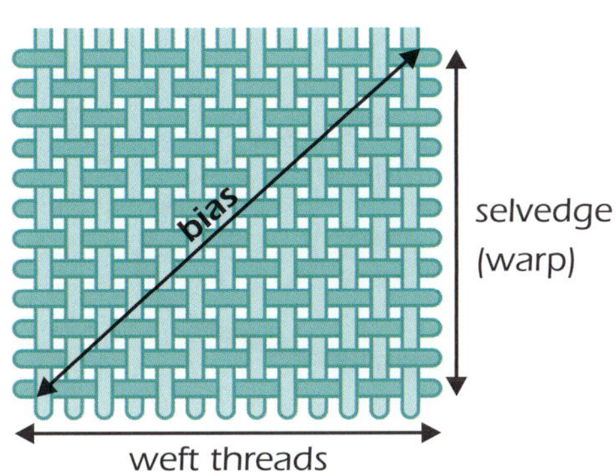

Piping – a common use for bias binding

Cutting out

1. Arrange pattern pieces on the fabric. Straight-of-grain arrows should run parallel with selvedge edges. Place fold arrows on fold. (Pattern instructions will suggest a layout.)
2. Pin in position.
3. Using a sharp scissors, cut around each pattern piece. Leave a 1.5cm seam allowance if not already allowed. (Most patterns include this allowance, in which case cut fabric to the exact size of pattern pieces.)
4. Keep fabric flat on the table with one hand. Do not lift the fabric up to cut it. Cut notches outwards.
5. Transfer important pattern markings such as buttonhole location using tailor tacks and possibly tailor's chalk and a tracing wheel and carbon, as pictured here.

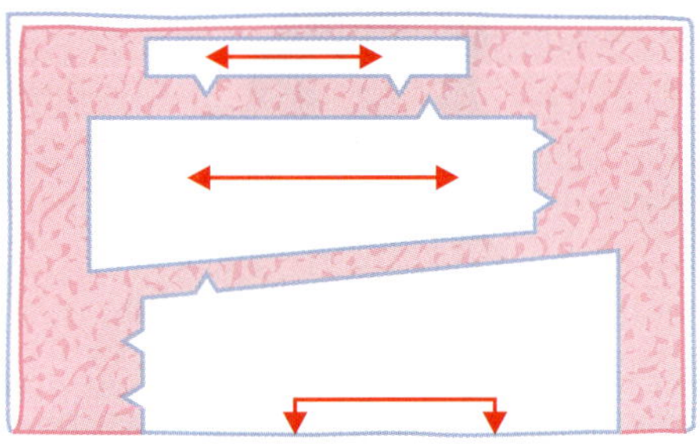

Tailor tacking

Tracing wheel and carbon

Tailor's chalk

Homework Assignment 52 P. 195

Tailor tacking is always used; tailor's chalk and a tracing wheel may also be used.

CHAPTER 36

Practical Needlework Tasks

Unit 5 TEXTILE STUDIES

Teacher's CD-ROM

Slide presentation • Student activity pack

As part of the Junior Certificate Textile Studies section, you must make two simple textile items:

- A household item.
- An item of clothing.

Your finished pieces will not be examined directly, but you may be asked questions about one or other of them in section B, question 6 of your examination paper.

Household item

Sample brief

Design and make a household item. The item must be made from textiles and cost no more than €10 to make. You must be able to complete the item in approximately four weeks.

Analysis

What are the points that you must consider?

1. A textile must be used.
2. The item must be for the home.
3. It must cost no more than €10.
4. It must not be too difficult for you to make. Consider:
    - Your sewing skills.
    - The short time given to make the item.

Research

Look through books and magazines for ideas and cost of fabrics.

List possible solutions

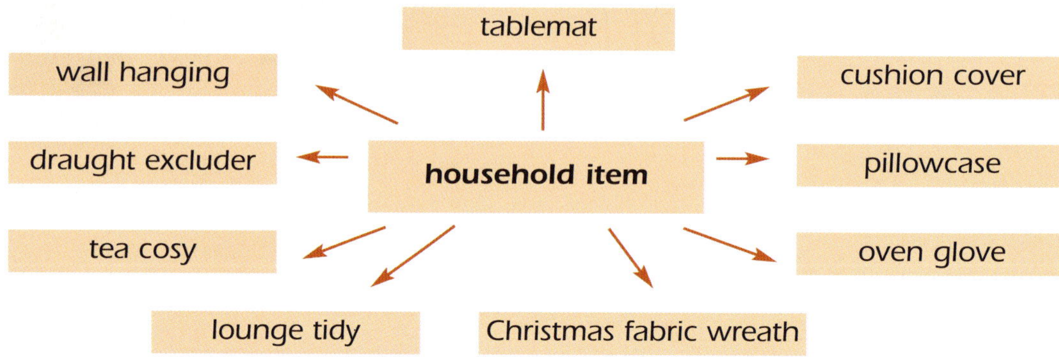

Decide on a solution

Give a reason.

Action

Make the item.

Evaluate

Did you do everything you were asked to do in the brief?

Making a household item – Christmas door wreath

You will need:

- Three strips of different but matching Christmas fabric, each 150cm x 15cm. (Depending on the fabric width, groups of six to nine students will be able to make their wreath from 1.5 metres of each fabric, thus making the project very cost effective.)
- Matching thread.
- Polystyrene beads or polyester wadding for stuffing.
- Two types of matching wide wired Christmas ribbon (60cm of one and 120cm of the other).
- 30cm of thin Christmas ribbon.
- Christmas decorations.

HOW TO MAKE THE WREATH

1. Cut out three strips of fabric 150cm x 15cm each. Fold right sides together and iron each one in half, then mark a stitching line 1.5cm in on the long and one short side. Tack to hold in place (see diagram 1).
2. Machine along the stitching line, then turn the fabric tube right side out.
3. Machine along the bottom of each tube 3cm up. This prevents the stuffing from going right to the bottom of the tube (see diagram 2).
4. Stuff the tubes, leaving space at the top of each one (if you are using polystyrene beads, cut the bottom off a large soft drinks bottle and use it with a measuring jug to funnel the beads down into each tube).
5. Sew the tube shut using either machine or hand sewing. Machine another line of sewing at the top of each tube 3cm down.
6. Machine three tubes together at the top. Plait them evenly (see diagram 3).
7. Sew the plait closed at the other end by sewing the three tubes together. Pull the plait into a round wreath shape.

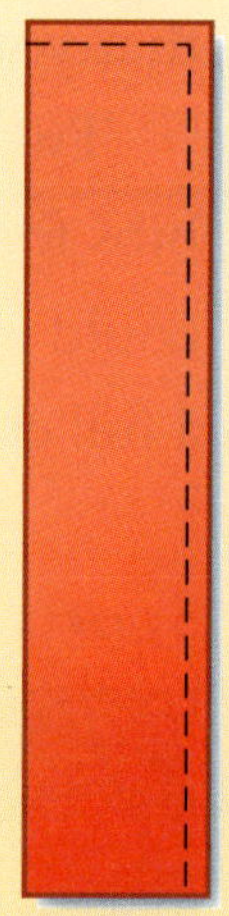

Diagram 1

Diagram 2

Diagram 3

8. Tie both ends of the plait together with half of the thin ribbon.
9. To decorate the wreath, cut the Christmas ribbon into 30cm lengths. Fold each length in two. Arrange the ribbon as shown in diagram 4. Staple or sew into place.
10. Using a glue gun, glue (or hand sew) the ribbon in place. Glue the Christmas decorations on top of the ribbons.
11. Loop the other half of the thin ribbon at the top of the wreath for hanging on the door.

Diagram 4

Item of clothing

The second textile item that you must make as part of the basic Junior Certificate Home Economics course is an item of clothing. The usual difficulty with this part of the course is finding ideas for an item of clothing that you will actually wear and make use of.

Two ideas are to make an apron for use in home economics class or sports bibs for use in PE class to distinguish teams from each other. Half of the class could make their bib in one colour and the other half in another, thus making a full class set and cutting down on costs because fabric can be bought in bulk.

Sports bib

You will need:

- A pattern.
- 0.25 metres (¼ metre) of bright washable fabric.
- Thick elastic (24cm per bib).
- Matching thread.

How to make the bib:

1. Make the pattern (see diagram below or use an old bib as a guide for making the pattern). Cut out the fabric.

2. Pin, tack and sew the shoulder seams together. Iron flat and neaten by either using zigzag or edge machining (see diagram 2).
3. Turn in all the raw edges twice, iron, tack and machine around to neaten (see diagram 3).
4. Tack and then machine the elastic securely on (see diagram 4).

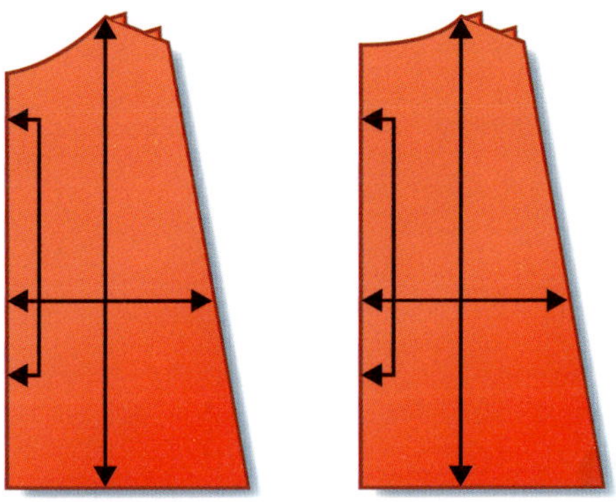
Diagram 1

Diagram 2

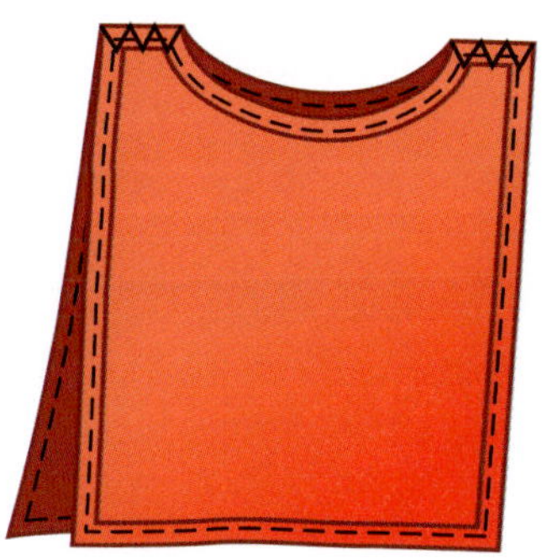
Diagram 3

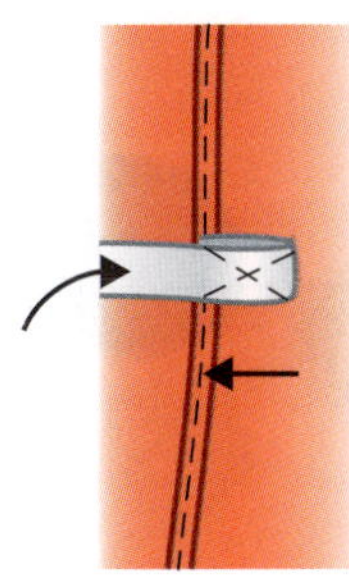
Diagram 4

Homework Assignment 53 P. 199

Test Yourself eTest.ie

Unit 6

Options

CHAPTER 37

Childcare Option

Slide presentation

Development of the foetus in the uterus (womb)

Revise pregnancy and birth, pp. 209–10, and nutrition during pregnancy, pp. 23–4.

While pregnancy generally lasts 40 weeks, many babies are born prematurely (less than 40 weeks) or are overdue (more than 40 weeks). Rapid development takes place in the uterus during pregnancy.

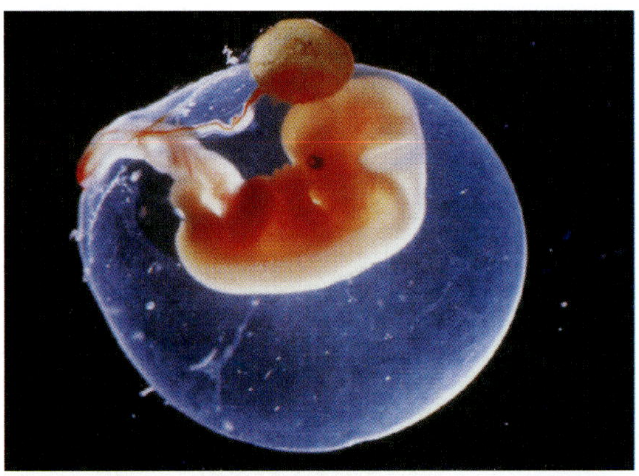

Six weeks

Week 6

The embryo is now approximately 2.5cm long. The heart is beating and arms and legs are beginning to form. It is important that the mother does not allow harmful substances such as alcohol to pass to the baby at this stage, as all the organs are forming.

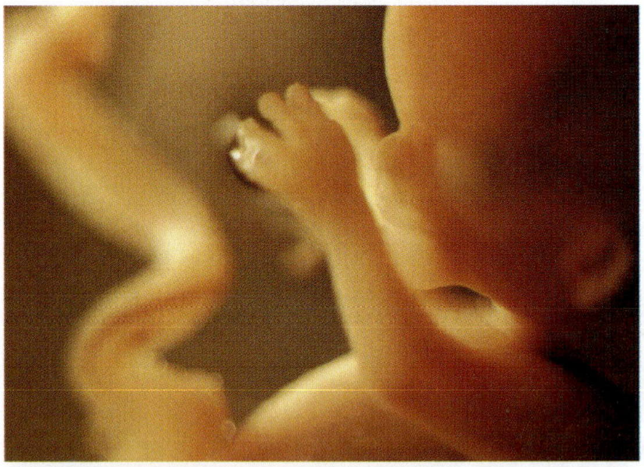

Twelve weeks

Week 12

The embryo is now called a foetus and is approximately 8.5cm long. All the organs, both external (outside) and internal (inside), are formed. They must now mature.

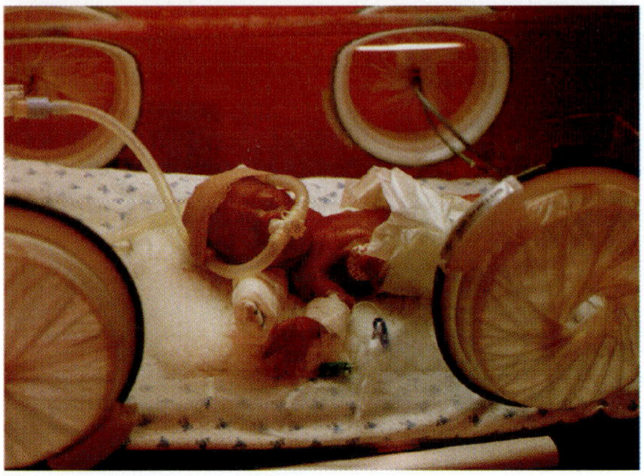

Twenty-eight weeks

Week 28

The foetus is now about 35cm long and weighs approximately 1.1kg (2.4lb). A baby born at this stage has a 75 per cent chance of survival in an intensive care baby unit.

Weeks 38 to 40

The baby is now at full term. He or she is covered in a waxy substance called vernix, which stops the baby's skin from drying out. Full-term babies are on average 48cm long and weigh approximately 3.4kg (7.5lb).

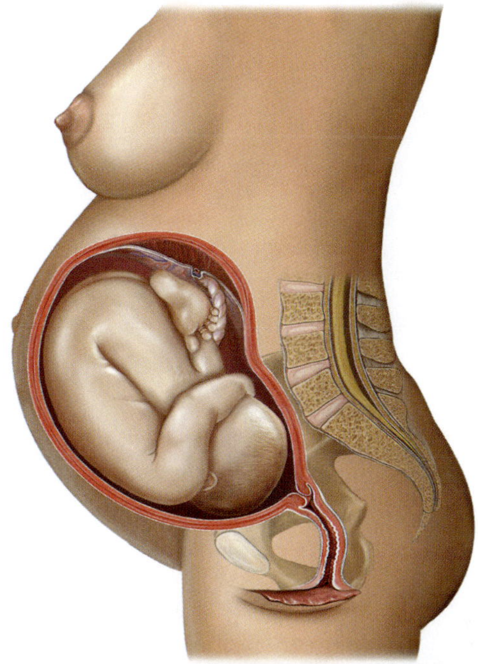

Child development

Child development means the development of every aspect of the child:

- Physical development.
- Intellectual and language development.
- Social and emotional development.

Fresh air and exercise are vital to healthy physical development

Physical development

- Increase in height and weight.
- Developing gross motor skills: This means co-ordinating large body movements, e.g. crawling, walking, running, jumping, etc.
- Developing fine motor skills: This means co-ordinating small body movements, especially with the hands, e.g. feeding with a spoon, picking up small objects, holding a pen or pencil.

Children should be given opportunities to learn and develop to their full potential

Intellectual and language development

Intellectual and language development are very closely linked.

Intellectual development

- Reasoning, e.g. if I eat my dinner, I will be allowed out to play.
- Problem solving, e.g. if I make the base of this block tower wider, it won't keep falling over.
- Concept formation (a pig is a pink animal with a curly tail).
- Concentration and memory.

Language development

- Listening and understanding.
- Talking, reading and writing.

Children learn a lot through imitation.

Social and emotional development

Social development

Social development involves three things: learning the norms (acceptable ways of behaving) in their particular society, e.g. eating with a knife and fork; how to relate well to others, e.g. sharing, turn taking; and developing a sense of right and wrong, e.g. it is wrong to throw litter on the ground.

Emotional development

Emotional development means learning to cope with feelings and development of self-esteem and self-image (how you see yourself).

Promoting healthy development

While **hereditary factors** (traits the child inherits from his or her parents) do influence a child's developmental progress, the child's **environment** (how the child is brought up) is equally (if not more) important.

Healthy physical development

Parents should:

- Provide a well-balanced diet containing plenty of freshly prepared food. Avoid excessive exposure to convenience and fast foods.
- Ensure the child gets plenty of fresh air and sleep.
- Ensure the child gets plenty of opportunity for physical activity and play, e.g. involve the child in sports from an early age.
- Give the child plenty of opportunities to practise their fine motor skills, e.g. feeding themselves. Later on, give them opportunities to write, draw, make and do activities, etc.

Healthy intellectual and language development

Parents should:

- Listen and talk to their child.

- Encourage their child's efforts.
- Read stories to their child and provide plenty of reading material for them, e.g. visit the local library weekly. Children should be exposed to books from an early age.
- Expose their child to a variety of interesting activities, such as cooking, gardening, nature walks, etc.
- A child who is exposed to these things stands a much better chance of reaching their full potential than a child who experiences few of these things.

Note: A major international study by the OECD in 2007 found that approximately 10 per cent of Irish children have severe literacy difficulties. Of these, 25 per cent had fewer than 10 books in their home.

Healthy social and emotional development

Parents should:

- Ensure that their child has a stable, secure family life with predicable routines.
- Give their child plenty of physical contact and affection.
- Give plenty of encouragement and praise.
- Set clear boundaries for their child, with fair and consistent discipline.
- Set a good example – much of a child's social behaviour is learned through imitation, e.g. if a child hears bad language, they will use bad language.
- Not overprotect their child. If a child is overprotected, this can cause the child to believe that their parents do not think them capable, which can in turn affect self-image and self-esteem.
- Give their child independence and an appropriate amount of responsibility, e.g. in dressing, feeding, tidying away toys, making their own decisions.

Stages of child development from birth to three years

The tables below outline the **norms** of development from birth to three years. Norms mean the average age at which children do certain things. There will be variation between children. Often a child may be more advanced in one area than another, e.g. may be fast to walk, but slower to speak.

Stage	Physical development	Intellectual and language development	Social and emotional development	Suitable toys and activities for age group
Birth	◎ At birth, reflexes are present, e.g. stepping reflex (see photo). ◎ No head control. ◎ Can see 25cm from nose.	◎ Startled by loud noises. 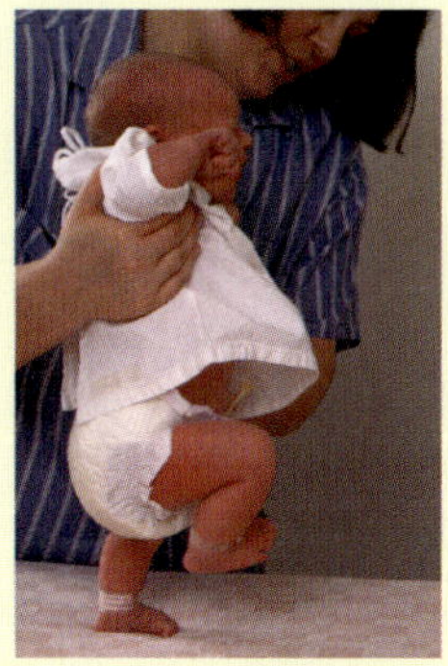	◎ Cries to make needs known.	◎ Plenty of physical contact, breastfeeding helps mother and baby to bond. ◎ Constantly talk in a soothing voice to the baby. ◎ Play music to the baby.
6 weeks	◎ When lying on front, can lift head up for a few seconds. 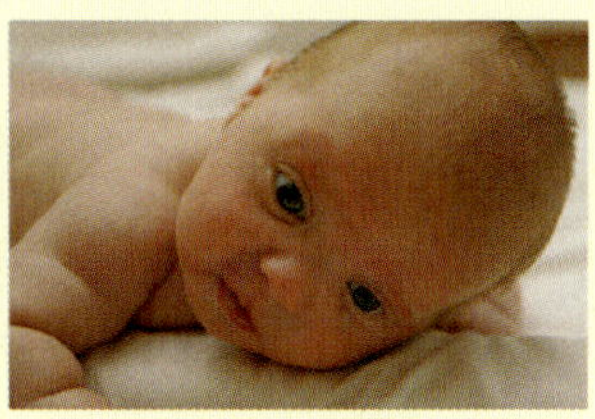	◎ Recognises familiar voices. ◎ Gurgles and coos.	◎ Smiles at about 6 weeks. ◎ Looks at parent's face intently when feeding. ◎ Cries to make needs known.	◎ Things to look at, e.g. mobiles. ◎ Plenty of close physical contact. ◎ Talk to and interact with the baby constantly. ◎ Music.
3 months	◎ Body is now uncurled, legs and arms are outstretched. ◎ Kicks vigorously. ◎ Head is steady. ◎ Plays with own hands.	◎ Chuckles. ◎ Turns head towards sounds. 	◎ Gets excited at voices, sounds, e.g. bath water running, sight of a bottle.	◎ Things to kick, e.g. baby gyms (home-made are just as good). ◎ Music.
6 months	◎ Sits with support, turning head from side to side to look around. ◎ Holds hands up to be lifted. ◎ When standing, can take weight on legs, enjoys bouncing up and down.	◎ Squeals aloud in play. ◎ Babbles tunefully, e.g. *a dah aroo goo ga*. Out of sight is out of mind – no sense of object permanence	◎ Still friendly towards strangers (fear of strangers develops around 7 months).	◎ Picture books. ◎ Bath toys. ◎ Toys to bang, e.g. drum with wooden spoon. Activity centres. 

Stage	Physical development	Intellectual and language development	Social and emotional development	Suitable toys and activities for age group
6 months (continued)	- Puts everything into mouth (see photo).	– will not look for a fallen or hidden object.		
9 months	- Can sit alone. - Rolls along on floor. - Attempts to crawl, sometimes succeeds. - Can stand holding on (see photo). - Passes toys from hand to hand. - Uses finger to point.	- Shouts to attract attention. Understands simple words, e.g. *bye-bye* or *no*. - Babbles *da da, ma ma*. Playful vocal sounds, e.g. if you say 'Jack has a bad cough', baby will pretend to cough.	- Can hold and bite a biscuit. Clings to known adult, fears strangers. Plays peek-a-boo. Claps hands.	- Songs and action rhymes. - Encourage crawling, give toys that roll. - Give finger foods. 
12 months	- Some babies 'bear walk' before walking. - May walk alone. - Can crawl upstairs (care is needed as they cannot come down safely). - Can pick up small objects, e.g. crumbs. - Points to what he or she wants.	- Knows own name. - Understands simple instructions, e.g. 'Give the ball to Daddy.' - Understands the use of everyday objects, e.g. hairbrush. - Waves bye-bye.	- Helps with dressing, e.g. holds foot out for shoe. - Likes to be constantly in sight of a familiar adult. - Can bring spoon to mouth, may tip it upside down and spill food.	- Picture books. - Push-along toys. - Fetching games, e.g. get teddy. - Songs and rhymes. 

Stage	Physical development	Intellectual and language development	Social and emotional development	Suitable toys and activities for age group
18 months	- Walks well carrying a toy. - Runs carefully with eyes fixed on the ground; will therefore bump into things. - Climbs onto adult chair and then turns around. - Makes scribbles and dots on paper. - Turns several pages of a book at once. - Starts to show left- or right-handedness.	- Recognises familiar faces in photos. - Uses 20+ recognisable words. - Imitates everyday activities, e.g. feeding a doll, brushing the floor.	- Can feed him or herself. - Can take off shoes, socks and hat. - Will play alone but still likes adult to be nearby. - Tells adult when nappy is soiled and wants it removed.	- Dancing to music. - Pull/push-along toys. - Crayons and paper. - Bricks. - Shape sorters. - Encourage child to 'help' with household chores. 
2 years	- Can run and avoid obstacles. - Walks upstairs and (often) down, holding rail or wall, two feet to a step. - Throws a ball without falling over. - Sits on a tricycle, but cannot use the pedals. - Can remove paper wrapping from a sweet. - Holds a pencil and scribbles. - Turns pages singly.	- 50+ recognisable words. - Two- or three-word sentences – girls often talk earlier than boys. - Refers to self by name. - Constantly asking the names of objects and people. - Can join in nursery rhymes and songs. - Enjoys pretend play.	- Spoon-feeds without spilling. - No comprehension of danger, e.g. will run out onto road. - Has temper tantrums (usually one or two per day). - Will not yet share willingly. - Plays near other children but not with them.	- Jigsaws. - Simple story books. - Play dough. - Painting. - Threading toys. - Musical instruments. - Tricycle. - Props for pretend play, e.g. a cash register for shop. 

Stage	Physical development	Intellectual and language development	Social and emotional development	Suitable toys and activities for age group
2 years (continued)			• Jealous of other siblings getting attention from important adults.	
3 years	• Rides a tricycle using the pedals. • Kicks ball forcibly. • Can avoid obstacles when running. • Can cut out with safety scissors. 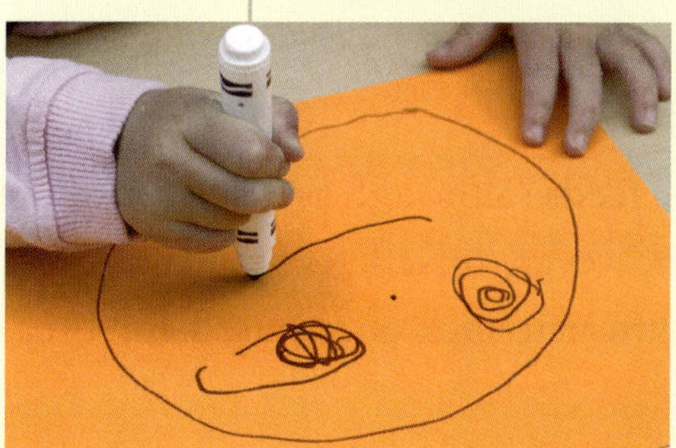 Cheap, simple activities such as drawing and colouring are excellent	• Can write X, V, H and T. • Draws a person with a head and one or two other parts/ features. • May know names of colours. • Covers entire page with paint, often uses only one colour. • Asks many questions: what, where, who.	• Eats with a fork and spoon. • Can pull pants up and down. • Toilet trained (step stool and training seat can help with independence – see photo). • Plays with other children. • Understands sharing. • Shows affection for other siblings.	• Story books. • Educational computer games. • Crayons, paint and paper. • Construction toys, e.g. Lego. • Sand and water play. • Cooking activities. • Encourage children to 'help' with household chores. • Large outdoor equipment, e.g. slide.
		• Loves stories, demands favourites over and over. • Counts to 10 or more but has little understanding of number.		• Make-believe toys.

Feeding

Babies feed on milk alone for the first four months of life. Babies may be bottle or breastfed.

Breastfeeding

Advantages:

- Nutrients are in the correct proportions for the baby's needs.
- Antibodies are passed from the mother to the baby; breastfed babies are better able to fight infection.
- Breast milk is totally sterile; no risk of food poisoning.
- Breastfeeding encourages bonding.
- Breast milk is free and always available.
- Breastfeeding helps mother regain her figure after pregnancy.
- Breastfed babies are less likely to be overweight, suffer from allergies, have colic or constipation.

Disadvantages:

- Strain on mother, who must do all the feeds (although breast milk can be expressed and used to bottle feed; however, mixed feeding like this is often not recommended because a different suck is required for breast and bottle feeding).
- Other members of the family, e.g. father, may feel left out.
- Breastfeeding can be sore to begin with.
- Lack of breastfeeding facilities or bad attitudes of others to breastfeeding in public.
- Because breast milk is more digestible, it does not stay in the stomach as long, so breastfed babies may therefore feed more often and sleep less.

Bottle-feeding

Advantages:

- Formula milks are now available that copy breast milk exactly.
- Bottle-feeding gives the mother more freedom; night feeds can be shared between parents.

Disadvantages:

- Badly made-up feeds can be dangerous; never put extra scoops of formula into the bottle, as it can cause the baby to dehydrate or become very constipated.
- Bottles that have not been sterilised properly can give the baby food poisoning and make him or her very ill.
- Formula milks are expensive and making up feeds is time consuming.
- Bottle feeds do not provide protection against infection and disease like breast milk does.

Formula milk

Infant formula milk is made from cow or soya milk. It is manufactured to resemble breast milk. Soya milk formula is given to vegan babies or babies with a cow's milk allergy.

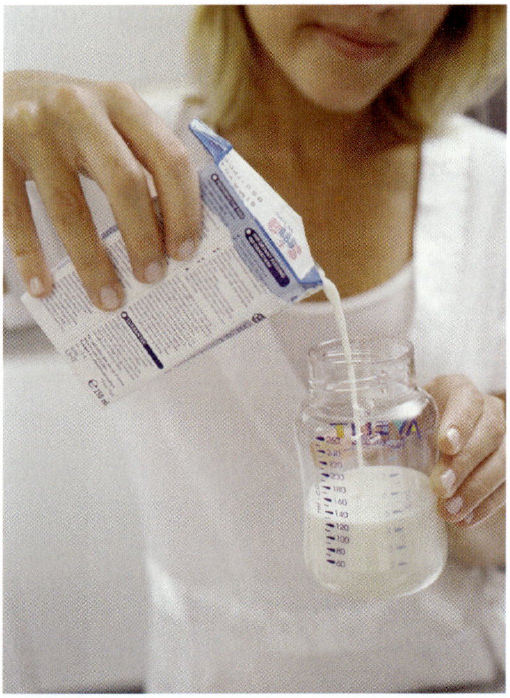

Ready-made formula feeds are available for travel, but they are too expensive to use all the time

Making up a formula feed

1. Wash your hands carefully.
2. Scrub all baby-feeding equipment thoroughly with a bottle brush, washing-up liquid and hot water; rinse.
3. Sterilise using one of the following four methods:
   - Boil everything in a saucepan with the lid on for three minutes.
   - Use a cold water sterilising tank. Sterilising fluid or tablets are added to cold water; bottles, etc. must be completely covered with fluid for 30 minutes.
   - Use a steam sterilising unit that clicks off automatically when the bottles are sterilised; follow manufacturer's instructions exactly.
   - Sterilisers for use in the microwave are also available; follow instructions exactly.
4. **First**, pour the exact amount of cool **boiled** water into the sterilised bottles.
5. **Second**, add the correct number of **level** scoops of dried formula milk (the pack will tell you how many scoops to add).
6. Replace the teat and lid and shake well.

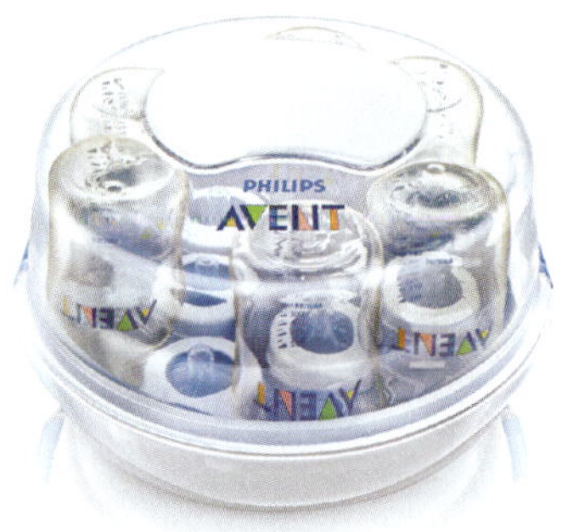

Microwave steam steriliser

Automatic steam steriliser

7. If you make up more than one feed, store the others in the fridge. Reheat carefully in a jug of boiling water (microwave reheating can be dangerous, as the outside of the bottle may be cool and the inside hot: shake well).
8. Hold the baby close when feeding. A baby should never be left alone to feed with a propped-up bottle.
9. Empty any leftover feed out. Rinse and wash the bottle, ready for sterilising.

Winding

All babies, but particularly bottle-fed babies, swallow some air while feeding. Winding is done to help bring up trapped wind and make the baby more comfortable. To wind a baby, hold him or her up against your shoulder or hold under their chin on your knee and gently rub or pat the baby's back until the wind is released. Cover your shoulder with a tea towel, as some feed may also come back up. Some babies may also need gripe water or colic drops to help.

Winding a baby

Weaning

Babies are usually ready for weaning at around 16 weeks. While babies may accept food earlier, babies should not be weaned too early, as their digestive systems are not developed enough to cope with solids. Breast- or bottle-fed babies have an instinct to feed, but eating solid food takes practice and babies may appear to be spitting out food even when they are not.

Baby rice and puréed fruits and vegetables are suitable first foods. Never add salt or sugar to feeds and avoid foods containing gluten (wheat), as it can be difficult to digest.

Remember, eating habits that last a lifetime are created in childhood. Avoid giving children sugary or high-fat foods.

Baby food can be made in bulk and frozen in ice cube trays. That way, it can be used as needed.

> Commercial baby foods have improved greatly in recent times and now there is a huge variety on the market. Such foods are very useful in emergencies but are expensive if used all the time.

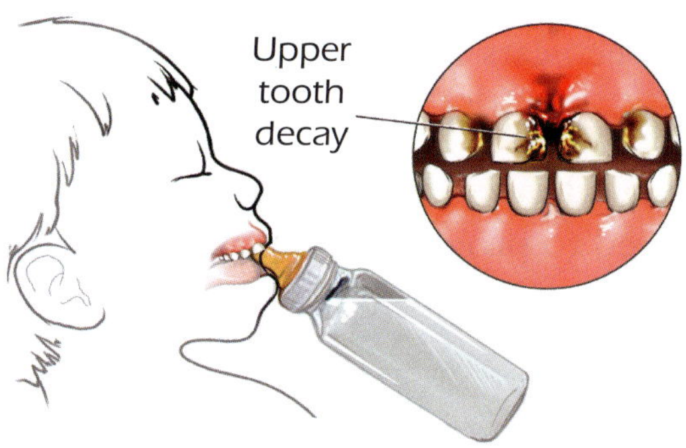

Bottle rot

Care of the teeth

A baby's teeth start to appear at around six to seven months. Even though baby teeth (also called milk teeth) only last until approximately age seven, it is important that they are well cared for.

- Never give babies juice to drink from a bottle, as this leads to bottle rot. Even young babies can drink small amounts at a time from a cup or spoon.
- Do not allow babies and toddlers to fall asleep with bottles of milk in their mouth, as this leads to bottle rot.
- Once baby teeth appear, clean them using a cotton bud or later a soft toothbrush. Teach toddlers to brush their own teeth as soon as they are able to.
- Do not bribe children with sweets or dip soothers in sugar: you are encouraging a sweet tooth and may cause tooth decay.
- Provide children with plenty of calcium-rich foods such as cheese, yoghurt and milk.

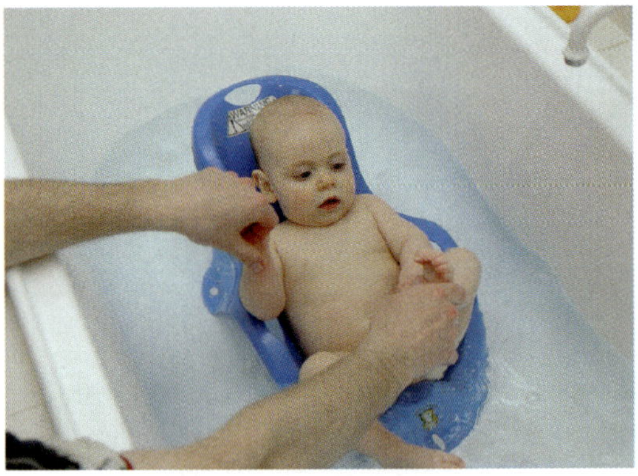

Bathing

Small babies need to be washed every day. Baby baths are available that allow even a very small baby to be supported and the freedom to kick their legs freely. If the baby cannot be given a bath, then they should be **'topped and tailed'**. This means that the baby's face and hands are washed first with the nappy area washed last in order to avoid spreading infection.

Toilet training

While there is no set age at which toilet training should begin, children often show signs of being ready at around three years old. Girls often toilet train earlier than boys, perhaps because they generally have better verbal skills at this age and are able to say that they have to go. The main thing about toilet training is that the child should be allowed to progress at their own pace in a relaxed atmosphere. A low potty is often used initially, and then, when the child progresses to the toilet, a trainer seat and step may be used.

Nowadays there seems to be a baby gadget for everything. Parents should be wary of spending money on unnecessary gadgets that are expensive and clutter up the house.

Clothing

A **layette** is the name given to the set of clothes needed for a newborn baby. It may include the following:

2 sleep suits (see photo on next page)
2 baby blankets
7 vests
7 babygros
3 cardigans
1 or 2 all-in snow suits
2 pairs of scratch mittens
7 bibs

A layette

Buying baby clothing

- Clothing should be bought big enough to last two to three months.
- Buy soft, flexible, washable fabrics with no hard seams or rough stitching.
- Clothing should be flame resistant.
- Clothing should be easy to put on and take off.
- Avoid buttons on inner garments, as they may press into the baby and be uncomfortable. Buttons on cardigans, etc. should be very well sewn on. Snap fasteners are safe and convenient.

Sleep suit

Nappies

While the majority of babies wear disposable nappies, for both economic and environmental reasons there has been a renewed interest in using cloth nappies and brands such as Bum Genius and FuzziBunz have become popular. Where disposable nappies are used, there are ecologically friendly brands available that do not contain plastic. Nappies should be disposed of carefully.

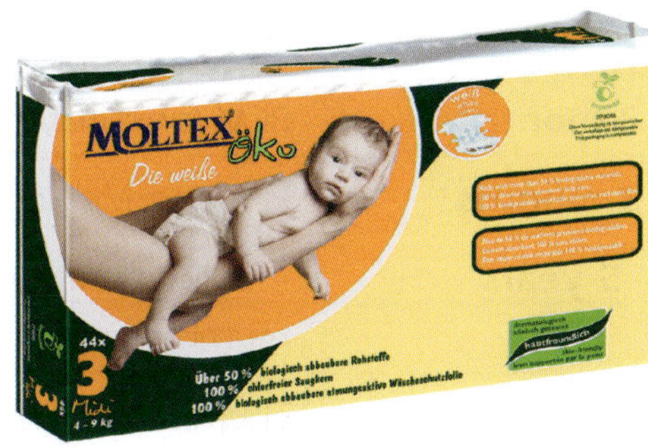

Eco-friendly nappies are available to buy online and in some supermarkets

Healthcare

All babies in Ireland are entitled to free healthcare provided by the Health Service Executive (HSE).

Baby clinics run by the HSE provide health and developmental checkups, e.g. sight, hearing and physical development. If they suspect a health or developmental difficulty, they will refer the baby on to a more specialised service.

A **public health nurse** visits every mother and baby within a few days of them being discharged from hospital. Public health nurses provide help and guidance on issues such as feeding, immunisations, etc.

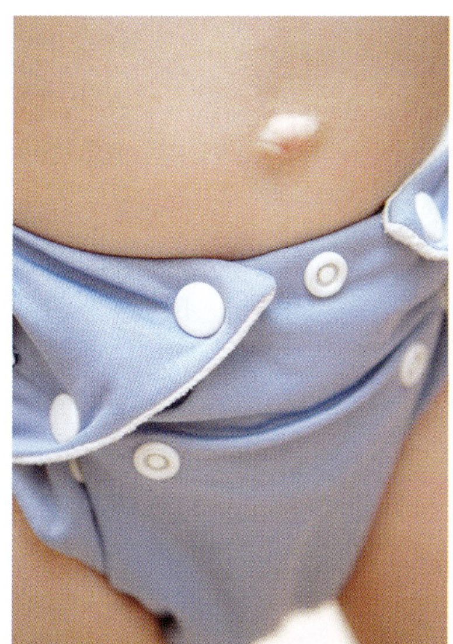

Modern cloth nappies are becoming more popular

Immunisation works by stimulating the immune system to produce antibodies to fight particular diseases. Because either an altered version of the virus or bacteria, e.g. measles, mumps, rubella, or only a component of the virus or bacteria, e.g. tetanus, diphtheria, whooping cough, is injected into the baby, immunisation shots cannot cause the disease itself. Immunisations are available free of charge from the GP. GPs keep records of what injections a baby has had, but parents should keep an accurate record also.

Babies born after 1 July 2008 follow the immunisation schedule shown in the table below.

Age	Immunisation
0–1 month	BCG (usually given while in hospital)
2 months	6 in 1 (diphtheria, tetanus, whooping cough, hib, polio and hepatitis B), PCV (pneumococcal conjugate vaccine)
4 months	6 in 1 (diphtheria, tetanus, whooping cough, hib, polio and hepatitis B), Meningococcal C
6 months	6 in 1 (diphtheria, tetanus, whooping cough, hib, polio and hepatitis B), Meningococcal C, PCV (pneumococcal conjugate vaccine)
12 months	PCV (pneumococcal conjugate vaccine)
13 months	Hib and Meningococcal C
4–5 years	4 in 1 (diphtheria, tetanus, whooping cough, polio), MMR – measles, mumps and rubella
11–14 years	TD (tetanus, diphtheria)

Childcare facilities

Because large numbers of families have both parents working, good childcare facilities have become very important in Ireland. There are a number of childcare options available to working parents:

- Childminder (may be a relative).
- Live-in babysitter or au pair.
- Crèche.
- Pre-school or Montessori.

Choosing childcare facilities

- Choose childcare facilities that have an open door policy (parents can walk in at any time).
- When visiting potential childcare facilities, parents should bring their child with them and observe how staff interact with him or her. Parents should observe if there are any children who are upset or not receiving attention.

- Look for a variety of equipment, toys and educational material, such as jigsaws, play dough, books, etc. Children should have access to a safe outside area.
- Children should not spend too much time watching TV or DVDs. Once a week is plenty.
- Rooms should be spacious and clean with plenty of natural light.
- Children should have a separate sleep/nap area – cots should not be used as play pens. Children should not be sleeping in recliners and pushchairs.
- Staff should be well trained and experienced. Parents should ask how long staff have been working there – a high staff turnover could indicate problems.
- There should be good routines for eating, playing and sleeping.
- Proper child to childcare worker ratios should be in place: 3:1 for babies under one year, 6:1 for children between one and three years, and 8:1 for children between three and six years.
- There should be clean nappy-changing facilities.
- Children should not have access to food preparation areas and meals prepared should be nutritionally balanced.
- Exits should be easily accessed in case of an emergency, fire drills should be posted and practised and fire blankets, extinguishers and smoke alarms should be present.
- Safety devices, e.g. socket covers, should be in place.
- There should be emergency procedures in place should a child become ill and a policy preventing children from attending while ill.
- Feedback should be given to parents daily on their child, e.g. what they have eaten, whether they have had wet and/or dirty nappies, etc. This is important should a child become ill after they leave for the day – doctors may require this information.

Babysitting guidelines

The Irish Red Cross produces an excellent handbook for babysitters and parents. It can be downloaded from the Irish Red Cross website at www.redcross.ie – click first on 'Services in Ireland' and then on 'Community

Services', where you will see a link for 'A Handbook for Babysitters and Parents'. Babysitting could be an interesting topic for a Junior Certificate childcare project.

Children with extraordinary abilities also have frequently unmet special needs

Children with special needs

All children have needs, for example the need for food, shelter, clothing, love, security and understanding. Children with disabilities or extraordinary abilities have these same needs together with some additional ones.

A **disability** is something that can restrict the individual or make some things more difficult to do.

Classification of special needs

Special needs can be classified in a number of ways.

1. **Incidence (how often the special need occurs)**
   - **High-incidence special needs:** These are special needs that occur relatively frequently in the general population but symptoms are not very severe, e.g. borderline general learning difficulty, dyslexia, eczema, high-achieving children.
   - **Low-incidence special needs:** These are special needs that do not occur frequently in the general population but symptoms can be severe, e.g. cerebral palsy, autism, Down's syndrome.

2. **Cause and/or area of development affected by the special need**
   - **Physical conditions:** Epilepsy, asthma, eczema, diabetes, HIV and AIDS, coeliac, dyspraxia.
   - **Inherited conditions:** Sickle cell anaemia, cystic fibrosis, haemophilia, Duchenne muscular dystrophy.
   - **Conditions affecting communication and control:** Dyslexia, dyscalculia, dyspraxia, autistic spectrum disorders, speech, language and communication impairment, emotional and behavioural difficulties, ADHD (attention deficit hyperactivity disorder).
   - **Conditions affecting cognitive development:** General learning disability (borderline, mild, moderate, severe), dyscalculia (math).

- **Complex conditions:** Down's syndrome, fragile X syndrome, hearing impairment, visual impairment, spina bifida, hydrocephalus, cerebral palsy.

Always treat a child with special needs as the individual they are. Ensure that the child is considered first and the special need second.

Some common conditions and disabilities explained

It must be pointed out that only a very basic explanation is offered here for these complex disabilities.

Asthma

- **Cause:** The airways of the lungs become narrowed. Allergies, infection, exercise, the weather or emotional upset may bring on an attack.
- **Effects:** Breathing becomes difficult. If an attack is severe, the child may become anxious and afraid and require medical attention.
- **Special needs:** Child must avoid things or situations they know bring on attacks, e.g. playing football on a cold foggy morning. A reliever inhaler is used to widen the airways again and bring breathing back to normal. A preventer inhaler is used to help prevent attacks from occurring in the first place.

Autism

- **Cause:** Unknown.
- **Effects:** Autism is a complex lifelong condition that affects the child's ability to socialise and communicate effectively. Some children with autism also have obsessive or ritualistic behaviour. Almost all will have an excessive need for sameness and routine in their lives.
- **Special needs:** Safety is a big concern. The child often has no sense of danger. Routine, special education, e.g. ABA (applied behavioural analysis).

Cerebral palsy

- **Cause:** The part of the brain that controls movement and posture is damaged or fails to develop. This may be caused by complications during pregnancy or accident/injury during or after birth.
- **Effects:** Movement of limbs is impaired or in other cases balance may be affected. Cerebral palsy ranges from mild to very severe – child may be unable to move or speak.

- **Special needs:** Physiotherapy, speech therapy, occupational therapy (helping person develop new life skills).

Coeliac

See pp. 31–2.

Cystic fibrosis

- **Cause:** Hereditary disease (passed on in the genes).
- **Effects:** Body mucus is very thick, causing breathing problems, severe chest infections and digestive problems.
- **Special needs:** Antibiotic therapy for lung infections, physiotherepy, digestive enzymes taken at every meal, lung transplant.

Diabetes

See pp. 32–3.

Down's syndrome

- **Cause:** Usually an abnormality on the twenty-first chromosome. Associated with maternal age, e.g. at age 25–29 the incidence is 1 in 1,100, whereas by age 40 the incidence is 1 in 100.
- **Effects:** Learning difficulties, characteristic physical appearance, frequent illness, prone to chest infections and heart conditions.
- **Special needs:** A stimulating environment and a positive attitude will help the child reach his or her full potential.

Dyslexia

- **Cause:** Dyslexia is inherited. It may be inherited from an uncle, aunt or grandparent.
- **Effects:** Dyslexia is a language-based learning disability in which a person has trouble reading and writing. It is estimated that while approximately 20 per cent of children have reading and writing difficulties, only about 3 per cent have dyslexia. Environmental factors such as a lack of books and reading at home are thought to be the main causes of reading difficulty, whereas children with dyslexia have difficulty reading despite adequate tuition.
- **Special needs:** Specific language learning techniques are used to overcome the problem. Use of technology, e.g. Dragon NaturallySpeaking (a computer program that converts the student's speech into text) helps the child with schoolwork.

Hearing impairment

- **Cause:** Can be hereditary or caused by infections such as rubella during pregnancy or meningitis in the child after birth.
- **Effects:** Degree of hearing loss can range from slight hearing loss to profound deafness.
- **Special needs:** Cochlear ear implants are becoming more common. Hearing aids, speech therapy, sign language.

Spina bifida

- **Cause:** True cause not known; both genetic and environmental factors thought to be involved (taking regular folic acid before and during pregnancy reduces the risk of spina bifida by 70 per cent).
- **Effects:** Gap in the bones of the spine exposing the spinal cord. Several different types of spina bifida; ranges from little or no disability to paralysis.
- **Special needs:** Children should be helped to partake in all the activities usual for their age group.

Visual impairment

- **Cause:** Hereditary or caused by infections during pregnancy or birth, e.g. rubella.
- **Effects:** Individual may be blind or partially sighted.
- **Special needs:** Many visually impaired children, if given good resources and support, do very well in mainstream schools.

Irish family law

The structure of the Irish family has changed dramatically over the past number of decades. As a result of all this change, Irish family law has needed to change and be updated. Some of the most common laws are listed and briefly explained below.

- **Family Law (Maintenance of Spouses and Children) Act 1976:** In the event of separation or divorce, the earning partner must provide reasonable maintenance in order to support children. Failure to do so may result in deductions at source.
- **Family Home Protection Act 1976:** Prevents the selling of the family home without the consent of both partners.
- **Family Law (Protection of Spouses and Children) Act 1981:** Gave the circuit and district courts power to grant barring and protection orders (added to by the Domestic Violence Act 1996).

- **Status of Children Act 1987:** Abolished status of illegitimacy and amended law on maintenance and succession rights for non-marital children. Allowed unmarried fathers to apply for guardianship of their children. Provided for blood tests to establish paternity.
- **Children Act 1989 and 2001:** Gave the HSE powers to care for children at risk.
- **Child Care Act 1991:** Gave powers to the HSE to care for children who were ill treated, neglected or sexually abused. (*Children First – The National Guidelines for the Protection and Welfare of Children* was published in 1999.)
- **Maintenance Act 1994:** Simplified procedures for recovering maintenance debts from other countries.
- **Family Law Act 1995:** Raised the minimum age for marriage to 18 and requires three months' written notice to the local registrar.
- **Domestic Violence Act 1996:** Extended safety, barring and protection orders to non-spouses, gave the health boards powers to apply for orders, allowed arrest without warrant for breach.
- **Family Law (Divorce) Act 1996:** Allowed divorce and remarriage.
- **Children Act 1997:** Recognised natural fathers as guardians, allowed children's views to be considered in guardianship, access and custody matters, allowed parents to have joint custody.
- **Education Act 1998:** Outlines the Department of Education and Science's role in providing education for all children under 18 years.
- **Education of Persons with Special Needs Act 2004:** Outlines the government's obligation regarding providing education to children with special needs.

In addition to the law, there are a number of organisations available to families experiencing difficulties.

- **Family Mediation Service:** This is a state-run service that helps couples who have decided to separate to sort out difficult issues such as custody of children, maintenance, etc.
- **Irish Catholic Marriage Advisory Council (CMAC):** Provides a counselling service to couples whose marriages are in difficulty.
- **Women's Aid:** Provides temporary accommodation and counselling for women victims of domestic violence and their children.
- **Gingerbread:** A support group for lone parents.
- **Alcoholics Anonymous, Narcotics Anonymous, Al-Anon** and

Alateen: Provide support for families and individuals affected by drug and alcohol abuse.

Childcare project

You will not be asked questions on the Home Economics written paper about the childcare option. Instead, the childcare option, like each of the other two options, is assessed through project work. Your project is worth 15 per cent of your final Junior Certificate mark at both Ordinary and Higher Levels.

For this project you must select a **topic** and then research and prepare a written report on it. The written report should **not** be more than **1,500 words** (approximately five full typed pages or nine written pages). You will not receive good marks for large amounts of writing copied closely from books or leaflets. Read the section below for ideas on how to research and present a good project.

Deciding on a topic

Some possible topics include:

- Feeding babies and young children.
- A child developmental study (where you choose a child and follow his or her development over a period of time).
- Experiences of being a teenage mother or lone parent.
- A babysitter's handbook.
- A guide for new parents.
- Make a child's toy as part of an overall study on child development.
- A study of childhood illness and immunisations.
- An investigation into childcare facilities in your area.
- An investigation into a particular special need.
- Safety and accident prevention in the home, first aid for babies.

Research methods

A good project will have two kinds of research:

1. **Primary research:** With this type of research, you gather information yourself. You can do this by using questionnaires, interviewing people, observing children at play and recording what you see, visiting a play school and recording what you see, etc.
2. **Secondary research:** With this type of research, you read and use other people's primary research. Secondary research is taken from books, the internet, magazines, information leaflets, etc. It is important that you do not copy straight from these sources into your project, as you will lose marks.

Presentation of project

Each of the following should be included.

1. **Contents page**.
2. **Acknowledgements:** You should thank anybody who helped you with your project, e.g. people who gave you information.
3. **Aims:** List what exactly it is you wish to investigate and find out. You should try to have approximately four or five good, strong aims.

> Example: If you chose to do your project on Down's syndrome, an example of an aim would be: 'I would like to find out what causes Down's syndrome.'

4. **Research:** You should give details of all the different research you undertook as part of the project. Remember, you must use both primary and secondary research.

> Example: If you chose to investigate the topic of breastfeeding for your project, you could say the following as part of your research section:
>
> *Primary research: I interviewed a mother who had breastfed both her children, asking her about her experience (please see Appendix 1 for interview questions asked).*
>
> *Secondary research: I looked up breastfeeding on the internet and also got a number of interesting leaflets from the health promotion corner in my local hospital.*

5. **Main content of project:** Give details about what you found out about your topic. It should be presented in an organised way and follow the aims of your project closely.

> Example: If you chose to do a project on children with type 1 diabetes, you would write here about (1) causes, symptoms and diagnosis, (2) living with diabetes (results of an interview with a parent of a child with diabetes), (3) statistics – results of internet investigation into how common it is in children, (4) sample menus for a child with diabetes, etc.

6. **Conclusions:** Present the most important findings of your project.

> Example: Having investigated the topic of breastfeeding on the internet, by interviewing a mother and by reading leaflets on the subject, I found that the main advantages of breastfeeding are that it passes immunity from infection on from mother to baby, etc.

7. **Evaluation:** In this section, you review your aims and decide how well you achieved them. Explain why you feel you achieved or did not achieve them. If you were to do this project again, list the changes you would make.

Example: One of the main aims of this project was to investigate the childcare options available for parents in this town. I certainly did this by carrying out thorough research and compiling a list of all childcare services available, etc.

8. **Bibliography/sources of information:** In this section, you should list where you got your information. Include books, magazines, leaflets, internet sites, etc.
9. **Appendix:** Include copies of interviews, questionnaires, letters you received, leaflets, etc.

Marking scheme

Below is a copy of the marking scheme used by examiners of your project. You should use it to make sure you have covered all areas.

Area	Marking criteria	Marks
Aim of project	Clear statement of aims Relevance to child development	10
Research methodology/ problem solving	Information-gathering techniques used and/or investigation of task	20
Content	Relevance to aim, depth of treatment, testing information, practical work, e.g. models, accurate information, organisation of materials	40
Conclusion	Conclusions drawn from results of investigation, to include a critical evaluation of any product produced against stated aims	10
Originality	Indication of original input by way of analysis, interpretation and/or development of topic by the candidate	10
Layout	Layout, spelling/writing skills, quality of graphics, etc., finish of product	10

CHAPTER 38

Design and Craftwork Option

Teacher's CD-ROM

Slide presentation

Craft has a long, rich history in Ireland. In the past, craft items such as knitted jumpers, baskets, woven fabrics, lace and embroidery would have been made in every household. Many such crafts were made firstly as functional items and only secondly as items of beauty.

The major sectors within the Irish craft industry today are pottery, glass, jewellery, textiles (particularly knitwear) and furniture. While Irish craft businesses are usually small in scale and spread all over the country, the industry does employ a significant number of people, particularly in isolated rural communities unsuited to large-scale manufacturing.

Nicholas Mosse pottery

Brenda Hoey jewellery

Tim Ryan knitwear

The Irish Craft Council

The Irish Craft Council, which was formed in 1971, is the national agency for the development of the craft industry in Ireland. The main aims of the council are to:

- Research and market Irish crafts at home and abroad.
- Encourage excellence in the Irish crafts industry.

- Provide training courses in various Irish crafts.
- Provide information to those interested in the craft industry.
- Run exhibitions to promote Irish crafts, e.g. in the RDS.
- Provide a directory of Irish crafts where Craft Council members have their own webpage.

For a broad view of the craft industry in Ireland today, visit the Craft Council's website at www.ccoi.ie or write to them at Crafts Council of Ireland, Castle Yard, Kilkenny; telephone (056) 776 1804.

Design and craftwork project

You will not be asked questions on the Home Economics written paper about the design and craftwork option. Instead, the design and craftwork option, like each of the other two options, is assessed through project work. Your project is worth 15 per cent of your final Junior Certificate mark at both Ordinary and Higher Levels.

Brief

For this project, you must design and make a simple, cost-effective craftwork item from a **textile**.

The design and craftwork folder

Together with the craft item, you must present a written folder, which must contain the following.

1. A table of contents:
   - Analysis of brief (points 2, 3 and 4 below).
   - Solution (points 5, 6, 7 and 8 below).
   - Evaluation (points 9 and 10 below).
2. A statement of what you have been asked to do.
3. A list of the most important things you have to consider.
4. Evidence that you investigated a number of different crafts before deciding on one.
5. Background information on the craft you have chosen. You could look on the internet for this, or in books and magazines from your Home Economics room or local library.
6. A plan of work similar to this sample plan:

- Week 1: Make a list of all the materials and equipment I need and go buy them.
- Week 2: Practise my craft on scraps of fabric.
- Week 3: Complete sample drawings and designs; choose one, etc.

7. A list of all materials and equipment you used for making the craft item, with costings.
8. A description with diagrams, sample designs, patterns, etc. of exactly how you made your craft item.
9. An evaluation of the craft item: does it meet the brief? Why?
10. Proposed modifications: what would you change if you were to do it again and why.

The craft item itself

Stage 1: Research and choose a craft. You will have to consult with your teacher and carry out research in books, magazines, craft shops, etc. **You cannot use craft kits.** Some possibilities are:

- Appliqué
- Crochet
- Cross-stitch
- Embroidery
- Knitting
- Lace making
- Patchwork
- Quilting
- Rug making
- Weaving

Note: Tie-dying, batik, stencilling or painting fabric can be used but only **in addition to** a stitch-based craft, which must make up the main part of your work. For example, if you decided to create an underwater sea scene, you could paint parts of the background undersea colours before using textured embroidery and beading to create the scene.

Stage 2: Decide what to make that would best suit your craft. Some possibilities are:

- Cushion covers (suits most of the crafts above).
- Lampshade (weaving, pleating, appliqué, embroidery).

- Peg bag (appliqué, embroidery, cross-stitch).
- Picture (appliqué, embroidery, cross-stitch, lace making).
- Rug (rug making).
- Table wear – placemats, napkins, tablecloths, tray cloths and table runners (most crafts above).
- Wall hanging (patchwork, appliqué, embroidery).

Stage 3: Practise your craft. You should practise on old scraps of material: keep these and present them in your design folder.

Stage 4: Finalise your design on paper.

Stage 5: Make your craftwork item.

Sample craft items

Knitted cushions are now very fashionable. You could add unusual buttons, a little beading or embroidery to make yours unique.

Peg bag made out of strong cotton fabric (it can be further stiffened with iron-on fabric interfacing) and decorated with appliqué and embroidery

CHAPTER 39

Textile Skills Option

Teacher's CD-ROM

Slide presentation

This option gives you the opportunity to make an item of clothing and to learn about career opportunities in the textile industry, for example as a clothing designer.

Using patterns and basic garment construction

Before beginning this chapter, please revise Chapter 35. Pay particular attention to the following:

- Using a pattern envelope.
- Choosing fabric for sewing.
- Pattern layouts.
- Transferring pattern markings.
- Cutting out pattern pieces.

Taking body measurements

Before you buy a pattern or fabric, you will need to know your correct body measurements.

General guidelines

- Use a tape measure that has not been stretched and do not pull it too tight, as it will not give the correct reading.
- Remove outer garments, such as jumpers, so that you are not measuring over too much bulk.
- Ask a friend to help, as it is very difficult to take your own measurements correctly.
- Check all measurements twice, as it is easy to make mistakes.

For most garments, you need to measure your:

1. Chest (male) or bust (female).
2. Waist.
3. Hips.

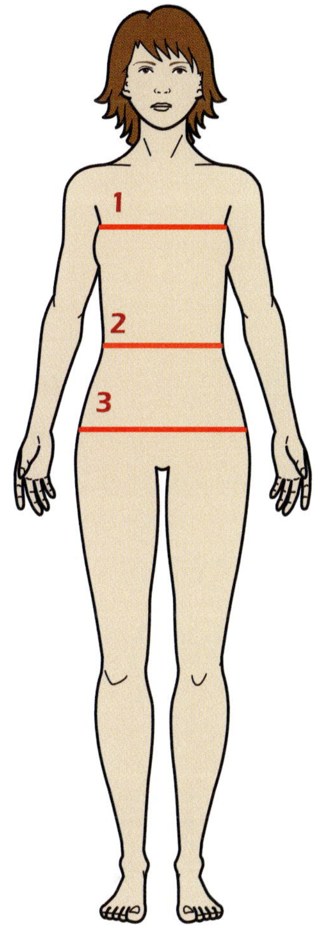

For all of these, measure around the fullest (widest) part. To find your natural waistline, tie a piece of string around your waist: where it rests comfortably is your natural waistline.

You may need additional measurements for some garments:

1. **Back length:** From the bone at the bottom of your neck to your natural waistline.
2. **Sleeve length:** From your shoulder to your wrist, keeping your elbow bent.
3. **Outside leg:** From your waist down to where the bottom of the hem will be.
4. **Inside leg:** From your crotch to where the bottom of the hem will be.
5. **Neck width:** Measure around the neck and add 1.2cm to the result (so that collars will not be too tight).

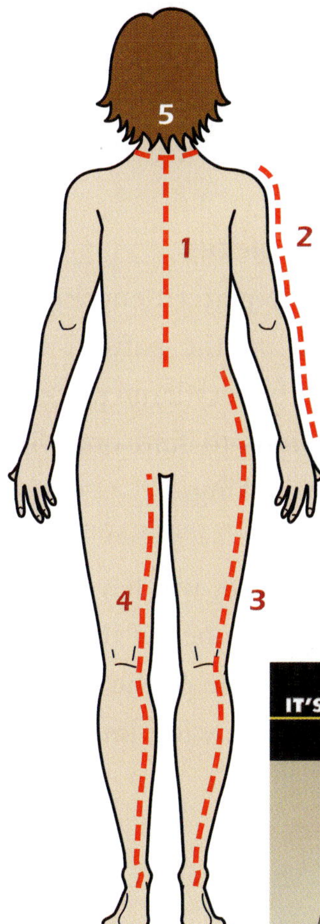

Making clothes

Choosing a pattern

Several different companies, such as Simplicity and Burda, manufacture commercial patterns. These companies display their patterns in pattern catalogues, which are available for you to look at in textile shops or you can view and buy from their range online. Most of these companies manufacture patterns that are suitable for beginners; these are often found in a special section of their catalogues or websites (www.simplicity.com or www.burdafashion.com).

Most patterns include more than one style (view) and a range of sizes

The pattern envelope

The pattern envelope front and back gives you information on:

- What the garment(s) should look like when finished.
- How much fabric you need for each view and size of garment.
- Which fabrics are suitable for the garment(s).
- Any extras, or **notions**, you need to make the garment(s).
- View of the back of the garment(s).

Inside the pattern envelope

Inside the pattern envelope, you will find two things:

- The actual pattern pieces.
- A set of instructions.

Pattern pieces

Inside the pattern envelope, you will find the pattern pieces for all the views pictured on the pattern envelope. Pattern pieces will be printed out on a number of very large pieces of tissue paper. You will have to study the pattern instructions to find out which pieces are needed for the particular garment you are making.

Pattern pieces will have the following information printed on them:

- The number of the pattern piece.
- The name of the pattern piece, e.g. skirt back.
- The following important markings.

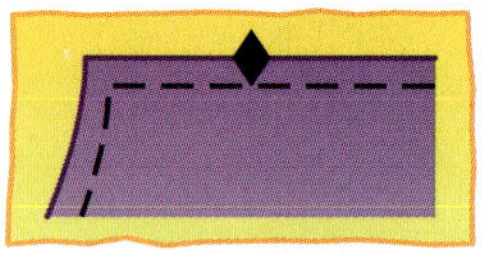

Notches

These show where the garment pieces should be joined. Cut notches outwards.

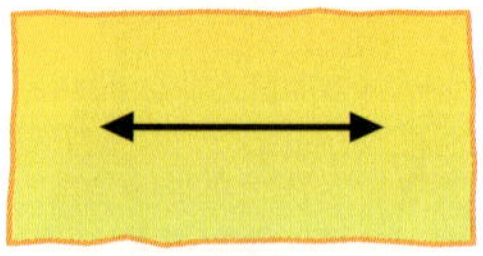

Straight grain

This arrow should be running along the selvedge (warp) of the fabric.

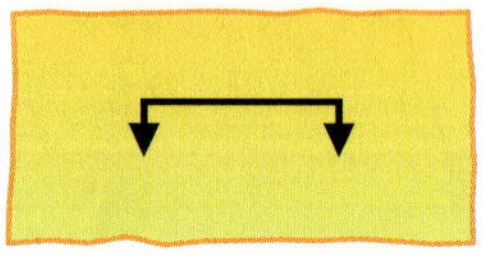

Fold line

This line should be placed along the fold of the fabric.

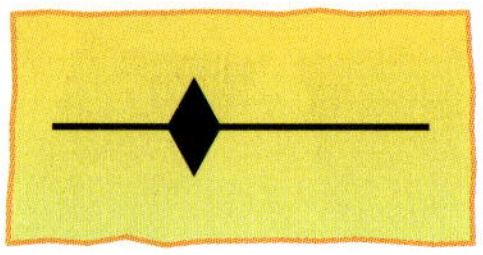

Cutting line

Most patterns have a cutting line that is 1.5cm outside the stitching line; this is where you cut out the fabric. **Note:** Some patterns do not have a cutting line, so you must allow the 1.5cm seam allowance yourself.

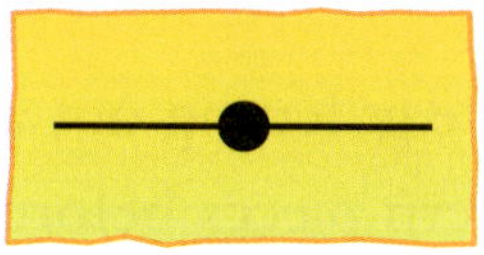

Balance marks

These show important points on the garment, such as the centre of the garment and the armhole.

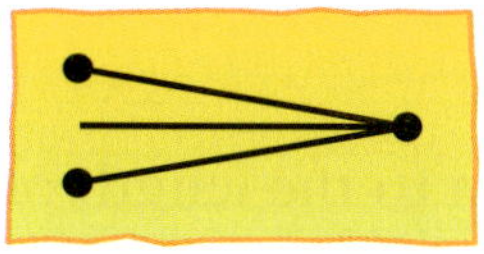

Construction marks

These show the position of darts, pockets, pleats, etc.

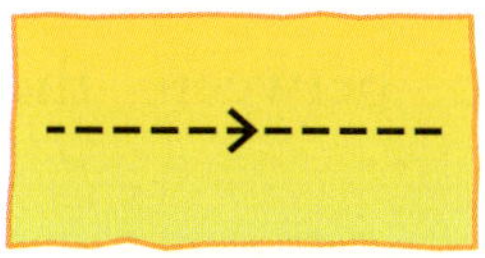

Stitching line

Machine along this line.

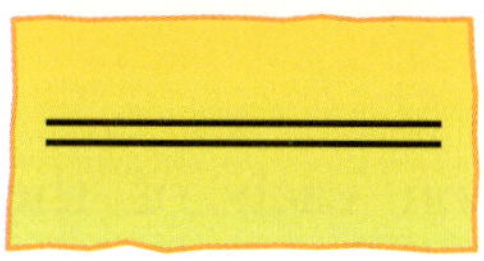

Alteration lines

It is at these lines that pattern pieces can be made longer or shorter (p. 352).

Button positioning marks

These should be marked with a tailor tack to show where buttons are to be placed.

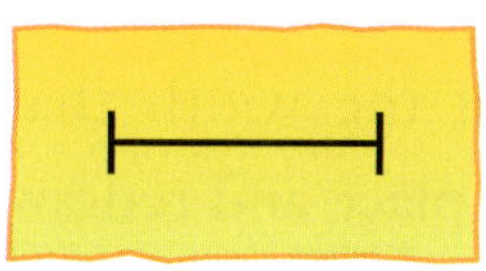

Buttonhole positioning marks

These show where buttonholes should be sewn. Notches, balance marks, button and buttonhole positioning marks should all be transferred from the tissue pattern to your fabric using tailor tacks (see Chapter 35, p. 305).

Stitching lines and construction marks may be transferred to fabric using a tracing wheel and paper.

Instruction sheets

These usually contain the following information:

- A sketch of the back of the garment(s).
- A labelled sketch of all the pattern pieces included.
- A list of the pieces needed for each view.
- Instructions for altering the pattern, e.g. making it longer.
- A sketch showing how pattern pieces can best be laid out on fabrics of different widths.
- Cutting instructions.
- Step-by-step instructions on how to make the garment.

Altering patterns

While small adjustments can be made on the garment itself, e.g. letting out a seam slightly, larger adjustments must be made on the pattern pieces before placing them on the fabric.

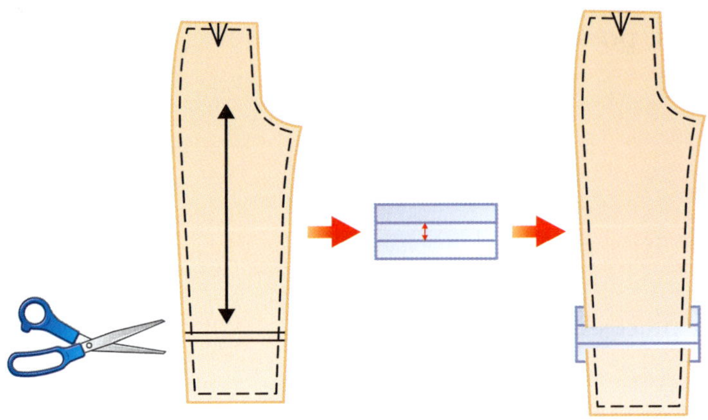

To lengthen pattern pieces

Example: You want to add 3cm to the length of a pair of trousers.

1. Cut the pattern piece between the alteration lines.
2. On another piece of paper, draw two parallel lines 3cm apart.
3. Lay one pattern piece on each of the parallel lines. Stick in place using masking tape.
4. Redraw the cutting line. Trim excess paper.

To reduce the length or width of a pattern

Fold the pattern piece on the alteration lines. The fold should measure half the width that you need to reduce. Tape into place and redraw the cutting line.

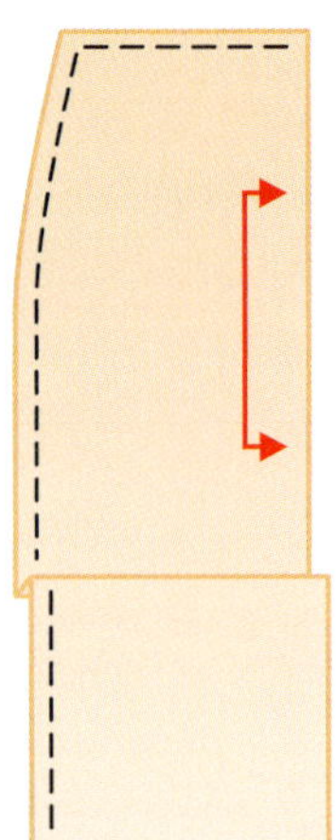

Decreasing length

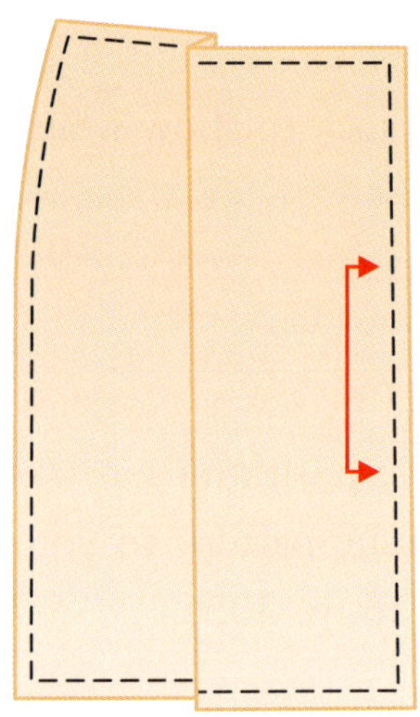

Decreasing width

To increase width

1. Draw two parallel lines on a piece of paper the correct distance apart. For example, if you want to increase width by 3cm, the lines should be 3cm apart.

Increasing width

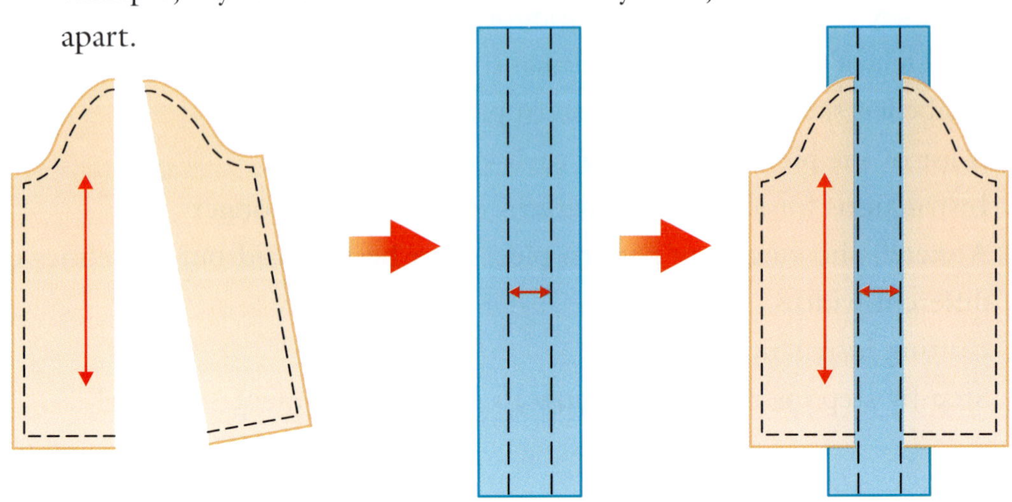

2. Tape the cut pattern piece along the two parallel lines. Redraw the fitting lines, etc.

Remember: If you increase the width of one part of the garment, the pieces it is attached to must also be increased to allow the pieces to join together.

Laying out pattern pieces

See also Chapter 35, pp. 310–12.

Your pattern instructions will include diagrams showing how your pattern pieces should best be laid out. Layouts will be different for different fabric widths.

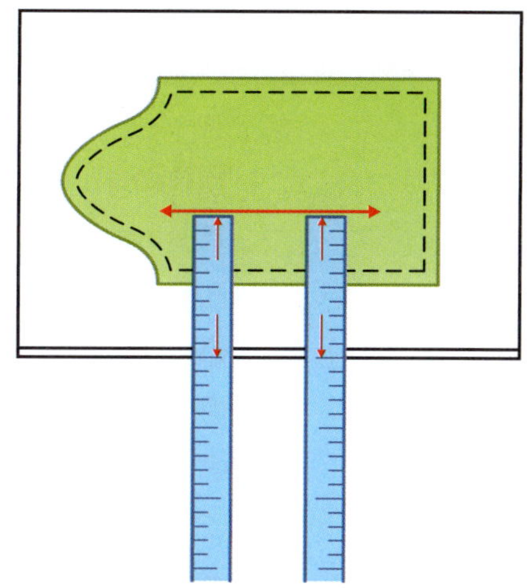

Laying pattern pieces using straight-of-grain lines

Generally

- Press fabric on the wrong side before beginning pattern layout.
- Fold the fabric right sides and selvedge edges together.
- Pattern pieces are generally placed on the fold or laid on the fabric using the straight-of-grain lines (see p. 312).

Using straight-of-grain lines

Lay the pattern pieces on the fabric so that the straight-of-grain arrow looks parallel with the selvedge edge. Pin one end of the arrow to the fabric. Measure from each end of the straight-of-grain arrow to the selvedge edge; when both ends are exactly the same distance from the selvedge, pin the other arrowhead in place. Then pin the rest of the pattern piece down.

Cutting out

See Chapter 35, p. 312.

Transfer of pattern markings

It is vital to transfer important pattern markings from the tissue pattern pieces to the fabric. There are three main methods for doing this.

1. Tailor tacks should always be used to show the location of important points on the pattern, e.g. end-of-bust darts, position of button and buttonholes.
2. Waxed paper and a tracing wheel are generally used to mark the sewing line. Two sheets of waxed paper are used, one against each piece of fabric

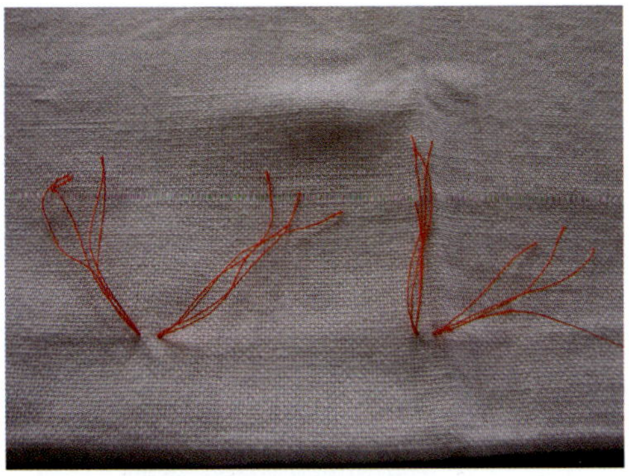

on the wrong side. The wheel is rolled along the sewing line and the line comes out on the fabric and can be used as a guide to keep tacking and sewing straight.

3. Tailor's chalk is sometimes used for marking the sewing line when pattern pieces have no seam allowance included.

Fitting

It is important that the garment you are making fits well before you sew it up. A garment that fits well will:

- Be neither too loose nor too tight.
- Hang well.
- Be comfortable and look well.

Guidelines

- Tack the large pieces, i.e. front and back pieces, of the garment together.
- Tack any darts in place.
- Try the garment on: sit, bend, raise your arms to see that the garment is not too tight. You will be able to loosen or tighten the garment by letting out or taking in some of your seam allowances.
- Check that shoulder seams lie on the shoulder and that the armhole is not too tight or too loose.
- Check that the waist of the garment is on the natural waistline.
- Mark alterations with chalk or pins; remove the garment and tack alterations; try the garment on again before sewing.

Pressing

Pressing is important to give your garment a finished, crisp look. Pressing is different from ironing: with pressing, you lift the iron and press down on the fabric, lift and press, etc.

Guidelines

- Press after each stage of construction, e.g. after sewing the side seams. Do not wait until the end to press everything, as you will not get as good a result.
- Usually press on the wrong side; if you must press on the right side, use a pressing cloth to protect the fabric.

- Use a steam iron set at the correct temperature for the fabric.
- Give the garment a final overall press when it is fully complete.

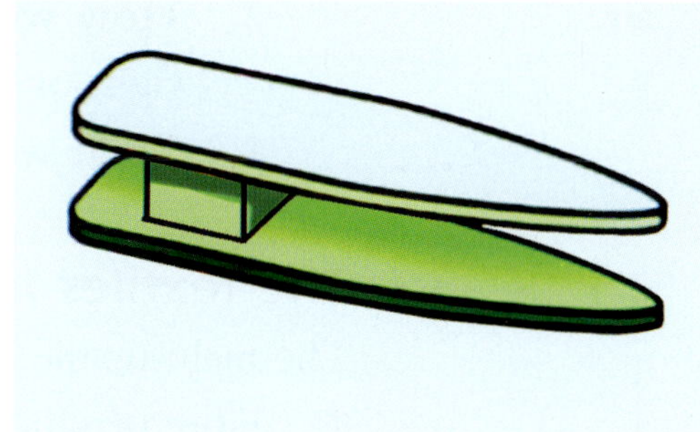
A sleeve board is used to press small areas of garments such as collars and sleeves

Textile skills project

While there will be questions on Textile Studies (Unit 5) on the final examination paper, the textiles skills option, like the other two options, is assessed through project work alone and is worth 15 per cent of your overall final mark for Home Economics. For this option you must complete an item of clothing (worth 80 marks) and present a written support folder (worth 20 marks), the details of which are outlined below.

Brief

Make an item of clothing that includes a minimum of two processes such as application of a collar, sleeves, zip, buttonholes, etc.

Support folder

You should include the following information in your support folder.

- Give details of what factors influenced you when choosing what garment to make, e.g. your sewing skills, availability of fabric, your body shape, fashion, your budget, if there was something you needed or a special occasion coming up, such as you made a child's dress because your aunt had a new baby girl.
- Give the details of the pattern you used and any changes you made to it.
- Give the details of the fabric you used, e.g. cost, amount you needed, type of fabric. Draw a wash care label for your garment.
- You could complete a fabric burning test to identify your fabric: present your results.
- Give details of the notions you had to purchase to complete the garment, and list and price them, e.g. buttons, zip, etc.
- What sewing equipment did you use? You could draw diagrams of some of the more unusual equipment, e.g. sleeve board.
- Evaluate your item of clothing under the following headings:
    1. **How well is it finished?** Evaluate every part of the garment: seams, seam finishes, collar, zip, buttons, buttonholes, hems, pockets, etc.

2. **How well does it fit?** Are there any puckers? Is the garment too tight or loose?
3. **What would you change next time round?**

The textiles industry

The main textile industries in Ireland are:

- Fibre production and research.
- Yarn production, e.g. making knitting wool.
- Fabric production, e.g. tweed, linen production.
- Textile product production, e.g. Aran sweaters, wool and tweed suits, linen table wear, carpets.
- Fashion design. Successful Irish designers include Paul Costello, Louise Kennedy, Quinn & Donnelly, John Rocha, Philip Treacy and Lulu Guinness.
- Retail, e.g. shop assistants.

Hats by the Irish designer Philip Treacy are sought after worldwide

For those interested in fashion design or in the textile industry generally (weaving, printing, etc.), a number of colleges around the country offer courses ranging from certificate to degree level. Ask your career guidance teacher for details.

Food tables

Composition of foods (per 100g)

	kcal	Protein (g)	Saturated fat (g)	Unsaturated fat (g)	Cholesterol (mg)	Carbohydrate (g)	Fibre (g)	Salt (mg)	Calcium (mg)	Iron (mg)	Carotene (µg)	Vitamin A (µg)	Vitamin D (µg)	Vitamin C (mg)	Water (g)
Cereal and cereal products															
Bran, wheat	206	14.1	0.9	0.6	0	26.8	39.6	28	110	12.9	0	0	0	0	8.3
Cornflour	354	0.6	0.1	0.4	0	92.0	N	52	15	1.4	0	0	0	0	12.5
Croissant	360	8.3	6.5	13	75	38.3	2.5	390	80	20	0	21	0.2	0	31.1
Brown flour (wheat)	323	12.1	0.2	1.0	0	68.5	6.4	4	130	3.2	0	0	0	0	14.0
White flour (wheat)	341	9.4	0.2	0.7	0	77.7	3.6	0.3	140	2.0	0	0	0	0	14.0
Wheat germ	357	26.7	1.3	5.3	0	44.7	N	0.5	55	8.5	0	0	0	0	11.7
Brown rice (boiled)	141	2.6	0.3	0.7	0	32.1	1.1	1	4	0.5	0	0	0	0	66.0
White rice (boiled)	138	2.6	0.3	0.8	0	30.9	1.0	1	18	12	0	0	0	0	68.0
Noodles	62	2.2	0.1	0.3	6	22.2	1.0	15	5	0.3	0	2	Tr	0	84.3
Spaghetti	104	3.6	0.1	0.4	0	22.2	1.8	Tr	7	0.5	0	0	0	0	73.8
White sliced bread	217	7.6	0.3	0.6	0	46.8	3.7	530	100	1.4	0	0	0	0	40.4
Brown bread	215	9.2	0.5	1.2	0	1.6	41.6	550	54	2.7	0	0	0	0	38.3
All-Bran	261	14.0	0.6	1.9	0	46.6	30.0	900	69	12.0	0	0	1.6	0	3.0
Bran flakes	318	10.2	0.4	1.2	0	69.3	17.3	1000	50	20.0	0	0	2.1	25	3.0
Coco Pops	384	5.3	0.4	0.5	0	94.3	1.1	800	20	6.7	0	0	2.1	0	3.0
Common Sense	357	11.0	0.7	2.9	0	74.0	N	900	50	6.7	0	0	2.1	0	3.0
Cornflakes	360	7.9	0.1	0.4	0	85.9	3.4	1110	15	6.7	0	0	2.1	0	3.0
Frosties	377	5.9	0.1	0.3	0	93.7	1.2	800	11	6.7	0	0	2.1	0	3.0
Muesli	363	9.8	0.8	4.4	Tr	72.2	8.1	380	110	5.8	Tr	Tr	0	Tr	7.2
Porridge (made with milk)	116	4.8	2.7	2.0	14	13.7	0.8	620	120	0.6	21	53	0	1	74.8
Rice Krispies	369	6.1	0.3	0.5	0	89.7	1.1	1260	10	6.7	0	0	2.1	0	3.0
Shredded Wheat	325	10.6	0.4	1.8	0	68.3	10.1	8	38	4.2	0	0	0	0	7.6
Shreddies	331	10	0.2	0.9	0	74.1	10.9	550	40	2.8	0	0	0	0	4.0
Smacks	386	8.0	0.4	1.1	0	89.6	N	20	20	6.7	0	0	2.1	0	3.0
Special K	377	15.3	0.3	0.6	0	81.7	2.7	1000	70	13.3	0	0	2.8	0	3.0
Start	355	7.9	0.3	1.1	0	81.7	9.3	500	40	15.0	0	0	3.1	37	3.0
Weetabix	359	11.0	0.4	1.6	0	75.7	11.6	270	35	7.4	0	0	0	0	5.6
Biscuits															
Chocolate digestives	524	5.7	16.7	9.1	22	67.4	2.9	160	110	1.7	Tr	Tr	Tr	0	2.2
Cream crackers	440	9.5	N	N	N	68.3	6.1	610	110	1.7	0	0	0	0	4.3
Ginger nuts	456	5.6	7.2	7.2	N	79.1	1.8	330	130	4.0	N	0	0	0	3.4
Jaffa cakes	363	3.5	N	N	21	67.8	N	130	55	1.5	0	14	0.1	2	18.0
Cakes, buns and scones															
Rice Krispie buns	464	5.6	10.7	6.8	5	73.1	0.8	450	28	4.0	25	Tr	0.8	0	1.6
Madeira cake (queen cakes)	393	5.4	8.8	7.2	N	58.4	1.3	380	42	1.1	N	N	N	0	20.2
Sponge cake (jam filled)	302	4.2	1.6	2.4	N	64.2	1.1	420	44	1.6	N	N	N	0	24.5
Chocolate Swiss roll	337	4.3	11.3		8.6	58.1	2.4	350	77	1.1	N	N	N	0	17.5
Plain scones	362	7.2	4.9	9.1	29	53.8	2.2	770	180	1.3	125	140	1.2	Tr	22.9
Fruit scones	316	7.3	3.3	8.1	27	52.9	3.6	710	150	1.5	N	N	N	Tr	25.3
Wholemeal scones	326	8.7	4.8	9.0	27	43.1	5.0	730	110	2.3	115	130	1.2	0	26.9
Pastry															
Wholemeal pastry (cooked)	499	8.9	11.8	19.6	43	44.6	6.0	360	24	2.4	130	135	1.4	0	7.4
Mince pies	423	4.3	7.4	12.1	25	59.0	2.8	310	75	1.5	82	77	0.8	0	12.0
Pizza (basic)	235	9.0	5.5	5.7	16	24.8	1.8	570	210	1.0	250	65	0.1	3	51.7

Composition of foods (per 100g)

	kcal	Protein (g)	Saturated fat (g)	Unsaturated fat (g)	Cholesterol (mg)	Carbohydrate (g)	Fibre (g)	Salt (mg)	Calcium (mg)	Iron (mg)	Carotene (µg)	Vitamin A (µg)	Vitamin D (µg)	Vitamin C (mg)	Water (g)
Desserts															
Bread and butter pudding	297	5.9	5.9	3.1	53	49.7	3.0	310	120	1.6	45	100	0.2	Tr	29.3
Christmas pudding	291	4.6	4.5	4.7	45	49.5	2.7	200	79	1.5	9	23	0.2	0	30.4
Fruit crumble	198	2.0	2.1	4.4	12	34.0	2.2	68	49	0.6	145	64	0.7	3	54.8
Apple tart	260	3.0	4.8	7.9	18	34.0	2.2	200	59	0.8	115	55	0.6	3	47.9
Pancakes	301	5.9	7.1	8.3	68	35.0	0.9	53	110	0.8	14	60	0.2	1	43.4
Milk and milk products															
Whole milk	66	3.2	2.4	1.2	14	4.8	0	55	115	0.05	21	52	0.03	1	87.8
Skimmed milk	33	3.3	0.1	Tr	2	5.0	0	55	120	0.05	Tr	1	Tr	1	91.1
Semi-skimmed milk (low fat)	46	3.3	1.0	0.5	7	5.0	0	55	120	0.05	9	21	0.01	1	89.8
Condensed milk	333	8.5	6.3	3.2	36	55.5	0	140	290	0.23	70	110	5.40	4	25.9
Evaporated milk	151	8.4	5.9	3.0	34	8.5	0	180	290	0.26	100	105	3.95	1	69.1
Human milk (colostrum)	56	2.0	1.1	1.4	31	6.6	0	47	28	0.07	135	155	1.03	7	88.2
Human milk (mature)	69	1.3	1.8	2.1	16	7.2	0	15	34	0.07	24	58	0.04	4	87.1
Baby milk formula	67	1.6	1.6	2.0	N	7.0	0	0.022	56	0.8	Tr	75	1.1		87.0
Soya milk	32	2.9	0.3	1.5	0	0.8	Tr	32	13	0.40	Tr	0	0	0	89.7
Cream (single)	198	2.6	11.9	6	55	4.1	0	49	91	0.1	125	315	0.14	1	73.7
Cream (double)	449	1.7	30	153	130	2.7	0	37	50	0.2	325	600	0.27	1	47.5
Cream (low fat)	148	3.0	8.3	4.3	40	4.3	0	49	99	0.1	54	190	0.10	1	78.9
Cheese (brie)	319	19.3	16.8	8.6	100	Tr	0	700	540	0.8	210	285	0.20	Tr	48.6
Cheese (cheddar)	412	25.5	21.7	10.8	100	0.1	0	670	720	0.3	225	325	0.26	Tr	36.0
Cheese (low-fat cheddar)	261	31.5	9.4	4.8	43	Tr	0	670	840	0.2	100	165	0.11	Tr	47.1
Cottage cheese	98	13.8	2.4	1.2	13	2.1	0	380	73	0.1	10	44	0.03	Tr	79.1
Edam	333	26	15.9	8.1	80	Tr	0	1020	770	0.2	150	175	0.19	Tr	43.8
Fromage frais (fruit)	131	6.8	13.7	4.7	70	13.8	Tr	35	86	0.1	N	82	0.04	Tr	71.9
Parmesan	452	39.4	20.5	10.4	100	Tr	0	1090	1200	1.1	210	345	0.25	Tr	18.4
Yoghurt (fruit)	105	5.1	1.5	1.0	10	15.7	N	82	160	Tr	16	39	0.04	1	73.1
Yoghurt (low-fat fruit)	90	4.1	0.4	0.2	4	17.9	N	64	150	0.1	4	10	0.01	1	77
Choc ice	277	3.5	10.8	5.9	30	28.1	Tr	91	130	0.1	5	1	Tr	N	N
Cornetto	260	3.7	6.7	5.5	2	34.5	N	91	120	N	N	N	Tr	N	N
Ice cream (vanilla)	194	3.6	6.4	2.7	31	24.4	Tr	69	130	0.1	195	115	0.12	1	61.91
Cheesecake	242	5.7	5.6	4.4	60	33.0	0.9	160	68	0.5	N	N	N	0	44.0
Jelly	61	1.2	0	0	0	15.1	0	5	7	0.4	0	0	0	0	84
Milk pudding	129	3.9	2.7	1.4	15	20.1	0.2	59	130	0.1	22	56	0.03	1	72.4
Trifle	166	2.4	5.2	3.5	33	19.5	0.5	63	68	0.3	33	70	0.17	4	68.1
Eggs and egg dishes															
Eggs (chicken)	147	12.5	3.1	5.9	385	Tr	0	140	57	1.9	Tr	190	1.75	0	75.1
Egg white	36	9.0	Tr	Tr	0	Tr	0	190	5	0.1	0	0	0	0	88.3
Egg yolk	339	16.1	8.7	16.6	1120	Tr	0	50	130	6.1	Tr	535	4.94	0	51.0
Scrambled eggs	247	10.7	11.6	8.6	350	0.6	0	1030	63	1.6	72	295	1.55	Tr	62.4
Omelette (cheese)	266	15.9	12.2	8.4	265	Tr	0	900	280	1.2	100	265	1.13	Tr	57.1
Quiche (plain)	314	12.5	10.3	10.2	140	17.3	0.7	340	260	1.0	100	185	0.93	Tr	46.7
Fats and oils															
Butter	737	0.5	54.0	22.4	230	Tr	0	750	15	0.2	430	815	0.76	Tr	15.6
Dairy spread (Dairygold)	662	0.4	28.1	41.2	105	Tr	0	760	14	Tr	845	800	5.80	0	22.0
Low-fat spread	390	5.8	11.2	27.5	6	0.5	0	650	39	Tr	985	920	8.00	0	49.9
Polyunsaturated margarine	739	0.2	16.2	61.1	7	1.0	0	800	4	0.3	750	775	7.94	0	16.0
Margarine (hard, e.g. Stork)	739	0.2	30.4	47.3	285	1.0	0	800	4	0.3	750	665	7.94	0	16.0

Composition of foods (per 100g)

	kcal	Protein (g)	Saturated fat (g)	Unsaturated fat (g)	Cholesterol (mg)	Carbohydrate (g)	Fibre (g)	Salt (mg)	Calcium (mg)	Iron (mg)	Carotene (µg)	Vitamin A (µg)	Vitamin D (µg)	Vitamin C (mg)	Water (g)
Fats and oils (continued)															
Margarine (soft)	739	0.2	26.9	51	225	1.0	0	800	4	0.3	750	860	7.94	0	16.0
Olive oil	899	Tr	14.0	80.9	0	0	0	Tr	Tr	0.4	N	0	0	0	Tr
Sunflower oil	899	Tr	11.9	83.2	0	0	0	Tr	Tr	Tr	Tr	0	0	0	Tr
Meat and meat products															
Bacon – boiled (lean)	167	29.4	3.6	5.2	36	0	0	1350	15	1.9	Tr	Tr	Tr	0	62.7
Bacon – gammon steak	172	31.4	1.9	2.7	19	0	0	2210	10	1.5	Tr	Tr	Tr	0	57.0
Bacon – rasher (back) fried	465	24.9	15.9	22.6	143	0	0	1910	13	1.3	Tr	Tr	Tr	0	29.7
Ham	120	18.4	1.9	2.7	68	0	0	1250	9	1.2	Tr	Tr	Tr	0	72.5
Minced beef (average)	229	23.1	6.5	8	83	0	0	320	18	3.1	Tr	Tr	Tr	0	59.1
Beef – stewing steak	223	30.9	4.7	5.8	82	0	0	360	15	3.0	Tr	Tr	Tr	0	68.4
Lamb (loin chop, grilled)	355	23.5	14.4	12.6	107	0	0	72	9	1.9	Tr	Tr	Tr	0	46.6
Lamb (cutlet, grilled)	370	23.0	15.3	13.4	107	0	0	71	9	1.9	Tr	Tr	Tr	0	45.1
Pork (loin chops)	332	28.5	9.0	13.4	108	0	0	84	11	1.2	Tr	Tr	Tr	0	46.3
Chicken – roast	148	24.8	1.6	3.5	96	0	0	81	9	0.8	Tr	Tr	Tr	0	68.4
Chicken liver (fried)	194	26.9	2.1	2.4	610	0	0	240	15	9.1	0	12230	N	13	64.2
Duck – roast	189	25.3	2.7	6.5	160	0	0	96	13	2.7	N	N	N	0	64.2
Lamb's liver (fried)	232	22.9	4.0	5.7	330	3.9	0.1	190	12	10.0	60	22680	0.5	12	58.4
Lamb's kidney (fried)	155	24.6	2.1	2.4	610	0	0	270	13	12.0	0	110	N	9	66.5
Beef burgers	264	20.4	8.0	8.5	81	7.0	1.3	880	33	3.1	Tr	Tr	Tr	0	53.0
Black pudding	305	12.9	8.5	11.7	68	15.0	0.5	1210	35	20.0	Tr	41	Tr	0	44.0
Corned beef	217	26.9	6.3	5.1	93	0	0	950	14	2.9	Tr	Tr	Tr	0	58.5
Liver pâté	316	13.1	8.4	12.8	169	1.0	Tr	790	15	7.1	130	7330	N	N	50.6
Sausage rolls	459	8.0	11.8	18.2	43	37.5	1.8	530	76	1.3	80	85	0.9	0	22.3
Pork sausages (fried)	317	13.8	9.4	13.7	53	11.0	0.7	1050	55	1.5	Tr	Tr	Tr	N	44.9
Pork sausages (grilled)	318	13.3	9.5	13.7	53	11.5	0.7	1000	53	1.5	Tr	Tr	Tr	N	45.1
Steak and kidney pie	176	14.8	7.0	10.3	141	15.2	0.7	660	35	2.8	50	80	0.5	1	49.0
White pudding	450	7.0	31.8		22	36.3	3.1	370	38	2.1	Tr	Tr	Tr	0	22.8
Beef curry with rice	137	8.8	1.9	2.2	21	16.9	N	260	N	N	N	Tr	Tr	Tr	68.9
Beef stew	120	9.7	3.3	3.5	30	4.6	0.7	330	15	1.1	1100	1	Tr	1	77.3
Chicken curry with rice	144	7.8	2.3	2.8	28	16.9	N	230	250	N	N	N	N	1	68.4
Bolognese sauce	145	8.0	3.1	7.1	25	3.7	1.1	430	23	1.4	1275	Tr	Tr	4	74.7
Chilli con carne	151	11.0	3.0	4.9	27	8.3	3.2	250	29	2.2	145	Tr	Tr	9	67.6
Irish stew	123	5.3	3.5	3.1	20	9.1	1.0	360	10	0.6	2	Tr	Tr	3	76.2
Lasagne	102	5.0	1.9	1.6	11	12.8	0.5	430	71	0.7	N	N	N	Tr	75.2
Shepherd's pie	118	8.0	2.4	3.2	28	8.2	0.7	450	16	1.2	15	15	0.1	3	75.6
Fish and fish products															
Cod (baked, butter added)	96	21.4	0.5	0.4	48	0	0	340	22	0.4	Tr	2	Tr	Tr	76.6
Cod (fried in batter: oil)	199	19.6	0.9	8.8	N	7.5	0.3	100	80	0.5	Tr	N	Tr	Tr	60.9
Haddock – (steamed)	98	22.8	0.2	0.4	48	0	0	120	55	0.7	Tr	Tr	Tr	Tr	75.1
Haddock (fried in crumbs)	174	21.4	0.7	7.1	N	3.6	0.2	180	110	1.2	Tr	Tr	Tr	Tr	65.1
Plaice (steamed)	93	18.9	0.3	1	50	0	0	120	38	0.6	Tr	Tr	Tr	Tr	78.0
Plaice (fried in batter)	279	15.8	1.5	15.5	N	14.4	0.5	220	93	1.0	Tr	Tr	Tr	Tr	52.4
Herring (grilled)	199	20.4	3.7	9.6	50	0	0	170	33	1.0	Tr	34	25.0	Tr	65.5
Mackerel (fried)	188	21.5	2.3	7.9	62	0	0	150	28	1.2	Tr	43	21.1	Tr	65.6
Salmon (canned)	155	20.3	1.5	5.9	34	0	0	570	93	1.4	Tr	35	12.5	Tr	70.4
Salmon (smoked)	177	17.8	0.8	3.2	50	0	0	1880	19	0.6	Tr	13	Tr	Tr	65.0
Tuna (canned in oil)	189	27.1	1.4	6.7	50	0	0	290	12	1.6	Tr	N	5.8	Tr	63.3
Tuna (canned in brine)	99	23.5	0.2	0.3	51	0	0	320	8	1.0	Tr	N	4.0	Tr	74.6

Composition of foods (per 100g)

	kcal	Protein (g)	Saturated fat (g)	Unsaturated fat (g)	Cholesterol (mg)	Carbohydrate (g)	Fibre (g)	Salt (mg)	Calcium (mg)	Iron (mg)	Carotene (µg)	Vitamin A (µg)	Vitamin D (µg)	Vitamin C (mg)	Water (g)
Fish and fish products (continued)															
Prawns (boiled)	107	22.6	0.4	0.9	81	0	0	1590	150	1.1	Tr	Tr	Tr	Tr	70.0
Fish cakes (fried)	188	9.1	1.0	8.3	17	15.1	0.6	500	70	1.0	Tr	Tr	Tr	Tr	63.3
Fish fingers (grilled)	56.2	15.1	2.8	5.7	35	19.3	0.7	380	52	0.8	Tr	Tr	Tr	Tr	56.2
Fish pie	105	8.0	1.2	1.5	19	12.3	0.9	250	37	0.4	15	28	0.2	2	75.7
Vegetables															
New potatoes (boiled)	75	1.5	0.1	0.1	0	17.8	1.2	9	5	0.3	Tr	0	0	9	80.5
Old potatoes (boiled)	72	1.8	Tr	0.1	0	17.0	1.4	7	5	0.4	Tr	0	0	6	80.3
Chips (home-made, fried in vegetable oil)	189	3.9	0.6	5.7	0	30.1	3.0	12	11	0.8	Tr	0	0	9	56.5
Chips (frozen, fried in vegetable oil)	273	4.1	2.5	10.4	0	36.0	3.5	29	15	0.9	Tr	0	0	16	40.3
Oven chips (baked)	162	3.2	1.8	2.2	0	29.8	2.8	53	12	0.8	Tr	0	0	12	58.5
Chips fried in animal fat	273	4.1	7.5	5.3	12	36.0	3.5	30	15	0.9	N	N	Tr	16	40.3
Potato waffles (baked)	200	3.2	1.0	6.7	0	30.3	N	430	32	0.5	Tr	0	0	36	52.7
Baked beans	84	5.2	0.1	0.1	0.3	15.3	6.9	530	53	1.4	74	0	0	Tr	71.5
Green/French beans	25	1.7	Tr	Tr	0	4.7	N	Tr	36	1.2	180	0	0	7	90.0
Lentils	105	8.8	0.1	0.4	0	16.9	3.3	3	22	3.5	N	0	0	Tr	66.7
Soya beans	141	14.0	0.9	4.9	0	5.1	8	1	83	3.0	6	0	0	Tr	64.3
Tofu	73	8.1	0.5	1.0	0	0.7	0.3	4	510	1.2	2	0	0	0	85.0
Peas (frozen)	79	6.7	0.3	1.0	0	9.7	7.3	94	35	1.6	405	0	0	12	75.6
Processed peas	99	6.9	0.1	0.4	0	17.5	7.1	380	33	1.8	60	0	0	Tr	69.6
Broccoli	24	3.1	0.2	0.5	0	1.1	N	13	40	1.0	475	0	0	44	91.1
Brussels sprouts	35	2.9	0.3	0.8	0	3.5	2.6	2	20	0.5	320	0	0	60	86.9
Cabbage	16	1.0	0.1	0.3	0	2.3	2.3	8	33	0.3	210	0	0	20	93.1
Carrots	24	0.6	0.1	0.2	0	4.9	2.8	50	24	0.4	7560	0	0	2	90.5
Cauliflower	28	2.9	0.2	0.6	0	2.1	1.6	4	17	0.4	60	0	0	27	90.6
Celery	7	0.5	Tr	0.1	0	2.5	1.6	60	41	0.4	50	0	0	8	95.1
Courgette (cooked)	63	2.6	0.6	4.0	0	2.6	N	1	38	1.4	500	0	0	15	86.8
Cucumber	10	0.7	Tr	Tr	0	1.5	0.7	3	18	0.3	60	0	0	2	96.4
Curly kale	24	2.4	0.2	1.0	0	1.0	2.6	100	150	2.0	3375	0	0	71	90.9
Garlic	98	7.9	0.1	0.3	0	16.3	N	4	19	1.9	Tr	0	0	17	64.3
Leeks	21	1.2	0.1	0.4	0	2.6	2.4	2	24	1.1	735	0	0	17	92.2
Lettuce	14	0.8	0.1	0.3	0	1.7	1.3	3	28	0.7	355	0	0	5	95.1
Mixed vegetables (frozen)	42	3.3	Tr	Tr	0	6.6	N	96	35	0.8	2520	0	0	13	85.8
Mushrooms	13	1.8	0.1	0.3	0	0.4	2.3	5	6	0.6	0	0	0	1	92.6
Onions	36	1.2	Tr	0.1	0	7.9	1.5	3	25	0.3	10	0	0	5	89.0
Parsnips	66	1.6	0.2	0.7	0	12.9	4.3	10	41	0.6	30	0	0	17	78.7
Peppers	20	2.9	N	N	0	0.7	N	7	30	1.2	175	0	0	120	85.7
Spinach	19	2.2	0.1	0.6	0	0.8	3.1	120	160	1.6	3840	0	0	8	91.8
Sweet corn (canned)	23	2.9	N	N	0	2.0	2.0	1140	8	1.2	140	0	0	14	92.5
Tomatoes	17	0.7	0.1	0.2	0	3.1	1.3	9	7	0.5	640	0	0	17	93.1
Turnip	12	0.6	Tr	0.1	0	2.0	2.0	15	48	0.2	20	0	0	10	93.1
Fruit															
Apples (eating)	47	0.4	Tr	0.1	0	11.8	2.0	3	4	0.1	18	0	0	6	84.5
Apricots	31	0.9	Tr	Tr	0	7.2	1.9	2	15	0.5	405	0	0	6	87.2
Avocado	190	1.9	4.1	14.3	0	1.9	N	6	11	0.4	16	0	0	6	72.5

Composition of foods (per 100g)

	kcal	Protein (g)	Saturated fat (g)	Unsaturated fat (g)	Cholesterol (mg)	Carbohydrate (g)	Fibre (g)	Salt (mg)	Calcium (mg)	Iron (mg)	Carotene (µg)	Vitamin A (µg)	Vitamin D (µg)	Vitamin C (mg)	Water (g)
Fruit (continued)															
Bananas	95	1.2	0.1	0.1	0	23.2	3.1	1	6	0.3	21	0	0	11	75.1
Blackberries	25	0.9	Tr	0.1	0	5.1	6.6	2	41	0.7	80	0	0	15	85.0
Blackcurrants	28	0.9	Tr	Tr	0	6.6	7.8	3	60	1.3	100	0	0	200	77.4
Cranberries	46	.6	tr	tr	0	9	4.6	2	8	.8	36	60	0	13.3	
Fruit cocktail (canned)	29	0.4	Tr	Tr	0	7.2	1.0	3	9	0.4	54	0	0	14	86.9
Fruit salad (homemade)	55	0.7	Tr	Tr	0	13.8	1.5	2	16	0.2	20	0	0	16	82.3
Gooseberries	19	1.1	N	N	0	3.0	2.9	2	28	0.3	110	0	0	14	90.1
Grapefruit	30	0.8	Tr	Tr	0	6.8	1.6	3	23	0.1	17	0	0	36	89.0
Grapes	60	0.4	Tr	Tr	0	15.4	0.8	3	23	0.1	17	0	0	3	81.8
Kiwi fruit	49	1.1	N	N	0	10.6	2.3	4	25	0.4	37	0	0	59	84.0
Lemons	19	1.0	0.1	Tr	0	3.2	4.7	5	85	0.5	18	0	0	58	86.3
Mandarin oranges	32	0.7	Tr	Tr	0	7.7	0.3	6	17	0.5	95	0	0	20	89.6
Melon	19	0.6	Tr	Tr	0	4.2	0.9	8	20	0.3	1000	0	0	26	92.1
Oranges	37	1.1	Tr	Tr	0	8.5	1.8	5	47	0.1	20	0	0	38	86.1
Passion fruit	36	2.6	0.1	0.2	0	5.8	N	19	11	1.3	750	0	0	23	74.9
Peaches (raw)	33	1.0	Tr	Tr	0	7.6	2.3	1	7	0.4	58	0	0	31	88.9
Peaches (canned in syrup)	55	0.5	Tr	Tr	0	14.0	0.9	4	3	0.2	75	0	0	5	81.1
Pears	40	0.3	Tr	Tr	0	10.0	2.8	3	11	0.2	18	0	0	6	83.8
Pineapple	41	0.4	Tr	0.2	0	10.1	1.3	2	18	0.2	18	0	0	12	86.5
Plums	36	0.6	Tr	Tr	0	8.8	2.3	2	13	0.4	295	0	0	4	83.9
Prunes (semi-dried)	141	2.5	N	N	0	34.0	12.8	11	34	2.6	140	0	0	Tr	31.1
Raisins	272	2.1	N	N	0	69.3	6.1	60	46	3.6	12	0	0	1	13.2
Raspberries	25	1.4	0.1	0.2	0	4.6	6.7	3	25	0.7	6	0	0	32	87.0
Rhubarb (stewed with sugar)	48	0.9	Tr	Tr	0	11.5	2.0	1	33	0.1	60	0	0	6	84.6
Strawberries	27	0.8	Tr	Tr	0	6.0	2.0	6	16	0.4	8	0	0	77	89.5
Nuts															
Almonds	612	21.1	4.7	48.6	0	6.9	12.9	14	240	3.0	0	0	0	0	4.2
Peanuts (roasted and salted)	602	24.5	9.5	40.7	0	7.1	6.9	400	37	1.3	0	0	0	0	1.9
Peanut butter	623	22.6	11.7	39.7	0	13.1	6.8	350	37	2.1	0	0	0	0	1.1
Walnuts	688	14.7	5.6	59.9	0	3.3	5.9	7	94	2.9	0	0	0	0	2.8
Sugars/snacks															
Honey	288	0.4	0	0	0	76.4	0	11	5	0.4	0	0	0	0	23.0
Jam (fruit)	261	0.6	0	0	0	69.0	1.0	16	24	1.5	Tr	0	0	10	29.8
Mincemeat	274	0.6	2.4	1.7	4	62.1	3.0	140	30	1.5	9	0	0	Tr	27.5
White sugar	394	Tr	0	0	0	99.9	0	Tr	2	0	0	0	0	0	Tr
Golden syrup	298	0.3	0	0	0	79.0	0	270	26	1.5	0	0	0	0	20.0
Treacle	257	1.2	0	0	0	67.2	0	96	500	9.2	0	0	0	0	28.5
Bounty bar	473	4.8	21.2	3.6	10	58.3	N	180	110	1.3	40	Tr	Tr	0	7.6
Milk chocolate	529	8.4	17.8	11.0	30	59.4	Tr	120	220	1.6	40	Tr	Tr	0	2.2
Crème eggs	385	4.1	16.8		N	58.0	Tr	55	120	0.8	55	47	0.6	0	5.3
Kit Kat	499	8.2	13.8	11.3	N	60.5	N	110	200	1.5	47	Tr	Tr	0	1.3
Mars bar	441	5.3	10.0	8.0	25	66.5	Tr	150	160	1.1	40	Tr	Tr	0	6.9
Twix	480	5.6	12.0	11.1	N	63.2	N	190	110	1.1	7	Tr	Tr	0	3.5
Popcorn	592	6.2	4.3	34.2	0	48.6	N	4	10	1.1	230	0	0	0	0.9
Crisps	546	5.6	9.2	21.9	0	49.3	10.7	1070	37	1.8	2	0	0	27	1.9
Crisps (low fat)	456	6.6	6.2	14.6	0	63.0	13.7	1070	36	1.8	2	0	0	14	1.1
Corn snacks (e.g. Monster-Munch)	519	7.0	11.8	18.7	0	54.3	N	1130	68	0.8	460	0	0	Tr	3.3

Composition of foods (per 100g)

	kcal	Protein (g)	Saturated fat (g)	Unsaturated fat (g)	Cholesterol (mg)	Carbohydrate (g)	Fibre (g)	Salt (mg)	Calcium (mg)	Iron (mg)	Carotene (µg)	Vitamin A (µg)	Vitamin D (µg)	Vitamin C (mg)	Water (g)
Drinks															
Cocoa (with whole milk)	76	3.4	2.6	1.3	13	6.8	0.2	70	110	0.2	20	50	0.03	Tr	84.6
Milkshake	90	2.9	2.0	1.0	10	13.2	Tr	55	100	1.0	51	21	0.05	1	80.0
Coca-Cola	39	Tr	0	0	0	10.5	0	8	4	Tr	0	0	0	0	89.8
Lucozade	67	Tr	0	0	0	18.0	0	28	4	Tr	0	0	0	3	81.7
Ribena (undiluted)	228	0.1	0	0	0	60.8	0	26	5	0.4	N	0	0	78	40.3
Orange juice	36	0.5	0	0	0	8.8	0.1	10	10	0.2	17	0	0	39	89.2
		Alcohol content (g)													
Beer	32	3.1				2.3	0	9	8	0.01	0	0	0	0	96.7
Cider	36	3.8				2.6	0	7	4	Tr	0	0	0	0	96.3
Lager	29	3.2				1.5	0	4	4	Tr	0	0	0	0	96.2
Red wine	68	9.5				0.3	0	10	7	0.9	0	0	0	0	97.7
White wine	66	9.1				0.6	0	4	9	0.50	0	0	0	0	98.2
Spirits, e.g. vodka	222	31.7				Tr	0	Tr	Tr	Tr	0	0	0	0	99.9
Soups and sauces															
Cream of chicken (tin)	58	1.7	3.8		N	4.5	N	460	27	0.4	0	0	0	0	87.9
Cream of mushroom (tin)	53	1.1	3.8		N	3.9	N	470	30	0.3	0	0	0	0	89.2
Cream of vegetable (tin)	37	1.5	0.7		N	6.7	N	500	17	0.6	18	0	0	0	86.4
Oxtail soup (packet)	27	1.4	0.5		N	3.9	0.3	400	11	0.3	0	0	0	0	92.5
Cheese sauce (whole milk)	197	8.0	7.5	6.4	39	9.0	0.2	450	240	0.2	105	150	0.55	1	66.9
White sauce (whole milk)	150	4.1	4.4	5.3	26	10.9	0.3	400	140	0.2	77	115	0.62	Tr	73.7
Mayonnaise (shop bought)	691	1.1	11.1	61.2	75	1.7	0	450	8	0.3	100	86	0.33	N	18.8
Tomato ketchup	98	2.1	0	0	0	24.0	N	1120	25	1.2	240	0	0	2	64.8

Please note the following: Tr = traces of the nutrient present. N = significant quantities of the nutrient present; values not known.